# Expository Discourse in Children, Adolescents, and Adults

# New Directions in Communication Disorders Research: Integrative Approaches

*Rhea Paul, Series Editor*

**Rhea Paul (Ed.)**
*Language Disorders from a Developmental Perspective: Essays in Honor of Robin S. Chapman*

**Elena L. Grigorenko and Adam J. Naples (Eds.)**
*Single-Word Reading: Behavioral and Biological Perspectives*

**Marilyn A. Nippold and Cheryl M. Scott (Eds.)**
*Expository Discourse in Children, Adolescents, and Adults: Development and Disorders*

# Expository Discourse in Children, Adolescents, and Adults

## Development and Disorders

Edited by

**Marilyn A. Nippold and Cheryl M. Scott**

Psychology Press
Taylor & Francis Group

New York   London

Psychology Press
Taylor & Francis Group
270 Madison Avenue
New York, NY 10016

Psychology Press
Taylor & Francis Group
27 Church Road
Hove, East Sussex BN3 2FA

© 2010 by Taylor and Francis Group, LLC
Psychology Press is an imprint of Taylor & Francis Group, an Informa business

Printed in the United States of America on acid-free paper
10 9 8 7 6 5 4 3 2 1

International Standard Book Number: 978-1-84169-892-2 (Hardback)

### Library of Congress Cataloging-in-Publication Data

Expository discourse in children, adolescents, and adults : development and
     disorders / editors, Marilyn A. Nippold, Cheryl M. Scott.
          p. ; cm. -- (New directions in communication disorders
          research--integrative approaches)
     Includes bibliographical references and index.
     ISBN 978-1-84169-892-2 (hardcover : alk. paper)
          1. Language disorders. 2. Communicative disorders. 3. Language acquisition.
     I. Nippold, Marilyn A., 1951- II. Scott, Cheryl M. III. Series: New directions in
     communication disorders research--integrative approaches.
          [DNLM: 1. Language Disorders. 2. Communication Disorders. 3. Language
     Development.  WL 340.2 E965 2010]

     RC423.E985 2010
     616.85'5--dc22
                                                                        2009032318

**Visit the Taylor & Francis Web site at**
**http://www.taylorandfrancis.com**

**and the Psychology Press Web site at**
**http://www.psypress.com**

# Contents

# Series Foreword

We are pleased to present this new volume in our series, *New Directions in Research on Communication Disorders: Integrative Approaches.* The purpose of this series is to provide researchers and professionals in the area of communication development, disability, and related fields with works that provide state-of-the-art information compiled by scientists and practitioners whose goal is to invite collaboration and integrate knowledge on a broad range of emerging issues that pertain to the understanding of human communication and its disorders.

In this volume, we examine an area of discourse that has been relatively understudied in the literature on language development: that of expository text. By this term, Professor Nippold, Professor Scott, and their authors refer to the use of language, in spoken and written form, to explicate facts and share complex knowledge in extended discourse units. The ability to engage in this kind of discourse, while it emerges early in childhood, requires many more years of growth—even into adulthood—to evolve toward the dense, abstract, decontextualized, highly organized, and structured products that are required for successful participation in academic and professional interactions. Moreover, as the authors of this volume amply demonstrate, its acquisition depends not only on the development of strong language skills but also on cognitive and metacognitive abilities as well as on the acquisition of specific knowledge.

Facility with expository discourse is crucial to success in academic settings, and this facility must extend to all modalities of language: understanding and use in both oral and written forms. Yet most students receive little direct instruction in the production and comprehension of exposition; rather, they are expected somehow to "pick it up" along the way. While the assumption that children will learn to process and produce expository texts on their own may hold true for some students with typical development, it is a virtual formula for failure for students with disabilities. Those with language-based learning disorders, hearing impairment, traumatic brain injury, high-functioning autism spectrum disorders, and attention and executive function difficulties are likely to experience deficits in the ability to manage these texts. Yet there are few assessment instruments developed specifically to examine students' abilities in expository discourse, particularly to examine them independent of reading problems. This volume makes a significant contribution to the understanding of these issues by providing detailed information on the typical development of expository discourse skill, elaborating on characteristics needed in tools to identify students who have particular difficulty with exposition, examining several approaches to direct instruction, and outlining the circumstances under which such instruction is most appropriate and effective.

An additional strength of the Nippold and Scott contribution is its international scope. While most books that deal with language and learning disorders in the school-age and adolescent population look parochially at studies of English, this volume provides information from a range of countries and languages. The broad perspective provided by this approach helps readers move beyond the narrow view of issues of language learning in older children that is seen in most other volumes on this topic.

Finally, the volume adheres strictly to an evidence-based approach to the discussion of assessment and intervention for expository discourse. The clinicians and scientists who collaborated on this volume provide a thorough and comprehensive review of empirical literature available to elucidate the development and disorders of exposition. This distinguished cohort has assembled a cogent review of what is currently known about these topics, interpreted it, and made it accessible to readers who may want to apply its content to their own clinical practice with struggling students as well as to those who aim to create new research paradigms that can extend what we currently know. We anticipate that readers with a range of interests who take advantage of the compendium of information offered here will be amply rewarded for their efforts.

**Rhea Paul**
*Series Editor*

## CHAPTER 1

# Overview of Expository Discourse: Development and Disorders

## Marilyn A. Nippold and Cheryl M. Scott

Expository discourse, the use of language to convey information, is frequently called on in learning environments where individuals are expected to listen, speak, read, write, and analyze new concepts. In schools, for example, this occurs as students learn about challenging subjects such as economics, astronomy, and mathematics.

## WHY IS EXPOSITORY DISCOURSE IMPORTANT?

Imagine that you are a 10th-grade adolescent attending a public high school in Los Angeles, California. In economics class, you and your classmates are about to view a video lesson that explains how consumer demand for products operates in the marketplace. First, however, you listen and take notes as your teacher defines key terms such as *law of demand*, *market demand curve*, *microeconomics*, and *marginal utility*. Following the video, you read a passage in your textbook (Clayton, 2005) that elaborates on the topic of consumer demand, illustrated by several tables and graphs. After completing the passage, you are assigned to write a report, due next week, in which you are to "analyze several magazine or newspaper ads to determine how the ads reflect or use the law of diminishing marginal utility" (p. 93). Next, your teacher organizes the class into small groups, and each is assigned to interview the manager of a different store (e.g., grocery store, department store, drugstore) concerning the "effect that sale prices have on consumer demand" (p. 91). To complete this assignment, your group will need to generate a list of questions to ask the manager, select a member to carry out the interview, analyze the results, write a summary, and present the findings to the class.

After economics class, you go to astronomy, where you are studying *comparative planetology*. Today you take an essay exam where you are asked to describe the differences between Jovian and terrestrial planets and to explain why Jovian planets are more massive than terrestrial planets (Chaisson & McMillan, 2005). That afternoon in math class, the notion of *limits* is introduced, a basic concept in calculus. To teach this concept, your teacher presents Zeno's paradox of the tortoise and Achilles, in which a tortoise challenges the Greek hero Achilles to a foot race. The tortoise boasts that as long as he has a head start of 10 meters, he will always be in front because, when Achilles reaches the tortoise's starting point, the tortoise also will have moved ahead and will continue to do so, however slowly. Your teacher asks the class to explain the flaw in the tortoise's assumption that "an infinite amount of time is required to cover a distance [that can be] divided into an infinite number of segments" (Smith, 1995, p. 648). After a lively discussion, a classmate responds as follows: "Even though a certain distance, say 1 mile, can be divided into an infinite number of smaller segments (1 = .50 + .25 + .125 + .0625 ...), those segments will always add up to 1. The distance is limited, and on reaching that limit, Achilles, the faster runner, will overtake the tortoise."

As these scenarios illustrate, school success in the 21st century requires proficiency with expository discourse. Although many students are proficient in listening, speaking, reading, and writing in the expository genre, others struggle to meet these expectations.

## PURPOSE OF THIS BOOK

This book was designed to provide information on the use and understanding of expository discourse in spoken and written language in school-age children, adolescents, and young adults. Recently, researchers have been investigating the development of this genre in typical students and in those with language disorders. Although there are many books that address the development of narrative discourse in both types of students, by comparison, contributions on expository discourse are sparse. This book has been designed to address this knowledge gap. Chapters 2 through 6 discuss the development of expository discourse, covering comprehension and production, and chapters 7 through 11 discuss the challenges faced by students with developmental or acquired language disorders, focusing on the nature of their problems and appropriate methods of assessment and intervention, given what has been learned from research. In this edited volume, invited authors include professors, research associates, and clinicians at universities in the United States, France, Israel, and New Zealand. Representing international perspectives, it contains information on speakers of English in addition to speakers of other languages, including French and Hebrew.

## CONTENT OVERVIEW

Chapter 2, written by Lynn Snyder and Donna Caccamise from the University of Colorado at Boulder (United States), addresses the comprehension of expository materials, offering insights into the challenging nature of this genre. As they point out, reading comprehension suddenly becomes quite difficult in fourth grade because textbooks used at this level employ the expository genre to teach important subjects such as history, social studies, and science. Prior to fourth grade, the narrative genre predominates in classroom materials. Many factors contribute to the greater difficulty of the expository genre over the narrative. For example, expository materials are more likely to include difficult vocabulary such as abstract nouns and other low-frequency words. In addition, they focus on new and unfamiliar topics that students are expected to learn by reading and listening to informative discourse. A student's prior knowledge or lack of it concerning a particular topic also contributes to the ease or difficulty with which expository materials are understood. The ability to integrate new information into an existing knowledge bank and to draw inferences from expository discourse is an additional requirement, along with the use of metacognitive strategies such as comprehension monitoring. Limitations in any of these factors can affect the degree to which a student gains meaning from expository discourse. Information contained in this chapter provides a strong foundation for teachers, speech-language pathologists, and other professionals whose goal it is to promote students' academic success, as discussed later in the book (e.g., chapter 9).

Whereas Snyder and Caccamise discuss the importance of domain knowledge for the comprehension of expository discourse, Marilyn A. Nippold from the University of Oregon (United States) describes in chapter 3 how knowledge of a particular domain influences the content, clarity, and complexity of language produced when an individual discusses a specific topic in the expository genre. For example, when school-age children, adolescents, and adults are asked to explain the rules and strategies of their favorite game or sport, they produce longer sentences with greater amounts of subordination compared to when they are speaking in a conversational genre about simpler topics such as pets, siblings, or friends. This pattern of significantly greater syntactic complexity in the expository genre has been documented not only in typically developing speakers but also in adolescents with a history of developmental language disorders. Thus, when asked to explain a complex topic about which they are knowledgeable, even younger individuals and those with language weaknesses rise to the occasion, tapping into the language competencies they do possess. Other studies reported in chapter 3 indicate differences in the content, clarity, coherence, and accuracy of expository discourse produced by experts versus novices when they are asked to write or talk about a particular topic such as baseball, football, chess, or politics. The roles of interest and motivation are also discussed in relation to the quality and quantity of expository discourse produced.

In chapter 4, Jean-Marc Colletta and Catherine Pellenq from Grenoble University (France) address a fascinating new topic of research: the development of gestures in relation to children's spoken explanations. In a detailed investigation of French-speaking children between the ages of 3 and 11 years, they examine developmental changes in the use of syntax, the lexicon, and gestures during expository discourse. Their findings show that young children typically produce short, simple explanations that refer to events happening in the current environment, accompanied by simple deictic pointing. In contrast, by the time children have reached preadolescence, they typically produce sustained explanations of complex phenomena that go beyond the immediate context (e.g., topics such as ancestral roots, family relationships, and childhood safety), characterized by multiple clausal embedding and the use of advanced connectives (e.g., *anyway, otherwise,* and *all the same*), accompanied by metaphorical gestures. For example, the authors report that when explaining how the world was once a safer place for children, a 10-year-old boy gestured with his hand metaphorically to represent the past as he glanced in a backward direction while verbalizing an adverb of time ("earlier on"). They claim that these attainments are linked to cognitive advances in the knowledge base, abstract thought, and language development, as argued by other authors (e.g., chapters 5, 6, 8).

In chapter 5, Ruth A. Berman and Bracha Nir from Tel Aviv University (Israel) report on their cross-sectional developmental investigation of expository discourse in written language. Their study included children and adolescents from fourth, seventh, and 11th grades who were native speakers of English or Hebrew. After viewing a wordless video depicting a conflict between people, participants wrote an essay on the topic of interpersonal conflict where they were requested to offer their own thoughts and opinions. The findings indicated important developmental changes. For example, in terms of content, older writers were more likely than younger ones to express opinions framed as broad generalizations, illustrated by relevant experiences drawn from their own lives. Whereas younger writers (fourth graders) tended to use modal verbs reflecting a prescriptive or judgmental attitude (e.g., people *should* get along), older writers (11th graders) tended to use modals that reflected a more flexible, objective attitude (e.g., it *may be possible* to prevent conflict). Moreover, older writers were more likely than younger ones to use the passive voice (e.g., people *are confronted by problems*) and to employ longer and syntactically more complex sentences containing multiple

January 29, 2010

Dear Customer:

Thank you for your purchase of *Expository Discourse in Children, Adolescents, and Adults: Development and Disorders*, edited by Marilyn A. Nippold and Cheryl M. Scott.

The contributor list was errantly left out at time of printing. The contributors are listed below, and this information will be inserted on page ix at reprint.

## Contributors

Ruth A. Berman, PhD
Tel Aviv University
Tel Aviv, Israel

Donna Caccamise, PhD
University of Colorado
Boulder, Colorado

Jean-Marc Colletta, PhD
Grenoble University
Grenoble, France

Esther Dromi, PhD
Tel Aviv University
Tel Aviv, Israel

Barbara J. Ehren, PhD
University of Central Florida
Orlando, Florida

Gail T. Gillon, PhD
University of Canterbury
Christchurch, New Zealand

Pazit Kotler, PhD
Tel Aviv University
Tel Aviv, Israel

Catherine Moran, PhD
University of Canterbury
Christchurch, New Zealand

Marilyn A. Nippold, PhD
University of Oregon
Eugene, Oregon

Bracha Nir, PhD
Tel Aviv University
Tel Aviv, Israel

Catherine Pellenq, PhD
Grenoble University
Grenoble, France

Dorit Ravid, PhD
Tel Aviv University
Tel Aviv, Israel

Cheryl M. Scott, PhD
Rush University Medical Center
Chicago, Illinois

Lynn Snyder, PhD
University of Colorado
Boulder, Colorado

Jeannene M. Ward-Lonergan, PhD
University of the Pacific
Stockton, California

We sincerely regret any inconvenience this may have caused you. Please let us know if we can be of any assistance regarding this title or any other titles that Psychology Press/Taylor & Francis publishes.

Best regards,

Psychology Press/Taylor & Francis

ISBN 978-1-84169-892-2 (HB)

subordinate clauses, elaborated noun phrases, and advanced connectives (e.g., *on the other hand* and *in other cases*). Developmental gains also occurred in the use of nonfinite verb forms, including gerunds, participles, and infinitives in the expository essays, and in the use of literate vocabulary, including, for example, abstract nouns and morphologically complex, polysyllabic, and low-frequency words. The authors argue these changes are associated with social, emotional, and cognitive development and with educational opportunity.

In chapter 6, Dorit Ravid, Esther Dromi, and Pazit Kotler, from Tel Aviv University (Israel) provide a fascinating discussion of the relationship between expository writing and the language of mathematics, which they call "mathematical discourse." In their research, Hebrew-speaking children and adolescents from fourth and seventh grades, respectively, were asked to write expository essays on the topic of friendship. The students were also asked to generate mathematical story problems based on a given set of facts. For example, one of the scenarios they were presented was as follows:

Avi, Einat, and Sa'ar collect *pugim* (small metal discs for playing). Sa'ar has 80 more *pugim* than Einat. Einat has twice as many *pugim* as Avi. Avi has 40 *pugim*. (p. 154)

The findings of their study indicated that language productivity in expository writing and mathematical discourse increased greatly between late childhood and early adolescence as measured by mean number of words and clauses produced. With respect to syntactic complexity, greater developmental gains occurred in mathematical discourse than in expository writing, primarily the result of a jump in the use of conditional (if–then) subordinate clauses. For example, a fourth grader posed the following problem using a simple sentence: "How many [pugim] did Einat and Sa'ar collect together?" (p. 154). In contrast, a seventh grader posed the following problem using a complex sentence containing a conditional (adverbial) clause that itself contains an embedded relative clause: "What would be the difference between Sa'ar and Einat if Einat gets 20% of the *pugim* Avi has?" (p. 155). Thus, it appears that, as young people gain an understanding of mathematical principles, they tap into their syntactic competence to express that knowledge.

Moving on to language disorders, chapter 7 by Jeannene M. Ward-Lonergan from the University of the Pacific (United States) contains information on studies that have examined expository discourse comprehension and production in school-age children and adolescents with developmental language impairments. Focusing on the language demands of the classroom, Ward-Lonergan explains how these students frequently experience difficulties with all aspects of expository discourse. For example, after listening to social studies lectures, they recall fewer details and draw fewer inferences compared to their peers with typical language development. Moreover, their production of expository discourse concerning academic topics is often limited in the amount of information conveyed and in the use of later-developing syntactic structures. Lingering grammatical errors may also be present. Reading comprehension for textbooks written in the expository genre is similarly impaired. Factors related to poor comprehension in students with language impairments include limited awareness of expository text structures, difficulty processing large amounts of information about unfamiliar topics, weak comprehension monitoring, and limited knowledge of literate vocabulary and syntactically complex sentences in expository texts. Regarding their ability to write formal expository essays, similar deficits typically occur in addition to numerous errors of spelling and punctuation, making it difficult for them to succeed academically. Given the extent of these deficits, it is imperative that students with language impairments receive intervention in school contexts designed to enhance their ability to comprehend and produce expository discourse in spoken and written modalities. Both of these important intervention topics are revisited by Ward-Lonergan in chapter 10.

Cheryl M. Scott from Rush University Medical Center, Chicago (United States), provides critical information in chapter 8 concerning the diverse ways in which expository discourse can be assessed, emphasizing spoken and written language production. These include large-scale writing assessments where students write essays in their classrooms, norm-referenced language tests that are individually administered, and language samples that are elicited and analyzed for syntactic and lexical complexity. Challenges associated with each of these approaches are discussed. For example, given their numbers, large-scale writing assessments are often scored quickly, with little attention to detail, and may not reflect the role of the knowledge base for strong expository performance. Norm-referenced tests examine linguistic complexity at a word or sentential level rather than at a text level and are more likely to examine narrative rather than expository discourse and to examine spoken rather than written language development. In contrast, language samples, while time consuming to elicit and analyze, can provide the most useful information about a student's proficiency with expository discourse, particularly when the individual is asked to talk about a complex topic (also see chapter 3) and the sample is analyzed in ways that reflect sophisticated linguistic attainments. These include, for example, the use of advanced syntactic structures such as elaborated noun phrases, sentences that contain multiple levels of subordination (clauses embedded within clauses), and literate vocabulary such as abstract nouns, adverbial conjuncts, and morphologically complex words (also see chapters 5 and 6). One particularly helpful feature of this chapter is the inclusion of sentences that were produced by children with typical and disordered language development and analyzed syntactically and lexically.

Given the challenging nature of expository discourse, chapter 9 by Barbara J. Ehren from the University of Central Florida (United States), provides welcome information on interventions designed for adolescents who struggle to comprehend textbooks written in the expository genre. For example, Ehren offers guidance from research on how the teacher or speech-language pathologist might intervene to promote adolescents' comprehension of textbooks from social studies, mathematics, and science classes, focusing on their ability to decode and understand technical vocabulary (e.g., *brinkmanship, federalist, quadratic, tessellation, colloidal,* and *cytokinesis*), to activate prior knowledge of the topic, and to use metacognitive strategies such as summarization, paraphrasing, self-questioning, and self-monitoring to identify the main ideas of a passage and draw inferences. Promoting the use of metacognitive strategies is particularly important because of their potential to build the adolescent's capacity as an independent learner. The importance of explicitly teaching adolescents about the structure of expository text and to identify key structural elements such as macrostructures (text grammars such as descriptions, sequences, and comparison/contrasts), signaling devices (e.g., headings, subheadings, and opening phrases such as "in this chapter, you will learn about ..."), and cohesive ties (linguistic devices such as conjunctions, relative pronouns, and ellipses) is also emphasized in order to build students' awareness of expository text, thereby increasing their comprehension. In addition, for students who struggle to understand complex syntax, it is important to heighten their awareness of the propositions or "idea units" that are contained within subordinate clauses. This is particularly challenging for students with language disorders because of the multiple levels of embedding that occur in sentences in expository text. Moreover, as emphasized elsewhere (e.g., chapters 3 and 8), the advantages of building the knowledge base in various subjects areas to ensure comprehension cannot be overstated.

In chapter 10, Jeannene M. Ward-Lonergan (University of the Pacific, United States) provides further direction for enhancing students' comprehension of expository texts, emphasizing a number of information processing techniques that teachers and speech-language pathologists can employ. Examples include focusing students' attention on the goals of a lesson, helping them activate and expand their knowledge of the topic, and encouraging students to monitor their own learning in order to build independence. The potential benefits of teaching students to employ strategies such as summarization, paraphrasing, and self-questioning are also highlighted, techniques that have been validated through intervention research with diverse learners. Also discussed are strategies such as semantic feature analysis that can be used to enhance students' knowledge of challenging vocabulary contained in texts used to teach science, mathematics, and social studies. The chapter also includes a helpful section on intervention for written expression in the expository genre. A topic that has received comparatively little attention from research, written expression is critical for academic success in the 21st century, as students are regularly assigned to write essays in which they must explain what they have learned from reading their textbooks and listening to their teachers' lectures. Research reported in this chapter supports activities that provide students with frequent opportunities to write expository essays, to discuss their ideas and the writing process, and to receive constructive feedback from teachers, speech-language pathologists, and even their peers.

In chapter 11, which completes this volume, Catherine Moran and Gail T. Gillon from the University of Canterbury (New Zealand) discuss some of the challenges faced by school-age children and adolescents who have suffered a traumatic brain injury (TBI). For many young people with TBI, difficulties with expository discourse manifest themselves in all aspects of later language development, including the use of literate vocabulary and complex syntactic structures, the production of relevant content, and organization of the information they wish to convey. Unfortunately, these problems often occur in youth with TBI despite their adequate performance on standardized language tests. Hence, the chapter focuses on the importance of assessing expository discourse in these youths, how to elicit samples of expository discourse, how to analyze a sample, and how to use the information to plan intervention to improve expository discourse production. Examples of tasks that can be used to elicit expository discourse are provided. As discussed elsewhere (e.g., chapters 3 and 8), the authors emphasize the importance of using tasks that are cognitively engaging and that require specialized knowledge to create a genuine need for the speaker to call on advanced linguistic structures. The chapter concludes with an intriguing case study of an adolescent who suffered a TBI, which resulted in difficulties with expository discourse. Intervention designed to boost the content and relevance of his discourse, using a graphic organizer, is clearly described.

## LOOKING TO THE FUTURE

Given the expanse of topics, domains, and disciplines that contribute to the study of expository discourse, it should not be surprising that the opportunities for future research into the development of expository competence are limitless. Although there are many themes to highlight when considering future research directions, based on the contributions to this volume, two seem particularly compelling.

### Expository Discourse Encompasses Many Types of Language

The theme that informational language comes in numerous forms and covers an infinite number of topics is embedded throughout the chapters of this volume. Most developmental researchers, studying children and adolescents with typical or diminished language abilities, have limited their inquiry to one type of expository discourse (the range of tasks and content used can be found in the review of findings summarized by Ward-Lonergan in chapter 7). Several researchers whose work is reported here, however, either in the programmatic sum of their work (Nippold in chapter 3) or in more direct comparisons (Ravid, Dromi, and Kotler in chapter 6), have begun to explore the effects of topic (e.g., content domain, level of expertise, and motivation) on linguistic form at the word, sentence, and discourse levels. Inclusion of a modality distinction, whether children are asked to tell or write about a topic, adds another dimension to the varieties of expository language. Modality comparisons have received some attention, but research designs that elicit both types of expository discourse from the same children are still rare.

It is not surprising, then, that educators, special educators, and the broader lay public have concerns about how the findings of one study may or may not generalize to other types of expository discourse. As discussed by Scott in chapter 8, broad state and national writing assessment programs have tried to circumvent the issue of variability of content knowledge among students. A common remedy is to construct writing prompts about experiential-based topics that presumably most students have experience with or opinions about (e.g., the advisability of school uniforms). However, this practice has vocal critics who claim that the resulting essays can be formulaic and sometimes trivial. Future employers may question how well the types of expository reading and writing practiced in elementary and secondary schools will transfer to the more fluid workplace contexts that call for communicating information clearly and quickly and most likely in online formats. Ehren (chapter 9) has discussed the fact that textbook discourse, which educators have often used when teaching informational language, may not be the best model. The inherent iterations of expository discourse might not be such an issue in assessment or intervention applications if it could be shown that competence is a self-contained "modular" skill such that a student with skills in one type is highly likely to be equally competent in another type. But this seems simplistic and unlikely. Referring to college writers, Richardson (2008) argued recently that the view of writing as a "basic skill" that is presumably acquired (or at least strengthened) in first-year composition courses is a literacy myth. Rather, he notes that acceptable writing in one disciplinary genre does not necessarily transfer to another.

If expository form follows function and if facility with one form may not transfer to all forms, as these scenarios seem to imply, how might researchers in the future deal with this issue? The first step is to document the type and extent of variability that occurs by studying children and adolescents in greater depth and over a longer period of time. The cross-sectional, static design (e.g., elicit one expository sample) is not well suited to addressing questions about any one student's basic ability to handle expository language. A better design would be to gather multiple samples on different topics, under different task conditions, probing all four modalities (listening, speaking, reading, and writing) over time (i.e., with longitudinal designs). In intervention studies, researchers can address some of these issues by casting a broader net for the measurement of training effects (see chapters 9 and 10). Extending the time frame for maintenance of training effects would be helpful as well. As noted in Ehren's reference to several systematic reviews of interventions for expository discourse in chapter 9, only a small fraction of investigations to date have measured maintenance beyond posttest results or transfer of skills.

## Expository Discourse as Cognitive and Linguistic Capability

A second theme highlighted in several chapters of this volume is the sheer cognitive complexity involved in comprehending and producing expository discourse. Researchers can and have parsed out the components of this complexity. There is domain-specific knowledge: The comprehension of informational language will be easier or harder on a continuum that corresponds to prior understanding and exposure to the topic. Writing or speaking about a topic will follow the same pattern; the more that is known about a topic, the easier it will be to produce a coherent text. Then there are the many cognitive processes required for comprehending expository discourse—processes captured in the construction-integration model described by Snyder and Caccamise in chapter 2. The comprehension of written expository texts is thought to require interactions between (a) background knowledge; (b) cognitive processes that support integration, inference, and executive functions; and (c) features of the text itself to an extent above and beyond that required for narrative comprehension. There is also the exquisite fine-tuning among developmental growth patterns in affective, social, and cognitive development with growth patterns in general language and literacy. In chapter 5, Berman and Nir show how this occurs when their older writers, capable of taking a more distanced and nuanced view of personal conflict, draw from a different set of modal auxiliaries and subject nominals when compared to younger writers who are more judgmental and dogmatic. Moreover, growth in the ability to engage in complex thought is reflected in the increasingly abstract and metaphorical nature of the gestures that accompany children's explanations of complex topics, as discussed by Colletta and Pellenq in chapter 4.

Shedding more light on these complex interactions that occur for children and adolescents with both typical and impaired language abilities will require some different research approaches. There have been very few studies that have explored the relationship between domain-specific knowledge and expository ability in depth (an exception, however, is Nippold's work with expert chess players, described in chapter 3). It is insufficient to say that two groups of children being compared in a treatment study, for example, are equated in terms of knowledge on the basis of performance within a normal range on a standardized cognitive measure (e.g., nonverbal intelligence or even verbal intelligence). To our knowledge, studies have not yet been designed that account for developmental variation in social cognition or attitudes of participant groups. Hence, the ability to account for variation in expository discourse comprehension and production as a function of domain-specific knowledge, social cognition, executive function abilities, and so forth is in need of research. Research designs that seem particularly well suited to these types of questions would include regression models and other techniques designed to highlight mediation effects and pathways in complicated cognitive systems.

Depending on the outcome of these studies, future research designed to enhance expository discourse by attending to the associated competencies will be appreciated, particularly by teachers, speech-language pathologists, and other professionals who work closely with school-age children and adolescents. Moreover, intervention studies that are cross disciplinary and collaborative in nature should be exceptionally exciting.

## REFERENCES

Chaisson, E., & McMillan, S. (2005). *Astronomy today* (5th ed.). Upper Saddle River, NJ: Pearson/Prentice Hall.

Clayton, G. E. (2005). *Economics principles and practices: Teacher wraparound edition.* Columbus, OH: Glencoe/McGraw-Hill.

Richardson, M. (2008). Writing is not just a basic skill. *Chronicle of Higher Education, 55*(11), A47.

Smith, K. J. (1995). *The nature of mathematics* (7th ed.). Pacific Grove, CA: Brooks/Cole.

## CHAPTER 2

# Comprehension Processes for Expository Text: Building Meaning and Making Sense
### *Lynn Snyder and Donna Caccamise*

Every time a reader sits down to read, there are two main parties to the transaction: the reader and the text to be read. Successful reading depends primarily on these two parts of the equation: the skills, knowledge, and processes that the reader brings and the linguistic characteristics of the text and genre to be read (McNamara, 2004; Perfetti, 1994). More specifically, comprehension of the text will depend on the reader being able to access relevant knowledge and engage higher-order information processes and strategies to understand or make sense of the text and its specific features that can be apprehended. When there is a good "match" between the reader and the features of the text or material, a deeper global level understanding of the text results (McNamara, 2007; McNamara & Kintsch, 1996; McNamara, Kintsch, Songer, & Kintsch, 1996). The same can be said of listening to connected discourse and understanding it. The purpose of this chapter is to examine both sides of the comprehension equation for expository material: the dynamic constructive and integrative processes, strategies, and knowledge that readers and listeners access and engage to understand expository information and the linguistic features of the expository information that can facilitate or hinder comprehension during the reading event. Before we examine the components of this transaction, however, we first turn our attention to the pressing need to look at these components in the context of processing expository material, that is, material that provides information.

## THE CHALLENGE OF EXPOSITORY TEXT

It is particularly important to examine the reader–text "match" and the interactions involved in comprehending expository information or text because they represent the greatest challenge for many readers. The definitional purpose of expository text is to inform. As a result, expository materials provide new information to the reader and listener and contain unfamiliar, low-frequency, often abstract vocabulary and concepts (Chall, 1993). Historically, readers and listeners have found this genre more difficult to comprehend than other, more familiar genres, such as narratives (Berkowitz & Taylor, 1981, Taylor & Samuels, 1983). This difficulty is acute for schoolchildren, especially during the fourth grade.

### The Great Shift

In schools across the United States, expository materials begin to present problems for students in the fourth grade when the curriculum shifts in such a way that a significantly larger proportion of the curriculum is presented in expository form, either in textbooks, magazine articles, newspapers, reference articles, hypertext articles on the Web, science lab explanations, or classroom lectures. In fact, Duke (2000) observed that until around third or fourth grade, most of the materials students read are narratives. Despite the range of exposure to the expository genre and informational text that surrounds students at home during the primary grades, very little of that genre is represented in classroom texts. Duke and Purcell-Gates (2003) reported that although primary grade students see a great deal of game-related print, other instructions, magazines, newspapers, brochures, pamphlets, trading cards, and other informational text at home in addition to storybooks, the proportion of what they see is quite dissimilar from that found in classrooms, where narrative texts and poetry are more consistently represented. In fact, Duke (2000) estimated that first graders see informational text 3.6 minutes a day in their classrooms. Consequently, when that proportion shifts abruptly around fourth grade, students seem to find the increased representation of expository materials in literacy and learning events a bit daunting. At the very least, it is simply less familiar to them because they have spent less time engaged with expository materials and demands prior to this shift.

It is not unusual, then, that Chall (1983, 1996) noted that by fourth grade, students are no longer engaged in "learning to read" or learning and mastering the foundational skills needed to break the orthographic code and gain access to the encoded meaning in text. Rather, they are engaged in "reading to learn," or reading with the purpose of discovering new information. As a result, when students have difficulty reading and understanding expository material, they demonstrate not only reading comprehension problems but also problems in learning their academic subjects, such as science, citizenship, health, and social studies (Chall & Jacobs, 2003; McNamara, Best & Castellano, 2003).

## The Fourth-Grade Slump

McNamara and her research team (Best, Floyd, & McNamara, 2004; Best, Ozuru, Floyd, & McNamara, 2006; McNamara, 2004) observed that it may not be coincidental that the alarming "fourth-grade slump" (Miechenbaum & Beimiller, 1998; Snow, 2002) reported annually in students' reading comprehension coincides with the abrupt transition to expository reading materials in fourth grade. Beck and McKeown (1991) commented that the "fourth grade slump can at least partially be explained by students' inability to make meaning of expository text" (p. 482).

The studies that were carefully conducted by McNamara's research group (Best et al., 2004, 2006; McNamara, 2004) contrasting students' comprehension of narrative versus expository texts make a strong case for the inherent difficulty of expository materials for third and fourth graders. This point is particularly salient in the findings from a study conducted by Best et al. (2006). In this experiment, they asked fourth-grade students to read two narrative and two expository texts and answer multiple-choice questions; half the questions addressed the global themes of the selections, and the other half focused on specific factual information contained in the text. Best et al. (2006) found that the students demonstrated better comprehension on the narrative texts. The major difference was found on the students' responses to the questions that addressed the deeper global meaning of the selections. The students did not show as deep a level of comprehension of the expository as the narrative selections. These findings underscore the differential difficulty that expository text poses for typically achieving fourth graders.

This transition is also reflected in the genres of the content represented in reading comprehension tests. A number of standardized measures of silent reading comprehension select passages from materials in students' curricula. As a result, their selections reflect the fourth-grade transition from narrative to expository text in their testing passages and affect student performance correspondingly. For example, using the range of narrative genre (e.g., including narrative accounts as well as stories) in a simple inspection of the passage selections on one form of a standardized test of reading comprehension indicated that the representation of narratives versus expository texts shifts from a predominance of narrative stories and narrative accounts (e.g., 8 out of 11 selections at the second-grade level) until fourth grade, when expository selections predominate (7 out of 12 selections). In short, expository material takes an increasingly central position in the reading and discourse activities of American classrooms beginning in fourth grade. The abrupt transition to expository materials occurs despite evidence that the expository genre is more difficult for students to comprehend at a deeper level, one that interacts with stored world knowledge and is incorporated into memory. The impact of this difficulty can have far-reaching consequences for students because it can actually limit their learning.

For these reasons, it is important to look at the reading equation in students' comprehension of expository material in terms of its two primary components. First, we examine the overall constructive and integrative nature of comprehension from the vantage point of the reader. We pay particular attention to automatic comprehension processes, inferential processing, the memory processes invoked, the effect of memory capacity, the way that information held in working memory is integrated into the mental representations being built, memory differences between good and poor readers, and the strategic processes readers and listeners engage to monitor, regulate, and repair their understanding. Second, we look at the other side of the equation: the expository text or material. There is evidence that text comprehension may be mediated by interactions between individual differences in comprehension processes, knowledge, and features of the text itself, such as genre and other linguistic variables (McNamara & Kintsch, 1996; O'Reilly & McNamara, 2002). Consequently, we consider the features of expository material as it interacts with individual differences in knowledge, the effect of genre, text coherence, and cohesion. Finally, we examine the effect of the modality of presentation—printed or spoken—on comprehension.

## THE READER AND THE COMPREHENSION PROCESS

### The Construction and Integration of Meaning During Comprehension

The leading paradigm for reading and listening comprehension takes a constructivist approach in which comprehension is viewed as an online iterative process during which an individual constructs and integrates meaning from discourse, creating a mental representation. Kintsch's (1988) characterization of this construction and integration process presents it as an automatic, that is, not effortful, process. It is only when these automatic, lower-level processes fail to construct a coherent representation of a selection that readers are thought to activate more analytic and effortful inferential processing and strategies. A good starting place is to examine the levels of processing invoked during comprehension.

### Levels of Processing

According to the construction-integration theory of comprehension (Kintsch, 1998), the mental representation of meaning found in discourse is described in terms of multiple levels of processing. These include the *text base* and the *situation model*.

**The text base** The *text base* is the level that includes all the information that is explicitly expressed by a text, organized and structured as the author expressed it. As readers/listeners construct a memory for the text base, they extract meaning from the linguistic forms (e.g., words, sentences, and paragraphs) by engaging processes that build coherence. These include bridging inferences that link pronominal referents to the appropriate person or item to which the pronoun is referring within and across sentences and between paragraphs across text. In addition, the process of transforming words into meaning units (referred to as propositions in this model) requires some degree of inferencing to make those connections. This is the minimum effort that a motivated reader must perform to build an accurate memory representation of the text base. With a coherent text base in episodic memory, a reader/listener can engage in several processes that are commonly found in classroom activities and assessments. They can recall the text base, answer questions about the text base, recognize text base components, and summarize the text base—all activities common to current comprehension assessments. Creating and accessing the text base is not, however, adequate to reach a deep—as opposed to a shallow—level of comprehension. For this, you need the situation model.

**The situation model** The *situation model* refers to the processing level where readers and listeners actively construct a sense or meaning of the text by combining their representation of the text base with prior knowledge, thereby constructing new knowledge. A reader with impoverished background knowledge on the subject of a given discourse will have difficulty creating a useful situation model. On the other hand, a good reader with background knowledge will actively engage with the text base, making inferences, accessing relevant background knowledge, and using comprehension strategies such as monitoring and other sense-making strategies to create his or her own unique interpretation of the discourse, which will update one's knowledge in memory. No longer is this discourse just an isolated piece of information held in episodic memory as it was when it was just the text base. Rather, it becomes part of one's long-term memory and background knowledge for future discourse processing. This goes beyond the intent of the author and becomes something far more elaborated than the text base, based on the reader/listener's prior knowledge, discourse context, and other influences, such as cultural and social. By creating a situation model, the reader/listener is able to go beyond regurgitating the explicit text and is able to use this knowledge by abstraction, generalization, and application. The complexity of the interactions that take place when constructive and integrative processes are activated to build meaning becomes more apparent under closer scrutiny, in particular, inferential processing and issues of memory and capacity.

## Drawing Inferences

Successful discourse comprehension requires the reader/listener to make inferences. When comprehending a text, a successful reader must minimally make local inferences that fill in coherence gaps created by what is left out of the surface code of the text. As we mentioned earlier, pronominal referents are an example of this type of local inferencing process. Inferencing at the deeper global level includes linking the text base with the situational model that is being derived by integrating the text base with background knowledge, the author's intent, the reader's goals, cultural influences, and so forth. One constraint on creating a situation model is that readers are more likely to construct inferences that refer to causal antecedents than to create causal consequences about items, topics, or events mentioned in the text (Cote, Goldman, & Saul, 1998; Graesser & Bertus, 1998; Trabasso & Magliano, 1996; Zwaan & Brown, 1996). Basically, causal antecedent inferences refer to "why" questions about information in the text. As this is about something past, it is easier to elaborate what is known. Causal consequences, on the other hand, are about the future and can be about vague and potentially unconstrained outcomes. Readers do not tend to go down this garden path.

An example of these two types of knowledge-based inferences can be demonstrated with the following sentence: "Campers are always instructed to put water on the campfire." An antecedent inference that could be made from the statement could include "Water puts out fires." Such an inference is quickly made. On the other hand, possible causal consequence inferences might include "Campfires can cause the loss of billions of dollars' worth of timber" or "The water thrown by campers on a fire can flood an entire campsite." One could speculate/make many inferences about the consequences of campers' fires and throwing water on them but with no a priori reason to do so. Thus, comprehenders tend not to make these inferences. When they do make causal inferences, processing times increase significantly, indicating an increased demand on cognitive resources. Research shows that comprehenders typically do not expend these resources for inferences that would likely be of marginal benefit since speculation typically does not predict actual outcomes (Graesser & Bertus, 1998).

Some researchers have suggested that these knowledge-based inferencing abilities vary considerably because of individual differences and the effect of flexible, trainable strategies used to create the situation model (e.g., Perfetti, 1994; Rayner & Pollatsek, 1989). However, Graesser and Bertus (1998) measured knowledge-based inferencing by adults reading expository text while accounting for age, working memory span, general world knowledge, reasoning ability, and reading frequency. They found no differences in the pattern of inference-making processes. Rather, the mechanisms used to construct situation models were as constrained and systematic as are the mechanisms at the more shallow levels of reading. Given the number of construction and integration processes that take place during comprehension, it is clear that memory also plays an important role when building an understanding of comprehension processes.

## Memory Processes During Comprehension

The construction-integration model is a two-stage comprehension process of construction and then integration of concepts and propositions. When the reader or listener encounters discourse, he or she first activates network nodes in long-term memory (LTM) that are triggered by the text. This involves a spreading activation of all possibly relevant nodes in the network at first, but those nodes with weaker strength are inhibited during the integration process.

This is believed to occur in a passive, bottom-up manner, with a stable text base emerging from continued input from reading or listening. Nodes that get repeated get reinforced in the forming text base and situation model; nodes that are not reinforced are inhibited. The simplest example of this is when an individual gives meaning to vocabulary used. Take the word "bank." There is evidence that when this word is encountered, multiple meanings are activated at first (e.g., riverbank vs. a bank full of money). The context provided by the text causes the wrong definition to be inhibited. While this explanation took some time to read, the actual process occurs in a matter of milliseconds. This has been described as a *search after meaning by convergence* (Long & Lea, 2005). In this view, the integration process involves memory retrieval during text processing as an unguided, passive activation process (for a more comprehensive explanation, see Caccamise & Snyder, 2005). Indeed, a number of studies have shown that the initial activation of background knowledge appears to be unaffected by the ultimate relevance of the information (e.g., Kintsch 1998; Lea, Mason, Albrecht, Birch, & Myers, 1998; Long, Seely, & Oppy, 1996; McKoon, Gerrig, & Greene, 1996).

Opposing this passive view of memory retrieval processes during integration is the idea that the reader or listener's search after meaning is an active, evaluation, memory-retrieval process. In this view, individuals basically ask "why" questions, activating information that will help them establish causal links to explain why actions, events, and states are mentioned (e.g. Graesser, Singer, & Trabasso, 1994; Long & Lea, 2005). However, Long and Chong's (2001) study of expository text found that activation and text relevance does not necessarily lead to integration. Much of comprehension research has focused on the construction side of comprehension processes because they are easier to operationalize and test. The integration part of the equation has so far proven difficult to study. Generally, discourse theorists currently believe that a combination of active, top-down processes and passive bottom-up processes will be at the heart of a complete theory of comprehension (e.g., Long & Lea, 2005). How this amount of processing can occur with such relative ease in comprehenders in spite of the traditional capacity limits assigned to working memory is of particular relevance to our understanding of comprehension.

## Memory Capacity

One of the knotty issues in explaining comprehension of expository information is memory capacity, that is, the amount of information that can be held in storage at any one time. For any search-after-meaning process (see the previous description) to be possible, one would have to posit a working memory the capacity of which is both flexible and large, in sharp contrast to past research on short-term memory (STM). It has well been documented that working memory or *short-term working memory* (STWM) has a very limited capacity. Van Dijk and Kintsch (1983) described components to be held in memory while reading that included perceptual and linguistic features, propositional structure, macrostructure, situation model, control structure, goals, lexical knowledge, schemata, general knowledge, and episodic memory for prior text. Clearly, on the surface of things, these are far more units of information than traditional notions of working memory can accommodate. Since this is obviously not a problem for successful readers, something more must be going on.

To deal with the inconsistency between working memory capacity and obvious working memory demands during reading, Ericsson and Kintsch (1995) proposed that there seems to be an expanded working memory that they call *long-term working memory* (LTWM) that can handle these operations with ease. Specifically, they suggested that working memory has two components: STWM and LTWM. The STWM is available under all conditions, has severe capacity limitations, and has been the subject of many laboratory memory experiments. (For example, George Miller's [1956] famous experiment defined STM as having the capacity of 7 ± 2 bits of information. While results are nuanced in terms of decades of follow-on research, the procedure paradigm tended to address small units, such as letters, numbers, and nonsense syllables.)

In contrast to STM, LTWM is viewed as an expert skill that is not capacity limited. It is described as that portion of LTM that is directly retrievable from cues in STM. This occurs in expert domains where strong stable links exist between cues in STM and the nodes that are automatically activated in LTM. Most things that adults do in their daily lives, such as driving and walking, are routine, and they are experts in these activities. Any expert domain has access to the benefits of LTWM. Successful reading comprehension is described as an expert skill in this framework (Kintsch, Patel, & Ericsson, 1999). Basically, using LTWM, readers will form links between new information in a text with relevant background knowledge in areas where they have well-structured background knowledge and experience (i.e., expertise). In this manner, the reader can create deep levels of comprehension that enable learning and use of the new information in novel ways (Kintsch, 2002; McNamara, de Vega, & O'Reilly, 2007).

## Integrating Information in Working Memory Into the Situation Model

Although research findings support both the more passive "convergence" and the more active "evaluation" hypotheses as explanations of the search for meaning, little is known about the relative balance of these processes or when one might occur instead of the other. One plausible scenario is that convergence processes are routine for most people, as information is activated and at least to some degree integrated in LTWM, but that evaluative processes might be more prone to the reader's goals and comprehension strategy skills. As suggested later in this chapter, skilled readers tend to monitor their comprehension and actively engage processes that serve to explain coherence gaps and integrate new knowledge with old, thus deepening their comprehension of discourse. We look to future research to provide more depth and understanding on this issue.

## Memory Differences Between Good and Poor Comprehenders

Although there appear to be no individual differences in the general profile of inference processes engaged while comprehending text, there are discernible differences between good and poor comprehenders in terms of actual memory processes. Palladino, Cornoldi, DeBeni, and Pazzaglia (2001) studied the relationship between reading comprehension ability and the ability to update memory. Good comprehenders were those who scored more than one standard deviation above the mean on an Italian comprehension test, while poor comprehenders scored at least one standard deviation below the mean. All subjects were matched for age and general logical intelligence as determined by a battery of tests on logical reasoning subtests present in standard group intelligence tests. They found that the updating process was not a simple inclusion/exclusion of relevant material in working memory, proposing that there is some mechanism that takes into account activation patterns and strength. Their data showed that working memory, based on selecting and updating relevant information and avoiding intrusion errors, was significantly worse for poor comprehenders as compared to good comprehenders. Carretti, Cornoldi, De Beni, and Romano (2005) conducted a follow-up study the findings of which suggested that the relationship between reading comprehension and working memory is mediated by the ability to control for irrelevant information, with poor comprehenders showing more intrusion errors that were maintained longer in working memory when compared to good comprehenders. This leads to the conclusion that poor comprehenders somehow have a less efficient inhibition mechanism when it comes to updating and using information in working memory, a finding supported by McNamara and McDaniel's (2004) work.

In short, comprehension of expository information is an active process, with the construction of understanding and integration of information comprehended taking place at an automatic level. When readers encounter difficulty, they engage more effortful processes that rely on knowledge and strategies. An LTWM accounts for the way in which readers are able to accomplish so much in building a deeper understanding of expository material and yet remain well within their resource and capacity limits.

What has also become very clear in all this is that knowledge pervades the entire process of constructing and integrating an understanding of expository discourse. It is crucial to the development not only of the text base level of understanding but also, more importantly, of the deeper-level situation model mental representation. In addition, knowledge is the linchpin of the construction of key inferences in expository materials.

## KNOWLEDGE AND THE COMPREHENSION OF EXPOSITORY VERSUS NARRATIVE MATERIAL

Kamhi (2007) suggested that those who struggle with reading comprehension may be dealing with the effects of diminished knowledge because comprehension depends heavily on knowledge, thus underscoring the prominent role of knowledge in the comprehension process. This observation is especially true when readers and listeners must deal with expository information. A productive way to examine this can be to look at it in two contexts: the aftermath of the "fourth-grade slump" in elementary education and studies that examine the contribution of knowledge to accuracy of reading comprehension of expository versus narrative texts.

### The Sequelae of the "Fourth-Grade Slump"

The crisis of the "fourth-grade slump" does not seem to go away as students mature and receive continued exposure to expository materials. Rather, the National Assessment of Educational Progress (NAEP) "national report card" (Lee, Grigg, & Donahue, 2007) reports surprisingly low percentages of students who read proficiently. These figures are essentially unchanged from 1992 to 2005. It is apparent that the reading comprehension scores of U.S. students seem to decline during middle school (Chall, 1993; Snow, 2002), resulting in what has sometimes been called the "eighth-grade cliff." Further, the low percentage of students reading proficiently remains unchanged during high school. The declining levels of reading comprehension in U.S. students across advancing grade levels draw our attention to the downward spiral that students face when they struggle to understand and learn from expository information. That is, when students have diminished comprehension of what they read or hear, it limits the scope and depth of knowledge that they acquire, in turn limiting what they can access to understand and learn other information contained in new expository materials (Alexander, Murphy, Woods, Duhon, & Parker, 1997).

Kintsch (1998) characterized learning from texts as the ability to use the information productively in new contexts because the text information is integrated with the reader's prior knowledge and becomes part of it so that it, too, can be accessed for comprehension and problem-solving activities in new contexts. The impact of early limitations in comprehension, then, can have far-reaching effects, especially because knowledge is a key player in the comprehension of expository material. If we consider the sequelae of the fourth-grade slump, it is easy to look to the continuing downward trend observed on NAEP testing the past several years. More focused and specific evidence of the role of knowledge in reading comprehension, however, is provided by studies that examine the effect of domain knowledge on reading comprehension of expository text.

## Domain-Specific Topic Knowledge

The effect of prior knowledge, especially domain-specific topic knowledge—as distinguished from general subject matter knowledge (Alexander & Jetton, 2000)—has been demonstrated to have the greatest impact on the comprehension of expository text (Alexander, Kulikowski, & Schultz, 1994; Chiesi, Spillich, & Voss, 1979; Haenggi & Perfetti, 1994). It has this differential impact because expository text communicates information unique to the domain in question. One cannot rely on general background knowledge to make sense of the more specific information conveyed in expository text. By contrast, narratives are thought to follow uniform discourse structures that contain a sequence of causally related events (Cain, 1996). Often, the events are very familiar to children and are thought to make fewer demands on children than expository texts (McNamara, Floyd, Best, & Louwerse, 2004).

The differential impact of expository text is highlighted by the findings of McNamara et al.'s (2004) study of students' comprehension during the incipient stages of the fourth-grade slump, that is, during the spring of third grade. They examined the effects of decoding skills and world knowledge on a sample of third-grade students' comprehension of narrative and expository texts. They found that better decoding skills resulted in better comprehension of the narrative text. In contrast, better comprehension of the expository text was accounted for by higher levels of world knowledge. These findings confirm the relative difficulty posed by expository texts for students about to transition into fourth grade and the role that knowledge plays in the comprehension of expository text. Further, they are consistent with the findings from this research team's other work with middle school and high school students (e.g., Best, Ozuru, & McNamara, 2004; McNamara, 2004; McNamara et al., 2003).

Studies confined to expository text per se provide a window into the extent to which knowledge impacts comprehension of expository text. Such studies indicate that more knowledgeable readers demonstrate greater use of deeper-level processes while reading expository text than less knowledgeable readers. This can be seen in their greater use of mental summarization, elaboration of main ideas, and reflective thinking about what has been read (Alexander et al., 1997) as well as in the generation of explanations of science texts (Chi, Feltovich, & Glaser, 1981) and analysis of history texts (Wineburg, 1991) than that observed in their less knowledgeable middle school, high school, and college peers.

Graesser and Olde (2003) asked college students who had been tested on a large battery of cognitive and personality measures to read an illustrated text on an everyday device for 5 minutes. Then they were presented with a scenario in which the device breaks. They were then allotted 3 minutes to produce questions about the possible causes for the breakdown and the repairs that might be made. Graesser and Olde found that the high-quality questions were posed by those students who also had high mechanical comprehension scores and electronics knowledge as ascertained by the cognitive assessment. Using more traditional experiments, Shapiro (2004) asked college students to read two texts on which they were then tested. Her first experiment used history texts the author created (fictional history); the second experiment used two texts about memory. Students' silent reading comprehension skills were also assessed with a standardized measure. She found that students' prior domain-specific knowledge (e.g., prior knowledge about memory and the topic of the selections) was more highly correlated with their comprehension of the selections than their assessed level of reading skill. In addition, their domain-specific knowledge was the only significant predictor of comprehension accuracy. These findings are buttressed by Samuelstuen and Bråten's (2005) finding that students' prior topic knowledge accounted for the most variance in their comprehension of expository text.

Finally, studies (McNamara & Kintsch, 1996; McNamara et al., 1996; O'Reilly & McNamara, 2002) have found that more knowledgeable readers demonstrate deeper understanding of expository texts that require numerous inferences. In fact, O'Reilly and McNamara (2002) found that more knowledgeable readers actually construct deeper and more accurate comprehension for texts that contain more conceptual gaps, generating more inferences.

These findings highlight the pervasive role of knowledge in the comprehension of expository materials. More knowledgeable readers answer more comprehension questions correctly and engage in deeper processing, including summarization, elaboration of main ideas, reflective thought, and formulation of better questions about problems and their solutions. Domain-specific knowledge, however, is not the "whole enchilada" of reading comprehension for expository text. When readers are faced with difficult material, they also engage in effortful strategic processing to scaffold their comprehension of expository text (Samuelstuen & Bråten, 2005), such as science texts (McNamara, 2004).

## STRATEGIC PROCESSING

The processes activated during the comprehension of expository information reflect some active engagement with the information presented. The active reader not only interacts with the information being presented but also makes sense of what has been heard or said relative to prior knowledge and the text already processed. However, it takes more than just being knowledgeable in the domain being addressed by the exposition; it often involves using that knowledge strategically.

It is thought that there is a range of strategies that are activated in the service of making sense, sometimes referred to as metacognitive strategies. *Metacognition* refers to an individual's awareness and knowledge of his or her own cognitive processes and ability to monitor and regulate them (Collins, Dickson, Simmons, & Kame'enui, 1998; Haller, Child, & Walberg, 1988). In this instance, it refers to being aware of whether one is comprehending what is being read or heard. Specifically, it involves monitoring one's understanding to determine whether what has been read or heard makes sense with what one knows and is consistent with the preceding discourse, deciding whether it needs to be repaired, and engaging the processes needed to repair the faulty interpretation.

Some comprehension processing is automatic and effortless, while other aspects, such as drawing inferences, are more effortful and active. Research, however, suggests that less accurate and/or shallow readers and listeners are more passive in their processing styles. Specifically, poor readers are less likely to reactivate text that is causally related to the sentence they are reading (Graesser et al., 1994), less likely to draw inferences that link the text they are reading to its theme (Trabasso & Magliano, 1996), and more likely to miss local semantic anomalies (e.g., *tranquilizing stimulants*; Hannon & Daneman, 2004) that make the text incoherent. This tends to result in inaccurate and/or shallow comprehension. Conversely, skilled or good readers are more likely to use these same reading strategies (Baker, 1994; Long & Golding, 1993; Long et al., 1996). Further, providing instruction on the use of active reading strategies does improve depth of processing and, not surprisingly, reading comprehension for less skilled and low-knowledge readers for both narrative and expository text (Kucan & Beck, 1997; McNamara, 2004; McNamara & Scott, 2001).

There is evidence that both strategic knowledge (Guthrie, Anderson, Alao, & Rinehart, 1999) and metacognition (Baker, 2002) influence higher-level processing of text. In addition, Ozuru, Best, and McNamara (2004) found that the effort and strategies that readers used to comprehend expository text were associated with their reading comprehension ability, with skilled readers making more elaborations at both the local or sentence level and the global or text level, linking and integrating information across the text than less skilled readers. Further, students' level of domain knowledge (high or low) did not have any influence on the frequency with which either type of elaboration was produced. Because our interest here is in processes as opposed to interventions, we look at specific metacognitive processes observed in listeners and readers as opposed to a discussion of the array of learning strategy interventions that have emerged over the past decade. Any disruption or inconsistency within and between one or more comprehension processes can result in comprehension failure that will require some repair. Consequently, listeners and readers monitor their understanding or comprehension and regulate and repair any disruptions in order to construct accurate interpretations of the expository discourse.

## Comprehension Monitoring

One of the most prominent metacognitive activities particularly relevant to listening and reading comprehension is *comprehension monitoring*. This term refers to an individual's ability to recognize when information that has been processed does not make sense in and of itself, seems inconsistent with the information that has preceded it, or is anomalous in meaning.

There is considerable evidence that skilled readers are always monitoring their comprehension. Kinnunen, Vauras, and Niemi (1998) suggested that it may range from just a momentary sense of whether one understands something to a range of actions aimed at maintaining comprehension and dealing with comprehension failures. The latter include such things as slowing down one's reading rate, rereading, stopping to search memory or think, or even ceasing to read altogether.

Some time ago, Baker and Anderson (1982) asked college students to read expository passages that contained inconsistencies related to the main points and details. The students were encouraged to reread earlier sections of the passages whenever they wanted. When the students encountered text inconsistencies, they spent more time reading sentences that contained information that conflicted with previously presented information, and they looked back more often at sentences containing inconsistencies. Further, they attended to the inconsistencies related to main points just as often as they did to those involving details.

Baker (1985) identified three standards or criteria that readers use to monitor their comprehension of text at the different levels of text processing: lexical, syntactic, and semantic. At a more local level, lexical criteria refer to whether one comprehends individual words. If the word is not understood or if the word has multiple meanings, then the individual may draw an inference—for better or for worse—about its meaning from the context, using immediate and prior context to engage in the selection of the correct sense of the word. The syntactic criteria refer to monitoring the acceptability of the syntax one has read or heard. Finally, the semantic criteria involve checking whether the semantic representations one is constructing are consistent with one's world knowledge and, especially, that the ideas are not contradictory. Baker found that children at different grade and skill levels applied these criteria differentially by grade and reading skill. She found that younger and poorer readers overrelied on the lexical or word meaning standard, while older and skilled readers applied all standards in their online monitoring of what they had read. (Similarly, Kinnunen and Vauras's [1995] eye movement study found that comprehension monitoring and text processing level were interdependent.) Those students, taught to monitor text for consistency between sentences, monitored their comprehension at the local or microstructure level. By contrast, those students taught to monitor at the lexical and syntactic levels actually attended to the propositional macrostructure of the text. Readers at every proficiency level engage in comprehension monitoring, moving along a continuum of cognitive complexity. Strategic readers, however, do more than just monitor their comprehension. In the face of comprehension failure, they actively regulate their understanding and repair inconsistencies (Pressley, El-Dinary, & Brown, 1992).

## Comprehension Regulation and Repair

Good comprehenders have been found to actively apply strategies to regulate and repair their understanding of expository material in an ongoing manner more often than less competent readers (Alexander & Jetton, 2000). Studies indicate that competent readers make greater use of their background knowledge and apply a variety of different kinds of strategies as they read (Pressley, 2000). These metacognitive strategies are used consciously and kept under the control of readers to regulate the attainment of their reading goal, the purpose for which they are reading the selection (Pressley, 2000; Trabasso & Bouchard, 2002). In fact, students with poor decoding skills have been found to develop strong text processing strategies and to exploit their background knowledge to compensate for their less fluent decoding (Strømso & Bråten, 2002; Strømso, Bråten, & Samuelstuen, 2003).

These regulation and repair strategies include producing explanations to oneself in order to elaborate and relate text information to other parts of the text read or to the readers' knowledge (Magliano, Trabasso, & Graesser, 1999), constructing the problem represented by the text and solving it (Deegan, 1995), rereading, engaging in backward and forward search strategies to cross-reference and identify information to verify or revise an interpretation (Chan, Cole, & Barfett, 1987), self-questioning, contrasting information found in the text with the reader's world and/or domain-specific knowledge, comparing main ideas with one another and the details in order to restore comprehension (Haller et al., 1988), questioning the author (Beck & McKeown, 2002), deciding whether to interpret the information literally or more liberally, and identifying portions of the information that remain confusing. All these studies provided evidence that the use of these self-regulation and repair strategies were related to good reading comprehension. In short, good comprehenders not only monitor expository information online at many levels but also access a number of strategies to keep that information logically consistent and coherent.

The myriad automatic and effortful processes engaged during comprehension are only one part of the equation. The reader or listener activates these during interaction with the properties of expository information. We now turn our attention to this part of the comprehension equation: the expository text itself.

## EXPOSITORY DISCOURSE

The comprehension of expository discourse or text is dependent on the range of processes just described and the individual's world and domain-specific knowledge. As identified earlier, these processes and knowledge also interact with the genre and features of the text itself. Information conveyed in the expository genre is often regarded more challenging for students to comprehend than that communicated in a narrative style. For accurate comprehension, there must be a sufficient "match" between the reader's knowledge and the expository genre, the text's coherence, and its cohesion for comprehension to be accurate.

### A Genre–Knowledge Interaction: Looking for a "Good Match"

When reading expository text, there must be a "match" between the reader's knowledge and the information contained in the text for comprehension to be successful. This, however, is less the case for narratives. Best et al. (2004) noted that readers are generally less familiar with information that they encounter in expository text. Because a definitional feature of expository text is the communication of unfamiliar information, they opined, why would the reader bother with it in the first place? In contrast, the purpose of reading narratives is to understand sets of plots and characters as well as for recreational purposes. Because readers often have schemas for plotlines and character types, they are less dependent on accessing domain-specific knowledge to make sense of narratives. In contrast, both the McNamara and Scott (2001) study with adults and the Best et al. (2004) study of young readers found that expository text comprehension was best accounted for by readers' prior knowledge. Without it, readers were unable to make the knowledge-driven inferences required by the expository text for accurate comprehension. As established earlier, many studies have demonstrated that readers' prior knowledge strongly influences their comprehension of expository texts (e.g., Afflerbach, 1990; Lundeberg, 1987). Those readers with greater knowledge of the domain addressed by the expository text are found to demonstrate a more accurate understanding of the information it contains (McNamara & Kintsch, 1996). As discussed earlier, Best et al. (2004) found that this was not the case for comprehension of narratives, in which decoding skills figured more prominently in children. In short, access to domain-specific knowledge seems to facilitate the comprehension of expository text. When domain-specific background knowledge is low, comprehension of the information conveyed in expository text is less complete. Other characteristics of text can influence the comprehension of expository text: its coherence and cohesion.

### Effects of Text Coherence and Cohesion

**Coherence**    The *coherence* of a text refers to its causal and logical semantic structures that make the relationships among the bits of information being conveyed articulate in a logical and reasoned manner. This text property has been found to play a crucial role in the accurate and deeper comprehension of expository text (van Dijk & Kintsch, 1983). Coherence occurs at both the local and the global level (Long & Lea, 2005). *Local coherence* refers to connections that occur among sequences of clauses. It is often achieved by the use of cohesive ties, especially those that are referential, such as anaphora. On the other hand, *global coherence* refers to information that is connected across the text, used for constructing the gist or the themes of the selection that support the construction of a situation model. It is thought that readers search for and evaluate their knowledge to construct meaning that is coherent or consistent (van den Broek, Risden, & Husebye-Hartmann, 1995). Consequently, the coherence of the text influences the types of processing activated and information integrated during the course of a reader's or listener's construction of the meaning or sense of the selection.

A number of studies have found that readers retrieve prior text information even when the incoming sentence is locally coherent with the sentences that immediately precede it (Albrecht & Myers, 1995; Lea, Kayser, Mulligan, & Myers, 2002; Long et al., 1996; McKoon et al., 1996). This effect is so robust that Albrecht and Myers found that individuals had no difficulty comprehending a locally coherent sentence that contradicted information presented much earlier in the text. The readers detected the inconsistency although local coherence was maintained. But activating information and detecting text consistency and/or relevance do not always lead to integration. Long and Chong (2001) found that both good and poor readers were slow to read a target sentence when it was inconsistent with information presented a sentence away, that is, on the local level. In contrast, only good readers showed the effect of inconsistency at the global level, in which information was separated by several sentences.

Researchers who have attended to the influence of text coherence on reading examined its effects on the quality and accuracy of readers' comprehension of what they have read. One well-known study found that those text revisions that increased the structural and explanatory coherence of texts by adding clarifying content and elaborations resulted in significantly increased memory for the ideas in a social studies text (Beck, McKeown, Sinatra, & Loxterman, 1991). Miller and Kintsch (1980) found that filling in background information as well as cohesive ties resulted in better comprehension for college students.

Improving a text's coherence, however, does not always result in improved comprehension for some individuals. McNamara et al. (1996) found that globally coherent text and more explanatory information in text did facilitate comprehension of a science text. But in a related experiment, they found that those readers who had low background knowledge about the topic being read benefited from a more coherent text. Conversely, their high-knowledge readers benefited more from a minimally coherent text because they engaged in more active processing to infer the causal relations in the text. Consequently, they processed the text at a deeper level than more coherent versions.

The construction-integration model provides us with a clear interpretation of these findings. According to the model, a well-written text with high coherence and explicit text should be easier to read, and, indeed it is, based on readers' ability to recall the text base (Kintsch, 1988, 1998; McNamara et al., 1996). The model also posits that active processing to construct meaning is important to achieve a sufficient situation model. That being the case, one would expect that a less coherent text will keep readers actively constructing meaning, leading to a better situation model as demonstrated by learning that allows transfer and generalization. Some reading strategies used by skilled readers to create this deep level of processing include making inferences through questioning the text and problem-solving operations. Indeed, McNamara et al. (1996) found support for this outcome. Specifically, they found that less knowledgeable readers did better with more coherent tests but that better/more knowledgeable readers did better with less coherent texts that required more active processing to fill in coherence gaps than the high-coherence texts. In a contrary fashion, the high-coherence texts seemed to promote a more passive reading pattern in the good/knowledgeable readers, while the low-coherence texts essentially required these knowledgeable readers to actively engage with the text, promoting increased thinking. Overall, this means that either a high-coherence or a low-coherence version of any text may not necessarily be the best text to use in classrooms where students with varying degrees of background knowledge, reading strategies, and constructive processes such as inferencing can be found.* The surface flow of the text also influences comprehension.

**Cohesion**    The surface flow of discourse, or its *cohesion*, is accomplished by the author's or speaker's explicit use of lexical and syntactic devices or cohesive ties that link it together (Halliday & Hasan, 1976). These include the use of anaphora, other pronominal reference, conjunctions, ellipses, collocation, reiteration, and the like. McNamara et al. (1996) also found that increasing the cohesion of text, that is, supplying missing cohesive ties, increased the reading comprehension of low-knowledge readers. Because these readers lacked the domain-specific knowledge needed to generate inferences when faced with texts lacking cohesion, their performance increased considerably when these ties were provided. As in the case with low-coherence text described earlier, this improvement of the text quality did not impact high-knowledge readers because they could already generate the inferences needed. Further, their performance was better for the low-cohesion texts

---

* While this chapter is not about specific interventions, it should be noted that there are promising emergent instructional strategies that can handle these individual differences in the classroom. This includes computer-driven tutoring where students can be guided individually through expository text with timely questions, cues, and prompts that model ideal comprehension strategies (e.g., Caccamise, Snyder, & Kintsch, 2008).

because inference generation involves a greater depth of semantic processing, resulting in enhanced memory and comprehension for what was read. Again, we see an interaction between knowledge and text features even at the surface level of text cohesion.

Analyses of the text cohesion of the books used in schools indicate that the expository text that the students, especially younger readers, must read for information and learning purposes is problematic. Graesser, McNamara, and Louwerse (2003) found that although the majority of the sentences in these books may be short and may contain familiar vocabulary words, the cohesive ties that younger, low-knowledge readers need to help them make the necessary connections among ideas are often lacking. Explicit surface-level linguistic devices that cue the relations among ideas being expressed in the text and foster coherence, such as causal conjunctions, were notably absent. McNamara et al. (1996) suggest that such low-cohesion texts can place low-knowledge readers at risk for being unsuccessful at comprehending expository text. This sets a less-than-ideal climate for reading and learning. The dilemma for educators and clinicians is to select text that plays the delicate line between the degree of text coherence and cohesion, the reader's knowledge, and strategic processing. In some ways, it could be likened to a search guided by the Goldilocks principle (with apologies to Landauer, Foltz, & Latham, 1998). Applying it in the context of the trade-offs in knowledge, coherence, and cohesion needed to create a viable reader–text "match," it might take the form of "this one has too little familiar information," "that one has too much explicit coherence and cohesion," and "this one's just right!"

In addition to the interaction between features of the text (i.e., its coherence and cohesion) and the individual's knowledge as core semantic processes are activated and engaged to build the comprehension of expository discourse, there is a final consideration that must be weighed. Information presented in the expository genre is communicated most frequently in two different sensory modalities: the auditory modality for spoken discourse, such as occurs in classroom lectures, documentaries, and museum and science reports, and the visual modality for written/printed discourse, such as observed in information conveyed via print or written words. Although much of oral language development, including the development of listening comprehension for discourse, typically precedes the development of reading comprehension, the two modalities of presentation themselves may influence an individual's ability to comprehend what is spoken or read.

## MODALITY DIFFERENCES

Language comprehension, especially listening comprehension, has long been thought to be a key component of reading. The ever-popular "simple view of reading" of Hoover and Gough (1990) rests on the assumption that reading is the product of the interaction between an individual's decoding skills and language comprehension ability. The latter, obviously, would seem to form the basis for the constructive and integrative processes of reading comprehension. In the context of this chapter, it is our intent to examine it from the perspective of constructive and integrative processing, with particular attention to the expository genre in order to determine the effects of modality on comprehension processes.

A number of early studies examined the effects of modality on the recall and summarization of text (e.g., Kintsch & Kozminsky, 1977; Smiley, Oakley, Worthen, Campione, & Brown, 1977). Although they found a robust relationship, they all used narrative texts. Snyder and Downey (1991) looked at the variance in silent reading comprehension scores for primarily expository texts in a standardized reading assessment, accounted for by variables from listening comprehension for narratives, such as gist accuracy. They found that for older typically achieving readers between 10.5 and 13 years of age, constructive comprehension variables from the listening comprehension task accounted for 23.7% of the unique variance in the reading comprehension scores. By contrast, this was not the case for the younger typically achieving students between 8 and 10.5 years of age in this same study. Variables related to syntactic processing accounted for the greater share of the variance with an additional 14.8% unique variance in their reading comprehension accounted for by constructive comprehension variables. These findings suggested that there is some positive relationship between constructive comprehension variables in the oral modality (albeit from a narrative task) and reading comprehension for primarily expository text. On the other hand, Sinatra (1990) has pointed out that her findings suggest that the processing of expository discourse may not be so strongly related for listening and reading, especially when the individual has to deal with lengthy or difficult texts.

Diakidoy, Stylianou, Karefillidou, and Papageorgiou (2005) studied the relationship between listening and reading comprehension for narrative versus expository text in second-, fourth-, and sixth-grade students. They found that the relationship between reading and listening comprehension for narratives increased with the advancing grade levels, with a corollary finding that the differences between the two modalities decreased in the higher grades. However, this was not the case for expository text. First of all, Diakidoy et al. found that the levels of expository comprehension were lower than narrative comprehension at all grades except second, when reading comprehension for narrative and expository texts was comparable. Further, the correlation between expository listening and reading was not significant at fourth grade and was modest at sixth grade. Expository listening and reading predicted variance in each other to a modest extent, between 12% and 14%, across the grade levels. Needless to say, the only consensus that seems to be available is that the expository genre seems difficult for schoolchildren to handle, regardless of the modality of presentation.

## COMPREHENSION OF EXPOSITORY DISCOURSE REVISITED

### Status of Comprehension of Expository Material

The research discussed points to comprehension of expository information as a case of both process and product. That is, readers and listeners engage in automatic processes to understand and make sense of expository information. They activate both their general and their domain-specific knowledge not only to construct an understanding of what they have read but also to integrate the successive pieces of information with their understanding of what has preceded them. Good comprehenders monitor what they are reading and listening to so that when they encounter inconsistencies in their understanding, they regulate them and actively engage strategies to repair the cognitive dissonance.

Further, because the purpose of the expository genre is to provide information, usually new information, characterized by low-frequency words and a high proportion of unfamiliar concepts, the expository genre is more difficult to comprehend. Readers and listeners need to activate more domain-specific knowledge to build an understanding of expository material and integrate it into their knowledge bank, which will then be engaged to process other expository materials. Inefficient comprehension processes lead to reduced levels of product, that is, new knowledge, in turn leading to a diminished ability to comprehend new materials in the same domain. Moreover, the coherence and cohesion properties of expository text interact with a reader's knowledge to promote active and/or strategic processing of the material. For the most part, the modality of presentation of the information seems to matter less in the issue of comprehension than the genre of the text. Most studies converge on the notion that expository discourse is simply more difficult to comprehend than narratives for many reasons related to processes needed to construct mental representations of what has been read and to the properties of the material being read. This led us initially to entertain the challenge of the fourth-grade slump, but this is not the final word.

## A HOPEFUL OUTLOOK

While these data sound challenging, there are a host of studies on evidence-based interventions that have proven very successful in improving students' comprehension of expository material. If we take this more pragmatic perspective, we find many recent studies that attest to the success of strategic learning interventions, especially for difficult text, such as science. The dominant feature of these interventions is their focus on promoting *deeper* comprehension. Their goal is not just the acquisition of a passive bank of domain-specific knowledge. Rather, their goal is a dynamic one: to promote readers' interaction with, within, and across levels of expository text so that this interaction occurs online; continuously builds, revises and updates, or integrates meaning; and makes sense of what has been heard and/or read.

For years, speech-language pathologists, special educators, and reading specialists have addressed and intervened in the remediation of deficits that involve both knowledge—linguistic and conceptual—and the higher-level processes that apprehend that knowledge with increasing success. As practitioners and researchers, it is this dual focus on process and product that will continue to advance our understanding of how readers and listeners comprehend expository discourse.

## REFERENCES

Afflerbach, P. P. (1990). The influence of prior knowledge on expert readers' main idea construction strategies. *Reading Research Quarterly, 25*(1), 31–46.

Albrecht, J. E., & Myers, J. L. (1995). Role of context in accessing distant information during reading. *Journal of Experimental Pscyhology: Learning, Memory, and Cognition, 21,* 1459–1468.

Alexander, P. A., & Jetton, T. L. (2000). Learning from text: A multidimensional and developmental perspective. In M. L. Kamil, P. B. Mosenthal, P. D. Pearson, & R.Barr (Eds.), *Handbook of reading research* (Vol. 3, pp. 285–310). Mahwah, NJ: Lawrence Erlbaum Associates.

Alexander, P. A., Kulikowski, J. M., & Schultz, S. K. (1994). How subject matter knowledge affects recall and interest on the comprehension of scientific exposition. *American Educational Research Journal, 31,* 313–337.

Alexander, P. A., Murphy, P. K., Woods, B. S., Duhon, K. E., & Parker, D. (1997). College instruction and concomitant changes in students' knowledge, interst, and strategy use: A study of domain learning. *Contemporary Educational Psychology, 22,* 125–146.

Baker, L. (1985). How do we know when we don't understand? Standards for evaluating text comprehension. In D. L. Forrest-Pressley, G. E. McKinnon, & T. G. Waller (Eds.), *Metacognition, cognition and human performance* (Vol. 1, pp. 155–205). New York: Academic Press.

Baker, L. (1994). Children's effective use of multiple standards for evaluating their comprehension. *Journal of Educational Psychology, 76,* 588–597.

Baker, L. (2002). Metacognition in comprehension instruction. In C. C. Block & M. Pressley (Eds.), *Comprehension instruction: Research-based best practices* (pp. 77–95). New York: Guilford Press.

Baker, L., & Anderson, R. (1982). Effects of inconsistent information on text processing: Evidence for comprehension monitoring. *Reading Research Quarterly, 17,* 281–294.

Beck, I. L., & McKeown, M. G. (1991). Social studies texts are hard to understand: Mediating some of the difficulties. *Language Arts, 68,* 482–490.

Beck, I. L., & McKeown, M. G. (2002). Questioning the author: Making sense of social studies. *Educational Leadership, 60*(3), 44–47.

Beck, I. L., McKeown, M. G., Sinatra, G. M., & Loxterman, J. A. (1991). Revising social studies text from a text-processing perspective: Evidence of improved comprehensibility. *Reading Research Quarterly, 26*(3), 251–276.

Berkowitz, S. J., & Taylor, B. M. (1981). The effects of text type and familiarity on the value of information recalled by readers. In M. Kamil (Ed.), *Directions in reading: Research and instruction* (pp. 157-161). Washington, DC: National Reading Conference.

Best, R. M., Floyd, R. G., & McNamara, D. S. (2004, November). *Understanding the fourth-grade slump: Comprehension difficulties as a function of reader aptitudes and text genre.* Paper presented at the 85th annual meeting of the American Educational Research Association, San Diego, CA.

Best, R. M., Ozuru, Y., Floyd, R. G., & McNamara, D. S. (2006). Children's text comprehension: Effects of genre, knowledge, and text cohesion. In *Proceedings of the 7th International Conference on Learning Sciences* (pp. 37–42). Mahwah, NJ: Lawrence Erlbaum Associates.

Best, R. M., Ozuru, Y., & McNamara, D. S. (2004). Self-explaining science texts: Strategies, knowledge and reading skill. In Y. B. Kofai, W. A. Sandoval, N. Enyedy, A. S. Nixon, & F. Herrerra (Eds.), *Proceedings of the 6th International Conference on the Learning Sciences* (pp. 89-96). Mahwah, NJ: Lawrence Erlbaum Associates.

Caccamise, D., & Snyder, L. (2008). Theory and pedagogical practices of text comprehension. *Topics in Language Disorders, 25,* 5–20.

Caccamise, D., Snyder, L. & Kintsch, E. (2008). Constructivist theory and the situation model: Relevance to the future assessment of reading comprehension. In C. Block & S. Parris (Eds.), *Comprehension instruction* (pp. 80-97). New York: Guilford Press.

Cain, K. (1996). Story knowledge and comprehension skill. In C. Cornoldi & J. Oakhill (Eds.), *Reading comprehension difficulties: Processes and intervention* (pp. 176–192). Mahwah, NJ: Lawrence Erlbaum Associates.

Carretti, B., Cornoldi, C., De Beni, R., & Romano, M. (2005). Updating in working memory: A comparison of good and poor comprehenders. *Journal of Experimental Child Psychology, 91*(1), 45–66.

Chall, J. (1983). *Stages of reading development.* New York: McGraw-Hill.

Chall, J. (1993). *The academic challenge: What really works in the classroom?* New York: Guilford Press.

Chall, J. (1996). *Stages of reading development* (2nd ed.). Fort Worth, TX: Harcourt Brace.

Chall, J., & Jacobs, V. (2003, Spring). The classic study on poor children's fourth grade slump. *American Educator, 27,* 14-15, 44.

Chan, L. K. S., Cole, P. G., & Barfett, S. (1987). Comprehension monitoring: Detection and identification of text inconsistencies by LD and normal students. *Learning Disability Quarterly, 10,* 114–124.

Chi, M., Feltovich, P., & Glaser, R. (1981). Categorization and representation of physics problems by experts and novices. *Cognitive Science, 5,* 121–152.

Chiesei, H. I., Spilich, G. J., & Voss, J. F. (1979). Acquisition of domain-related information in relation to high and low domain knowledge. *Journal of Verbal Learning and Verbal Behavior, 18,* 275–290.

Collins, V. L., Dickson, S. V., Simmons, D. C., & Kame'enui, E. J. (1998). *Metacognition and its relation to reading comprehension: A synthesis of the research* (Technical Report No. 23). Eugene: IDEA of the University of Oregon.

Cote, N., Goldman, S. R., & Saul, E. U. (1998). Students making sense of informational text: Relations between processing and representation. *Discourse Processes, 25*(1), 1–53.

Deegan, D. H. (1995). Exploring individual differences among novices reading in a specific domain: The case of law. *Reading Research Quarterly, 30,* 154–170.

Diakidoy, I. N., Stylianou, P., Karefillidou, C., & Papageorgiou, P. (2005). The relationship between listening and reading comprehension of different types of text at increasing grade levels. *Reading Psychology, 26,* 55–80.

Duke, N. K. (2000). 3.6 minutes per day: The scarcity of informational texts in first grade. *Reading Research Quarterly, 35,* 202–224.

Duke, N. K., & Purcell-Gates, V. (2003). Genres at home and at school: Bridging the known to the new. *The Reading Teacher, 57,* 30–37.

Ericsson, K. A., & Kintsch, W. (1995). Long-term working memory. *Psychological Review, 102,* 211–245.

Graesser, A., & Bertus, E. (1998). The construction of causal inferences while reading expository texts on science and technology. *Scientific Studies of Reading, 2*(3), 247–269.

Graesser, A. C., & Olde, B. (2003). How does one know whether a person understands a device? The quality of questions the person asks when the device breaks down. *Journal of Educational Psychology, 95,* 524–536.

Graesser, A. C., McNamara, D., & Louwerse, M. M. (2003). What do readers need to learn in order to process coherence relations in narrative and expository text? In A. P. Sweet & C. E. Snow (Eds.), *Rethinking reading comprehension* (pp. 82–98). New York: Guilford Press.

Graesser, A. C., Singer, M., & Trabasso, T. (1994). Constructing inferences during narrative text comprehension. *Psychological Review, 101,* 371–395.

Guthrie, J. T., Anderson, E., Alao, S., & Rinehart, J. (1999). Influences of concept oriented reading instruction on strategy use and conceptual learning from text. *Elementary School Journal, 99,* 343–366.

Haenggi, D., & Perfetti, C. (1994). Processing components of college-level reading comprehension. *Discourse Processing, 17,* 83–104.

Haller, E., Child, D. A., & Walberg, H. J. (1988). Can comprehension be taught? A quantitative synthesis of "metacognitive" studies. *Educational Researcher, 17,* 5–8.

Halliday, M. A., & Hasan, R. (1976). *Cohesion in English.* London: Longman.

Hannon, B., & Daneman, M. (2004). Shallow semantic processing of text: An individual-differences account. *Discourse Processes, 37*(3), 187–204.

Hoover, W. A., & Gough, P. B. (1990). The simple view of reading. *Reading and Writing, 2*(2), 127–160.

Kamhi, A. (2007). Knowledge deficits: The true crisis in education. *The ASHA Leader, 12,* 28–29.

Kinnunen, R., & Vauras, M. (1995). Comprehension monitoring and the level of comprehension in high- and low-achieving primary school children's reading. *Reading and Instruction, 5*(2), 143–165.

Kinnunen, R., Vauras, M., & Niemi, P. (1998). Comprehension monitoring in beginning readers. *Scientific Studies of Reading, 2,* 353–375.

Kintsch, W. (1988). The role of knowledge in discourse comprehension: A construction-integration model. *Psychological Review, 95*(2), 163–182.

Kintsch, W. (1998). *Comprehension: A paradigm for cognition.* New York: Cambridge University Press.

Kintsch, W. (2002). On the notions of theme and topic in psychological process models of text comprehension. In M. Louwerse & W. van Peer (Eds.), *Thematics: Interdisciplinary studies* (pp. 157–170). Amsterdam: Benjamins.

Kintsch, W., & Kozminsky, E. (1977). Summarizing stories after reading and listening. *Journal of Educational Psychology, 69*(5), 491–499.

Kintsch, W., Patel, V., & Ericsson, K. A. (1999). The role of long-term working memory in text comprehension. *Psychologia, 42,* 186–198.

Kucan, L. & Beck, I. (1997). Thinking aloud and reading comprehension research: Inquiry, instruction, and social interaction. *Review of Educational Research, 67,* 271-299.

Landauer, T., Foltz, P., & Latham, D. (1998). Introduction to latent semantic analysis. *Discourse Processes, 25,* 259–284.

Lea, B., Kayser, P., Mulligan, E., & Myers, J. (2002) Do readers make inferences about conversational topics? *Memory and Cognition, 30*(6), 945–957.

Lea, R. B., Mason, R. A., Albrecht, J. E., Birch, S. L., & Myers, J. L. (1998). Who knows what about whom: What role does common ground play in assessing distant information. *Journal of Memory and Language, 39*(1), 70–84.

Lee, J., Grigg, W. S., & Donohue, P. (2007). *National Assessment of Educational Progress Nation's Report Card: Reading.* Jessup, MD: Educational Document Publications Center.

Long, D. L., & Chong, J. L. (2001). Comprehension skill and global coherence: A paradoxical picture of poor comprehenders' abilities. *Journal of Experimental Psychology: Learning, Memory and Cognition, 27,* 1424–1429.

Long, D. L., & Golding, J. M. (1993). Superordinate goal inferences: Are they automatically generated during comprehension? *Discourse Processes, 16,* 55–74.

Long, D. L., & Lea, R. B. (2005). Have we been searching for meaning in all the wrong places? Defining the "search after meaning" principle in comprehension. *Discourse Processes, 39,* 279–298.

Long, D. L., Seely, M. R., & Oppy, B. J. (1996). The availability of causal information during reading. *Discourse Processes, 22,* 145–170.

Lundeberg, M. A. (1987). Metacognitive aspects of reading comprehension: Studying understanding in legal case analysis. *Reading Research Quarterly, 22*(4), 407–432.

Magliano, J. P., Trabasso, T., & Graesser, A. C. (1999). Strategic processes during comprehension. *Journal of Educational Psychology, 91,* 615–629.

McKoon, G., Gerrig, R. J., & Greene, S. B. (1996). Pronoun resolution without pronouns: Some consequences of memory-based text processing. *Journal of Experimental Psychology: Memory, Learning, and Cognition, 22,* 919–932.

McNamara, D. S. (2004). SERT: Self-explanation reading training. *Discourse Processes, 38*(1), 1–30.

McNamara, D. S., Best, R., & Castellano, C. (2003). *Learning from text: Facilitating and enhancing comprehension.* Available: http://www.speechpathology.com/articles/article_detail.asp?article_id=45

McNamara, D. S., Floyd, R. G., Best, R., & Louwerse, M. (2004). World knowledge driving comprehension difficulties. In Y. B. Kafai, W. A. Sandoval, N. Enyedy, & A. S. Nixon (Eds.), *Proceedings of the 6th International Conference of the Learning Sciences* (pp. 326–333). Mahwah, NJ: Lawrence Erlbaum Associates.

McNamara, D. S., de Vega, M., & O'Reilly, T. (2007). Comprehension skill, inference making, and the role of knowledge. In F. Schmalhofer & C.A. Perfetti (Eds.), *Higher level language processes in the brain: Inference and comprehension processes* (pp. 233-253). Mahwah, NJ: Lawrence Erlbaum Associates.

McNamara, D. S., & Kintsch, W. (1996). Learning from text: Effects of prior knowledge and text coherence. *Discourse Processes, 22,* 247–288.

McNamara, D. S., Kintsch, E., Songer, N. B., & Kintsch, W. (1996). Are good texts always better? Interactions of text coherence, background knowledge, and levels of understanding in learning from text. *Cognition and Instruction, 4*(1), 1–43.

McNamara, D. S., & McDaniel, M. (2004). Suppressing irrelevant information: Knowledge activation or inhibition? *Journal of Experimental Psychology: Learning, Memory, and Cognition, 30*(2), 465–482.

McNamara, D., & Scott, J. (2001). Working memory capacity and strategy use. *Memory and Cognition, 29*(1), 10–17.

Meichenbaum, M., & Beimiller, A., (1998). *Nurturing independent learners: Helping students take charge of their learning.* Cambridge, MA: Brookline Books.

Miller, G. A. (1956). The magical number seven, plus or minus two: Some limits on our capacity for processing information. *Psychological Review, 63,* 81–97.

Miller, J. R., & Kintsch, W. (1980). Readability and recall of short prose passages: A theoretical analysis. *Journal of Experimental Psychology: Human Learning and Memory, 6*(4), 335–354.

O'Reilly, T., & McNamara, D. S. (2002, November). *Text coherence effects: Interactions of prior knowledge and reading skill.* Paper presented at 43rd annual meeting of the Psychonomic Society, Kansas, City, MO.

Ozuru, Y., Best, R., & McNamara, D. S. (2004). Contribution of reading skill to learning from expository texts. In K. Forbus, D. Gentner, & T. Regier (Eds.), *Proceedings of the 26th Annual Meeting of the Cognitive Science Society* (pp. 1071–1076). Mahwah, NJ: Lawrence Erlbaum Associates.

Palladino, P., Cornoldi, C., De Beni, R., & Pazzaglia, F. (2001). Working memory and updating processes in reading comprehension. *Memory and Cognition, 29*(2), 344–354.

Perfetti, C. A. (1994). Psycholinguistics and reading ability. In M. A. Gernsbacher (Ed.), *Handbook of psycholinguistics* (pp. 849–894). San Diego, CA: Academic Press.

Pressley, M. (2000). What should comprehension instruction be the instruction of? In M. L. Kamil, P. B. Mosenthal, P. D. Pearson, & R. Barr (Eds.), *Handbook of reading research* (Vol. 3, pp. 545–561). Mahwah, NJ: Lawrence Erlbaum Associates.

Pressley, M., El-Dinary, P. B., & Brown, R. (1992). Skilled and not-so-skilled reading: Good information processing and not-so-good information processing. In M. Pressley, K. R. Harris, & J. T. Guthrie (Eds.), *Promoting academic competence and literacy: Cognitive research and instructional innovation* (pp. 91–127). San Diego, CA: Academic Press.

Rayner, K., & Pollatsek, A. (1989). *The psychology of reading.* Old Tappan, NJ: Prentice Hall.

Samuelstuen, M. S., & Bråten, I. (2005). Decoding, knowledge, and strategies in comprehension of expository text. *Scandinavian Journal of Psychology, 46,* 107–117.

Shapiro, A. M. (2004). How including prior knowledge as a subject variable can change the outcomes of learning research. *American Educational Research Journal, 41,* 159–189.

Sinatra, G. M. (1990). Convergence of listening and reading processing. *Reading Research Quarterly, 25*(2), 115–130.

Smiley, S. S., Oakley, D. D., Worthen, D., Campione, J., & Brown, A. L. (1977). Recall of thematically relevant material by adolescent good and poor readers as a function of written vs. oral presentation. *Jounal of Educational Psychology, 69,* 381–387.

Snow, C. E. (2002). *Reading for understanding: Toward an R&D program in reading comprehension.* Santa Monica, CA: RAND.

Snyder, L. S., & Downey, D. M. (1991). The language-reading relationship in normal and reading-disabled children. *Journal of Speech and Hearing Research, 34,* 129–140.

Strømso, H. I., & Bråten, I. (2002). Norwegian law students' use of multiple sources while reading expository texts. *Reading Research Quarterly, 37,* 208–227.

Strømso, H. I., Bråten, I., & Samuelstuen, M. S. (2003). Students' strategic use of multiple sources during expository text reading: A longitudinal think-aloud study. *Cognition and Instruction, 21,* 113–147.

Taylor, B., & Samuels, S. J. (1983). Children's use of text structure in the recall of expository material. *American Educational Research Jounal, 20,* 517–528.

Trabasso, T., & Bouchard, E. (2002). Teaching readers how to comprehend text strategically. In C. C. Block & M. Pressley (Eds.), *Comprehension instruction: Research based practices* (pp. 176–200). New York: Guilford Press.

Trabasso, T., & Magliano, J. P. (1996). How do children understand what they read and what can we do to help them? In M. Grades, P. van den Broek, & B. Taylor (Eds.), *The first R: A right of all children* (pp. 160-188). New York: Columbia University Press.

van den Broek, P., Risden, K., & Husebye-Hartmann, E. (1995). The role of readers' standards for coherence in the generation of inferences during reading. In R. F. Lorch & E. J. O'Brien (Eds.), *Sources of coherence in reading* (pp. 353-374). Hillsdale, NJ: Lawrence Erlbaum Associates.

van Dijk, T., & Kintsch, W. (1983). *Strategies of discourse comprehension.* New York: Academic Press.

Wineburg, S. S. (1991). On the reading of historical texts: Notes on the breach between school and academy. *American Educational Research Journal, 28,* 495–520.

Zwaan, R., & Brown, C. M. (1996). The influence of language proficiency and comprehension skill on situation-model construction. *Discourse Processes, 21*(3), 289–327.

## STUDY GUIDE QUESTIONS

1. The "fourth-grade slump" is thought to be due to a change in
   a. class schedule.
   b. curriculum.
   c. classroom narratives.
   d. text genre.
2. When readers make inferences, they do so by
   a. processing the surface code of the text.
   b. linking the text base with the information needed.
   c. using syntactic knowledge to create and build meaning.
   d. memorizing the explicit text.
3. Domain-specific topic knowledge has the greatest impact on the comprehension of
   a. expository text.
   b. political rhetorical text.
   c. science fiction.
   d. narrative text.
4. The coherence of a text refers to its
   a. causal and syntactic structures.
   b. causal and logical structures.
   c. surface flow of discourse.
   d. anaphoric reference.
5. Modality differences refer to
   a. narrative versus expository text.
   b. expository versus listening.
   c. listening versus reading.
   d. narrative versus listening.

## CHAPTER 3

# Explaining Complex Matters: How Knowledge of a Domain Drives Language
## Marilyn A. Nippold

The game of chess is not merely an idle amusement. Several very valuable qualities of the mind, useful in the course of human life, are to be acquired or strengthened by it, so as to become habits, ready on all occasions. For life is a kind of chess, in which we have often points to gain, and competitors or adversaries to contend with, and in which there is a vast variety of good and ill events that are, in some degree, the effects of prudence or the want of it.

—Benjamin Franklin (1800, p. 19)

Franklin's quote from an essay concerning important lessons about life that can be learned through the game of chess—foresight, circumspection, caution, and perseverance—is an example of how an understanding of complex matters and the will to express that knowledge can inspire the eloquent use of language. *Epistemology* is the branch of philosophy that studies human knowledge (Steup, 2007), posing fundamental questions, such as, what is knowledge, where does it come from, and how can it be examined? Ancient Greek philosophers such as Plato (427–347 B.C.) and Socrates (469–399 B.C.)

frequently debated questions such as these. Yet it was not until the 19th century that Scottish philosopher James Frederick Ferrier (1808–1864) formally coined the term *epistemology* (Wikipedia, 2008), or "theory of knowing" (Ferrier, 1875, p. 77), claiming that the goal of philosophy was to establish a body of reasoned truth.

This chapter focuses on epistemology but poses a different sort of question: how does an individual's knowledge of a domain drive the use of complex language? The ability to articulate one's knowledge of a complex topic—expository discourse—has long been of great interest to educators, prompting scholars more than a century ago to write books on the subject. For example, in 1896, Hammond Lamont, an English professor at Harvard University, wrote a book for college students titled *Specimens of Exposition* (Lamont, 1896), in which he presented examples of expository essays—drawn from varied fields of inquiry such as science, history, economics, and government—that attempted to explain complex phenomena (e.g., the construction of the steam engine, the nature of peace, and the U.S. Constitution) in an understandable fashion. According to Lamont, the quality of an essay improved when information was well organized, key terms were defined, and major points were illustrated with examples.

During that same era, additional books were written that provided detailed instruction in how to write effectively about complex matters. In 1901, Gertrude Buck and Elisabeth Woodbridge, English professors at Vassar College and Yale University, respectively, published a book titled *Expository Writing* (Buck & Woodbridge, 1901), emphasizing that authors could do their best work only when they had a sincere interest in the topic and were motivated by a genuine purpose, such as to truly inform the reader. Several years later, Frances Perry, an English professor at Wellesley College, published *An Introductory Course in Exposition* (Perry, 1908), arguing that expository writing was an essential activity because it could assist students in acquiring skills of "keen observation, deliberation, sound critical judgment, and clear and concise expression" (p. 5).

More than a century later, educators continue to emphasize the importance of expository discourse. For example, in written language, as reflected in published state standards, high school students in the United States are expected to write essays and reports where they "convey information and ideas from primary and secondary sources accurately and coherently; anticipate and address readers' potential misunderstandings; use technical terms accurately; and document their sources." Similarly, in spoken language, students are expected to "communicate supported ideas across the subject areas using oral, visual, and multi-media forms in ways appropriate to the topic, context, audience, and purpose; to make connections and transitions among ideas and elements; and to demonstrate control of eye contact, speaking rate, volume, enunciation, inflection, gestures, and other nonverbal techniques" (http://www.ode.state.or.us). In chapter 8 of this volume, Cheryl M. Scott discusses the assessment of expository discourse in children and adolescents in the context of formal speaking and writing tasks.

Given these high expectations for speaking and writing in the public schools today, the extensive resources devoted to assessment, and the fact that school success, especially beyond fourth grade (as explained by Snyder and Caccamise in chapter 2 of this volume), depends on the ability to speak, listen, read, and write in the expository genre, it is important that school-based professionals such as speech-language pathologists and teachers have access to information on the development of expository discourse in children, adolescents, and adults. Although much has been written about the development of conversational and narrative discourse (e.g., Berko Gleason & Bernstein Ratner, 2009; Clark, 2003; Nippold, 2007; Owens, 2008; Pence & Justice, 2008), comparatively little has been written about expository discourse. Fortunately, however, interest in studying the development of this genre in spoken and written modalities has increased in recent years, paralleling a growing awareness that information exchange through clear and precise communication is critical for educational success in the 21st century.

Accordingly, this chapter discusses research that examines the development of expository discourse in children, adolescents, and adults. Studies that focus on speakers with typical language development are included, as are some that include speakers with language impairments, emphasizing spoken language. Next, the chapter discusses research that examines the role of domain knowledge in relation to the complexity of expository discourse produced in spoken and written language. The role of interest and motivation in relation to the quality of expository discourse is also discussed. Finally, the chapter offers some possible implications of this body of research for education.

## DEVELOPMENT OF EXPOSITORY DISCOURSE

Although educators have expressed a long-standing interest in expository discourse and a high regard for its practical advantages, developmental studies of this genre have been undertaken only recently. In an attempt to fill this void in the literature, Nippold and colleagues conducted a series of studies that examined the use of complex syntax in spoken expository discourse in children, adolescents, and adults (Nippold, 2009; Nippold, Hesketh, Duthie, & Mansfield, 2005; Nippold, Mansfield, & Billow, 2007; Nippold, Mansfield, Billow, & Tomblin, 2008, 2009; Nippold, Moran, Mansfield, & Gillon, 2005).

In those studies, syntax was the primary focus because, as the structural foundation of sentences (Crystal, 1996), it enables a language user to express unique thoughts and ideas in an organized fashion. Specifically, the use of complex sentences can greatly increase the efficiency of communication by replacing a string of simple sentences ("I have a dog. His name is Boris.

Boris is brown and white") with one integrated unit that includes at least one subordinate clause ("I have a dog named Boris who is brown and white"). Major types of subordinate clauses include relative ("I like cats *that have green eyes*"), adverbial ("*When we get home*, let's play hide-and-go-seek"), and nominal clauses that function as objects ("Grandpa said *we're going to Disneyland*") (Crews, 1977; Quirk & Greenbaum, 1973). On entering kindergarten, most children can produce complex sentences containing all types of subordinate clauses (Diessel, 2004). Despite the sophisticated level of language use that routinely occurs in young children, the production of longer sentences containing multiple subordinate clauses that express increasingly abstract thoughts continues to develop throughout childhood, adolescence, and into adulthood (Berman & Verhoeven, 2002; Loban, 1976; Nippold, Hesketh, et al., 2005; Nippold, Moran, et al., 2005; Nippold et al., 2007; Verhoeven et al., 2002). Relevant to this chapter is the research finding that tasks that require a speaker to explain complex matters (e.g., strategies needed to win a game of chess) can stimulate children, adolescents, and adults to employ higher levels of linguistic sophistication compared to less formal tasks where they are talking about simpler, more common topics (e.g., pets, siblings, birthday parties) (e.g., Nippold, 2009; Nippold, Hesketh, et al., 2005). In other words, tasks that are cognitively challenging help to bring out a speaker's linguistic competence.

## Speakers with Typical Language Development

In a study of sentence complexity in expository discourse, Nippold, Hesketh, et al. (2005) interviewed groups of children, adolescents, and adults whose mean ages were 8, 11, 13, 17, 25, and 44 years old ($n$ = 20 per group). All participants were typically developing English speakers living in the northwestern United States. Each interview began with a conversation about common topics such as family, friends, pets, school, or work. After the conversation had ended, the Favorite Game or Sport (FGS) task was presented where the participant was asked to talk about a favorite activity and to explain the goals, rules of play, how to win, and some key strategies that every good player should know. The purpose of using the FGS task was to allow participants to speak from the comfort of a familiar knowledge base as they explained a complex topic.

Both the conversational and the expository tasks were effective in prompting the participants to express themselves verbally, and for the FGS task a wide variety of activities were discussed. These included, for example, board games such as Monopoly, Clue, Sorry, and chess and sports such as basketball, baseball, football, cross-country running, tennis, and rowing. To measure syntactic complexity, each conversational and expository sample was transcribed and entered into the computer program *Systematic Analysis of Language Transcripts* (SALT; Miller & Chapman, 2003), where it was segmented into T-units. A T-unit is a complete sentence that contains one main (independent) clause ("He has to move here") and optionally may contain one or more subordinate clauses ("*If he is here*, he has to move here") (Loban, 1976). Additionally, each instance of a finite subordinate clause was coded, including relative ("He just beat Topalov, *who was the best in the world*"), adverbial ("I learned how to play *when I was three years old*"), and nominal ("Capture the King is where *you do not have to say 'check'*") clauses. As defined by Quirk and Greenbaum (1973), a "finite clause always contains a subject as well as a predicate, except in the case of commands and ellipsis" (p. 310). Nonfinite clauses—those that do not contain a subject (e.g., infinitives and participles)—were not coded, to be consistent with previous research that examined syntactic development beyond the preschool years (e.g., Hunt, 1970; Loban, 1976). Then, for each sample, mean length of T-unit (MLTU) was computed, which is the average number of words per T-unit. Clausal density was also computed, which is the total number of main and subordinate clauses produced divided by the total number of T-units produced. These two factors are considered to be efficient measures of syntactic development in school-age children, adolescents, and adults (Nippold, 2007).

The results of the study indicated that syntactic complexity was substantially higher in the expository genre than in the conversational genre for all six age-groups on all key variables including MLTU, clausal density, and relative, adverbial, and nominal clause use. Moreover, age-related increases in syntactic complexity were observed into adulthood, with older speakers generally producing longer utterances with greater amounts of subordination than younger speakers, in both the conversational and the expository genres. To illustrate these developmental differences, Figure 3.1 contains portions of the expository transcripts from two participants in the study, an 11-year-old girl and a 26-year-old man, both of whom were talking about competitive running. Both excerpts, consisting of 10 T-units, have been entered into SALT and coded for the use of main and subordinate clauses. For this portion of the interview, the girl produced an MLTU of 10.80 words and a clausal density score of 1.70, whereas the man produced an MLTU of 19.20 and a clausal density score of 2.30. In addition to these quantitative differences, it is apparent from their interviews that the man's knowledge of the sport far surpasses the girl's, particularly as reflected in their explanations of strategies that could be used to win a cross-country race. These patterns suggest that knowledge of the topic makes an important contribution to the use of complex syntax in expository discourse.

This trend is consistent with this author's perspective that two critical factors that underlie syntactic development beyond the preschool years are intellectual stimulation and cognitive advances. As a person acquires information through education, work, and other life experiences; asks meaningful questions; draws logical inferences; and makes generalizations, that person's knowledge base and depth of understanding continuously expand, fueling the need to use complex language to express those thoughts efficiently.

**Speaker 1: 11-year-old girl**

My favorite sport is [IC] track and cross-country. In track, there's [IC] long distance and short distance. But I usually run [IC] short distance because I can go [ADV] a lot faster when it's [ADV] short distance. And cross-country it's [IC] long distance all the time. And you never get [IC] to do short distance. And I did [IC] it last year. That's [IC] the long distance. In long distance, I start [IC] off slow so I have [ADV] energy at the end. So I just go [IC] at a good pace that I know [REL] I can keep [NOM] up with while I keep [ADV] running. And then right at the end I just go [IC] as fast as I can [ADV].

**Speaker 2: 26-year-old man**

When I was [ADV] in high school, we were taught [IC] some different strategies as far as racing tactics that we could use [REL] to fool your opponent, tire them out more quickly. A couple of different things that I used [REL] to do was [IC] a lot of surging, which involves [REL] you racing along. And then you'll run [IC] harder for a short period of time or a burst of speed over a short period of time. And you do [IC] it maybe five or six times throughout the race, different lengths and different bursts. And just try [IC] to tire out your opponent so you can break [ADV] away from them and win the race. Another tactic is [IC] when you have [ADV] a lot of corners in a race and you can turn [ADV] a corner and not be seen by your opponent, put [NOM] in a surge. So when your opponent comes [ADV] around the corner, you're [IC] farther ahead than you were [ADV] before. And that's [IC] a mental tactic because it tends [ADV] to make them want [NOM] to give up. That's [IC] one of my favorites. Other people that have [REL] good sprint speed will just hang [IC] on whomever until the last half to quarter mile.

**Figure 3.1.**   Portions of the expository interviews of an 11-year-old girl (from the author's files) and a 26-year-old man, talking about competitive running. Each excerpt has been segmented into T-units and coded for finite clauses (IC, independent [main] clause; ADV, adverbial clause; REL, relative clause; NOM, nominal clause). The clause type is indicated immediately after its finite verb. (From Nippold, M. A., Hesketh, L. J., Duthie, J. K., & Mansfield, T. C., *Journal of Speech, Language, and Hearing Research, 48*, p. 1064, 2005.)

In a subsequent investigation, Nippold, Moran, et al. (2005) compared the development of conversational and expository discourse in American and New Zealand children, adolescents, and adults. In each country, 20 speakers from each of three age-groups—11, 17, and 25 years old—participated. All individuals were native speakers of standard American or standard New Zealand English who were typically developing. Each participant was interviewed individually using the same conversational and expository discourse tasks as used in the previous study (Nippold, Hesketh, et al., 2005). Then all samples were transcribed and analyzed using the same procedures as described previously.

For the FGS task, popular topics of discussion included basketball, baseball, football, and soccer for the Americans and rugby, cricket, netball, and surfing for the New Zealanders. The results indicated that the expository task elicited language samples with substantially greater syntactic complexity in both cultures for all age-groups than did the conversational task, with differences occurring for MLTU, clausal density, adverbial clause use, and nominal clause use. Across cultures, age-related growth was revealed in MLTU, clausal density, and relative clause use in both genres and in nominal clause use in conversation. Speakers from the two cultures performed similarly, although the New Zealanders tended to use slightly less complex language than the Americans, especially during conversational discourse. Figure 3.2 illustrates these developmental, cultural, and genre-related findings for the factor of MLTU.

As reported previously, the FGS task elicited a wide range of topics in speakers of all ages in studies involving English-speaking cultures (Nippold, Hesketh, et al., 2005; Nippold, Moran, et al., 2005). Recognizing the multitude of ways to examine expository discourse, Nippold et al. (2007) employed a peer conflict resolution (PCR) task in a developmental study of the use of complex syntax in this genre. Typically developing American English speakers ($n = 60$) from three age-groups—11, 17, and 25 years old—were individually interviewed. The task involved two scenarios that concerned conflicts between young people. One conflict occurred in a work setting, and the other occurred in a school setting. To begin the session, the interviewer read a peer conflict scenario aloud to the participant, who was asked to listen carefully and then to retell the story to the interviewer. For example, one of the stories, "The Fast-Food Restaurant," involved two individuals who were working at a restaurant and sharing the duties of taking out the garbage (undesirable) and working the grill (desirable). One day, the worker who was assigned to perform the undesirable task complained of a sore arm and asked the other worker to switch jobs. However, the worker with the desirable task was reluctant to do so, not wanting to miss the chance to perform an enjoyable job. After the participant had retold the story successfully, the interviewer began to ask a series of questions that were designed to prompt the individual to engage

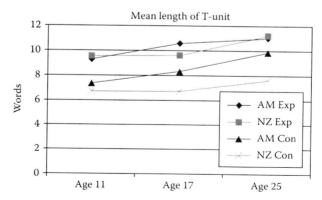

**Figure 3.2.** Mean length of T-unit for American (AM) and New Zealand (NZ) youth in the expository (Exp) and conversational (Con) discourse tasks.

in expository discourse while reflecting on interpersonal issues, such as the nature of the problem depicted in the story, how it might be resolved, and what the eventual outcome might be if it were handled in that way.

The results of the study indicated age-related increases in the use of complex syntax as measured by MLTU, clausal density, and relative and nominal clause use, with the adults outperforming the children on each of these measures. Although the mean raw scores of the adolescents exceeded those of the children on these measures, only the differences between the adults and the children reached statistical significance. Informal inspection of the transcripts from speakers of different age-groups suggested that older speakers, compared to younger ones, had greater insights into interpersonal conflicts, were better able to consider a conflict from more than one perspective, and could offer a greater number of strategies to resolve a conflict amicably. To illustrate these differences, portions of the transcripts from an 11-year-old girl and a 28-year-old woman who participated in the study are shown in Figure 3.3. Each excerpt has been segmented into T-units and coded for finite clauses. For this section of the interview, consisting of seven T-units for each speaker, the girl produced an MLTU of 11.43 words and a clausal density score of 1.71; in contrast, the woman produced an MLTU of 34.43 words and a clausal density score of 3.86. Although knowledge of interpersonal conflicts was not directly measured in this study, these patterns suggest that a speaker's knowledge of the topic influences the use of complex syntax in expository discourse.

## Speakers With Language Impairments

Studies involving speakers with language impairments have revealed similar patterns. As part of a longitudinal investigation of language development, Nippold et al. (2008) examined conversational and expository discourse in a large cohort of adolescents ($n = 444$) (mean age = 13 years) who were living in the midwestern United States. When they were in kindergarten, participants had been identified as having typical language development (TLD), specific language impairment (SLI), or nonspecific language impairment (NLI), based on the results of formal testing. Although the SLI group had demonstrated nonverbal cognition within average limits, the NLI group had performed below average in this area. At eighth grade, each participant was interviewed using the conversational and FGS tasks that had been used in two previous studies that focused on typically developing speakers (Nippold, Hesketh, et al., 2005; Nippold, Moran, et al., 2005). All samples were transcribed and analyzed as before.

As with the two previous studies, the FGS task elicited discussion of a wide variety of games and sports in all three groups. The results indicated that MLTU, clausal density, and relative, adverbial, and nominal clause use were greater in the expository genre than in the conversational genre for all three groups of adolescents. Although the groups did not differ in syntactic complexity on the conversational task, the TLD group outperformed both the

**Interviewer: What is the main problem here?**

Girl:    It's [IC] Jane's turn to work on the grill. And she doesn't want [IC] to lose that opportunity.

Woman:  The main problem is [IC] that Jane is [NOM] being asked to give up something that she does not want [REL] to give up.

**Interviewer: Why is that a problem?**

Girl:    Because Kathy's arm hurts [IC]. But Jane doesn't want [IC] to give up her position.

Woman:  It's [IC] a problem for Jane because she doesn't want [ADV] to make the sacrifice to switch tasks from a fun task to a very not so fun task. And I imagine [IC] that's [NOM] a problem for Kathy because if Jane's not willing [ADV] to switch, then Kathy will be [ADV] left needing to complete a task which is [REL] her turn to do but which will cause [REL] her pain.

**Interviewer: What is a good way for Jane to deal with Kathy?**

Girl:    Jane can say [IC], "You can be [NOM] the grill for awhile and then I'll be [NOM] the grill for awhile and we can just switch [NOM] off."

Woman:  I think [IC] a good way would be [NOM] for Jane to tell Kathy that she will be willing [NOM] to help out by taking out the garbage if it's going [ADV] to cause Kathy harm to do so, but letting her know that she really enjoys [NOM] working on the grill, and letting her know that it will be [NOM] a sacrifice for her to make this trade, and perhaps to request that sometime in the future when Kathy's arm is [ADV] better, that they might switch [NOM] tasks again so that Jane will be [ADV] able to have a time when she will get [REL] to work on the grill instead of taking out the garbage.

**Interviewer: Why is that a good way for Jane to deal with Kathy?**

Girl:    Because she just started [IC] chewing her out, "Well, it's [NOM] your turn to do the garbage, I did [NOM] mine." Then that would just make [IC] Kathy feel [NOM] even worse.

Woman:  It's [IC] a compassionate approach to Kathy's situation. If she has [ADV] an injured arm, it seems [IC] like it would be [NOM] a good way to deal with that. But it also ensures [IC] that Jane will be [NOM] able to still have her chance to work at the grill at some point.

---

**Figure 3.3.**   Responses of an 11-year-old girl and a 28-year-old woman (from the author's files) to the same questions asked by the interviewer during the "Fast-Food Restaurant" scenario on the peer conflict resolution task. Utterances have been segmented into T-units and coded for finite clauses (IC, independent [main] clause; ADV, adverbial clause; REL, relative clause; NOM, nominal clause). The clause type is indicated immediately after its finite verb. (From Nippold, M. A., Mansfield, T. C., & Billow, J. L., *American Journal of Speech-Language Pathology, 16,* 179–188, 2007.)

SLI and the NLI groups on the expository task, particularly in terms of MLTU. Thus, only the FGS task was sensitive to syntactic deficits in adolescents.

As part of a larger effort to monitor the progress of adolescents having a history of early language impairments, Nippold et al. (2009) administered the PCR task to the same groups of adolescents in the midwestern United States who had been examined when they were in eighth grade (Nippold et al., 2008). For this particular study, adolescents (*n* = 426) with an early history of TLD, SLI, or NLI were retested when they were in 10th grade (mean age = 15 years). The procedures used for eliciting, transcribing, and analyzing the language samples were identical to those that had been employed in the developmental study discussed previously (Nippold et al., 2007).

The results of the study indicated that on the PCR task, the TLD group outperformed both the SLI and NLI groups on the factors of MLTU, clausal density, and nominal clause use, thus confirming the continued presence of syntactic weaknesses in adolescents with a history of language impairments. As with the developmental study (Nippold et al., 2007), participants' knowledge of interpersonal relationships was not formally measured. However, informal analyses of the language samples suggested that many of the adolescents with language impairments, particularly those in the NLI group, were less sophisticated in their understanding of interpersonal conflicts and how they might be resolved, compared to the adolescents with typical development. For example, compared to the adolescents in the TLD group, those in the NLI group were less likely to offer multiple solutions, to view the conflict from both character's perspectives, or to describe the emotions of the individuals involved. Future studies that measure adolescents' knowledge of peer relationships in association with the content and complexity of their explanations during tasks such as the PCR should be conducted, giving consideration to cognitive and linguistic differences between language groups.

## DOMAIN KNOWLEDGE AS THE FOUNDATION FOR EXPRESSION

Relevant to this issue, several investigators have formally examined knowledge of a specific domain in relation to the production of expository discourse in typically developing individuals, using a design that controls for the amount of knowledge a speaker or writer possesses on a topic. In general, they have found that knowledge of the domain is associated with the content, quality, and quantity of discourse produced.

In one such study, Voss, Vesonder, and Spilich (1980) examined differences in text production as a function of topic knowledge in young adults ($n = 20$). The participants were university students who had taken a knowledge test on the subject of baseball, worth 45 possible points. On this test, one-half of the participants had obtained a high score (mean = 41.3) ("high-knowledge group"), and the other half had obtained a low score (mean = 13.9) ("low-knowledge group"). The groups did not differ in verbal ability based on scores from a standardized reading test. All participants were asked to write a 350-word passage in which they described a fictitious baseball game. Results indicated that the high-knowledge group was more likely to elaborate on specific game actions than the low-knowledge group and that the low-knowledge group was more likely to make irrelevant comments compared to the high-knowledge group. Whereas the high-knowledge writers focused more attention on the game itself, the low-knowledge writers focused more attention on the players, fans, and psychological issues. Thus, it was concluded that knowledge of a particular domain influences the content of writing.

In view of the findings of Voss et al. (1980) regarding differences in text production in adults with high versus low knowledge of baseball, McCutchen (1986) studied the effects of knowledge of a domain on the quality of essays produced by school-age children. Boys from grades 4, 6, and 8 (n = 30) had taken a 30-item quiz that examined their understanding of football terminology and the rules of play. At each grade level, one-half of the boys had demonstrated "high knowledge" of football, and the other half had demonstrated "low knowledge" of the sport. The high- and low-knowledge groups did not differ in verbal ability based on reading scores from a standardized achievement test. Each boy was asked to write an essay on the topic of football as if he were a sports reporter for a newspaper. All essays were analyzed for local cohesion by identifying the use of coordinating (e.g., and, but, so) and subordinating (e.g., if, when, while) conjunctions to determine how well sentences connected to each other. Essays were also analyzed for content by counting the number of topic-related details produced.

The results indicated that, at each grade level, the high-knowledge group produced a greater percentage of locally connected sentences than did the low-knowledge group. High-knowledge boys also produced more details about specific football plays than did low-knowledge boys. Thus, there were important differences in both the coherence and the content of essays produced depending on the background knowledge of the writer. This suggests that when speech-language pathologists, teachers, and other professionals encounter children who struggle to produce coherent and detailed essays, it may be helpful to examine the extent to which the writer is knowledgeable about the topic.

Indeed, there is evidence that building a child's knowledge of a domain may improve the quality of expository writing. Chambliss, Christenson, and Parker (2003) conducted a study of fourth-grade children (n = 20) who wrote expository essays on environmental pollution. Children were instructed to write their essays to be understood by younger students at their school. Prior to the writing assignment, the children had participated in a classroom-based science program where they learned about various types of pollution affecting water, air, and land. The program, which spanned several weeks, involved small-group activities such as building an ecosystem (e.g., an aquarium), helping it thrive through daily care, introducing "pollutants" such as salt and vinegar (to represent acid rain), and examining the impact on the ecosystem. The students also read informative texts on pollution, discussed the topic with their teacher, and created charts to help them organize their knowledge of the effects of pollution on living organisms.

Chambliss et al. (2003) reported that, following instruction, children wrote essays that reflected an understanding of cause-and-effect relationships, logical sequencing, and the ability to synthesize new information in ways that could be understood by younger readers. They also reported that children wrote using their own words (they did not copy from the texts) and personalized the information, making up scenarios to illustrate scientific concepts based on their own knowledge, experiences, and reasoning. However, the children reportedly had had little prior experience with scientific writing. Without the controls that a pre–post design would bring, the authors could not measure the amount of growth that occurred as a result of the instructional program. Nevertheless, the findings of this investigation are promising.

To illustrate, a portion of an essay written by one child in the study, "Juanita," is shown in Figure 3.4. This excerpt exemplifies many positive features such as causal reasoning, personalized examples, and clear explanations. In addition, it can be seen that she expresses herself efficiently through the use of complex sentences containing all major types of subordinate clauses, including relative ("Oil is a kind of liquid *that is usually the color black*"), adverbial ("But *when it spots one*, the fish has oil on it"), and nominal ("You ask *how can oil affect our plants and animals?*"). Notably, Juanita also produces complex sentences containing multiple subordinate clauses ("Let's say *a fish was swimming by* and *there was some oil*") and embedding where one subordinate clause is attached to another ("Well, do you know *what is in that fish you are eating for dinner?*").

To formally examine Juanita's use of syntax, this author entered her complete essay into SALT, segmented the writing into T-units, and coded it for all main and subordinate clauses. This process yielded a total of 34 main clauses, 18 subordinate clauses (3 adverbial, 9 nominal, and 6 relative), a clausal density score of 1.53, and an MLTU of 8.71 words. Bearing in mind that Juanita wrote this essay for younger children, a process that may have caused her to simplify her sentences, she nevertheless evidences a sophisticated level of syntactic development during this expository writing activity.

---

Oil is [IC] a kind of liquid that is [REL] usually the color black. The oil affects [IC] our plants and animals. You ask [IC] how can oil affect [NOM] our plants and animals? Well, let me tell [IC] you, my friend, how it can [NOM]. For an example, a bird tries [IC] to get a meal. But when it spots [ADV] one, the fish has [IC] oil on it. But the bird does not know [IC]. Then it goes [IC] down, misses, and gets oil on its wings. Then the bird gets [IC] affected and cannot fly well. Then we go [IC] to the fish. Let's say [IC] a fish was swimming [NOM] by and there was [NOM] some oil. The oil gets [IC] on the fish. Now the fish cannot swim [IC]. Now for a plant, the oil can cover [IC] a pond with plants in it. When the oil has covered [ADV] the whole pond, it blocks [IC] the sunlight and air. So the plants will die [IC]. Did you know [IC] that oil can affect [NOM] a whole food chain with one drop of oil on where it starts [NOM]? Let's see [IC]. First, the oil gets [IC] to the plant. So the plant dies [IC]. Then the animal that eats [REL] the animal that eats [REL] the plant dies [IC] and so on.

---

**Figure 3.4.**   Written by "Juanita," a fourth-grade student. Juanita's essay has been segmented into T-units and coded for finite clauses (IC, independent [main] clause; ADV, adverbial clause; REL, relative clause; NOM, nominal clause) by this author, who corrected errors of spelling, capitalization, and punctuation. The clause type is indicated immediately after its finite verb. (Excerpted from Chambliss, M. J., Christenson, L. A., & Parker, C., Written Communication, *20*, p. 435, 2003. With permission from Sage Publications.)

Chambliss et al. (2003) suggested that having the students carry out expository writing activities deepened their understanding of scientific concepts by requiring them to reflect on what they had learned from the science program, to integrate it with what they already knew, and to explain it to others. However, the researchers cautioned that future research is necessary to examine the "epistemic potential," or teaching value, of expository writing. Their findings also suggested that it is beneficial to build a child's knowledge base through a variety of activities as a prerequisite for strong expository writing. Although many factors contribute to successful writing (e.g., vocabulary, spelling, and punctuation), if students struggle with expository writing assignments, it may be worthwhile to investigate their understanding of the topic as a possible limiting factor.

In a fascinating study of young adults, Jones and Read (2005) interviewed university students ($n = 36$) about complex political issues to determine if a speaker's level of background knowledge concerning a given topic impacts the organization and coherence of expository discourse produced. Participants in their investigation had been classified as "experts," "intermediates," or "novices," based on their level of understanding (high, moderate, or low, respectively) of major international events, as measured by investigator-constructed political knowledge tests and awareness scales. Each participant was interviewed about a political topic and asked to talk about historical information and key individuals, groups, and countries involved. Each interview was audio taped, transcribed, and analyzed using a complex coding system.

As predicted, the experts provided significantly longer and more complicated explanations than the intermediates or novices, reflecting greater organization and coherence and a deeper appreciation of underlying causal relationships, critical details, and a historical focus on the topic. Additionally, the experts were more likely to discuss the issues in a dynamic manner, mentioning the changing nature of events and relationships, compared to the other two groups, whose explanations reflected a more static view of the circumstances. Jones and Read (2005) provided examples of transcripts of speakers from each of the three groups who were discussing the same topic, the Israeli–Palestinian conflict. Excerpts from those transcripts are contained in Figure 3.5. It is intriguing to contrast the expert with the intermediate speaker, who discussed the issues in a simplified manner, and with the novice, whose explanation was even simpler.

Because of an interest in the relationship between language and thought, this author compared the syntactic complexity of these three speakers. To accomplish this, the complete transcripts from the expert, intermediate, and novice, provided by Jones and Read (2005), were entered into SALT, segmented into T-units, and coded for main and subordinate clauses. For the expert, this process yielded 68 main clauses, 23 subordinate clauses (7 adverbial and 16 nominal), a clausal density score of 1.34, and an MLTU of 10.56 words. For the intermediate, it yielded 16 main clauses, 3 subordinate clauses (all nominal), a clausal density score of 1.19, and an MLTU of 8.38 words. Contrastively,

**Expert** (p. 60):
The conflict started [IC] at the turn of the century. Jews in Europe decided [IC] they needed [NOM] a homeland. They thought [IC] Palestine was [NOM] their homeland because they believe [ADV] that they had lived [NOM] there and they had established [NOM] their own kingdom. They tried [IC] to establish a connection with the European politicians because they wanted [ADV] to establish their own state in Palestine. Britain needed [IC] some help from the Jewish community in Europe during WWI. The price for that help was [IC] a promise from the British government to help the Jews establish their own state in Palestine. However, the Arabs helped [IC] the British against the Ottoman Empire. The Arabs were given [IC] promises of establishing their own independent Arab state.

**Intermediate** (p. 59):
There is [IC] a conflict between the Israelis and the Palestinians. Two people are fighting [IC] over an area of land. The Israelis believe [IC] that the area is [NOM] the Holy Land. The Israelis believe [IC] the land has belonged [NOM] to the Jews since thousands of years ago. Until the 1950s, the Jews were not living [IC] there. Israel was given [IC] that land area after WWII. The Palestinians were living [IC] there. The Palestinians considered [IC] it their own land.

**Novice** (p. 59):
There is [IC] a conflict between Israel and the Palestinians. The Palestinians want [IC] to take over Israel. They are [IC] in a fight. The war is centered [IC] in the Gaza Strip. It is [IC] guerilla warfare.

**Figure 3.5.**    Excerpts of transcripts from speakers having different levels of knowledge, discussing the Israeli–Palestinian conflict. Each excerpt has been segmented into T-units and coded for finite clauses (IC, independent [main] clause; ADV, adverbial clause; REL, relative clause; NOM, nominal clause) by this author. The clause type is indicated immediately after its finite verb. (From Jones, D. K., & Read, S. J. *Discourse Processes, 39*(1), 45–80, 2005.)

for the novice, it yielded only 5 main clauses, 0 subordinate clauses, a clausal density score of 1.0, and an MLTU of 6.60 words. Although this analysis is based on only one speaker per category, these patterns suggest that a person's knowledge of a topic influences the level of syntactic complexity employed such that the greater the depth of understanding, the greater the need for longer T-units with greater subordination.

The study conducted by Jones and Read (2005) prompted Nippold (2009) to examine language productivity and syntactic complexity in children in relation to their knowledge of the topic of discussion, the game of chess. This topic was chosen because chess is a complex activity that requires logical thinking and careful planning as well as knowledge of specific rules, goals, and strategies (Eales, 1985; Fine, 1967). Typically developing school-age children (*n* = 32) (mean age = 10 years, 11 months) who played chess participated in an individual interview that involved three speaking tasks: (a) a general conversation about common topics such as family, friends, and pets; (b) a chess conversation about topics such as how long they have played the game, why they enjoy chess, and their familiarity with famous chess players; and (c) a chess explanation about topics such as how the pieces move, the rules and goals of chess, and strategies needed to win a game of chess. The interviewers, who were university students, had little or no experience playing chess, creating a situation where the child was genuinely informing the adult about the topic of discussion. Each section of the interview was transcribed, entered into SALT, and analyzed for total T-units produced, MLTU, and clausal density. In addition, a U.S. master chess player served as a judge who anonymously reviewed the transcripts of all expository interviews. The judge's task was to classify each child as a relative "expert" or relative "novice" chess player based on how well the child had responded to the questions concerning the pieces, rules, goals, and strategies of chess. Then the performance of the experts ($n = 14$) and novices ($n = 18$) was compared on language productivity and syntactic complexity. It was predicted that the experts would outperform the novices on these measures during the expository task.

However, the results of the study did not support this prediction, as there were no differences between groups in language productivity or syntactic complexity. Rather, the findings indicated that, for both groups, the chess explanation task elicited the greatest amount of language output as measured by the total number of T-units produced and the greatest amount of complex syntax as measured by MLTU and clausal density. It was also found that MLTU and clausal density were greater during the chess conversation than during the general conversation. In other words, all children, regardless of their status as experts or novices, displayed their best performance when they talked about chess in the expository genre and their next-best performance when they talked about chess in the conversational genre. In contrast to these two speaking tasks, the general conversational task elicited the least amount of productivity and complexity.

Although the groups did not differ in language productivity or syntactic complexity, there was an important difference between groups, reflected in the judge's evaluation of their chess explanations. Namely, the experts displayed greater accuracy and clarity in their answers to the interviewers' questions compared to the novices, reflecting a more advanced level of understanding. Although the novices were less sophisticated in their understanding of chess, apparently their knowledge of the game was sufficient to enable them to perform as well as the experts in terms of language productivity and syntactic complexity. It is possible that other factors, such as interest and motivation, may have influenced the children's performance as well. Informal observation of the interviews suggested that many of the children were less interested in talking about common topics during the general conversation but became increasingly excited, speaking more quickly and with greater animation, as they began talking about chess. Because the children knew more about chess than did the interviewers, they were particularly enthusiastic in explaining how to win a game of chess, a pattern that occurred with both the experts and the novices. Thus, it is intriguing to examine what the children said during their interviews. Figure 3.6 contains excerpts from the three speaking tasks of a 12-year-old boy who participated in the study. During the general conversation, he produced only 21 T-units, an MLTU of 7.10, and a clausal density score of 1.10. His performance improved during the chess conversation, where he produced 31 T-units, an MLTU of 8.97, and a clausal density score of 1.35. Then, during the chess explanation, where his extensive knowledge of chess was revealed, he produced 51 T-units, an MLTU of 10.63, and a clausal density score of 1.61. Comparisons across excerpts such as this suggest that when school-age children are asked to discuss complex topics about which they are knowledgeable, interested, and motivated, they demonstrate an exceptionally high level of productivity and complexity that is

---

**General Conversation**

Interviewer: Do you have any pets at home?
Child: I have [IC] one guinea pig.
Interviewer: Really? Can you tell me about your guinea pig?
Child: She usually just stays [IC] in her little igloo. She loves [IC] her vitamins. And every morning, she will come [IC] out squeaking for her vitamin. And she also loves [IC] coming outside and eating on grass in our lawn.

**Chess Conversation**

Interviewer: How often do you play chess in a typical week?
Child: Once. Every Wednesday.
Interviewer: Who do you play with the most?
Child: Oh, whoever is at chess club that week.
Interviewer: Can you name any famous chess players?
Child: Oh, I can [IC] name a fair amount. Anand, Kasparov, Karpov, Ponomariov. Everyone who ends in "ov."
Interviewer: Can you tell me about one of them?
Child: Topalov is [IC] a very tactical player. And Kasparov is [IC] a very defensive player. And I think [IC] he just retired [NOM]. Like he was [IC] world champion twice now. And he just beat [IC] Topalov who was [REL] the best in the world.

**Chess Explanation**

Interviewer: Now can you tell me the rules that players need to follow?
Child: That is [IC] a fair amount of rules. Let's [IC] see. If your king is [ADV] being attacked, you have [IC] to move it out of there. And if you can't [ADV], you have [IC] to block it. And if you can't [ADV], you have [IC] to take the piece that is attacking [REL] your king. And if you can't [ADV], then you lose [IC] because you are [ADV] in checkmate and you can't move [ADV] anything but your king. You can't move [IC] a piece that is attacking [REL] your king. I can't think [IC] of anything else.

---

**Figure 3.6.** Excerpts from the three speaking tasks of a 12-year-old boy who participated in the study of expository discourse in chess players. Utterances have been segmented into T-units and coded for finite clauses (IC, independent [main] clause; ADV, adverbial clause; REL, relative clause; NOM, nominal clause). The clause type is indicated immediately after its finite verb. (From Nippold, M. A., *Journal of Speech, Language, and Hearing Research*, 2009, *52*(4), 856–871.)

not apparent when they are discussing simpler, more general topics that offer less intellectual stimulation.

## THE ROLE OF INTEREST AND MOTIVATION

In the Nippold (2009) study of chess players, the factors of interest and motivation were not objectively measured but were noted subjectively during the interviews. Nevertheless, there is evidence from research that interest and motivation are important ingredients in the quality of an individual's verbal expression, a point that was argued many years ago by English professors Buck and Woodbridge (1901).

Peters (1989) conducted a qualitative study of sixth-grade students ($n = 5$) who were participating in a series of writing sessions at school. Students were interviewed about their own compositions over a period of several months. Peters reported that students were most enthusiastic about the writing process and did their best work when they were allowed to personalize the information. For example, one day, their teacher assigned them to write about countries they had been studying. One student wrote about England, imagining that he had visited London, where he met famous people (e.g., Margaret Thatcher), took pictures of landmarks (e.g., Tower of Big Ben), and attended a meeting of Parliament. Another student imagined she was traveling around the world, writing postcards to a friend by describing pictures in her social studies textbook.

The findings of Peters's (1989) study showed that allowing students to write about topics they were genuinely curious about (e.g., travel, public safety, or the Civil War) encouraged them to seek new information that they incorporated into their essays, a result that supports the epistemic value of expository writing activities (Chambliss et al., 2003). This is the view that the act of explaining some aspect of a complex domain will help to build the individual's knowledge of the domain. Peters's study also suggested that giving students the freedom to entertain the reader with exciting or humorous anecdotes encouraged them to express what they knew, a result that supports the view that interest and motivation are critical to good writing (Buck & Woodridge, 1901). Although in public schools today students are frequently required to write expository essays about topics driven by state-mandated curricula, it is important to allow students the flexibility to perform these tasks in ways that will bring out their best performance.

## SUMMARY

Studies reported in this chapter indicate that spoken and written expository discourse tasks can prompt language users of all ages, including children, adolescents, and adults, to employ higher levels of syntactic complexity compared to tasks where they are communicating less formally about simpler topics. For example, there are marked differences in complexity when speakers are explaining the rules of basketball, tennis, or chess compared to when they are talking about their pets, family, or friends. This pattern has been reported in populations with typical as well as impaired language development. Studies also indicate that individuals who have greater depth of knowledge or expertise with respect to a particular domain such as political conflicts, games, or sports tend to express themselves with greater organization, accuracy, coherence, and logic compared to their less knowledgeable peers. Having a strong interest in the topic and a genuine need to express that knowledge also appears to contribute to the quality of expository discourse produced. Future studies are needed to explore these patterns more fully.

## IMPLICATIONS FOR EDUCATION

Since the late 1800s and early 1900s, educators (e.g., Buck & Woodbridge, 1901; Lamont, 1896; Perry, 1908) have written about the importance of spoken and written expository discourse for success in life, a view that continues to be endorsed by modern educational systems. Given the research that has been reported in this chapter, it is worthwhile to speculate on some possible implications it may hold for education.

School-based professionals such as speech-language pathologists and teachers often seek to encourage children, adolescents, and young adults to tap into their own linguistic competencies for the purpose of expressing themselves more effectively. To accomplish this goal, it may be useful to engage students in expository discourse tasks that are interesting and motivating and that require specialized knowledge of the topic. For example, if working with middle school students who demonstrate weaknesses in expressive language development, the professional may begin by helping the students learn a popular game or sport that is highly valued by their peer group. Perhaps a typical peer could be recruited to act as a tutor who explains the activity to a small group of students in need of assistance. Then the students could be coached on how to explain the game or sport in their own words "so that others will know how to play." Following successful practice sessions, the students could be asked to display their new knowledge by actually teaching younger children how to play under the continued guidance of the professional. Throughout these activities, the professional can encourage students to employ complex syntax so as to communicate the essential ideas in a clear, organized, and efficient manner. After achieving success with a popular peer activity, the students could progress to other subjects that require precise explanations. Motivating topics might include, for example, how to build an aquarium, how to create a map of the school grounds, how to score a cross-country race, or how to make a prom dress. Once students have achieved success with practical topics such as these, they may be ready to approach more challenging academic topics that arise in economics, science, or math classes. Although schools may be expected to follow predetermined curricula in classes such as these, given the importance of knowledge, interest, and motivation as factors influencing the quantity and quality of language produced, students may be more successful if they are encouraged to speak and write about topics that they find personally meaningful.

It has been argued that expository discourse activities have the potential to build an individual's knowledge base (Chambliss et al., 2003). Given the theme of this chapter that knowledge of a domain provides the foundation for expression, this would support a symbiotic relationship between knowledge and language in which each of these mental constructs continuously drives the other to higher levels of excellence. Future research is necessary to explore this relationship in school-age children, adolescents, and adults.

## REFERENCES

Berko Gleason, J., & Bernstein Ratner, N. (2009). *The development of language* (7th ed.). Boston: Pearson.

Berman, R. A., & Verhoeven, L. (2002). Cross-linguistic perspectives on the development of text-production abilities: Speech and writing. *Written Language and Literacy, 5*(1), 1–43.

Buck, G., & Woodbridge, E. (1901). *A course in expository writing*. New York: Holt.

Chambliss, M. J., Christenson, L. A., & Parker, C. (2003). Fourth graders composing scientific explanations about the effects of pollutants: Writing to understand. *Written Communication, 20*(4), 426–454.

Clark, E. V. (2003). *First language acquisition*. Cambridge: Cambridge University Press.

Crews, F. (1977). *The Random House handbook* (2nd ed.). New York: Random House.

Crystal, D. (1996). *Rediscover grammar* (2nd ed.). Essex: Longman.

Diessel, H. (2004). *The acquisition of complex sentences*. Cambridge: Cambridge University Press.

Eales, R. (1985). *Chess: The history of a game*. Oxford: Facts on File Publications.

Ferrier, J. F. (1875). *Philosophical works of the late James Frederick Ferrier* (Vol. 1): Institutes of metaphysic (3rd ed.). Edinburgh: William Blackwood and Sons.

Fine, R. (1967). *The psychology of the chess player*. New York: Dover.

Franklin, B. (1800). The morals of chess. In H. D. Symonds & T. Hurst (Eds.), *Chess made easy: New and comprehensive rules for playing the game of chess* (3rd ed., pp. 19–25). London: J. Cundee.

Hunt, K. W. (1970). Syntactic maturity in school children and adults. *Monographs of the Society for Research in Child Development, 35*(1, Serial No. 134).

Jones, D. K., & Read, S. J. (2005). Expert-novice differences in the understanding and explanation of complex political conflicts. *Discourse Processes, 39*(1), 45–80.

Lamont, H. (1896). *Specimens of exposition*. New York: Holt.

Loban, W. (1976). *Language development: Kindergarten through grade twelve*. Urbana, IL: National Council of Teachers of English.

McCutchen, D. (1986). Domain knowledge and linguistic knowledge in the development of writing ability. *Journal of Memory and Language, 25,* 431–444.

Miller, J. F., & Chapman, R. (2003). SALT: Systematic Analysis of Language Transcripts [Computer software]. Madison: University of Wisconsin, Waisman Center, Language Analysis Laboratory.

Nippold, M. A. (2007). *Later language development: School-age children, adolescents, and young adults* (3rd ed.). Austin, TX: PRO-ED.

Nippold, M. A. (2009). School-age children talk about chess: Does knowledge drive syntactic complexity? *Journal of Speech, Language, and Hearing Research, 52*(4), 856–871.

Nippold, M. A., Hesketh, L. J., Duthie, J. K., & Mansfield, T. C. (2005). Conversational versus expository discourse: A study of syntactic development in children, adolescents, and adults. *Journal of Speech, Language, and Hearing Research, 48*, 1048–1064.

Nippold, M. A., Mansfield, T. C., & Billow, J. L. (2007). Peer conflict explanations in children, adolescents, and adults: Examining the development of complex syntax. *American Journal of Speech-Language Pathology, 16*, 179–188.

Nippold, M. A., Mansfield, T. C., Billow, J. L., & Tomblin, J. B. (2008). Expository discourse in adolescents with language impairments: Examining syntactic development. *American Journal of Speech-Language Pathology, 17*, 356–366.

Nippold, M. A., Mansfield, T. C., Billow, J. L., & Tomblin, J. B. (2009). Syntactic development in adolescents with a history of language impairments: A follow-up investigation. *American Journal of Speech-Language Pathology, 18*(3), 241–251.

Nippold, M. A., Moran, C., Mansfield, T. C., & Gillon, G. (2005, July). *Expository discourse development in American and New Zealand youth: A cross-cultural comparison.* Poster session presented at the 10th International Congress for the Study of Child Language, Freie Universitat, Berlin, Germany.

Oregon Department of Education. Available: http://www.ode.state.or.us/. Retrieved August 17, 2009.

Owens, R. E. (2008). *Language development: An introduction* (7th ed.). Boston: Pearson.

Pence, K. L., & Justice, L. M. (2008). *Language development from theory to practice.* Upper Saddle River, NJ: Pearson/Merrill/Prentice Hall.

Perry, F. M. (1908). *An introductory course in exposition.* New York: American Book Company.

Peters, B. T. (1989). What sixth graders can teach us about form and competence. *Language Arts, 66*(2), 171–183.

Quirk, R., & Greenbaum, S. (1973). *A concise grammar of contemporary English.* New York: Harcourt Brace Jovanovich.

Steup, M. (2007). Epistemology. In E. N. Zalta (Ed.), *The Stanford encyclopedia of philosophy (winter edition).* Available: http://plato.stanford.edu/archives/win2007/entries/epistemology

Verhoeven, L., Aparici, M., Cahana-Amitay, D., van Hell, J., Kriz, S., & Viguie-Simon, A. (2002). Clause packaging in writing and speech: A cross-linguistic developmental analysis. *Written Language and Literacy, 5*(2), 135–162.

Voss, J. F., Vesonder, G. T., & Spilich, G. J. (1980). Text generation and recall by high-knowledge and low-knowledge individuals. *Journal of Verbal Learning and Verbal Behavior, 19*, 651–667.

Wikipedia. (2008). Epistemology. Retrieved January 17, 2008, from http://en.wikipedia.org/w/index.php?title=Epistemology&oldid=184893678

## STUDY GUIDE QUESTIONS

1. Expository discourse is the use of language to
   a. tell stories.
   b. argue or persuade.
   c. convey information.
   d. have a conversation.

2. Interest in expository discourse among educators began to emerge
   a. during the late 1800s.
   b. after World War II.
   c. during the 1960s.
   d. during the early years of the 21st century.
3. What is true about adolescents with a history of language impairments?
   a. Lingering syntactic deficits are obvious in conversational discourse.
   b. They use less subordination in expository discourse than in conversational.
   c. MLTU is no longer an important marker of syntactic development.
   d. Syntactic weaknesses are revealed by expository discourse tasks.
4. Research reported in this chapter suggests that key factors contributing to the quality of a person's spoken or written expository discourse include
   a. knowledge, interest, and motivation.
   b. personality, income, and social status.
   c. temperament, creativity, and optimism.
   d. persistence, patience, and drive.
5. It has been suggested that school-age children and adolescents who struggle with expository discourse tasks might be helped by having them
   a. participate more frequently in organized sports such as soccer.
   b. learn a new game or sport and attempt to teach it to others.
   c. memorize important names and dates of historical events.
   d. spend more time playing with younger children.

## CHAPTER 4

# The Development of Multimodal Explanations in French Children
## Jean-Marc Colletta and Catherine Pellenq

In this chapter, we focus on the development of explanatory abilities in French children attending nursery school and grade school. Even if young children are unable to produce written explanatory texts, there is nothing to stop them from formulating oral explanations. It is the "why" type of explanation that we intend to examine here and, more specifically, the way it develops with age. Furthermore, since speech acts are multimodal, children's explanatory verbal productions are frequently accompanied by bodily movements (hand and head gestures, facial expressions, changes of posture). The observation of gesture associated with speech provides data of considerable interest to anyone in the field of discourse development and the evolution of abstract thought.

In the first section, "Discourse Development and Explanatory Abilities in Speech," we begin by defending the idea that the study of the way in which explanations develop is a valuable starting point in gaining an understanding of how children come to master the academic (i.e., monologic) uses of discourse. In the next section, "Monologic Discourse and Gesture Development," we report certain data that shed light on the importance of gesture in spoken communication as well as other data that suggest that the gestural system associated with speech undergoes an undeniable development. In the third section, we document the methodological choices made for the study that underlie the results and analyses presented in this chapter. This comparative study consists of two facets, one relating to the explanatory behavior of children aged 6 to 11 years and the other relating to the equivalent behavior in younger children aged 3 to 6 years. In the fourth section on the development of explanatory abilities in French children, we present the most significant results of this study, showing that spoken explanations are more complex in older children than in younger ones. These results argue in favor of the idea that the ability to verbalize monologic explanations develops with age.

The gestural aspects of children's explanations are discussed in the remaining sections. It would appear that gestures relating to abstract dimensions and discourse cohesion are most prominent among the gestures that accompany the explanations produced by children aged 6 years and older (fifth section). While the utilization of such gestures is well documented in adults, their high rate in this corpus may seem surprising. Nevertheless, a semiotic analysis of these gestures reveals that they are based on the same properties as those observed in adults: abstract pointing and spatial metaphors (sixth section). In contrast, a comparison with the gestures produced by younger children indicates that they are practically absent in the latter. This finding is consistent with the hypothesis that the gestural system associated with speech develops through childhood (seventh section). The conclusion proposes a summary of this set of observations and results and addresses the implications both for explanatory development and, more generally, for language and cognitive development.

## DISCOURSE DEVELOPMENT AND EXPLANATORY ABILITIES IN SPEECH

Language acquisition is far from complete when a child enters primary school, and, as many authors have pointed out, 6-year-old children have mastered very few textual abilities that go along with monologic discourse (Fayol, 1997; Halliday, 1975; Hickmann, 2003; Jisa, 2004; chapters 1 and 5 in this volume). There are several reasons for the late mastery of monologic discourse, which we define here as the individually controlled use of language.

First, monologic discourse, like narratives and other facets of academic discourse, is language built at a textual level (Adam, 1999; Bartlett, 1964; Fayol, 1985; Mandler & Johnson, 1977; Roulet, Fillietaz, & Grobet, 2001; van Dijk, 1985), and its use is based on the ability to understand and generate linguistic information organized at this additional level. Second, monologic discourse displays specific properties of coherence and cohesion (Halliday & Hasan, 1976; Lundquist, 1980; Weinrich, 1989) that have no equivalent in conversation, which is constructed from the sequencing of short speech turns. At the same time, these properties define the written use of language with the result that later language development proves to be directly related to the acquisition of literacy (reading and writing) abilities (Jisa, 2004; Tolchinsky, 2004). Third, monologic discourse is language that is underpinned by reference displacement, decontextualization, and cognitive decentration. These involve cognitive abilities not exhibited by young preschool children (Golder, 1996; Hickmann, 2003; Karmiloff-Smith, 1979). Nevertheless, the studies of text production in children focus primarily on the development of textual abilities in terms of writing (Fayol, 1997). Consequently, little is known about the way children over 5 years of age come to perform oral monologic discourse.

However, for anyone interested in monologic discourse acquisition, the development of the ability to produce spoken explanations is of particular importance for a variety of reasons. First, unlike narratives, which are built from distinct sequences, explanations do not necessarily require an internal textual organization. Of course, there is such a thing as an "explanation" in the strict sense of the term, that is to say, a causal explanation in cases where there is an explanandum, that is, a phenomenon or behavior to be explained and an explanans or cause, reason, or motivation for this phenomenon or behavior (Veneziano & Hudelot, 2002; Veneziano & Sinclair, 1995). At the structural level, causal explanations necessarily link two sequences in the textual form <P because Q> (Adam, 1992). Whereas in writing a relationship is established between these two components in explanatory texts, this is not necessarily the same in spoken communication, where the dynamic of spoken exchanges means that the explanandum and explanans tend to be split over two speech turns:

**Speaker 1:**   why P
**Speaker 2:**   because Q

The second reason relates to the heterogeneity of the explanatory forms: Because spoken explanations may take the simple form with a single clause <because Q>, we might expect them to appear before narratives in children's language production. This is indeed the case: Studies of narrative development show that children are scarcely able to produce a narrative before the age of 5 years (Fayol, 2000), whereas the first explanations appear even before the end of their second year (Veneziano, 1998). Of course, these are not genuine causal explanations, and the productions observed at this age are really justifications: Children provide a reason for their demands, refusals, or behavior. For example, they may stretch their arm out toward their cup that is out of reach, look at the accompanying adult, and say "want drink" in order to justify the request or push away an extra spoonful of food while saying "not hungry" to justify the refusal. Another specific characteristic of these initial verbalizations is that they do not include the connector "because," which does not appear until the child's third year (Diessel, 2004; Kail & Weissenborn, 1984; Veneziano & Sinclair, 1995). In addition, children rarely verbalize the explanandum with the result that the adult has to identify it himself or herself in the context.

The third reason for our interest in the development of explanations comes from the observations set out previously. Purely at the linguistic level, there is an immense gap between children's first verbalized situational explanans and the explanatory written texts that they are able to draft during their final years of grade school. By then, they can dissociate themselves from the immediate situation and have acquired a decontextualized use of language, and, additionally, they have assimilated the constraints relating to cohesion and coherence that underlie the use of the textually organized forms of language both in individually controlled speech and in writing.

A priori, one might therefore imagine that the development of explanations between the ages of 3 and 11 years acts as a window into the development of monologic discourse. During the study described in this chapter, we tested the hypothesis that the ability to produce spoken explanations develops throughout nursery school, preschool, and grade school toward the production of textual uses of language.

## MONOLOGIC DISCOURSE AND GESTURE DEVELOPMENT

For more than half a century, since the pioneering work of Birdwhistell (1952), Scheflen (1964), Condon and Ogston (1966, 1967), and Kendon (1972, 1980), researchers have been interested in the scientific study of communications conveyed by body signals. The observations made by specialists in the study of gestures have led us to consider situation-based spoken communication to be a flow of multimodal information coming from the words, the voice, and the body.

Naturally, this observation may appear trivial: After all, don't we greet a friend with our hand or head while also using words? Don't we smile at the same time as offering an excuse? Don't we nod our heads to answer a question in the affirmative? However, the studies undertaken by gesture specialists tell us much more than these simple observations that relate only to the accomplishment of everyday language acts. When someone starts speaking to defend a point of view, offer an explanation, or recount an event, the person's face is frequently seen to express mental states and emotions while the head and hands move to express the speaker's thoughts. These face, head, and hand movements, sometimes accompanied by changes of posture, are known as "coverbals." They serve a number of functions, the most important of which are listed here (Colletta, 2004; Cosnier & Vaysse, 1997; Kendon, 2004; McNeill, 1992; see definitions and examples in Appendix 4.A at the end of this chapter):

- The identification of discourse objects with deictic or directional pointing when they are present and localizable in the physical communication setting or nearby
- The representation of discourse objects by means of gestures that depict or mime concrete referents and symbolize abstract referents
- The expression of emotions, mental states, and everyday language acts

- The structuring of language production through the emphasizing of basic components of speech (syllable, word, word group)
- Discourse cohesion by means of gestural anaphora and the marking of interclause relations, discourse units, and discourse structure
- Synchronization between speakers and the coordination with each other's behavior during social interaction

It is true that some speakers "move" more than others when they are talking and that some express a lot with their faces and little with their hands while others do the opposite, and it is also true that variables such as age, gender, and cultural environment influence gestures just as they impact communication behavior in general. However, it is still the case that, beyond our individual differences, we are all able to use our bodies to accompany our speech and that, when we do so, our gestures are coexpressive with our speech (Kendon, 2004). By calling on coverbal resources, we are able to perform multimodal messages in which the visual signals provide information that is sometimes redundant and sometimes complementary or supplementary to the vocoverbal signals. However, while we now possess a substantial volume of multimodal observations concerning adult speakers and social interactions between adults in English and other languages (Brookes, 2004, 2005; Kendon, 1990, 2004; McNeill, 1992, 2000; Poggi & Magno Caldognetto, 1997; Poyatos, 1992), including French (Bouvet, 2001; Calbris, 2003; Calbris & Porcher, 1989; Léonard & Pinheiro, 1993), the multimodal study of children's language is not so far advanced.

Although many descriptions of young children's communicative behavior are available (for more details, see Guidetti, 2003; Iverson & Goldin-Meadow, 1998; Marcos, 1998), we still know little about the way multimodal speech develops after the age of 2 years, once the child has gone past the preverbal stage. A few studies have focused on the nonverbal behavior of children age 3 and above (Cosnier, 1982; Garitte, Le Maner, & Le Roch, 1998; Goldin-Meadow, 2003; McNeill, 1992; Montagner, 1978). Although the results of these studies are not always consistent, they nevertheless lead us to hypothesize about the development of the gestural system associated with speech. In other words, the use of hand and head gestures, facial expressions, and changes of posture directly linked to speech should vary with age and develop as the child gains new cognitive and linguistic abilities. The fact that new gestural behaviors (pointings, representational gestures) emerge at the same time as new linguistic abilities in younger children (Bates, Benigni, Bretherton, Camaioni, & Volterra, 1979; Butcher & Goldin-Meadow, 2000; Capirci, Caselli, Iverson, Pizzuto, & Voltera, 2002; Capirci, Iverson, Pizzuto, & Voltera, 1996; Goldin-Meadow & Butcher, 2003, Özçaliskan & Goldin-Meadow, 2005) is consistent with this hypothesis.

In the study presented here, we attempted to test the hypothesis that the gestural system associated with speech develops in ways that abstract and discourse gestural behaviors appear and grow in the course of language acquisition. To do so, we observed the oral explanatory behavior of children between the ages of 3 and 11 years. Apart from confirming the existence of this development, the semiotic study of the gestures that accompany the spoken explanations yields some fascinating observations that we consider in greater detail in the fifth and sixth sections of this chapter.

## METHODOLOGICAL ISSUES

In recent years, we collected two corpuses of children's explanations. We had two objectives in doing so. First, we wanted to gather a set of data that was otherwise almost or totally nonexistent at the time, and, second, we wanted to study the development of multimodal explanatory abilities between the ages of 3 and 11 years.

The first set of data was taken from video recordings of children aged from 6 to 11 years engaged in conversation with an adult (Colletta, 2004). Sixty children from grade school were filmed in groups of three children of the same age. The interviews focused on family and social topics, and their main purpose was to prompt the children to produce causal explanations and verbal reasoning. These recordings enabled us to derive an initial corpus of 232 spoken explanations.

The second set of data was taken from video recordings of nursery school and preschool classroom interactions during teaching sessions. Twenty-four sessions were chosen for their exemplary value as classroom activities used by teachers to elicit causal explanations from young children aged from 3 to 6 years (Colletta, Simon, & Lachnitt, 2005; Colletta, Simon, Vuillet, & Prévost, 2004). Language sessions, experiments relating to the topics of air and water, art workshops, and sessions involving logical reasoning were filmed in six nursery schools. These recordings yielded a second corpus of 268 spoken explanations.

All 500 explanations present in these two corpuses were formulated by children in response to a "why" question asked either by an adult (interviewer or teacher) or by another child. Because of the widely divergent educational contexts and discourse topics, the semantic and thematic aspects of these causal explanations could not be taken into account. We therefore restricted our observations to the formal aspects of the collected data. Each explanation was verbally transcribed, and the transcriptions were checked several times by different people.

Each explanation was then carefully analyzed. We measured its duration as well as its linguistic content: number of syllables, number of clauses, and number of connectives. Duration is an interesting parameter since it provides information about the child's ability to manage varying lengths of explanatory speech turns. The number of syllables provides additional information about children's verbal production abilities but tells nothing about their discourse capacity. In contrast, the fact that a child produces an explanation composed of several clauses linked by connectives, which represent genuine tools for the establishment of textual cohesion, provides direct information about his or her monologic discourse abilities. In line with our aim, which is to study the gestural and not solely the verbal aspects of children's explanations, we also measured the number of coverbal movements performed by the child while formulating his or her explanation.

The coverbal movements were identified using a somewhat complex procedure that needs to be explained in greater detail. A prior examination based on our initial data (Colletta, 2000) allowed us to construct a classification of children's coverbal movements. The head and hand gestures, facial expressions, and changes of posture that we observed were found to be very similar to those found in adult studies. Whether children use them in the same manner as adults remains an unanswered question, but we found that children's coverbal gestures can be assigned to the same categories as those set out in the second section of this chapter and defined in Appendix 4.A. Two categorization tests were later constructed from the corpus, and 122 university students were asked to classify and code the coverbal movements that were shown to them during the experiment.

The results (Colletta, 2000) indicated that some gestures were easily classified, while others proved harder to code. We learned that coverbal gestures can be coded with a fair level of interjudge agreement (65% overall agreement) by persons who have never been trained to do so, thus indicating that everyone has some knowledge of the functions and meanings of coverbal gestures. Further, there was a very high level of agreement (up to 90%) for pointing gestures, synchronization gestures, expressive gestures, and concrete representational gestures (see Appendix 4.A for definitions). Moreover, agreement was poor (as low as 40%) for abstract representational gestures and gestures that mark discourse cohesion (see Appendix 4.A for definitions). It is worth noting that all gestural categories that were easy to code play an active role in the construction of reference or in the expression/detection of communicative intentions. Other categories of gestures may prove to be more important for the speaker him- or herself than for the listener during the speech production process.

As part of the current debate concerning the role of gesture in speech, some researchers (Feyereisen, 1994; Hadar & Butterworth, 1997; Krauss, Chen, & Gottesman, 2000; Krauss, Dushay, Chen, & Rauscher, 1995; Levelt, 1989) have claimed that gesture has no real communicative purpose because of its fuzzy semiotic properties (for instance, the meaning of a coverbal gesture is highly dependent on its context). Others, like McNeill (McNeill, 2005; McNeill & Duncan, 2000), Kita (2000), and Ruiter (2000), claim that gesture plays a crucial role in communication and that the listener pays close attention to it while processing the speaker's message, which is both audible and visual. We claim that both postulates may be true, depending on the category of gestures investigated in each study, whether they have an obvious communicative purpose (deictic gestures, concrete representational gestures, expressive gestures) on the one hand, or whether they help the speaker during the speech production process (abstract representational gestures, gestures that mark discourse cohesion, and beats that mark the structure of speech) on the other.

In the present study, all the coverbal movements performed by the children aged from 6 to 11 years were identified and coded by several independent coders. The coverbal movements performed by the children aged from 3 to 6 years (second set of data) were identified and coded by two independent coders. We now present the main results arising from this study.

## THE DEVELOPMENT OF EXPLANATORY ABILITIES IN FRENCH CHILDREN: FROM CLAUSE TO TEXT

The results presented in Table 4.1 come from the fusion of the two sets of data, thus giving us a complete picture of the formal changes observed in explanatory behavior from nursery school (children ages 3 to 4 years) to the last grades of primary school (children ages 9 to 11 years).

These results show a gradual increase on all of our measures. This is not surprising: As children get older, the duration of their entire explanations gets longer, and their explanations contain more syllables, more clauses, and more connectives (i.e., linguistic elements that relate two or more clauses or bigger discourse units; connectives are formed with coordinate conjunctions, subordinate conjunctions, adverbs, and formulaic constructions like "for example," "all the same," "on the other hand," and so on). However, as shown in Table 4.2, this change also has a qualitative aspect. The 500 explanations

**Table 4.1**  Mean Scores and Standard Deviations Based on 500 Explanations

| Measures per Explanation | 3–4 Years | 4–5 Years | 5–6 Years | 6–7 Years | 7–9 Years | 9–11 Years |
|---|---|---|---|---|---|---|
| Duration[a] | 2.10 | 4.43 | 4.05 | 7.00 | 9.38 | 10.56 |
|  | (0.82) | (3.15) | (2.77) | (4.72) | (6.54) | (5.80) |
| Syllables[b] | 7.13 | 12.35 | 13.08 | 23.23 | 30.69 | 39.32 |
|  | (3.36) | (7.38) | (7.97) | (13.85) | (18.16) | (20.12) |
| Clauses[b] | 1.13 | 1.44 | 1.61 | 2.37 | 3.28 | 3.70 |
|  | (0.41) | (0.82) | (0.87) | (1.25) | (2.10) | (2.02) |
| Connectives[b] | 1.08 | 1.40 | 1.70 | 3.10 | 3.47 | 4.67 |
|  | (0.53) | (1.06) | (1.11) | (2.25) | (2.27) | (2.78) |
| Coverbal gestures[b] | 0.31 | 0.75 | 0.98 | 2.23 | 2.48 | 3.47 |
|  | (0.47) | (0.89) | (1.27) | (2.56) | (2.94) | (3.06) |

[a]  seconds
[b]  number

**Table 4.2**  Proportion of Simple and Complex Explanations as a Function of Age (%)

|  | 3–4 Years | 4–6 Years | 6–9 Years | 9–11 Years |
|---|---|---|---|---|
| Simple explanations | 97 | 79 | 39 | 17 |
| Complex explanations | 3 | 21 | 61 | 83 |

can be assigned to two categories on the basis of their textual structure: "simple explanations" and "complex explanations." Simple explanations contain either one clause only, as in Example 4.1,[*] or two or more clauses that are simply juxtaposed with no logical or chronological link between them, as in Example 4.2 (the second clause corresponds to a second reason given by the child and is linked to the first clause by a conversational leap so that the connector "et" (and) has no obvious logical meaning in this speech turn):

## Example 4.1: Girl, 4 Years Old

| Explanandum: | pourquoi elle pleure la p'tite fille? |
| | why is the little girl crying? |
| Explanans: | parce qu'elle est punie |
| | because she was punished |
| Textual structure: | <because P1[†]> |

## Example 4.2: Girl, 3.5 Years Old

| Explanandum: | pourquoi tu dis que c'est de la fraise? |
| | why do you believe it's strawberry juice? |
| Explanans: | parce que c'est rouge et ça sent la fraise |
| | because it's red and it smells of strawberry |
| Textual structure: | <because P1 and P2> |

Complex explanations contain at least two clauses that are bound together, either logically or chronologically, as in Examples 4.3 and 4.4:

## Example 4.3: Boy, 5.5 Years Old

| Explanandum: | pourquoi le ballon s'est-il envolé si vite? |
| | why did the balloon fly away so fast? |
| Explanans: | parce qu'il a mis beaucoup d'air alors ça avance encore plus |
| | because he put a lot of air in it so that it moves faster |
| Textual structure: | <because P1 so that P2> |

---

[*] Transcription conventions used for all examples are found in Appendix 4.B.
[†] P1, P2, P3, etc. = clause 1, clause 2, clause 3, etc.

**Example 4.4: Boy, 6 Years Old**

| | |
|---|---|
| Explanandum: | pourquoi est-ce que ça peut faire mal? |
| | why can it hurt you? |
| Explanans: | parce que si tu lances en arrière ça tombe sur |
| | la tête et après ben t'es mort |
| | because if you throw it in the air it falls on your |
| | head and then you will die |
| Textual structure: | <because if P1, P2 and then P3> |

As Table 4.2 shows, the proportion of complex explanations increases greatly with academic age, from 3% in the explanations produced by the younger children to 83% in the explanations observed in the older ones. This is proof that, with increasing age, children tend to produce increasingly long explanations with an ever-richer verbal information content and a greater presence of explicit logical or chronological links expressed by connectives that link clauses. We also observe a constant diversification of the way these connectives are used with increasing age, as shown in Table 4.3.

This change from the use of simple explanation to the use of complex explanation, as well as the constant diversification in the use of connectives, leads older children to verbalize genuine monological explanatory discourse, such as explanations built out of coherent and logical/chronological relations between clauses, like in Example 4.5:

**Example 4.5: Boy, 9 Years Old**

| | |
|---|---|
| Explanandum: | pourquoi les parents d'un enfant ne sont-ils pas |
| | originaires d'une même famille? |
| | why don't a child's parents come from the same |
| | family? |
| Explanans: | c'est parce que [...] nos parents i' z'avaient des |
| | parents – qui: sont nos grand parents [...] et:: – i' |
| | sont pas fait d' la même famille pas'que si i' sont |
| | faits d' la même famille et qu'i' z'auraient fait un |
| | bébé – ben ça aurait fait un enfant handicapé |
| | quoi – et ça peut pas [...] sinon: i' s'rait pas un |
| | papa et maman – seront frère et sœur |
| | because our parents had their parents, who |
| | are our grandparents, and they are not from the |
| | same family because if they were and if they |
| | had had a baby, well he would have been hand- |
| | icapped, and that can't be the case otherwise |
| | they wouldn't be a dad and a mum, they would |
| | be brother and sister |
| Textual structure: | <because P1, P1', and P2 because if P3 and if |
| | P4, P5 and P6; otherwise, P7, P8> |

**Table 4.3**  Types of New Connectives Collected in Each of the Main Age-Groups

| | |
|---|---|
| 3–4 years | parce que (because), quand (when), et (and) |
| 4–5 years | si (if), alors (then), mais (but), donc (thus), même (even), or (now), à cause de (because of), après (later), maintenant (now), avant (before), aussi (so) |
| 5–6 years | alors que (while), tandis que (whereas), comme (as), au début (at the beginning), puis (then), et puis (and then) |
| 6–7 years | par exemple (for example), sinon (otherwise), pour (for, to) |
| 7–9 years | pourtant (nevertheless), par contre (on the other hand), autrement (otherwise), quand même (all the same) |
| 9–11 years | soit (either… or), puisque (because), de toute façon (anyway) |

From our point of view, and even though our analyses relate only to the form of the explanations and not to their content, all the observed developments indicate the gradual emergence in children of the ability to produce coherence, that is, speech organized as monologic discourse. Let us now consider the multimodal aspects of children's explanations.

## THE CLOSE RELATIONSHIP BETWEEN DISCOURSE AND GESTURE

Table 4.1 not only shows a gradual increase in the linguistic content of explanations with age but also indicates a similar increase in the use of coverbal gesture. The data provided by children aged from 6 to 11 years reveal two interesting findings. First, there are significant correlations between the linguistic productivity measures and the gestural productivity of explanations. We found a correlation of .72 between the number of syllables and the number of coverbal gestures and a correlation of .70 between the number of clauses and the number of coverbal gestures (Colletta, 2004). In other words, the more linguistic information there is, the more gestural information is associated with it. This finding is consistent with the multimodal speech processing hypothesis put forward by McNeill (2005), Kita (2000), and Ruiter (2000) (see the third section of this chapter).

The second finding suggests that there are very close relationships not only between gesture and monologic productivity generally but more precisely between gesture and the type of monologic discourse. The main purpose of the interviews we conducted with grade school children was to elicit causal explanations. However, the children also debated freely about various subjects, reported events they had witnessed, and described objects or places they were familiar with. Thus, together with the 232 explanations, we extracted 23 debating sequences, 32 narratives, and 25 descriptions (for more details, see Colletta, 2004). The duration, linguistic content, and gestural content of these debates, narratives, and descriptions were measured. The coverbal gesture was coded using the same method as for the causal explanations. Among the representational movements (see Appendix 4.A), the gestures of the concrete, which proved easy to code in the categorization experiment reported in the third section of this chapter, were counted separately. The gestures of the abstract, which proved difficult to code, were counted together with the discourse cohesion gestures, which also proved difficult to code. As mentioned in the third section of this chapter, we claim that abstract representational gestures, together with discourse cohesion gestures and beats, express primarily the speaker's enunciative efforts rather than the deliberate intention to communicate a visual message that is complementary or supplementary to the utterance.

As Table 4.4 shows, we found that children use specific coverbal resources with each type of monologic discourse task (Colletta, 2004). They use a large number of concrete representational gestures while describing and narrating, many expressive gestures while debating, and mainly abstract and discourse cohesion gestures while explaining.

The most striking phenomenon here is the high rate of abstract and discourse cohesion gestures in children's explanatory discourse. Adult speakers use discourse cohesion gestures and beats in spoken monologic discourse in order to segment their verbal production (background vs. foreground, narrative frame vs. comment, thesis vs. antithesis) and mark its cohesion (Bouvet, 2001; McNeill, 1992). In addition, they use abstract representational gestures in spoken explanatory discourse in order to convey abstract thought, thanks to the spatial metaphorical properties of such gestures (Calbris, 2003; McNeill, 1992). Do children over 6 years of age use abstract representational gestures when they provide causal explanations in speech as adult speakers do? Do younger children also use abstract and discourse cohesion gestures when giving causal explanations? Let us first consider the abstract thought question in the next section and subsequently the question relating to gesture development (the seventh section).

**Table 4.4**   Proportion of Coverbal Movements in Four Discourse Tasks (%)

|  | Abstract and Discourse Cohesion Gestures | Expressive Gestures | Concrete Representational Gestures | Synchronization Gestures |
|---|---|---|---|---|
| Explaining | 52.50 | 28.50 | 17.50 | 1.50 |
| Describing | 22.00 | 17.50 | 57.50 | 3.00 |
| Narrating | 29.50 | 23.50 | 42.00 | 5.00 |
| Debating | 19.00 | 56.00 | 10.00 | 15.00 |

## ABSTRACT AND DISCOURSE COHESION GESTURES
## IN CHILDREN'S SPOKEN EXPLANATIONS

The main types of abstract representational gestures and discourse cohesion gestures identified in children ages 6 to 11 years are defined and illustrated in this section.

### Indirect Pointing

Unlike deictic or directional pointing, indirect pointing does not indicate a referent that is physically and directly perceptible or localizable in the communication setting. We have identified at least two types of indirect pointing: anaphoric pointing, which has been amply described in studies of the gestural language used by individuals who are deaf in which it plays the linguistic role of a reference pronoun, as well as another type of pointing we called "substitution pointing." Anaphoric pointing makes it possible to designate a referent previously assigned to a location in the frontal space when the subject subsequently points to the same spot that is thought to represent it. To illustrate, Example 4.6 shows a speaker who, while describing where he lives, makes locative gestures (a and b) on the table to represent the location of two blocks of flats in his district, followed by two anaphoric gestures (c and d). The first one designates the initial block on the left and the second one the other block on the right:

### Example 4.6: Boy, 7 Years Old, Locative and Anaphoric Gestures

(a)     (b)     (c)     (d)

Là t'as un immeub' qui fait <u>comme ça</u> et: – <u>comme ça</u> – <u>ben celui qu'est peint c'est pas celui qu'est peint</u> – c'est <u>l'autre</u>
There you've got a block <u>like that</u> and – <u>like that</u> – <u>well the one that's painted isn't the painted one</u> – it's <u>the other</u>
(two hands locating the blocks on the table)
(R hand points > L)                                    (R hand points > R)

Anaphoric gestures can also be used for abstract referents. In Example 4.7, a speaker is explaining that a child in a family generally gets the father's name. He positions abstract entities in the front space before selecting the required ones, thanks to the anaphoric properties of his gestures: He uses his index finger to locate on his right the mother's family name (a) and then the ring finger to locate the father's family name on his left (b); he then points to the left (c) to select the latter while saying the father's name again:

**Example 4.7: Boy, 11 Years Old, Anaphoric Gesture on (c)**

(a)                          (b)                          (c)

i' z'ont une mère <u>elle s'appelle Martin</u> – et l'autre – <u>le père</u> Martinez
– et ben: ça – le nom <u>d' famille ça s'ra Martinez</u>
they've got a mum <u>she's called Martin</u> – and the other – <u>the dad</u>
<u>Martinez</u> – and well it – the <u>family name will be Martinez</u>
(R index > R)               (R ring > L)               (R hand points > L)

Substitution pointing is based not on coreference but on substitution: The object, action, or person designated by pointing corresponds not to the referent but to a substitute in the physical setting. In Example 4.8, the speaker evokes the possible danger of badly placed objects that may fall and cause injury. She gives the example of a drum placed on a shelf in the room in which the interview was held; after designating the drum by means of direct pointing, she touches the top of her head to evoke the head of a child hit by this badly placed object while walking underneath it:

**Example 4.8: Girl, 8 Years Old, Substitution Pointing**

comme le tambour là-bas – et ben – par exemple [...] <u>i' va tomber</u>
<u>sur la tête</u> et [...]
like the drum there – and well – for example [...] <u>it'll fall on your head</u>
and [...]

(touches the top of her head)

### Introduction of a New Referent

By means of a hand or head movement, the speaker locates a new object of discourse toward one spot in the frontal space or in one direction (right, left, up, or down). We show examples of the gestural introduction of a new referent in the following examples:

## Example 4.9: Boy, 7 Years Old, Gestural Introduction of a New Referent

moi j'ai plus d'arrière-grand-père ni d'arrière-gra'-mère – pas'que
mon arrière-<u>grand-pè::re</u> heu:: – il a fait la guerre
I've no longer got a great grand-dad or a great-grandma – not just my
great <u>grand-dad</u>, eh – he fought in the war

(head > R)

## Example 4.10: Boy, 7.5 Years Old, Gestural Introduction of a New Referent

pas'que […] – et ma am' – ma – mo<u>n aut' mamie</u> – elle a <u>fait maman</u>
because […] – and my gra – my – my<u> other granny</u> – she <u>had mum</u>
(head > R)                                    (head > L)

In the two previous examples, the new referents introduced as gestures at the same time as verbally are persons related to the speaker. In Example 4.9, the gesture refers to an ancestor ("my great grand-dad") who is positioned to the speaker's right by means of a quick sideways movement of the head; in Example 4.10, the two people (granny, mum) are positioned in two different directions, again by means of two quick head movements, the first to the right and the second to the left. In the next example, however, the referent is not a concrete referent but an abstract one: a moment in the day ("this afternoon"), which the speaker locates on the right, again by means of a quick sideways head movement:

## Example 4.11: Girl, 9 Years Old, Gestural Introduction of a New Abstract Referent

> ma maman elle c'est tous les jours que: elle travaille du matin –
> comme – <u>c't' après midi</u> là – ben elle s'ra à la maison [...]
> my mum every day she works in the morning – like – <u>this afternoon</u>
> – well, she'll be at home [...]
>
> (head + chest > L)

Finally, the referent can be introduced by means of a metaphorical gesture. In the next two examples, the referent is introduced with a votive gesture (i.e., hand forward with the palm up). The metaphorical properties of this gesture have been analyzed in detail by Calbris and Porcher (1989) and McNeill (1992) and are now well known: The hand represents a container, and the hollow of the hand suggests an invisible content that corresponds to the subject of the discourse offered to the partner in the conversation and to which the speaker wants to draw the partner's attention.

### Example 4.12: Boy, 7.5 Years Old, Metaphorical Introduction of a New Referent

> et d'abord on est obligé d'avoir des parents – si moi chus fait – chus
> bien <u>fait par quelqu'un</u>
> and you've got to have parents – if I was made – then <u>I was made
> by someone</u>
>
> (R hand > R in votive gesture)

### Example 4.13: Girl, 10 Years Old, Metaphorical Introduction of a New Referent

> ben – quand i' t'arrive des pro<u>blèmes tu</u> peux leur en parler: tu heu [...]
> well – if you have pro<u>blems you</u> can talk to them about it: you
> uh [...]
>
> (R hand > R in votive gesture)

## Symbolizing Time and Aspect

The gestures that symbolize time and aspect and that have been recorded by Calbris (1985) and Calbris and Porcher (1989) are also present in children's gestural repertoire. These are generally built on the basis of a left/right opposition (a gesture to the left designates the past, while a gesture to the right designates the future or vice versa) or, less frequently, on the basis of a front/back opposition (the back designates the past, and the front designates the future). Here is an example:

### Example 4.14: Boy, 10 Years Old, Metaphoric Gesture for Time

pas'que – avant – <u>avant dans l' temps</u> – on pouvait faire c' qu'on veut y avait pas de truc de drogue [...]
because – before – <u>earlier on</u> – you could do what you wanted and there were no drugs and stuff [...]

(gaze + L hand > L)

The speaker in Example 4.14 evokes a past period of time ("before, earlier on") and locates it at the top left of his frontal space by means of a gesture accomplished with the left hand while simultaneously looking in the same direction. The production of gestures that support the expression of time or aspect is generally accompanied either by an adverb ("avant/before" in Example 4.14) or by a noun or prepositional phrase relating to time or aspect ("dans le temps/earlier on" in the same example).

## Symbolizing a Process, an Action

Some children exhibit gestures that serve as metaphors for processes and actions. The most frequent of these is a cyclical movement of the hand (the hand draws one or more circles in the air) that goes with verbs such as "faire/do," "fabriquer/make," "devenir/become," or "conquérir/conquer." The metaphorical functioning of these gestures, based on the circular shape and the mode of repetition, has been excellently analyzed by Calbris and Porcher (1989) and Calbris (2003). Two other examples of gestural metaphors for processes are given here:

### Example 4.15: Boy, 11 Years Old, Metaphoric Gesture for a Process

Puisque le <u>père – i' garde – c'est lui qui:</u> – qui garde le nom d' famille [...]
Because the <u>father keeps it – it's him who</u> – who keeps the family name [...]

(R hand closes to form a fist)

### Example 4.16: Boy, 11 Years Old, Metaphoric Gesture for a Process

(a)                                    (b)

Pas'que les jeunes (xxx) – i' <u>viennent heu d'apprendre</u> – alors [...]
Because the young ones (xxx) – <u>have just learned</u> – well [...]
(L hand makes a grasping gesture, illustrated in two sequential photos here)

In Example 4.15, the gesture of closing the hand as a fist symbolizes gathering, putting back together. It is a metaphor for the verb "garder/keep" in the sense of "conserve." The gesture in Example 4.16 mimics the act of seizing something (here illustrated by means of two photos, a and b) that symbolizes the concept of learning, as if, for the speaker, learning signifies the acquisition of new knowledge.

## Symbolizing a Quantity

Some gestures symbolize an indefinite quantity linguistically marked by indefinite determiners such as "des/some," "quelques/some," or "plusieurs/a few." They are hand or head gestures designating a poorly defined area in the frontal space performed together with a side-to-side gaze. This imprecise designation of space turns out to be a metaphor for an indefinite entity. See this example:

## Example 4.17: Boy, 11 Years Old, Metaphoric Gesture for a Quantity

t'es trop p'tit pour aller heu – heu sortir le soir pas'que y <u>a- y a des</u>
<u>voleu::rs</u> y a – et t'es heu (xxx)
you're too small to go um – um go out in the evening because there
are <u>there are thieves</u> there are – and you are um (xxx)
(head and eyes moving through the space from L to R)

Here, the speaker combines a head gesture and a side-to-side gaze to express the idea that an indefinite number of people representing a potential danger ("thieves") could be present in town during the evening or night, and that is the reason why children should not go outside late in the evening. Other gestures symbolize a large quantity linguistically marked by determiners such as "tous or toutes/all." In Example 4.18, for instance, the speaker's hand gesture—hand open and moving through space from left to right and then from right to left—seems to enclose all the immediate frontal space and draw a field that metaphorically represents the concept of entirety encoded by the determiner "toutes/all":

## Example 4.18: Boy, 11 Years Old, Metaphoric Gesture for a Quantity

et là quand heu quand il aura fini <u>toutes ses études</u> il aura quarante-
cinq ans – enfin- [...]
and when he's finished <u>all his studies</u> he'll be forty-five years old
– well- [...]
(head and R hand sweep through space from L to R)

## Symbolizing Modality

A gesture of frequent use is the emblematic symbol of negation that consists of shaking the head from left to right. When talking about this gesture, one initially thinks of its pragmatic uses, for example, when it accompanies a negative response, as in Example 4.19, or when, in the absence of speech, it accompanies and reinforces an act of denial or refusal. However, this gesture also has referential meanings when performed with assertive utterances. It then acts as the metaphorical representation of ignorance (in Example 4.20, where the speaker admits not knowing how to act in the event of danger in the home), inability (in Example 4.21, where the referent is a small child unable to accomplish household tasks), or obligation (in Example 4.22, in which the speaker evokes situations in which he has to give way to the demands of his younger brother):

### Example 4.19: Boy, 7 Years Old, Emblematic Gesture of Negation

Sp.A: on peut s'amuser quand on a fini not' travail
Speaker A: we can have some fun when we've finished our work
Speaker B: <u>non – non – non – non non</u>
Speaker B: <u>no – no – no – no no</u>
(symbol of negation)

### Example 4.20: Boy, 8 Years Old, Negation Gesture as a Metaphor for Ignorance

pas'que après ch' peux m'é' – heu m'électrogu' - m'électrocuter: ou faire brûler la maison –
et <u>moi je sais pas</u> – 'fin: on m'a expliqué comment fallait m' dégager mais:
because I might e' – uh elegro' - electrocute myself or burn myself at home –
and <u>I don't know</u> – anyway I've been told how to get out of it but
(symbol of negation)

### Example 4.21: Girl, 8.5 Years Old, Negation Gesture as a Metaphor for Inability

et si on est petit par exemple – <u>eh ben on peut pas faire à manger pa'squ'on n'</u> sait pas faire
and if you're small, for example – <u>you can't do the cooking because you don't</u> know how
(symbol of negation)

### Example 4.22: Boy, 7 Years Old, Negation Gesture as a Metaphor for Obligation

'près i' dit – maman: c'est ma voitu::re – a'ors chu's obligé <u>d' lui donner</u> p'squ' i' va m' [...]
then he said – mum: it's my car – so I had to <u>give it to him</u> or he'd have [...]
(symbol of negation)

## Symbolizing Opposition

Finally, we collected gestures of opposition that were mostly oriented around the left/right axis in order to distinguish between or oppose two referential entities: The hand or head designates the right-hand side and then the left-hand side or vice versa. Example 4.10 has already provided an illustration of this since the two head movements used by the speaker are polarized around the lateral access and thus accentuate the distinction between the two referents (granny/mum). However, this opposition may also be symbolized in other ways. In Example 4.23, for instance, it is based on the use of a listing gesture: The speaker states the possibility that, within a family, the two parents may be of a different ethnic origin and symbolizes this difference by means of a listing movement.

### Example 4.23: Boy, 10 Years Old, Gesture Symbolizing Opposition

(a)    (b)

y a une CM1 – ses pa' – <u>un parent – son papa il est – heu::noir – et sa maman – elle est blanche</u> […]
there's a kid at school – his pa' – <u>one parent – his dad i – um::black – and his mum – she's white</u> […]
(points to his L thumb with his R index finger) (points to his L index finger with his R index finger)

## THE DEVELOPMENT OF GESTURE IN CHILDREN'S EXPLANATIONS: TOWARD ABSTRACTION

Not all the types of gesture that we have just reviewed are abstract to the same degree or in the same regard. We have identified two types of indirect, nondeictic pointing: substitution pointing and anaphoric pointing. The first is based on the identification in the communication setting of an object that has characteristics similar to those of the object of discourse and therefore relies purely on perceptual analogy. The second exhibits an additional level of abstraction in that it refers to time and not just to space. Indeed, it becomes necessary to establish a relation between two types of phenomena: a discourse object (the referent) and a location in the frontal space randomly chosen to represent it on the one hand and the successive pointings to this spot that reactivate the initial relation on each occasion on the other. It is this reactivation that makes anaphoric pointing a genuine tool for discourse cohesion, thus making it possible to maintain referential continuity. Anaphoric pointing therefore presumes the individually controlled use of language and can be considered as an index of the ability to produce monologic discourse.

The gesture that introduces a new referent locates the referent at a spot in the frontal space that is randomly chosen to represent it. It corresponds to some extent to the initial stage of anaphoric pointing. However, whether the referent is concrete or abstract, the gesture used to assign it a location operates as a pointing gesture with simple indexical properties, while the gesture that simultaneously acts as a metaphor for the introduction of a new referent (the votive gesture in examples 12 and 13) is based on conceptual analogy (Johnson, 1987) and is therefore more complex. It is therefore necessary to distinguish between the simple gestural introduction of a new referent and the metaphorical gestural introduction of a new referent, and there is every reason to believe that the former appears in children far earlier than the latter.

Like the metaphorical gestural introduction of a new referent, the gestural expression of time and aspect, processes, quantity, and opposition are based on conceptual analogy since they require the establishment of relations between two representations (one of the source, the other of the target) on the basis of a shared starting point for comparison (the metaphorical functioning of gestures has been described in detail by McNeill, 1992). The gestures that symbolize processes or quantities have provided us with excellent examples of this metaphorical functioning in children's coverbal gesture alongside the metaphors of time, aspect, and opposition, which are based on the body schema.

We still need to mention the case of gestures that express modes such as ignorance, inability, impossibility, or obligation. These are abstract for two reasons: first, because of their content given that the modes themselves are abstract concepts, and, second, because of their functioning, which is also metaphoric (the use of the symbol of negation results in the expression of ignorance as lack of knowledge, inability as lack of ability, and obligation or necessity as a situation in which there is no choice). Nevertheless, the sign used to express these modes (the gesture of negation) is an emblematic gesture with an undeniably conventional character, and it is plausible that young children learn to use it simply by imitating adults. Concerning this issue, we do not possess the necessary data to assess the level of complexity required by the modal use of the gesture of negation.

To summarize, gestures based on perceptual analogy (substitution pointing) and the establishment of a location (the gesture that simply introduces a referent) do not imply a high degree of abstraction and probably appear earlier in children's coverbal repertoires than gestures that form relations between discourse segments (anaphoric pointing) and gestures that are based on conceptual analogy (metaphorical representational gestures). However, further observations are now required to identify the age and conditions necessary for the emergence of these latter gestures. Let us now turn away from the corpus and the gestures produced by grade school children and look at the more general picture.

As shown in the fifth section of this chapter, children aged 6 to 11 years used a high rate of abstract and discourse cohesion gestures during their explanations. We still need to check whether the proportion of such gestures when all categories are taken together is as high in younger, nursery school and preschool children as it is in children aged 6 years or more. To do this, it is necessary to compare the types of coverbals produced by the two groups of children in our two sets of observations.

As Table 4.5 shows, there is a clear difference in the results: Unlike grade school children, children aged between 3 and 6 years produce very few abstract representational gestures and discourse cohesion gestures. Indeed, the gestures that accompany their explanations are primarily concrete gestures and, more specifically (even though this is not apparent from the table), deictic gestures that were counted together with concrete representational gestures.

It is true that the two sets of observations are not strictly comparable since the explanations produced by the grade school children related to family and social knowledge, whereas those produced by the nursery school and preschool children related to distinctly more varied content. In the latter case, the frequent use of deictic gestures can also be explained by the fact that many of the school activities used media (posters, albums, study sheets) that promote the use of gestural deictic. However, given the two sets of data, we have to acknowledge the almost total absence of indirect pointing, gestural introduction of new referents, and metaphorical gestures in younger children, whereas these gestures represent half the coverbal repertoire exhibited by children aged 6 years and more.

In other words, and in the light of these two sets of observations, the study of the coverbal gestures that accompany children's explanations indicates that the use of these gestures increases with age and that they change in nature during cognitive and language development. With increasing age, children are able to produce the representational gestures, making it possible to symbolize the abstract concepts that are not yet present in younger children's thought since they do not possess the necessary knowledge and cognitive

**Table 4.5**  Proportion of Coverbal Movements as a Function of Age (%)

|  | Abstract and Discourse Cohesion Gestures | Expressive Gestures | Concrete Representational Gestures |
|---|---|---|---|
| 3–6 years | 8.00 | 3.50 | 88.50 |
| 6–11 years | 53.00 | 29.00 | 18.00 |

tools. Increasing age also brings gestures that contribute to the maintenance of referential continuity, and these discourse cohesion gestures are clearly absent in young children whose textual abilities are still limited. The presence of these gestural categories in children's explanations and, more generally, in their linguistic behavior is of particular interest since it testifies to new cognitive (in terms of abstract representations) and discourse (in terms of individually controlled speech) abilities.

## CONCLUSION

The first spoken explanations are observed in children in their second year. These take the form of justifications rather than real causal explanations. They are very short, are dependent on the context, and exhibit no textual properties. Much later, at the age of 8 years, children are able to draft short written explanatory texts in the context of classroom activities and at the teacher's request. But what happens in the intervening period? How do children come to produce explanatory texts? Do they exhibit textual abilities in oral mode, that is, when producing spoken explanations, before they can do so in writing?

The inability to answer these questions was a starting point for the two collections of data that we presented in this chapter. The first consisted of gathering spoken explanations during interviews with children aged from 6 to 11 years, while the second consisted of obtaining spoken explanations from children aged from 3 to 6 years during classroom activities. Although developments were clear within each corpus, we needed to harmonize the two sets of data in order to gain a more complete understanding of the development of explanations between the first (3–4 years) and last (10–11 years) years of French primary school. We therefore compared the 500 explanations collected not in terms of their content (given the differing nature of the contexts in which they were observed) but instead in terms of their linguistic form and coverbal gestures.

The results of this study reveal two types of development in children's explanations: (a) development of the linguistic forms of the explanations, which, in general terms, progress from clause to text, and (b) development of the gestures that accompany the explanations, which, in general terms, progress from the concrete to the abstract and toward the marking of discourse cohesion. In fact, the older the children are, the longer and richer in terms of linguistic information their explanations become. This change also has a qualitative aspect: Explanations performed by the older children show far more interclausal relations because of an increase with age in the number of clauses and connectives per explanation. Thus, as children get older, their explanations exhibit more and more textual relations, and they gradually come to verbalize genuine monological explanatory discourse.

At the same time, as children become older, the more they make use of coverbal gesture since the increase in gestural information goes hand in hand with the increase in linguistic information. Furthermore, we can observe a change in the type of gestures they use. Nursery school and preschool children use concrete representational gestures and deictic pointings (88.5%) and make no use of abstract or discourse cohesion gestures, whereas grade school children use many of the latter (53%). To sum up, 6-year-old children who verbalize explanations begin to use abstract representational gestures and discourse cohesion gestures that are quasi-nonexistent in younger children.

The linguistic and gestural changes are closely related. The reason why discourse cohesion gestures are almost nonexistent in the coverbal repertoire of children under 6 years of age is that their use depends on the speaker's textual ability to verbalize monologic explanatory discourse, which at this age is still a challenge. This ability does not emerge before first grade in our data (Table 4.1). From then on, explanations contain more than two clauses and two connectives and begin to resemble explanatory texts.

A pending question would be the role played by coverbal gesture in this process. Do the changes in gesture reveal linguistic acquisitions that occur within an independent process of monologic discourse development, or does gesture play an active role in this development because of its cohesion and segmentation properties? Results from studies on the role of gesture in language acquisition show that a new linguistic acquisition is often preceded by a change in the gestural behavior of the child. For instance, the emergence of the pointing gesture before the end of the first year is a major milestone in the acquisition of a lexicon by the child; it shows the understanding of the semiotic principle "one signal for one referent" (Bates et al., 1979). A few months later, during the one-word period, the child performs word/gesture combinations. Some of them are redundant, and others are not. Nonredundant combinations have been proven to be good precursors of the two-word utterance stage (Butcher & Goldin-Meadow, 2000; Capirci et al., 1996, 2002; Goldin-Meadow & Butcher, 2003; Özçaliskan & Goldin-Meadow, 2005).

Would there be a similar developmental schema for monologic discourse acquisition? More precisely, we can hypothesize that gestural anaphora may precede linguistic anaphora in the child's first attempts to verbalize interclause relations and then be followed by more elaborate monologic spoken texts. Evidently, we need to collect new data to answer this question.

Another interesting point is the change toward the use of gestures of the abstract. It is closely related to the ongoing debate on the link between language and thought. McNeill (1992, 2005), Kita (2000), Goldin-Meadow (2003), and others postulate that gesture is a window into thought. As McNeill (1992) points out,

> Gestures and speech occur in very close temporal synchrony and often have identical meanings. Yet they express these meanings in

completely different ways. … Gestures exhibit images that cannot always be expressed in speech, as well as images the speaker thinks are concealed. … These gestures are the person's memories and thoughts rendered visible. Gestures are like thoughts themselves. (pp. 11–12)

In our study, we focused on the abstract gestures performed by grade school children. We called "abstract representational gestures" those gestures that introduce a new referent, that represent an abstract referent, or that use metaphoric properties. As previously mentioned, these gestures are not abstract to the same degree or in the same regard. Furthermore, psychologists would argue that concrete representational gestures are also abstract to an extent. For instance, a gesture that draws the image of a ball needs to extract certain properties of the object "ball" (Barsalou, 2003). All the same, the higher rate of metaphoric gestures in explanatory behavior of the older children illustrates a change in the way that the physical and social world is represented. It would be most beneficial to examine closely this developmental change with a more experimental protocol.

The picture we have of the explanatory and gestural development in our study has given rise to further questions that need to be fine-tuned in terms of both the linguistic form of children's explanations and the level of the coverbal resources that children deploy when producing their explanations. New data that we are currently gathering in schools will help us provide a more precise description of this dual development toward monologic discourse and abstract gestures. This ongoing project, funded by the Agence Nationale pour la Recherche in France, also has an interlanguage dimension (cooperation with U.S., Italian, and South African collaborators) that additionally will enable us to assess the impact of language and culture on the development of multimodal explanations.

## REFERENCES

Adam, J.-M. (1992). *Les textes: Types et prototypes. Récit, description, argumentation, explication, dialogue*. Paris: Nathan.

Adam, J.-M. (1999). *Linguistique textuelle: Des genres de discours aux textes*. Paris: Nathan.

Barsalou, L. W. (2003). Abstraction in perceptual symbol systems. *Philosophical Transactions of the Royal Society of London, 358*, 1177–1187.

Bartlett, F. (1964). *Remembering: A study in experimental and social psychology*. Cambridge: Cambridge University Press.

Bates, E., Benigni, L., Bretherton, I., Camaioni, L., & Volterra, V. (1979). *The emergence of symbols: Cognition and communication in infancy*. New York: Academic Press.

Birdwhistell, R. L. (1952). *Introduction to kinesics: An annotation system for the analysis of body motion and gesture*. Washington, DC: Foreign Service Institute, U.S. Department of State.

Bouvet, D. (2001). *La dimension corporelle de la parole*. Paris: Peeters.

Brookes, H. (2004). A repertoire of South African quotable gestures. *Journal of Linguistic Anthropology, 14*(2), 186–224.

Brookes, H. (2005). What gestures do: Some communicative functions of quotable gestures in conversations among Black urban South Africans. *Journal of Pragmatics, 37*, 2044–2085.

Butcher, C., & Goldin-Meadow, S. (2000). Gesture and the transition from one- to two-word speech: When hand and mouth come together. In D. McNeill (Ed.), *Language and gesture* (pp. 235–257). Cambridge: Cambridge University Press.

Calbris, G. (1985). *Espace-temps: Expression gestuelle du temps. Semiotica, 55*(1–2), 43–73.

Calbris, G. (2003). *L'expression gestuelle de la pensée d'un homme politique*. Paris: CNRS Editions.

Calbris, G., & Porcher, L. (1989). *Geste et communication*. Paris: Credif-Hatier.

Capirci, O., Caselli, M. C., Iverson, J., Pizzuto, E., & Volterra, V. (2002). Gesture and the nature of language in infancy: The role of gesture as a transitional device en route to two-word speech. In D. F. Armstrong, M. A. Karchmer, & J. V. Van Cleve (Eds.), *Essays in honor of William C. Stokoe: The study of signed languages* (pp. 213–246). Washington, DC: Gallaudet University Press.

Capirci, O., Iverson, J., Pizzuto, E., & Volterra, V. (1996). Gesture and words during the transition to two-word speech. *Journal of Child Language, 23*, 645–673.

Colletta, J.-M. (2000). A propos de la catégorisation fonctionnelle des kinèmes co-verbaux. In *Actes des XXIIIèmes Journées d'Etude sur la Parole, Aussois-France, 19–23 juin 2000* (pp. 229–232), Grenoble: Institut de la Communication Parlée, INPG et Université Stendhal-Grenoble III.

Colletta, J.-M. (2004). *Le développement de la parole chez l'enfant âgé de 6 et 11 ans: Corps, langage et cognition*. Hayen: Mardaga.

Colletta, J.-M., Simon, J.-P., & Lachnitt, C. (2005). Les conduites explicatives orales à l'école maternelle. In J.-F. Halté and M. Rispail (Eds.), *L'oral dans la classe: Compétences, enseignement, activités* (pp. 137–151). Paris: L'Harmattan.

Colletta, J.-M., Simon, J.-P., Vuillet, J., & Prévost, C. (2004). Les conduites explicatives en maternelle: Premiers résultats d'une étude développementale. In *Communication affichée au Colloque International "Acquisition, Pratiques Langagières, Interactions et Contacts," Paris, 25–26 juin 2004, Actes sur CDRom, Equipe d'accueil EA 170-Calipso*. Paris: Université de la Sorbonne Nouvelle-Paris III.

Condon, W. S., & Ogston, W. D. (1966). Sound film analysis of normal and pathological behavior patterns. *Journal of Nervous and Mental Disease, 143*, 338–347.

Condon, W. S., & Ogston, W. D. (1967). A segmentation of behavior. *Journal of Psychiatric Research, 5*, 221–235.

Cosnier, J. (1982). Communications et langages gestuels. In J. Cosnier, J. Coulon, A. Berrendonner, & C. Orecchioni (Eds.), *Les voies du langage: Communications verbales, gestuelles et animales* (pp. 255–304), Paris: Dunod-Bordas.

Cosnier, J., & Vaysse, J. (1997). Sémiotique des gestes communicatifs. *Nouveaux Actes Sémiotiques, 9*(52–54), 7–28.

Diessel, H. (2004). *The acquisition of complex sentences* (Cambridge Studies in Linguistics, 105). Cambridge: Cambridge University Press.

Fayol, M. (1985). *Le récit et sa construction, une approche de psychologie cognitive*. Neuchâtel: Delachaux et Niestlé.

Fayol, M. (1997). *Des idées au texte: Psychologie cognitive de la production verbale, orale et écrite*. Paris: Presses Universitaires de France.

Fayol, M. (2000). Comprendre et produire des textes écrits: L'exemple du récit. In M. Kail & M. Fayol (Eds.), *L'acquisition du langage: Vol. 2. Le langage en développement: Au-delà de trois ans* (pp. 183–213). Paris: Presses Universitaires de France.

Feyereisen, P. (1994). *Le cerveau et la communication.* Paris: Presses Universitaires de France.

Garitte, C., Le Maner, G., & Le Roch, E. (1998). La communication gestuelle dans une situation conversationnelle entre pairs du même âge de 6 à 10 ans. *Cahiers d'Acquisition et de Pathologie du Langage, 18,* 71–89.

Golder, C. (1996). *Le développement des discours argumentatifs.* Neuchâtel: Delachaux et Niestlé.

Goldin-Meadow, S. (2003). *Hearing gesture: How our hands help us think.* Cambridge, MA: Harvard University Press.

Goldin-Meadow, S., & Butcher, C. (2003). Pointing toward two-word speech in young children. In S. Kita (Ed.), *Pointing: Where language, culture, and cognition meet* (pp. 85–107). Mahwah, NJ: Lawrence Erlbaum Associates.

Guidetti, M. (2003). *Pragmatique et psychologie du développement : Comment communiquent les jeunes enfants.* Paris: Belin.

Hadar, U., & Butterworth, B. (1997). Iconic gestures, imagery and word retrieval in speech. *Semiotica, 115,* 147–172.

Halliday, M. A. K. (1975). *Learning how to mean: An exploration in the development of language.* London: Edward Arnold.

Halliday, M. A. K., & Hasan, R. (1976). *Cohesion in English.* London: Longman.

Hickmann, M. (2003). *Children's discourse: Person, space and time across languages.* Cambridge: Cambridge University Press.

Iverson, J., & Goldin-Meadow, S. (Eds.). (1998). *The nature and functions of gesture in children's communication* (New Directions for Child Development, 79). San Francisco: Jossey-Bass.

Jisa, H. (2004). Growing into academic French. In R. A. Berman (Ed.), *Language development across childhood and adolescence* (pp. 135–190). Amsterdam: Benjamins.

Johnson, M. (1987). *The body in the mind: The bodily basis of meaning, imagination and reasoning.* Chicago: University of Chicago Press.

Kail, M., & Weissenborn, J. (1984). L'acquisition des connecteurs: Critiques et perspectives. In M. Moscato & G. Piérault-Le-Bonniec (Eds.), *Le langage, construction et actualisation* (pp. 101–118). Rouen: Presses Universitaires de Rouen.

Karmiloff-Smith, A. (1979). *A functional approach to child language.* Cambridge: Cambridge University Press.

Kendon, A. (1972). Some relationships between body motion and speech. In A. Siegman & B. Pope (Eds.), *Studies in dyadic communication* (pp. 177–210). Elmsford, NY: Pergamon.

Kendon, A. (1980). Gesticulation and speech, two aspects of the process of utterance. In M. R. Key (Ed.), *The relationship of verbal and nonverbal communication* (pp. 207–227). The Hague: Mouton.

Kendon, A. (1990). *Conducting interaction: Patterns of behavior in focused encounters.* Cambridge: Cambridge University Press.

Kendon, A. (2004). *Gesture: Visible action as utterance.* Cambridge: Cambridge University Press.

Kita, S. (2000). How representational gestures help speaking. In D. McNeill (Ed.), *Language and gesture* (pp. 162–185). Cambridge: Cambridge University Press.

Krauss, R. M., Chen, Y., & Gottesman, R. F. (2000). Lexical gestures and lexical access: A process model. In D. McNeill (Ed.), *Language and gesture* (pp. 261–283). Cambridge: Cambridge University Press.

Krauss, R. M., Dushay, R. A., Chen, Y., & Rauscher, F. H. (1995). The communicative value of conversational hand gestures. *Journal of Experimental Social Psychology, 31,* 533–552.

Léonard, J.-L., & Pinheiro, M.-B. (1993). Énonciation et non-verbal: Aspects de la cohésion linguistique dans un récit oral poitevin. *Langage et Société, 65,* 39–68.

Levelt, W. J. M. (1989). *Speaking: From intention to articulation.* Cambridge, MA: MIT Press.

Lundquist, L. (1980). *La cohérence textuelle: Syntaxe, sémantique, pragmatique.* Copenhagen: Nyt Nordisk Forlag Arnold Busk.

Mandler, J. M., & Johnson, N. S. (1977). Remembrance of things parsed: Story structure and recall. *Cognitive Psychology, 9,* 111–151.

Marcos, H. (1998). *De la communication prélinguistique à la communication linguistique: Formes et fonctions.* Paris: L'Harmattan.

McNeill, D. (1992). *Hand and mind: What gestures reveal about thought.* Chicago: University of Chicago Press.

McNeill, D. (2005). *Gesture and thought.* Chicago: University of Chicago Press.

McNeill, D. (Ed.). (2000). *Language and gesture.* Cambridge: Cambridge University Press.

McNeill, D., & Duncan, S. D. (2000). Growth points in thinking for speaking. In D. McNeill (Ed.), *Language and gesture* (pp. 141–161). Cambridge: Cambridge University Press.

Montagner, H. (1978). *L'enfant et la communication.* Paris: Stock-Laurence Pernoud.

Özçaliskan, S., & Goldin-Meadow, S. (2005). Do parents lead their children by the hand? *Journal of Child Language, 32,* 481–505.

Poggi, I., & Magno Caldognetto, E. (1997). *Mani che parlano: Gesti e psicologia della comunicazione.* Padua: Unipress.

Poyatos, F. (1992). *Advances in nonverbal communication.* Amsterdam: Benjamins.

Roulet, E., Filliettaz, L., & Grobet, A. (2001). *Un modèle et un instrument d'analyse de l'organisation du discours.* Bern: Peter Lang.

Ruiter (de), J. P. (2000). The production of gesture and speech. In D. McNeill (Ed.), *Language and gesture* (pp. 284–311). Cambridge: Cambridge University Press.

Scheflen, A. E. (1964). The significance of posture in communication systems. *Psychiatry, 27,* 316–321.

Tolchinsky, L. (2004). The nature and scope of later language development. In R. A. Berman (Ed.), *Language development across childhood and adolescence* (pp. 233–247). Amsterdam: Benjamins.

van Dijk, T. A. (Ed.). (1985). *Handbook of discourse analysis.* Orlando, FL: Academic Press.

Veneziano, E. (Ed.). (1998). *La conversation, instrument, objet et source de connaissance* (Psychologie de l'interaction, 7–8). Paris: L'Harmattan.

Veneziano, E., & Hudelot, C. (2002). Développement des compétences pragmatiques et théories de l'esprit chez l'enfant: Le cas de l'explication. In J. Bernicot, A. Trognon, M. Guidetti, & M. Musiol (Eds.), *Pragmatique et psychologie* (pp. 215–236). Nancy: Presses Universitaires de Nancy.

Veneziano, E., & Sinclair, H. (1995). Functional changes in early child language: The appearance of references to the past and of explanations. *Journal of Child Language, 22,* 557–581.

Weinrich, H. (1989). *Grammaire textuelle du français.* Paris: Didier-Hatier.

# APPENDIX 4.A: MAIN FUNCTIONAL TYPES
# OF COVERBAL GESTURES

## Pointing Gestures

Hand or head gestures directed toward the referent of discourse that helps to identify it or localize it in situ. We may distinguish the following:

## Deictic Pointing

The speaker points to an object or a person directly present and perceptible in the physical context. It may be the following:

> The object he is talking about: "it is that book on the table"
> A place in the immediate physical setting: "leave your jacket over there on the sofa please"
> The interlocutor while addressing to him: "and what is your opinion on this subject?"
> Himself while saying: "as for me …," "I think, …", etc.

**Directional pointing.**    The speaker shows where to localize the referent when it is not directly perceptible. For instance, while answering a question about the place of a building, a park, or a river nearby, the speaker points into its absolute direction:

> "the museum you are looking for is in that direction, at three hundred yards from here."

**Indirect pointing.**    Some pointing gestures do not permit identification or location of a referent in (or from) the communication setting. These gestures, called "substitution pointing" and "anaphoric pointing," are defined later in this appendix.

## Representational Gestures

Hand gestures, head gestures, facial expressions or other body movements that help to represent a concrete referent (object, person, place, event) or symbolize an abstract referent. McNeill (1992) calls "iconic gestures" those that represent concrete referents and "metaphoric gestures" those that symbolize abstract ideas and concepts. Yet representational gestures are more or less iconic, and all gestures of the abstract are not based on metaphor, as this study shows. We may distinguish the following:

**Representational gestures of the concrete.**    Examples:

- Gestures depicting objects and their properties: The speaker gives the size of the referent with both hands while saying "the fish was as big as this"; the speaker draws a picture of the referent in the air with his finger while saying, "the pipe is curved like this"

- Locative gestures describing places: The speaker uses hand gestures to place in the frontal space or to construct the topological relations between the referents while describing a place or a route: "when you pass the bridge, you find a small church on your right, then you cross High Street ...".
- Locative gestures tracing moves: The speaker shows the directions of a character's moves with the hands or the head while narrating: "when he heard the dog, the cat jumped over the bin but the dog went on after him barking" (these gestures are called "observer viewpoint gestures" in McNeill's [1992] classification).
- Gestures miming processes and actions: The speaker mimes an action using a rotating gesture, "it opens like this," or mimes the action performed by a character while narrating: "he carefully climbed up the ladder" (these gestures are called "character viewpoint gestures" in McNeill's [1992] classification).
- Gestures miming person's attitudes or behavior: The speaker mimes the attitudes or behavior of a person or a character using gestures, facial expression, the whole body, and sometimes the voice as well when he reports speech: "and you know what she answered? 'you'll have to do it on your oowwwn 'cause I'm too tiiiired darling'! couldn't believe it!"

**Representational gestures of the abstract.**   Several illustrations are given in the sixth section of this chapter. We may distinguish the following:

- Substitution pointing: The speaker points to an object or a person directly present and perceptible in the physical context, and this object or person represents the referent of discourse on the basis of perceptual analogy. For instance, while narrating an event, the speaker points to the window as she says, "... then the little girl, she climbed on the windowsill, and she fell ...". See example 8 for another illustration.
- Gestural introduction of a new referent: The speaker uses a hand or a head gesture to arbitrarily locate the referent in the frontal space. See examples 9, 10, and 11.
- Metaphorical gestural introduction of a new referent: The speaker uses a votive hand gesture to arbitrarily locate the referent in the frontal space, and the hand, palm up, represents a container for an invisible content that is a metaphor of the referent. See examples 12 and 13.
- Gestural expression of time, processes, opposition, quantities, and other abstract concepts: The speaker uses hand or head gestures to perform gestural metaphors of these concepts. All metaphoric gestures are based on conceptual analogy. See examples 14, 15, 16, 17, 18, and 23.

- Gestural expression of modalities: The speaker uses hand or head gestures, facial expressions, and other bodily movements to express assertive modalities like certainty versus doubt, possibility versus impossibility, ability versus inability, and so on. See examples 20, 21, and 22.

## Discourse Cohesion Gestures

These are hand or head gestures that have representational properties like the previous ones and at the same time play a role in the marking of discourse cohesion and structure as well as other movements, such as postural changes, that do not have any representational properties and nevertheless share the same discourse properties. We may distinguish the following:

**Anaphoric pointing.**   After having assigned a referent to a location in the frontal space using a gestural introduction of a new referent, the speaker points again to the same spot while mentioning the same referent. Thus, as for the maintaining of reference, anaphoric pointing plays in visual modality the same role as linguistic anaphora in the auditory modality. See examples 6 and 7.

**Connectivity gestures.**   Short hand or head gestures that mark the transitions and symbolize the relations between clauses and bigger discourse units. Examples:

- The speaker points to the left as to refer to the future while recounting the following event during narration: "The three companions left home in the morning and walked all day long. <u>In the evening</u>, they were about to enter the forest ..."
- The speaker performs a short chasing hand or head gesture while using a connective like "anyway," "okay," or "right" while closing a parenthetical comment and getting back to the main discourse.

**Segmentation and demarcation gestures.**   Hand or head gestures as well as postural changes that mark clauses and bigger discourse units. Examples:

- The speaker tilts the head and chin to the right while expressing a first point of view, then tilts it to the left to express a second and opposite point of view: "<u>on the one hand it can help the poor to survive</u>, ... <u>on the other hand it doesn't help them to gain any financial autonomy</u> !"

## Speech Structuration Gestures

These are short binary hand or head movements called "beats" as well as other movements, such as a shrug of eyebrows, that closely accompany the speech flow. Contrary to the previous ones, these movements have no representational properties. Together with prosody, they rather help to mark short linguistic units (syllables, words) that the speaker wishes to accentuate. Examples:

- Head beats while enumerating: "several countries will sign on this treaty, for example Australia, Japan, China, India and also New Zealand" [unclear syntax: "among which"]
- Hand beats and prosodic accentuation while arguing: "is this our children's future? No, then we MUST take the RIGHT DEcisions."

## Expressive Gestures

These are facial expressions as well as other body movements with which they can combine to express speech acts, emotions, and mental states. Following Kendon (2004), we may distinguish the following:

**Performative gestures.** These are used either to accomplish speech acts (questions, yes and no answers, requests, commands, and so on) through bodily means of expression or to reinforce their illocutionary value when they are verbalized. Examples:

- Head nod as an affirmative answer or performed while answering "yes"
- Head shake as a negative answer or performed while answering "no"
- Shrug of shoulders performed while answering "I don't know" or "sorry, I don't care"
- Index finger to the lips while saying "hush!"

**Framing gestures.** These are used to express emotions and mental states linked to the content of the linguistic utterance. Examples:

- Smiling face to express fun while recounting a funny event
- Face expressing fear while reporting on a dramatic event
- Face expressing reflection while searching for words
- Use of the gestural quotation marks to express enunciative distance with regard to the utterance

## Synchronization Gestures

These are head and hand gestures, facial expressions, gaze, and other body movements that help speakers to coordinate their behavior during the social interaction. We may distinguish the following:

- *Phatic signals* performed by the speaker during his speech turn to beg the interlocutor's attention and signal his immediate intentions to go on or stop speaking
- *Feedback signals* performed by the interlocutor during the speaker's speech turn: head nods and facial expressions that may accompany audible feedback signals like "hum," sighs, or grunts

## APPENDIX 4.B: TRANSCRIPTION CONVENTIONS

- For all examples, we used orthographic transcription.
- Conventions relating to the linguistic data (all examples):

  Speech items that are difficult or impossible to identify are signaled by parentheses (xxx)

  Interruptions in transcription are identified by three dots in brackets: [...]

  Elisions are identified by an apostrophe: "ben moi j' l'ai dit"

  Hesitations are identified by "um" or "uh"

  Vocalic prolongations are identified by two colons: "et::"

  Pauses are identified by a dash: -

- Conventions relating to the gestural data (Examples 4.6 through 4.23 and Appendix 4.A):

  Each occurrence of a gesture is signaled on the transcription line by the underlining of the segment of speech corresponding to its stroke or duration.

  The gestures (position and configuration) are generally represented using photographs, except in the case of Examples 4.19 through 4.22, which require no illustration given the symbolic nature of the gesture of negation. The eyes of some speakers are covered in order to preserve their anonymity.

  The direction of the movements is represented by an arrow on those photographs where it is required.

  Each gesture is briefly described immediately below the line containing the speech.

  Abbreviations used:

  R = right

  L = left

  U = up

  D = down

  Fr = front

  Ba = back

  > = towards

## STUDY GUIDE QUESTIONS

1. Monologic discourse development
   a.  develops early.
   b.  is identical to conversational or dialogic discourse development.
   c.  relies on linguistic acquisitions that are not exhibited by the young child.
   d.  relies on linguistic acquisitions and cognitive abilities that are not exhibited by the young child.
2. The study of children's explanations provides information on discourse development because
   a.  its basic textual structure is presented in its simple as well as complex forms.
   b.  its basic textual structure is complex.
   c.  explanatory discourse and narrative discourse share the same basic discourse properties.
   d.  only older children are able to verbalize explanations.
3. Coverbal gesture
   a.  has no clear or precise communicative function.
   b.  is not linked with speech.
   c.  is not able to symbolize abstract ideas.
   d.  serves several functions, including representational and expression functions.
4. Does gesture that occurs with verbal explanations develop with age?
   a.  No, it does not develop with age.
   b.  Yes, the use of gesture decreases while verbal explanations develops.
   c.  Yes, it expresses increased abstract thought with the development of age.
   d.  Yes, but it develops independently from speech.
5. Gestures that occur with verbal explanations
   a.  have no representational meaning.
   b.  are mostly abstract representational gestures and discourse cohesion gestures.
   c.  are mostly expressive gestures.
   d.  are the same gestures as those that occur with narratives and other discourse genres.

## CHAPTER 5

# The Language of Expository Discourse across Adolescence

## *Ruth A. Berman and Bracha Nir*

This chapter considers the language that characterizes expository texts produced by schoolchildren and adolescents. In the present context, "language" refers to local linguistic usage—in the sense of lexical items and syntactic constructions rather than thematic content on the one hand or global-level discourse organization on the other (Berman & Nir-Sagiv, 2007, 2009b). That is, our concern here is with how expository style is expressed linguistically rather than what ideas are voiced or how they are structured within a given text (Britton & Black, 1985; Katzenberger, 2004). Several motivations underlie this decision. First, prior research in different languages shows that expository discourse manifests highly specific linguistic features (Biber, 1989, 2007) and that children are sensitive to this from early school age on (Berman & Nir-Sagiv, 2004, for Hebrew; Jisa, 2004, for French; Reilly, Zamora, & McGivern, 2005, for English). Second, these text-embedded linguistic usages show clear developmental trends, flourishing from late adolescence on. Besides, written expository texts constitute a privileged vantage point for studying more advanced and sophisticated forms of expression by means of what Blank (2002) terms "book language" (Berman, 2007; Ravid, 2004).

As a point of departure, we start by characterizing what is meant by "expository texts" in the present context. Expository discourse has been identified as a "macrogenre" (Grabe, 2002) that can be divided into various subgenres, such as encyclopedic entries, procedural instructions, newspaper articles, and research papers (Nippold, 2004; Pappas & Pettigrew, 1998; Swales, 1990). Beyond such genre-based distinctions, a given piece of expository discourse may also express a range of rhetorical functions (Paltridge, 2002; Werlich, 1976) or different "modes of discourse" (Du Bois, 1980; Smith, 2003), such as classification, comparison, definition, description, explanation, illustration, and persuasion.

In eliciting the database we analyze in this chapter, a deliberate attempt was made to differentiate expository texts that discuss an abstract topic from narratives that recount a specific personal experience. This database forms part of a large-scale cross-linguistic project conducted in seven countries, funded by a Spencer Foundation major grant to principal investigator Ruth Berman for the study of developing literacy in different contexts and differ-ent languages (Berman & Verhoeven, 2002b).* Texts were elicited in several countries, from students in four different age-groups, on the basis of the same initial 3-minute wordless video film showing unresolved situations of moral, social, and physical conflict (Berman & Katzenberger, 2004). This served as a trigger for eliciting an open-ended discussion of ideas concerning the socially relevant topic of interpersonal conflict. Participants of different ages (fourth graders aged 9 to 10 years, seventh graders aged 12 to 13, 11th graders aged 16 to 17, and graduate school adults aged in their 20s and 30s) and in differ-ent countries (France, Iceland, Israel, the Netherlands, Spain, Sweden, and the United States [California]) were asked to write a composition and give a talk in which they expressed their ideas on the topic of "problems between people." The same participants were also asked to write and tell a story about an incident where they had been involved in a situation of "problems between people" so that each participant produced four different texts in randomized order (personal experience narrative and expository discussion, both written and spoken). This design was observed in all seven countries, with 20 partici-pants in each of four age-groups producing all four texts.

This chapter, then, concerns texts that aimed at an expository discussion of the topic of interpersonal conflict or "problems between people" and deliberately disregards the narrative texts produced by the same participants on the same topic. In the elicitation of the expository discussion texts, participants were explicitly instructed *not* to summarize the film and *not* to tell a story but to give their thoughts and opinions on the subject in order to elicit an expository discussion. Beyond that, however, they were not given further prompts or directives. Since our goals were research oriented rather than pedagogically motivated (Macbeth, 2006), participants were deliberately not given any scaffolding instructions on how to structure their texts or what kind of language to use. Importantly, our database relies on "authentic" materials and as such combines features of both natural and what has been termed "contrived" or specially designed and structured linguistic data (Speer, 2002a, 2002b).

A deliberate outcome of our design, then, is that the texts considered here are in a genre that is clearly distinct from the "narrative mode" (Bruner, 1986;

---

* Data are taken primarily from the English- and Hebrew-language samples, with thanks to Judy Reilly of San Diego State University for giving us access to the English materials.

Georgakopoulou & Goutsos, 2000; Longacre, 1996). In fact, most of the participants in our sample fulfilled the elicitation requirements—in different languages
and across the four age-groups. They used markedly different language in the
stories they told and wrote compared with the texts analyzed here (Berman &
Verhoeven, 2002a; Reilly et al., 2005; Tolchinsky & Rosado, 2005), and they
produced texts that are in some basic sense "expository" since all of them contained at least one idea, opinion, or claim. For example, in the Hebrew subsam-
ple, "all participants, even in the youngest age group, made some kind of general
statement or expressed some opinion at the beginning of the texts they produced when asked to discuss the topic of 'problems between people'" (Berman &
Katzenberger, 2004, p. 66). In this, they gave expression to what we define as a
fundamental property of expository discourse: it proceeds categorically and "top
down," from broad generalizations to more detailed specification of content, and
it is built around generalized propositions as superordinate categories that need
to be further elaborated and subcategorized (Berman & Nir-Sagiv, 2007).[*]

Despite all the care taken with the original research design as well as
in formulating elicitation procedures, the "expository" texts we derived
represent an essentially mixed type of discourse. Some of the texts were to
one extent or another "argumentative" (Crammond, 1998), while several were
mainly "informative" (Giora, 1990), often providing a definition of the topic.
Younger participants, particularly, tended to adopt largely a "problem-solving"
orientation (Paltridge, 2002). In fact, although this was explicitly specified
in our elicitation procedures, relatively few participants observed a canonic
"discussion" mode, defined as discussing "an issue in the light of some kind of
'frame' or position," as providing "more than one point of view on the issue,"
and/or recommending "a final position on the issue" (Macken-Horarik, 2002,
p. 22). These elements could be discerned in relatively few of the texts across
the sample of 40 participants per age-group for both English and Hebrew:
none in grade school, only one or two in junior high school, and some half a
dozen of the high school students.

These different orientations to the task of writing an essay on the abstract,
socially relevant topic of interpersonal conflict are illustrated next from the
English-language texts. Example 5.1, from a 9-year-old, represents a monotonic
set of prescriptions in problem-solving mode.[†]

---

[*] These ideas are consistent with psycholinguistic analyses of expository texts as proceeding
from general to specific (Giora, 1985), or from "move-ons" to "expands" (Britton, 1994), and
with linguistic analyses of expository discourse as made up of "core" and "satellite" elements
(Mann & Thompson, 1988).

[†] For consistency and ease of exposition, the sample texts presented here are all of written essay
versions, although all participants also produced oral talk versions on the same topic. A range
of analyses comparing the expository texts in the two modalities revealed little difference
between the written and oral versions in terms of overall global text structure. Similar trends
also emerged for the two modalities in local linguistic expression, although by and large the
oral expository texts in both English and Hebrew used rather less sophisticated lexicon and
fewer complex syntactic structures than their written counterparts (Bar-Ilan & Berman, 2007;
Berman & Ravid, 2009; Nir-Sagiv, Bar-Ilan, & Berman, 2008).

### Example 5.1: Composition Written by Fourth-Grade Boy: Problem Solving

*I think people should discuss their problems or maybe even ask a grownup or someone older than yourself, and people really should get along. I think people should treat everyone the same.*

The excerpt in Example 5.2, the first half of a junior high school text, is also predominantly problem-solving in orientation, but it is, quite typically among the older participants, far more "mixed" since it includes other modes as well, such as definition by illustration and evaluation.

### Example 5.2: Composition Written by Seventh-Grade Girl: Problem Solving Plus Definition and Evaluation

*There are many conflicts in the world like stealing, cheating, and doing criminal type things* [DEFINITION BY ILLUSTRATION]. *There are many possible ways to solve conflicts like talking the problem out or confessing to what you did* [PROBLEM SOLVING]. *For cheating, it is bad to do that because people need to know your true academic ability, so what you could do is study for a test or quiz. Having conflicts in the world is very bad because that is what makes the world not peaceful at times* [EVALUATION] …

The high school text in Example 5.3 is also "mixed," but in marked contrast to the younger children's texts, it constitutes a canonic discussion that is framed by a prototypical definition and that weighs the (linguistically overtly marked) pros and cons of two different perspectives on the topic. It also recounts two past episodes to illustrate its claims, the first an experience the writer had of conflict with her swimming coach, the second a conflict a friend of hers had with two classmates—indicated by three dots in Example 5.3.[*]

### Example 5.3: Composition Written by 11th-Grade Girl: Discussion (Berman, 2008, p. 744)

*Conflict is opposing ideas or stances between two or more people.* [DEFINITION] *In many ways it is a necessary part of life. On the other hand it can cause disruption and chaos in the relationships of those involved.* [POSITIONS] *When people have a difference of opinion, a conflict is usually the result. This is a good way for those differences to be put aside.* [EVALUATION]
*For example, I recently started swimming under a new coach …* [ILLUSTRATIVE EPISODE]

---

[*] Underlined items are discourse connectives (sentence-modifying adverbials and coordinating and subordinating conjunctions) that are discussed later in the chapter under the heading "Clause Linking Connectivity."

*In that way conflict can be a good thing. The results were better than the situation that was achieved beforehand.* [EVALUATION]
*In other cases, conflict can ruin a friendship.* [POSITION] *My friend was very close friends ...* [ILLUSTRATIVE EPISODE]
*This is a situation in which conflict was a bad thing.* [EVALUATION]
*If the conflict cannot be resolved, then the relationship will suffer. In my case, I avoid conflict at all costs, sometimes to the point where I void my own opinion in order to prevent a conflict. On the one hand, I very seldom argue with people* [PERSONAL POSITION], *but on the other hand, my ideas may go unheard, or a friendship will be based on a fake foundation.* [EPISTEMIC POSITION]*
*There is a happy medium somewhere though. Hopefully, someday I will realize when a conflict is necessary and use it intelligently not as a fight but as a discussion to solve a common problem.* [EPISTEMIC PROBLEM SOLVING]

The text in Example 5.3 illustrates several facets of maturely proficient text construction. It demonstrates the cognitively demanding ability to introduce narrative-like, past tense–anchored episodic illustrations in the course of constructing expository discourse—analogous to the ability of skilled narrators to provide expository-like, atemporal generalizations to round out their recounting of narrative events (Berman & Nir-Sagiv, 2004, 2007). It indicates that interpretive evaluation not only is a mark of skilled narration (Labov, 1972; Ravid & Berman, 2006) but also may constitute an important elaborative element to expository discourse (see also Georgakopoulou & Goutsos, 2000; Martin & Rose, 2002), and it shows that cognitively anchored positions concerning the topic at issue are a hallmark of mature expository discussion (Reilly, Jisa, Baruch, & Berman, 2002; Reilly et al., 2005).

The next section, which makes up most of this chapter, describes and illustrates the language used in the texts we analyzed in different linguistic domains, for which we were able to identify patterns of lexical and syntactic expression that appear particularly genre sensitive and hence typical of expository discourse. The four domains detailed here are (a) temporality, particularly in use of verb tense and modal expressions; (b) clause structure, including passive and impersonal constructions; (c) clause combining by coordinate and subordinate constructions; and (d) lexical usage.

## PATTERNS OF LANGUAGE USE IN EXPOSITORY TEXT PRODUCTION

We now turn to the primary objective of this chapter to consider the nature of the language used in expository discourse as identified across the texts that we elicited. Importantly, the texts in our database reflect a large range of commonalities—not necessarily in thematic content or preferred discourse

---

* The term *epistemic* here refers to cognitively anchored perspectives on future contingencies, as discussed at some length later in this chapter.

mode but in linguistic expression. These shared properties are manifested at the interface between the lexicon and syntax in different domains of linguistic structure. Our analysis thus deliberately takes into account what linguists term the "lexicon–syntax interface," for example, to claim that structural syntactic factors play a role in the behavior of lexical items (Hale & Keyser, 2002). In fact, earlier analyses of both narrative and expository texts revealed a strong relationship between the criteria we adopted for lexical usage and different measures of syntax, such as clause length, use of relative clauses, and noun phrase complexity (Berman & Nir-Sagiv, 2007, 2009b). Moreover, lexicon and syntax also correlated in largely similar ways across English and Hebrew, two typologically different languages. These findings for vocabulary–syntax correlations in texts produced from middle childhood across adolescence underscore the strong connection between command of the lexicon and grammatical development—previously demonstrated mainly with respect to young preschool children (e.g., Bates & Goodman, 1999; Marchman & Bates, 1994; Marchman & Thal, 2005). They support a psycholinguistic view of grammar and the lexicon as "inseparable" components of language knowledge and language use (Bates & Goodman, 1997), and they are consistent with the analyses proposed here, in which lexical elements are shown to be the building blocks out of which clause-level syntax is constructed.

Against this background, the following domains are analyzed in subsequent sections: temporal expression in the categories of tense and mood; clause type—impersonals, passives, and so on with different kinds of subject nominals; clause-linking connectivity through coordination and subordination; and lexical selection as expressing register or style of usage. Developmental patterns (from ages 9 to 10 years through young adulthood) and cross-linguistic commonalities and contrasts are highlighted in the analyses.

## Temporal Expression: Tense, Aspect, and Mood

Studies in different languages reveal that most of the predicates in the expository texts in our sample are in a generic present tense form akin to the "simple present" of English (Kupersmitt, 2006; Ragnarsdóttir, Cahana-Amitay, van Hell, Rosado, & Viguié, 2002). This is because they relate mainly to currently relevant or generalized states of affairs. In general, expository discourse is largely "atemporal" in the sense that it is not anchored in a clearly demarcated time frame (marked by tense) or in a specific perspective (expressed through grammatical aspect).* Unlike narratives, expository discourse does not recount (actual or fictitious) events that occurred at some typically well-

---

* This generalization needs to be qualified in at least two cases: (a) proficient essayists may deliberately include specific past-anchored illustrative episodes as evidence for their generalizations, as in the full version of the high-schooler's text in (3) (Berman & Nir-Sagiv, 2007); and (b) in the discourse mode of what Biber (2007, July) has termed "procedural descriptions," past tense may be used in the methodology section of scientific articles, where researchers describe what they did in gathering evidence.

defined point in past time, and, unlike sportscasts or picture descriptions, expository texts do not relate to events that are in the course of occurring, so they are largely lacking in aspectual markings of the kind encoded by English progressive forms. And, indeed, throughout our database of more than 1,000 expository texts, participants across age-groups and languages relied heavily on present tense forms, unmarked for progressive or perfect aspect, in talking and in writing about the topic of problems between people. This is clearly illustrated by the opening of the text excerpted in Example 5.3 and in the first part of the middle school text in Example 5.4a.

### Example 5.4a: First Part of Composition Written by Seventh-Grade Boy (Berman, 2008, p. 743)

*I <u>think</u> there <u>are</u> many problems and conflicts in the world. I also <u>think</u> different people <u>handle</u> these problems in different ways. Some people <u>make</u> little problems out to be big conflicts. The world <u>has</u> many huge problems that <u>need</u> to be dealt with a lot quicker than some people's little problems.*

These timeless present tense generalizations—like those using the verb forms underlined in Example 5.4a—are fleshed out by a shift to "irrealis" mood. This term refers to propositions that relate to contingencies projected onto possible future worlds, including forms that in languages like French or Spanish can be grammatically marked by conditional and subjective inflections on the verb. In English, relating to future eventualities is typically achieved by use of a special category of items in the form of grammatical modals (e.g., English *can, may, might, must, should, will*) and their corresponding semimodal expressions (e.g., *be able to, be likely to, be liable to, have to, ought to, be going to*). Such elements serve to express an attitude as to whether a given proposition or state of affairs is desirable, necessary, possible, or likely. They are illustrated by the examples in the fourth grader's text in Example 5.1: *I think people <u>should</u> discuss their problems … and people really <u>should</u> get along*; from the seventh grader in Example 5.2: *what you <u>could</u> do is study for a test or quiz*; and the 11th grader in Example 5.3: *conflict <u>can</u> ruin a friendship, my ideas <u>may</u> go unheard, a friendship <u>will</u> be based on a fake foundation.* They also occur in the conclusion to the seventh grader's text in Example 5.4b.

### Example 5.4b: Continuation of Composition Written by Seventh-Grade Boy (Berman, 2008, p. 743)

*Some problems <u>can lead</u> to many bad conflicts, which happens a lot at schools, on the street, and many other places. Little problems <u>can be</u> easily <u>set aside</u>, while big problems <u>might take</u> thinking and some action. Different people <u>can lead</u> to many problems and differences in opinions also lead to many problems. I think if you are a good person, you <u>can overcome</u> most problems in life.*

Expressions like these occurred in no fewer than 20% of the clauses in the expository texts written in English (Reilly et al., 2005), while in other languages, which use rather different linguistic devices for relating to future contingences (impersonal constructions like French *il faut* and Hebrew subjectless constructions or conditional and subjunctive inflections in Spanish), these were used in around 15% of all clauses (Kupersmitt, 2006; Reilly et al., 2002). It might be the case that these types of generalized propositions were particularly well suited to the topic presented to participants in the present study. They appear quite common in another set of similar texts elicited from other Hebrew-speaking participants in the same age-groups asked to discuss the topic of violence in schools (Berman, 2003; Berman & Ravid, 1999). On the other hand, such statements are less common in *biographical* texts elicited from Hebrew-speaking sixth and 11th graders asked to describe the life of a public figure or family member as well as in more closely "expository" texts constructed by the same students selected out of 10 possible topics—war, cinema, the city of Tel Aviv, clocks, cats, higher academic studies, football, the Palestine Liberation Organization, the zoo, and sculpture (Ravid & Zilberbuch, 2003).

This particular linguistic system—use of modal expressions—also shows an interesting *developmental shift*. Across languages, the modals used by the youngest age-group (fourth graders) were typically a "deontic" type of term in prescriptive statements (like the *should* clauses in Example 5.1). They show that children at this stage of development refer mainly to obligations and prohibitions, reflecting socially determined and normatively prescriptive judgmental attitudes toward the topic of interpersonal conflict. Older speaker-writers, on the other hand, from adolescence up, use mainly "epistemic" modals—like the terms *can*, *cannot*, and *will* in Example 5.3—that express possible or probable states of affairs in some future world and so reflect a more distanced or objective view on the same topic. This is an interesting instance of a quite general trend in language development: the actual forms are mastered early on, but their meanings expand and their functions diversify over time, reflecting a noteworthy interplay between linguistic and cognitive development.

Another quite general facet of developing abilities in expository text construction is that, with age, the *range of forms* used within a given linguistic category expand and diversify. In the case in point, the linguistic subsystems of tense, aspect, and mood are increasingly recruited across adolescence to create a more richly varied "temporal texture": alongside the invariant present tense, greater reliance on past progressive and past perfect aspectual forms, together with a wider range of modal expressions, reflects a general cognitive shift from adherence to one dominant expressive option to a more flexibly variegated use of language. Moreover, not only do the forms themselves diverge with age, but they also acquire increasingly more variegated *functions*. In expository discourse, this means that the present tense serves initially among younger children in the context of vaguely timeless generalities (e.g., *Fighting is not good*, *It is not nice to fight*), whereas the generic propositions of older participants are more concretely anchored in specific states of affairs and situations (e.g., a high school student starts his text as follows: *Conflicts are large problems, particularly in high school. Although conflict never goes away, high school is a major focal point of conflict because of the extreme amount of new tension that students are confronted with*) (Berman, 2008, p. 743). From high school on, participants typically anchor their statements about the topic of conflict in specific situations, such as peer pressure, sibling rivalry, or teacher–student differences of perception. In contrast, among the younger children, the only more concrete type of anchoring is provided by direct reference to the scenes depicted in the video clip (e.g., *It is not good to cheat, if someone loses a purse you should return it*) (Berman & Katzenberger, 2004; Kupersmitt, 2006; Tolchinsky, Johanssen, & Zamora, 2002).

## Clause Types: Subjects and Predicates

We consider next clause-internal constructions and verb-argument relations. First, in keeping with their largely non–action-oriented thematic content (Longacre, 1996), expository texts make use of *existential and copular constructions* (e.g., in Example 5.2, *There are many conflicts in the world, Having conflicts is very bad*). Along similar lines, expository discourse is also often couched in terms of *impersonal constructions*: these occur without any surface subject in languages like Hebrew and Spanish and with expletive subjects like *it* or *il* in English and French for making different kinds of general statements. Among younger students, such propositions are often evaluative in character (e.g., from middle school texts, *it is bad to cheat, it is wrong to do all these things*), whereas in more mature texts they express a range of nonjudgmental, cognitively motivated "propositional attitudes" (e.g., *It is often the case that …, On the surface, it appears to be …*). These constructions serve to express a less active, patient-oriented perspective in preference to a dynamic or agent-oriented perspective—and they increase with age, particularly from high school up (Berman & Nir-Sagiv, 2004; Jisa & Viguié, 2005; Tolchinsky & Rosado, 2005).

For related reasons, expository texts rely heavily on *passive voice* (e.g., in Example 5.3, *If the conflict cannot be resolved, a friendship will be based*) to shift away from a personalized or agent-oriented perspective. That is, rather than focusing on who did what to whom, such constructions enable speaker-writers to take the undergoer as the point of departure for commenting on a given state of affairs. For example, a high school boy writes that "students are confronted with problems," "students are thrust into realization of the 'real world,'" "students are exposed to many new people" (see also Example 5.5). By using these typically passive constructions, this adolescent treats "students" as being subjected to certain situations rather than as an actor in the perpetration of events. This option is favored by speaker-writers of Germanic languages like English and Dutch (Jisa, Reilly, Verhoeven, Baruch, & Rosado, 2002), which lack generically impersonal constructions that are readily accessible to speaker-writers of languages like Hebrew (Berman & Nir-Sagiv, 2004) or Spanish (Tolchinsky & Rosado, 2005).*

---

* In Hebrew and Spanish, and to a lesser degree in French, another readily available means for downgrading of agency is by means of so-called "middle voice" constructions—with the clitic *se* in Romance languages (Kemmer, 1993) and use of verb-morphology in Semitic languages (Berman, 1979).

From the point of view of nominal reference, expository texts rely heavily on *generic pronouns*, such as English *they* and *one*, French *on*, or the second-person pronoun used impersonally in different languages, for example, in Example 5.2, *confessing to what <u>you</u> did, people need to know <u>your</u> true academic ability, what <u>you</u> could do is study* (Berman, 2005; Jisa, 2004; Reilly et al., 2005). In addition to these generic and impersonal pronouns, expository texts are typically highly "nominal" since, as noted earlier, in discussing an abstract topic, speaker-writers rely on lexical noun phrases as a frame of content for anchoring their generalizations. Thus, a high school boy uses a complex noun phrase with a relative clause embedded in a single highly "nominal" sentence: *The <u>pressures</u> that <u>society</u> places on <u>people</u> today seem to be a great <u>cause</u> of the <u>problems</u> and <u>conflict</u> that arise between <u>human beings</u> in the modern <u>world</u>* (Ravid, van Hell, Rosado, & Zamora, 2002).

Moreover, with age and, again, increasingly from high school on, expository writing is characterized by a rich range of lengthy and *complex noun phrases* (Ravid & Berman, in press). For example, the following "heavy" noun phrases occur in the expository text written by a high school boy, ranging from four to seven words in length, with head nouns underlined: *a <u>result</u> of insecurity, another <u>source</u> of conflict, many <u>people</u> in this world, close <u>contact</u> with someone unknown, their dominant <u>status</u> amongst a group, the other person's <u>point</u> of view, <u>students</u> who are unfamiliar with another student, the <u>relationships</u> in which they are involved.*

Taken together, these features reflect the fact that in expository texts, clause-internal information is packaged in a way that expresses an impersonal, relatively objective, nonagentive, and hence generally rather distanced, discourse "stance" (Berman, 2005; Berman, Ragnarsdóttir, & Strömqvist, 2002). These different facets of expository prose are illustrated by the (single underlined) <u>heavy noun phrases</u> combined with the (heavy underlined) <u>generic pronouns</u> and the (double underlined) <u>passive constructions</u> in the high school text in Example 5.5.

### Example 5.5: Composition Written by 11th-Grade Boy (Berman, 2008, pp. 743–744)

*Conflict is a <u>large problem</u> particularly in High School, although it never goes away. High school is <u>a major focal point of conflict</u> because of <u>the extreme amount of new tension</u> that <u>students are confronted with</u>. Coming from <u>a sheltered environment</u> with <u>the close supervision and intervention of parents and teachers</u>, <u>students are thrust into realization of the so called "real world"</u> where <u>you</u> must now make choices and resolve problems on <u>your</u> own. While <u>you</u> are never really on your own, this new freedom can give the overwhelming feeling of distancing <u>yourself</u> from <u>your</u> parents control. <u>Students are exposed to many new people</u> and begin to form social cliques or groups. These groups not only follow <u>racial and ethnic lines</u> but also <u>the class bracket</u> that <u>they are placed in</u>, such as advanced or* remedial. This can have <u>an impact on people</u> because of the exposure or lack of it or <u>jealousy and envy</u>. <u>Peer pressure</u> is <u>one of the main causes of conflict</u> which never goes away but that students have <u>a hard time</u> learning to cope with. While conflict is not a <u>necessarily bad thing</u>, it does help prepare people for <u>the real world</u> which is full of <u>conflict and problems</u>.

The cluster of expressive options selected for representing clause-internal verb-argument relations in expository texts like the one in Example 5.5 gives voice to an overall stance that is particularly well suited to the academic, reflective nature of expository discussion as a discourse genre.

## Clause-Linking Connectivity

Interclause connectivity in discourse can be achieved both lexically and syntactically. Consider, first, *lexical connectives*, be they sentence connectors like *however*, coordinators like *but*, or subordinators like *although*. These play an important role in the segmentation of discourse in general, particularly in the case of expository discourse, which is lacking in a default principle of organization, such as sequentiality in narratives. In the expository texts in our sample, lexical conjunctions express a range of semantic relations (among younger participants mainly causal), subsequently also expressing more abstract and metatextual notions like hypotheticality, adversativity, or contrast (Katzenberger & Cahana-Amitay, 2002). Examples include the underlined expressions in the following excerpts from high school texts, a sentence-connecting adverbial in (a) and a subordinating conjunction in (b): (a) *Many people are insecure about themselves and the relationships in which they are involved.* <u>*Thus*</u> *fighting another person out of unfounded jealousy occurs;* (b) <u>*While*</u> *conflict is not necessarily a good thing, it does help prepare people for the real world.* Other examples of such lexical connectives, both single words and multiword expressions, are illustrated by the underlined items in the high school text in Example 5.3. As shown there, these lexical connectives are an important means of realizing the discourse mode of "discussion," as defined earlier, since they serve to explicitly present, compare, and contrast different positions on an issue. Marking of such logical relations between clauses or sentences increases in explicitness, variety, and depth with age, reflecting metatextual abilities that emerge only in late adolescence. Younger children marked such relations overtly only occasionally, usually by means of everyday colloquial items like *so* and *but*. More explicit and sophisticated lexical items, like the adverbial connectives *for example*, *as a result*, *in contrast*, and *on the other hand* and the subordinating conjunctions *although* and *while* (in the contrastive sense of *whereas* rather than to mark temporal simultaneity), were largely lacking in our database of texts produced by writers before high school age.

A second major device for achieving textual connectivity is through clause combining (Haiman & Thompson, 1988) or *syntactic packaging* (Berman & Slobin, 1994). This has generally been accorded less attention in research on language acquisition, with the important exception of Scott's (2004) analysis of "clause connectivity" in schoolchildren's written and oral texts. As detailed for analysis of narrative texts in English, Hebrew, and Spanish (Berman, 1998; Berman & Nir-Sagiv, 2009a; Nir-Sagiv & Berman, in press; Scott & Windsor, 2000), connectivity is typically achieved by stringing together coordinate clauses and/or by expressing dependency relations between two or more clauses by complementation (e.g., *Some people feel that the conflict must be avoided at all costs*), by relative clauses, and/or by different kinds of adverbials—both finite (e.g., *Hopefully I will realize when a conflict is necessary*) and nonfinite *In order to co-exist peacefully, everybody just needs to compromise*). An example of a particularly dense kind of syntactic packaging is revealed by the cluster of four clauses linked together in the following excerpt from the essay of a high school boy, with only the main clause unmarked by underlining: *The pressure to do well may cause stress, which in turn can cause even more problems* [RELATIVE] *if this stress is taken out on others* [ADVERBIAL, CONDITIONAL].

Three types of dependent clause-linking constructions were particularly favored in the expository texts in our sample: relative clauses, conditional adverbial clauses, and nonfinite infinitival (e.g., *in order to co-exist peacefully, to do well*) or participial clauses (e.g., *Many times the problem can be figured out by simply talking things out or getting to the root of the problem*). The occurrence of relative clauses, adverbial clauses, and nonfinite dependent clauses in general showed a marked age-related increase, most noticeably from high school up. Relatedly, complex packages of several clauses together, like those illustrated here (e.g., with the two nonfinite participial clauses of manner linked by coordination through the lexical item or), were found only in the high school and adult texts, and their distribution was affected not only by development but also by target-language typology. For example, nonfinite subordination with participles and gerunds was far more common in English and Spanish than in Hebrew (Kupersmitt, 2006).

Alternation in use of nonfinite verb forms (infinitives, participles, or gerunds) as the main verb in a clause is illustrated by such constructions as *possible ways to solve problems* in Example 5.2, *a discussion to solve* in Example 5.3, or more sophisticated gerundive or participial uses, such as *freedom of distancing yourself* ... and *a hard time learning to cope* with peer pressure in Example 5.5. Interestingly, in more advanced language use, these nonfinites typically occur as complements of nouns rather than of verbs (e.g., *ways to solve, freedom of distancing*). Again, this demonstrates the interplay between different linguistic systems, in this case between clause-internal heavy noun phrases and use of nonfinite subordination for between-clause linkage.

## Lexical Selection and Level of Style

A range of measures of vocabulary has been applied to the expository texts in our database in both English and Hebrew. These include (a) *word length*, measured by number of syllables and, in English, by number of letters as well, comparing the number of polysyllabic words (three syllables or more) across the variables of age and text type (Nir-Sagiv, 2005); (b) *lexical density*, in both languages, measured by the proportion of open class items or content words (nouns, verbs, or adjectives) out of the total words per text (Nir-Sagiv, Bar-Ilan, & Berman, 2008; Ravid, 2004; Strömqvist et al., 2002); (c) *register*, in the sense of level of usage, specified as formal versus colloquial for English (Bar-Ilan & Berman, 2007) and as high, neutral, or low for Hebrew (Nir-Sagiv, Sternau, Berman, & Ravid, 2008; Ravid & Berman, 2009); and (d) *noun abstractness*, measured by a condensed version of the 10-point scale developed by Ravid (2006), ranging nouns in terms of semantic content from concrete, imageable, and specific at one end to abstract, generic, and derivationally complex at the other (Berman & Nir-Sagiv, 2007).* All these criteria of lexical usage revealed clear and significant age-related differences in the expository texts we analyzed for both English and Hebrew. Across the board, younger children—grade schoolers in middle childhood (aged 9–10 years) and young teenagers in middle school (aged 12–13 years)—score lower on a range of measures of lexical usage than high school adolescents and graduate student adults.

Consider, for example, the domain of linguistic register, a topic that has been relatively unexplored to date in developmental perspective (exceptions are the sociolinguistically motivated studies of English-language usage in Corson, 1984; Romaine, 1984). Here, "register" refers to level of usage, ranging from everyday casual or colloquial to more formal, elevated styles of language use. All languages manifest usage variation along such dimensions, but some show more extreme differentiation than others, and each language makes these distinctions in specific ways in terms of both communicative context and linguistic features. Accordingly, Gayraud (2000), for example, evolved an original set of criteria for stipulating level of usage or register in her study of a comparable set of expository texts produced by French-speaking school children and adolescents. And in our studies, too, we applied markedly different criteria to English and Hebrew for evaluating register level in our texts in the two languages (Bar-Ilan & Berman, 2007; Nir-Sagiv, Bar-Ilan, & Berman, 2008, for English; Nir-Sagiv et al., 2008; Ravid & Berman, 2009, for Hebrew). Across the database, in English, French, and Hebrew, the lexicon turned out to be a critical facet in lowering or elevating level of style. Thus, expository discourse typically deploys high-register and quite formal means of linguistic expression and reliance on the "literate lexicon" (Ravid,

---

* Another accepted means of assessing text-embedded vocabulary usage is that of *lexical diversity,* defined as proportion of different words out of the total words in a text. This procedure, as enhanced and motivated in Malvern, Richards, Chipere, and Durán (2004) in the form of so-called VOCD, and applied automatically in the CHILDES programs (MacWhinney, 2000), relates to word types in the sense of different word forms, rather than of different lexemes, and so was considered less relevant to the advanced level of language command under consideration here (see also Strömqvist et al., 2002).

2004). In English, expository texts in general and written essays rather more than oral discussions across the board favored long, low-frequency, and morphologically complex words of Latinate origin. Interestingly, use of words of Greco-Latin origin was also shown by Corson (1984) to be a distinguishing feature of the language use of adolescents from different social and ethnic backgrounds.

Relevant features of the expository lexicon are illustrated by the underlined items in Example 5.6, with each content word (noun, verb, or adjective) marked for historical origin as L(atinate) or G(ermanic).

### Example 5.6: Composition Written by 11th-Grade Boy (Berman, 2008, p. 754)

*Many people-L contend-L that the issue-L of conflict-L is an issue-L of good-G against evil-G, the final-L battle-L, the Apocalypse-L, etc. However, the issue-L of conflict-L should not be addressed-L as an issue-L requiring-L a complete-L solution-L, but rather a restraint-L. If one must think-G of conflict-L as a problem-L, then conflicts-L should be referred-L to as a necessary-L evil-G in modern-L society-L. Many important-L things-G arise-G out of conflict-L, including-L differing-L opinions-L and aesthetic-L differentiation-L and originality-L. On the other hand-G, conflict-L can result-L in a violent-L eruption-L, namely war-G. To resolve-L the issue-L of conflict-L, a cure-L should not be sought-G. Instead, people-L should learn-G to be able to harness-G the extent-L of a conflict-L, to keep-G things-G under control-L. Only when conflicts-L become-G out of control-L do they result-L in violent-L outbursts-G and become-G an evil-G.*

In terms of lexical density (i.e., the proportion of content words out of total words per text), nearly half the words in the essay in Example 5.6 are open class items (64 out of 139), and most of these (47 out of 64, or 73%) are Latinate in origin. Many of them are also morphologically complex (e.g., *differing, differentiation, originality*, and *eruption*).

In content, these typically abstract nouns and adjectives reinforce our earlier observations about the highly nominal nature and distanced stance of expository discourse. Thus, again, different factors conspire together to create the special language of expository texts—in the case in point, lexical category (content words in general and nouns in particular), semantic content (abstract, general concepts), and linguistic form (polysyllabic, morphologically complex).

## Interplay of Linguistic Expression and Thematic Content

The different domains of language use that we identified as typifying expository discourse conspire together in the construction of texts characteristic of the genre. This is clearly illustrated in the 11th grader's text in Example 5.7, showing the interplay between different domains of expository language use that we consider here: atemporality (generic present) and future projections (modal expressions), stativeness (copula, existential, and other nondynamic predicates), and a nonagentive, generic discourse stance (passives, expletives, impersonal, and middle-voice constructions).

## Example 5.7: Composition Written by 11th-Grade Boy

*Basically what a conflict is is that it is a problem or an issue between two people or between a group of people. A conflict can be started over a big or little issue or about something that can be blown out of proportion. Most of the time conflicts can be resolved fairly quickly or they can drag out for long periods of time. The only real way for a conflict to be resolved is for both sides or parties to be willing to resolve it. Most of the time from what I have seen is that most of the conflicts are about issues that are blown way out proportion and can be resolved within a few minutes. Some may take longer because the people do not want to admit that they were wrong in accusing the other person of something they did not do or that they did it and do not realize that they hurt someone.*

The sample text in Example 5.7 also demonstrates how clause-level and between-clause use of morphosyntactic constructions and the lexicon interact with the *thematic content* of texts. While not at the focus of our concerns in this chapter, it is worth noting that the language used by respondents of different ages reflects differences in the topics that they talk and write about in relation to the shared theme of interpersonal conflict and the attitudes that they adopt with respect to this domain of human experience. For example, the study of Reilly et al. (2002) demonstrates how types of subject nominals interact with modal expressions (e.g., *you should, people must, situations of conflicts are liable to ...*) to present attitudes that are largely socially judgmental and prescriptive among the younger children compared with more cognitively and objectively oriented attitudes to the topic of interpersonal conflict among high school students and adults. Moreover, as noted earlier in the section on clause types, the younger children tend to rely heavily on generic use of the second-person pronoun *you* in these contexts. For example, a fourth-grade girl starts her essay as follows: *I do not think fighting is good. You do not make friends that way. If you do not fight, you can have many many friends. But when you fight, you can hurt the person's feelings you are fighting with ...* (Berman, 2008, p. 742). And another 9-year-old girl writes along much the same lines: *If you see someone in a conflict, then you should not get into them* [sic]. *You should tell an adult, and use that as a lesson.... . You should also never get into conflicts yourself ...* (in this connection, see also Berman, 2005; Reilly et al., 2005). Older students and adults tend to express their attitudes to the topic of interpersonal conflict in more distanced terms, often by relying on an impersonal or abstract subject. They may use impersonal pronouns as subjects standing for entire propositions, for example, from the essays written by two adults: *It is exhiliarating to imagine a world devoid of conflict …* ; *It is a valuable exercise … to try to put oneself in the shoes of the other. This could help to make for a more pleasant confrontation.* In other cases, older participants express their attitudes with abstract nominals as subjects, as in the following examples from the opening to the essay of a high school boy, *The primary cause for problems and conflicts between individuals today would seem to stem from …,* or, as in the opening to a man's expository essays, *Whether in the political, career, or interpersonal realm, discussions must be managed carefully …,* and, from the essay of another man, *Open and thoughtful communication has the potential to reveal each person's needs and desires.* Taken together, these examples reflect not only a difference in the type of attitudes expressed by younger compared with older speaker-writers but also the interaction between different linguistic means—here, lexical modals and subject nominals—for expressing these attitudes in expository discourse.

These ideas are highlighted in Tolchinsky and Rosado's (2005) analysis of five different Spanish constructions that share the discourse feature of agency downgrading. They note that "account must be taken of the fact that the emergence of passives and the *increment in use of other forms occurs together with a change in the thematic content of the texts*" (p. 226, emphasis added). This conclusion is confirmed by the findings of Reilly et al. (2005) for use of passive constructions in the expository texts written in English, where they note that "agents in the adult passives frequently take the form of abstract nominals as opposed to the animate agents (often to be inferred) typical of the younger children's texts" (p. 202). Berman and Katzenberger's (2004) analysis of text openings in the Hebrew sample of our project likewise notes a marked difference in thematic content, in what schoolchildren talk and write about in discussing problems between people in the early teenage years (12- to 13-year-olds) compared with the younger, preschool children. This difference in the topics that participants in different languages are concerned with in their texts can be explained by general social, cognitive, and moral development in these age-groups (Flavell, Miller, & Miller, 1993; Hersch, Paolitto, & Reimer, 1979; Moshman, 1998; Steinberg, 2005).

## SUMMARY AND CONCLUSIONS

The point of departure for this chapter was an attempt to characterize what the term "expository texts" involves in the present context. Critical to any evaluation of the type of discourse considered here is the fact that we relate exclusively to materials that are "raw" in several senses. First, in methodology, participants were not given any explicit instructions about how to construct their texts or what kind of language to use. Investigators were specifically instructed not to say things like "be as expressive as possible, try to formulate your ideas clearly and concisely, pay careful attention to spelling and grammar." Nor were participants aided in the task of text construction by outlines or suggestions as to possible thematic content. This could explain in part why it was so difficult to pinpoint precisely what kind of discourse we were analyzing in our sample. True, all participants made at least one generalized statement about the topic of interpersonal conflict or problems between people (Kupersmitt, 2006). And in this sense, they all departed to some extent from the video film that served as an initial trigger for data elicitation. On the other hand, across languages, the younger participants tended to construct texts around topics that were directly anchored in the concrete situations depicted in the video (e.g., cheating on exams, being unwelcoming to a new student, or roughhousing on the playground) far more than the high school students and adults (Berman & Katzenberger, 2004; Tolchinsky et al., 2002).

A second "raw" feature of our database is that the texts we elicited were "unedited" since—while no time limit was imposed on participants and they were allowed to take notes—not one of them wrote a draft copy that they then used as a basis for revision. Moreover, the texts were "nonexpert" since they were produced by young speaker-writers who were not necessarily fully proficient essayists. Even the adult participants in our study, while well-educated and literate members of their speech community (graduate school students majoring in the humanities and sciences), were not professional writers, journalists, or language specialists. This made our database particularly suitable for evaluation in developmental rather than pedagogical terms. In other words, we assume that developmental changes across time that we detected in the expository texts produced in middle childhood compared with early and late adolescence are due to a combination of general social cognitive development on the one hand and the evolution of "linguistic literacy" on the other (Ravid & Tolchinsky, 2002). Enhanced literacy in the present context thus refers to the impact of increased exposure to and familiarity with literate, school-based materials rather than the effect of direct classroom teaching as such.

Most of this chapter was concerned with patterns of language use in expository text production rather than with thematic content or global text organization (Berman & Ravid, 2009). To this end, we examined linguistic forms used in different domains and on different levels—including means of expressing the discourse function of temporality, clause structure, interclausal connectivity, and lexical repertoire. Our analysis highlights the interplay between the forms favored by speaker-writers on the one hand and different facets of target-language structure on the other. For example, as an instance of the lexicon–syntax interface, modal terms in English typically occur together with verbs in the passive voice, while they are commonly used in subjectless impersonal constructions in Hebrew and Spanish.

The findings reported here for patterns of linguistic usage in expository text construction are in line with studies in a range of other domains that reveal late adolescence (in the case in point here, 16- to 17-year-old high school students) as a watershed in affective, social, and cognitive development. Across the lexical and syntactic domains analyzed here, there was a marked and significant cutoff point dividing the language use of high school students and adults from the younger, grade school and middle school participants in the study. This, again, suggests a complex interplay between consolidating literacy, general intellectual growth, and later language development (Berman, 2007; Nippold, 2007). Expository text construction appears to be a particularly fruitful area for observing the closely intertwined facets of development that consolidate in late adolescence since it requires speaker-writers to concurrently recruit linguistic, cognitive, and social abilities that develop in tandem rather than in isolation. These different factors are closely combined in the production of maturely proficient expository discourse, as illustrated, for example, by the developing use of modal terms like *can*, *be able to*, and *be possible* for the expression of propositional attitudes relating to the topic of interpersonal conflict. Thus, *linguistically*, there is increased variation in the morphosyntactic constructions and lexical items deployed in this domain; *cognitively*, such terms become more mentalistically oriented to epistemic reflections on possible future contingencies rather than restricted to subjective evaluations of what should or should not happen, while the *social* attitudes such terms express relate with age less to judgmental and prescriptive culturally conditioned norms and more to conclusions drawn from the personal experiences of the individual speaker-writer.

In conclusion, as directions for future research, further analysis is called for to assess the effect of modality by comparing oral discussions with written expository essays at different stages of development. Another fruitful line of study would be to compare linguistic expression in domains like those considered here in other subgenres of expository discourse—for example, encyclopedic, descriptive, or procedural—with the aim of fine-tuning characterizations of different expository modes of expression. Finally, in keeping with the goals of the present volume, we suggest that the type of analyses reviewed in this chapter for expository language use in different target languages might usefully be extended to populations from different socioeconomic backgrounds as well as to those with learning and language disorders.

## REFERENCES

Bar-Ilan, L., & Berman R. A. (2007). The Latinate-Germanic divide and register differentiation in developing text production across adolescence. *Linguistics, 45*, 1–35.

Bates, E., & Goodman, J. (1997). On the inseparability of grammar and the lexicon: Evidence from acquisition, aphasia, and real time processing [Special issue]. *Language and Cognitive Processes, 12*, 507–586.

Bates, E., & Goodman, J. (1999). The emergence of grammar from the lexicon. In B. MacWhinney (Ed.), *The emergence of language* (pp. 27–80). Mahwah, NJ: Lawrence Erlbaum Associates.

Berman, R. A. (1979). Form and function: Passives, middles, and impersonals in Modern Hebrew. *Berkeley Linguistic Society, 5,* 1–27.

Berman, R. A. (1998). Typological perspectives on connectivity. In N. Dittmar & Z. Penner (Eds.), *Issues in the theory of language acquisition* (pp. 203–224). Bern: Peter Lang,

Berman, R. A. (2003). Genre and modality in developing discourse abilities. In C. L. Moder & A. Martinovic-Ziv (Eds.), *Discourse across languages and cultures: Typological studies in language series* (pp. 329–356). Amsterdam: Benjamins.

Berman, R. A. (2005). Introduction: Developing discourse stance in different text types and languages [Special issue]. *Journal of Pragmatics, 37*(2), 105–124.

Berman, R. A. (2007). Developing language knowledge and language use across adolescence. In E. Hoff & M. Shatz (Eds.), *Handbook of language development* (pp. 346–367). London: Blackwell.

Berman, R. A. (2008). The psycholinguistics of developing text construction. *Journal of Child Language, 35,* 735–771.

Berman, R. A., & Katzenberger, I. (2004). Form and function in introducing narrative and expository texts: A developmental perspective. *Discourse Processes, 38,* 57–94.

Berman, R. A., & Nir-Sagiv, B. (2004). Linguistic indicators of inter-genre differentiation in later language development. *Journal of Child Language, 31,* 339–380.

Berman, R. A., & Nir-Sagiv, B. (2007). Comparing narrative and expository text construction across adolescence: A developmental paradox. *Discourse Processes, 43,* 79–120.

Berman, R. A., & Nir-Sagiv, B. (2009a). Clause-packaging in narratives: A cross-linguistic developmental study. In J. Guo, E. Lieven, S. Ervin-Tripp, N. Budwig, S. Özçalişkan, & K. Nakamura (Eds.), *Cross-linguistic approaches to the psychology of language: Research in the tradition of Dan I. Slobin* (pp. 149–162). New York: Taylor & Francis.

Berman, R. A., & Nir-Sagiv, B. (2009b). Cognitive and linguistic factors in evaluating expository text quality: Global versus local? In V. Evans & S. Pourcel (Eds.), *New directions in cognitive linguistics* (pp. 421–440). Amsterdam: Benjamins.

Berman, R. A., & Ravid, D. (1999). *The oral/literate continuum: Developmental perspectives.* Final Report to Israel Science Foundation, Jerusalem.

Berman, R. A., & Ravid, D. (2009). Becoming a literate language user: Oral and written text construction across adolescence. In D. R. Olson & N. Torrance (Eds.), *The Cambridge handbook of literacy* (pp. 92–111). Cambridge: Cambridge University Press.

Berman, R. A., & Slobin, D. I. (1994). *Relating events in narrative: A cross-linguistic developmental study.* Hillsdale, NJ: Lawrence Erlbaum Associates.

Berman, R. A., & Verhoeven, L. (2002a). Cross-linguistic perspectives on the development of text production abilities in speech and writing [Special issue]. *Written Languages and Literacy, 5* (Pts. 1 and 2).

Berman, R. A., & Verhoeven, L. (2002b). Developing text production abilities across languages and age groups. *Written Language and Literacy, 5*(1), 1–44.

Berman, R. A., Ragnarsdóttir, H., & Strömqvist, S. (2002). Discourse stance. *Written Languages and Literacy, 5*(2), 255–290.

Biber, D. (1989). A typology of English texts. *Linguistics, 27,* 3–43.

Biber, D. (2007, July). *Merging corpus linguistic and discourse analytic research goals: Discourse units in biology research articles.* Plenary lecture presented to 10th International Pragmatics Association, Göteborg, Sweden.

Blank, M. (2002). Classroom discourse: A key to literacy. In K. G. Butler & E. R. Silliman (Eds.), *Speaking, reading, and writing in children with language learning disabilities* (pp. 151–174). Mahwah, NJ: Lawrence Erlbaum Associates.

Britton, B. K. (1994). Understanding expository text: Building mental structure to induce insights. In M. A. Gernsbacher (Ed.), *Handbook of psycholinguistics* (pp. 641–674). New York: Academic Press.

Britton, B. K., & Black, J. B. (1985). *Understanding expository text*. Hillsdale, NJ: Lawrence Erlbaum Associates.

Bruner, J. (1986). *Actual minds, possible worlds*. Cambridge, MA: Harvard University Press.

Corson, D. (1984). The lexical bar: Lexical change from 12 to 15 years measured by social class, region, and ethnicity. *British Educational Research Journal, 10,* 115–133.

Crammond, J. G. (1998). The uses and complexity of argument structures in expert and student persuasive writing. *Written Communication, 15*(2), 230–268.

Du Bois, J. W. (1980). Beyond definiteness: The trace of identity in discourse. In W. Chafe (Ed.), *The pear stories: Cognitive, cultural, and linguistic aspects of narrative production* (pp. 203–274). Norwood, NJ: Ablex.

Flavell, J. H., Miller, P. H., & Miller, S. A. (1993). *Cognitive development* (3rd ed.). Englewood Cliffs, NJ: Prentice Hall.

Gayraud, F. (2000). *Le Développement de La Différentiation Oral/Écrit Vu à Travers Le Lexique*. Unpublished doctoral dissertation, Université Lyon 2, Lyon, France.

Georgakopoulou, A., & Goutsos, D. (2000). Mapping the world of discourse. The narrative vs. non-narrative distinction. *Semiotica, 131*(1/2), 113–141.

Giora, R. (1985). A text-based analysis of non-narrative texts. *Theoretical Linguistics, 12,* 115–135.

Giora, R. (1990). On the so-called evaluative material in informative text. *Text, 4,* 299–319.

Grabe, W. (2002). Narrative and expository macro-genres. In A. M. Johns (Ed.), *Genre in the classroom: Multiple perspectives* (pp. 249–268). Mahwah, NJ: Lawrence Erlbaum Associates.

Haiman, J., & Thompson, S. A. (Eds.). (1988). *Clause combining in grammar and discourse*. Amsterdam: Benjamins.

Hale, K., & Keyser, S. J. (2002). *Prolegomenon to a theory of argument structure*. Cambridge, MA: MIT Press.

Hersh, R. H., Paolitto, D. P., & Reimer, J. (1979). *Promoting moral growth: From Piaget to Kohlberg*. London: Longman.

Jisa, H. (2004). Growing into academic French. In R. A. Berman (Ed.), *Language development across childhood and adolescence* (pp. 135–162). Amsterdam: Benjamins.

Jisa, H., Reilly, J., Verhoeven, L., Baruch, E., & Rosado, E. (2002). Passive voice constructions in written texts. *Written Languages and Literacy, 5,* 163–182.

Jisa, H., & Viguié, A. (2005). A developmental perspective on the role of "on" in written and spoken expository texts in French. *Journal of Pragmatics, 37,* 125–142.

Katzenberger, I. (2004). The development of clause packaging in spoken and written texts. *Journal of Pragmatics, 36,* 1921–1948.

Katzenberger, I., & Cahana-Amitay, D. (2002) Segmentation marking in text production. *Linguistics, 40*(6), 1161–1184.

Kemmer, S. (1993). *The middle voice*. Amsterdam: Benjamins.

Kupersmitt, J. (2006). *Relating to time in narrative and expository texts: A cross-linguistic, developmental study of linguistic temporality*. Unpublished doctoral dissertation, Bar-Ilan University, Ramat Gan, Israel.

Labov, W. (1972). *Language in the inner city*. Philadelphia: University of Pennsylvania Press.

Longacre, R. E. (1996). *The grammar of discourse* (2nd ed.). New York: Plenum.

Macbeth, K. P. (2006). Diverse, unforeseen and quaint difficulties: The sensible responses of novices learning to follow instructions in academic writing. *Research in the Teaching of English, 41,* 180–207.

Macken-Horarik, M. (2002). "Something to shoot for": A systemic functional approach to teaching genre in secondary school science. In A. M. Johns (Ed.), *Genre in the classroom: Multiple perspectives* (pp. 4–17). Mahwah, NJ: Lawrence Erlbaum Associates.

MacWhinney, B. (2000). *The CHILDES project: Tools for analyzing talk* (3rd ed.): *Vol. 1. The format and programs*. Mahwah, NJ: Lawrence Erlbaum Associates.

Malvern, D., Richards, B., Chipere, N., & Durán, P. (2004) *Lexical diversity and language development: Quantification and assessment*. Basingstoke: Palgrave Macmillan.

Mann, W. C., & Thompson, S. A. (1988). Rhetorical structure theory: Toward a functional theory of text organization. *Text, 8*(3), 243–281.

Marchman, V., & Bates, E. (1994). Continuity in lexical and morphological development: A test of the critical mass hypothesis. *Journal of Child Language, 21,* 339–366.

Marchman, V., & Thal, D. (2005). Words and grammar. In M. Tomasello & D. I. Slobin (Eds.), *Beyond nature-nurture: Essays in honor of Elizabeth Bates* (pp. 139–164). Mahwah, NJ: Lawrence Erlbaum Associates.

Martin, J. R., & Rose, D. (2002). *Working with discourse: Meaning beyond the clause*. London: Continuum.

Moshman, D. (1998). Cognitive development beyond childhood. In W. Damon, D. Kuhn, & R. S. Siegler (Eds.), *Handbook of child psychology* (5th ed.): *Vol. 2. Cognition, perception and language* (pp. 947–978). New York: Wiley.

Nippold, M. A. (2004). Research on later language development: International perspectives. In R. A. Berman (Ed.), *Language development across childhood and adolescence: Psycholinguistic and cross-linguistic perspectives* (pp. 1–8). Amsterdam: Benjamins.

Nippold, M. A. (2007). *Later language development: School-age children, adolescents, and young adults* (3rd ed.). Austin, TX: PRO-ED.

Nir-Sagiv, B. (2005, July). *Cross-linguistic and developmental perspective on word length as criterion for vocabulary complexity*. Paper presented at the annual meeting of the International Association of the Study of Child Language, Berlin, Germany.

Nir-Sagiv, B., Bar-Ilan, L., & Berman, R. A. (2008). Vocabulary development across adolescence: Text-based analyses. In I. Kupferberg & A. Stavans (Eds.), *Language education in Israel: Papers in honor of Elite Olshtain* (pp. 47–74). Jerusalem: Magnes Press.

Nir-Sagiv, B., & Berman, R. A. (in press). Complex syntax as a window on contrastive rhetoric. *Journal of Pragmatics*.

Nir-Sagiv, B., Sternau, M., Berman, R. A., & Ravid, D. (2008). Register differentiation as a feature distinguishing school-age usage across the variables of genres (narrative/expository) and modality (written/spoken). *Script: The Israel Journal of Language and Literacy 1,* 71–103. [in Hebrew]

Paltridge, B. (2002) Genre, text type, and the English for Academic Purposes (EAP) classroom. In A. M. Johns (Ed.), *Genre in the classroom: Multiple perspectives* (pp. 73–90). Mahwah, NJ: Lawrence Erlbaum Associates.

Pappas, C. C., & Pettigrew, B. S. (1998). The role of genre in the psycholinguistic guessing game of reading. *Language Arts, 75,* 36–44.

Ragnarsdóttir, H., Cahana-Amitay, D., van Hell, J., Rosado, E., & Viguié, A. (2002). Verbal structure and content in written discourse: Narrative and expository texts. *Written Languages and Literacy, 5,* 95–124

Ravid, D. (2004). Emergence of linguistic complexity in later language development: Evidence from expository text construction. In D. Ravid & H. Bat-Zeev Shyldkrot (Eds.), *Perspectives on language and language development* (pp. 337–356). Dordrecht: Kluwer.

Ravid, D. (2006). Semantic-pragmatic development in textual contexts during the school years: The Noun Scale. *Journal of Child Language, 33,* 4.

Ravid, D., & Berman, R. A. (2006). Information density in the development of spoken and written narratives in English and Hebrew. *Discourse Processes, 41,* 117–149.

Ravid, D., & Berman, R. A. (2009). *Developing linguistic register across text types: The case of Modern Hebrew. Pragmatics and Cognition, 17,* 108–145.

Ravid, D., & Berman, R. A. (in press). Developing noun phrase complexity across adolescence. A text imbedded cross-linguistic analysis. *First Language.*

Ravid, D., & Tolchinsky, L. (2002) Developing linguistic literacy: A comprehensive model. *Journal of Child Language, 29,* 419–448.

Ravid, D., van Hell, J., Rosado, E., & Zamora, A. (2002). Subject NP patterning in the development of written and spoken text production. *Written Language and Literacy, 5,* 68–95.

Ravid, D., & Zilberbuch, S. (2003). Morpho-syntactic constructs in the development of spoken and written Hebrew text production. *Journal of Child Language, 30,* 395–418.

Reilly, J. S., Jisa, H., Baruch, E. & Berman, R. A. (2002). Lexical modals in expression of propositional attitudes. *Written Language and Literacy, 5,* 183–218.

Reilly, J. S., Zamora, A., & McGivern, R. F. (2005). Acquiring perspective in English: Use of pronouns, modals, and passives in two genres [Special issue]. *Journal of Pragmatics, 37,* 185–208.

Romaine, S. (1984). *The language of children and adolescents: The acquisition of communicative competence.* Oxford: Blackwell.

Scott, C. (2004). Syntactic ability in children and adolescents with language and learning disabilities. In R. A. Berman (Ed.), *Language development across childhood and adolescence* (pp. 111–134). Amsterdam: Benjamins.

Scott, C., & Windsor, J. (2000). General language performance measures in spoken and written narrative and expository discourse of school-age children with language learning disabilities. *Journal of Speech, Language and Hearing Research, 43,* 324–339.

Smith, C. S. (2003) *Modes of discourse: The local structure of texts.* Cambridge: Cambridge University Press.

Speer, S. A. (2002a). "Natural" and "contrived" data: A sustainable distinction? *Discourse Studies, 4*(4), 511–525.

Speer, S. A. (2002b). Transcending the natural/contrived distinction: A rejoinder to Ten Have, Lynch, and Potter. *Discourse Studies, 4*(4), 543–548.

Steinberg, L. (2005). Cognitive and affective development in adolescence. *Trends in Cognitive Sciences, 9,* 69–74.

Strömqvist, S., Johansson, V., Kriz, S., Ragnarsdóttir, H., Aisenman, R., & Ravid, D. (2002). Toward a cross-linguistic comparison of lexical quanta in speech and writing. *Written Language and Literacy, 5,* 45–69.

Swales, J. (1990). *Genre analysis.* Cambridge: Cambridge University Press.

Tolchinsky, L., Johansson, V., & Zamora, A. (2002). Text openings and closings: Textual autonomy and differentiation. *Written Language and Literacy, 5,* 219–254.

Tolchinsky, L., & Rosado, E. (2005). The effect of literacy, text type, and modality on the use of grammatical means for agency alternation in Spanish [Special issue]. *Journal of Pragmatics, 37,* 209–238.

Werlich, E. (1976). *A text grammar of English.* Heidelberg: Quelle & Meyer.

## STUDY GUIDE QUESTIONS

1. Expository texts differ from narratives in that they
   a. may contain at least one idea, opinion, or claim.
   b. must contain at least one idea, opinion, or claim.
   c. typically focus on events and descriptions.
   d. typically reveal a subjective discourse stance.
2. Expository texts are largely "atemporal" because
   a. they consist mainly of timeless generalizations.
   b. the verbs they use are mainly nonfinite.
   c. the verbs they use are either in simple or progressive aspect.
   d. they refer to situations in the distant past or future.
3. What is the function of modal expressions in expository discourse?
   a. They alternate with timeless generalizations in the present tense by relating to future eventualities.
   b. They reveal social and personal attitudes to the state of affairs under discussion.
   c. They show developmental differences between middle childhood and adolescence.
   d. All of the above.
4. Passive voice is used in expository discourse in order to
   a. express a relatively less involved approach to a given state of affairs.
   b. highlight the role of the agent in the situation under discussion.
   c. use more complex types of syntactic structures.
   d. make it possible to discuss hypothetical states of affairs.
5. Expository texts rely heavily on the nominal lexicon because
   a. nouns are more descriptive than verbs.
   b. individuals play an important role in expository discourse.
   c. nouns refer to the concepts related to in making generalized statements.
   d. personal pronouns are necessary for making generalized statements.

## CHAPTER 6

# Linguistic Complexity in School-Age Text Production: Expository versus Mathematical Discourse

*Dorit Ravid, Esther Dromi, and Pazit Kotler*

Language knowledge and language use increase and diversify immensely in the school years, linking spoken and written abilities and reflecting cognitive growth and the acquisition of new knowledge domains such as mathematics and sciences. Each new discipline learned at school entails learning new lexical items and domain-specific uses of syntactic constructions, thus enriching general language proficiency in schoolchildren. Mathematics is one of the central disciplines taught in grade school from early on, as it underlies all the exact sciences. The mathematical domain requires linguistic thinking of a novel kind—in fact, children need to learn a genre-specific type of "language": on the one hand, the symbolic and formal system of referring to mathematical entities and processes and, on the other, the mathematically oriented domain-specific usage of lexical items and syntactic constructions that might have different meanings in mathematics than in general language (Mestre, 1988).

At the same time that mathematical cognition and genre-specific language emerge and consolidate, schoolchildren are also taught to present, discuss, and explain their thoughts about objects and concepts, processes, and states in informational and expository discourse, especially in the highly expressive written language modality (Berman & Ravid, 2008). The questions this chapter asks and attempts to answer have to do with possible connections between the microstructure (i.e., linguistic properties) of expository text and the language of mathematics, as defined previously and elaborated later. To what extent do they interact in the cognition of schoolchildren across development?

A model of domain-general cognitive development and processing comes from Karmiloff-Smith's (1992) theory of interactive specialization, according to which development comes about as a result of back-propagating interactions between gene, brain, behavior, and the environment. Karmiloff-Smith's Representational Redescription (RR) model is an explanatory framework for the increasing accessibility and explicitness of children's representations to higher thinking. This data-driven process is domain general, operating in each specific domain at different time frames, and is constrained by the contents and level of explicitness of representations in each knowledge domain. The RR process involves recoding information that is stored in one representational format into a denser version of the previous one, making it gradually more explicit and interconnected across differential knowledge domains—and hence more available to conscious thought.

This model can be used to account for the quantitative and qualitative developments occurring in children's cognitive processes concurrently in both expository writing and mathematical thinking. Cognitive changes across later childhood and adolescence include the development of executive control and systems of self-repair, which govern the ability to set goals, plan and monitor procedures, and choose and change strategies. These cognitive abilities, especially procedural monitoring, are critical for both the ability to write expository text as well as for using language in mathematical discourse. In both domains, precision of expression is crucial, and it requires goal setting, planning, and analysis of procedures and their output.

A number of studies indicate that a relationship may be found between language and mathematical thought. In a study on learning algebra and evaluating language proficiency in 1,500 junior high school students, MacGregor and Price (1999) show that high language and algebra scores were almost always related. Dehaene, Spelke, Pinel, Philippe, and Tsivkin (1999) report that training Russian–English bilingual adults on precise addition versus estimation in one language led to faster performance in that language; after training, reaction times on both tasks declined, especially in the participants' mother tongue. According to these authors, the mathematical knowledge acquired by such training is stored in a language-specific format. Interestingly, studies of special populations support a possible linkage between language proficiency and mathematical knowledge. Thus, several studies pointed out a relationship between language impairment and mathematical impairment (Delazer, Girelli, Semenza, & Denes, 1999; Fazio, 1996, 1999; Montis, 2000) as well as excellence in both in a population of gifted children (Krutetskii, 1976).

This chapter aims to explore the relationship between types of linguistic proficiency as expressed in these two domains—expository and mathematical discourse—by examining texts produced by Hebrew-speaking school-aged children and young adolescents.

## LATER LANGUAGE DEVELOPMENT

The past decade or so has seen increasing interest in studying language development across the school years (Berman, 2004; Nippold, 2007). Later language development constitutes the precursor to the complex linguistic abilities of adults, which differ markedly from those of children and even from those of adolescents (Berman, 2007; Ravid & Zilberbuch, 2003b; chapter 5 in this volume). Three major phenomena characterize later language development. One phenomenon is the fact that new items, categories, and constructions emerge and surge where none or few existed before. For example, school-related lexical items such as *continent* or *identity* are acquired from written language. In Hebrew, derivational categories such as denominal i-final adjectives (e.g., *harari*, "mountainous") or derived abstract nominals (e.g., *muxanut*, "preparedness") emerge and consolidate in the school years (Ravid, 2004; Ravid & Avidor, 1998), and constructions requiring change in perspective that were hardly in use in childhood, such as medial passives and verbal passives, become prevalent (Berman, 2004; Kaplan, 2008). At the same time, novel pathways arise for interconnecting and amalgamating formerly unrelated elements and systems, creating rich and complex linguistic schemas, patterns, and architectures. Moreover, better, faster, more efficient, and more explicit modes emerge for representing language, thinking about it, and accessing its structures and functions. The changing nature of later language development and its relationship with other cognitive domains make it an interesting arena of investigation.

During the school years, knowledge and use of the lexicon change dramatically (Anglin, 1993; Nir-Sagiv, Bar-Ilan, & Berman, 2008; Best, Dockrell, & Braisby, 2006; Nippold, 2002). An extended content vocabulary yields greater lexical diversity and encodes semantically more specific and more abstract categories and concepts (Ravid & Cahana-Amitay, 2005; Seroussi, 2004; Strömqvist et al., 2002). Derivational morphology acquires an increasingly important role at the interface between vocabulary and syntax. The adolescent lexicon thus comes to include higher-register, morphologically complex, semantically diverse, abstract, and lexically specific items, such as denominal adjectives and nominalizations (Nippold, 2007) as well as extensions of concrete terms to more metaphorical usages (Carlisle, 2000; Levin, Ravid, & Rapaport, 2001; Ravid, 2006). Syntax relies increasingly on more marked, less frequent constructions such as passive voice, center-embedded clauses, and nonfinite subordination (Friedman & Novogrodsky, 2004; Ravid & Saban, 2008; Scott, 2004; Tolchinsky & Rosado, 2005). Text-embedded syntactic development is attested to by increasing morphosyntactic versatility as well as by diverse and complex syntactic architecture at all syntactic levels from phrase and clause to syntactic package and text segment (Berman & Nir-Sagiv, 2009a; Ravid, van Hell, Rosado, & Zamora, 2002; Scott & Windsor, 2000). These developmental changes in school-age language knowledge are accompanied by denser and more explicitly accessible linguistic knowledge and a metalinguistic ability to verbalize judgments of grammaticality and contextual appropriateness (Karmiloff-Smith, 1992).

A new consortium of maturing language capabilities thus makes it possible to spell out, hone, and customize linguistic expression so as to articulate the adolescent and adult mind. These changes in linguistic abilities witnessed across childhood and adolescence and their consequent mobilization in the service of adult communication could not be envisioned without the platform of written language—*the language of literacy*, increasingly the main expressive tool of adolescents and young adults (Berman & Ravid, 2008). Written texts are more informative and planned than spoken texts and encourage revision, review, and rewriting. Freed from the pressures of online processing of the spoken modality, writing is more likely to foster complex language than speech (Biber, 1988; Halliday, 1989; Ravid & Berman, 2006). To extend our knowledge about how linguistic complexity evolves in different types of written, school-type discourse, this chapter examines written expository texts and mathematical problems across middle childhood and early adolescence. The relationship between the language of expository texts on the one hand and the language of mathematical discourse on the other is of interest for two reasons. First, learning mathematics is often mediated by academic language typical of expository discussion (Sfard, 2002). Second, mathematical skills develop and consolidate at the same time as do higher-order language abilities in later language development so that advances in one domain may imply progress in the other.

## LINGUISTIC COMPLEXITY

The view of linguistic complexity in later language development (Ravid, 2004) relies strongly on the idea of a "lexicon–syntax interface" (Berman & Nir-Sagiv, 2009b; Ravid & Zilberbuch, 2003b), that is, that lexical items and syntactic constructions conspire to make a given piece of language more or less "complex." Linguistic complexity in texts is composed of two interrelated components: *lexical complexity* and *syntactic architecture*. The first term, *lexical complexity*, is defined along the two dimensions of lexical density and diversity. *Lexical density* refers to the amount of lexical content in the text as measured by the proportion of content-class words in the text out of the total number of words or by the number of content words per clause (Strömqvist et al., 2002). *Lexical diversity* refers to the amount of novel lexical content in the text as measured by the ratio of word tokens to word types (Richards & Malvern, 1997).

The second term, *syntactic architecture*, is defined in terms of several distinct though interrelated factors at differing levels of intraclausal and interclausal structure: *length*, *depth*, and *diversity*. *Length* refers to the number of words per syntactic unit (phrase, clause, or clause package), *depth* is measured by the number of complex governed nodes in the unit, and *diversity* indicates different types of syntactic units clustered together. Underlying this analysis is the assumption that lexical and syntactic complexity are closely interconnected and need to be analyzed in conjunction. Specifically, lexical complexity is a crucial component of the syntactic architecture of a text since lexical elements constitute the necessary building blocks for syntax at the level of phrase structure. For example, synthetically bound morphology rather than more periphrastic analytic options,* a source of morphosyntactic complexity in Hebrew, would be impossible without high lexical density and diversity of nouns (Cahana-Amitay & Ravid, 2000). Relatedly, complexity of the internal construction of noun phrases (with a lexical noun as head) is a major source of complex syntactic architecture (Ravid, 2006; Ravid & Zilberbuch, 2003a; Seroussi, 2004).

## EXPOSITORY DISCOURSE

An important distinction in the study described in this chapter is the difference between expository and mathematical discourse, which can be captured by the term *genre*. Genre definitions vary depending on the perspective taken by genre researchers. Steen (1999) defines genres as cognitive representations or schemas that are part of the mental repertoire of most participants in a discourse community (see also Paltridge, 1997). Ravid and Tolchinsky (2002) regard genres as text types defined by function, social-cultural practices, and communicative purpose. Text *genre* also has an important impact on the selection of rhetorical/expressive devices and grammatical constructions (Berman & Nir, 2004). A major genre distinction is that which distinguishes narratives from other types of discourse (Bruner, 1986). Narratives focus on people and their actions and motivations and express the unfolding of events in a temporal framework. In contrast, expository texts focus on ideas and concepts and express the unfolding of claims and argumentation in a causal context (Mosenthal, 1985; chapter 5 in this volume).

We chose expository writing for this study, given converging evidence of its status as the habitat of informative, complex, and abstract academic language as early as in grade school (Berman, 2005; Berman & Nir-Sagiv, 2007; Ravid, 2004, 2006; Ravid & Zilberbuch, 2003b). As Britton (1994)

---

* Hebrew has a number of optional bound inflections that have analytic counterparts. For example, the phrase *ha-bayit shelax*, "the-house yours-Fm," can be replaced by the bound morphological option *beytex*, "Your, Fm house." The bound options are morphophonologically more opaque and rarely occur in everyday speech. They are typical examples of later language developments acquired during the school years (Levin et al.,2001).

points out, expository texts aim to create a thematic structure in the reader's mind. From a thematic point of view, expository discourse is organized around a "discourse topic proposition" (Giora, 1985), consisting of "move-on" statements or "core" propositions elaborated by illustrative or delimiting "satellite" discourse elements (Matthiessen & Thompson, 1988). The ideas for expository production derive from general world knowledge and academic learning, and its construction requires familiarity with an array of logical relations and rhetorical devices, subject to an open modular schema (Britton, 1994; Mosenthal, 1985). As a result, expository texts show a close connection between the quality of discourse structure and thematic content, depending "not only on how the flow of information is organized but also on the logical consistency and originality of the propositional content which it conveys" (Berman & Katzenberger, 2004, p. 89). Given their focus on abstract ideas and concepts, expository texts are characterized by general, static, objective, distant, and detached discourse stance (Berman, 2005; Ravid & Cahana-Amitay, 2005), typically expressed by school-type literate lexical items, less familiar morphosyntactic constructions, and complex syntactic architecture (Berman & Nir-Sagiv, 2009b; Ravid, 2004).

Findings from texts produced by grade school children indicate that they know that expository discourse is used to make generalizations and voice opinions (Nippold, 2007; Reilly, Zamora & McGivern, 2005; Tolchinsky & Rosado, 2005), but they still find it difficult to construct a well-organized piece of expository discourse (Berman & Katzenberger, 2004). But at the same time and very pertinent to our aims, when viewed from the bottom-up perspective of language complexity measures (Ravid, 2004), even grade schoolers produce expository texts that are richer and more complex in linguistic expression than narrative texts (Ravid et al., 2002). These measures reveal facets of the inherent cognitive complexity of expository discourse that are not necessarily reflected in top-down analyses of global text organization (Berman & Nir-Sagiv, 2007; chapter 5 in this volume). We aim to make use of linguistic complexity measures to characterize and relate the language of expository text to that of mathematical discourse in grade school children and junior high schoolers based on their ability to create verbal problems in mathematics (henceforth *mathematical problems*).

## MATHEMATICAL DISCOURSE

Relating verbal to mathematical language in the context of mathematical problems requires a systematic framework of analysis. Mestre (1988) suggests such a framework by designating four linguistic proficiencies that might impact mathematical problem solving. The first is general reading comprehension, which underlies the ability to read and understand mathematical problems. A second proficiency involves knowledge of mathematically oriented domain-specific lexical items and syntactic constructions that might have different meanings in mathematics than in general language. For example, in mathematical discourse, the word *product* needs to be understood as designating the result of the multiplication procedure. A third proficiency closely related to the second one is the context-sensitive ability to move back and forth between mathematics-specific and language-general meanings so as to produce and comprehend both when necessary. To illustrate this point, Mestre uses the following problem presented to monolingual and bilingual (Spanish/English) high school students:

> Mr. Smith noted the number of cars, C, and the number of trucks, T, in a parking lot, and wrote the following equation to represent the situation: 8C=T. Are there more cars or trucks in this parking lot? Why? (p. 218)

Eleven out of the 14 monolingual and bilingual participants in that study said that according to the equation, there are more cars than trucks because the numeral 8 precedes C, whereas the correct answer is that there are more trucks than cars: The number of cars has to be multiplied by 8 to get to the number of trucks. The mistake of those students derived, according to Mestre, from a left-to-right parsing strategy following the English orthography.

Finally, familiarity with the symbolic and formal language of mathematics is necessary to solve mathematical problems. Spanos, Rhodes, and Corasaniti Dale (1988) label the notions of mathematical discourse and symbolic mathematical language together as "mathematical register." The complexity of the syntactic, semantic, and pragmatic characteristics of mathematical register derives from the intricate relationship between conceptual and procedural knowledge in mathematics. This classification is not always a simple task. These two types of knowledge are assumed to be distinct yet related, and there is no fixed order in their acquisition (Rittle-Johnson & Siegler, 1998). Teachers often report cases of students who are able to carry out a certain procedure yet fail to apply it when necessary to new situations and problems (Silver, 1987). Placing mathematical procedures within various contexts and emphasizing procedures and concepts while striving for comprehension and conceptualization of the procedures involved creates the necessary connections among knowledge units and consequently results in a mental model leading to "real" understanding of mathematical issues. This rich and complex consideration of mathematics is termed *mathematical discourse*.

Mathematical discourse is a specific text genre that uses lexical items and linguistic constructions to communicate mathematics and whose management requires the combination of mathematical abilities on the one hand and language abilities on the other. In a case study concerning a child with dyscalculia, Montis (2000) shows how linguistic intervention in the understanding of fractions improved her mathematical functioning. This improvement, according to Montis, indicates that the primary source of her mathematical difficulty does not stem from the actual mathematical concept of fractions but rather is linguistic in nature—"from failing to understand the standard way one talks about and writes fractions" (p. 552). Learning about mathematics, like any other subject, involves the development of a certain type of discourse. Such learning is defined as "a process of changing one's discursive ways in a certain well-defined manner" (Sfard, 2002, p. 8) since it enables the learner to communicate with an expert interlocutor by invoking and extending discursive skills. Being able to produce and comprehend mathematical discourse, like other discourse types, is a result of cognitive development, accumulating experience, and schooling. This chapter describes a recent study involving the specific subgenre of mathematical problems as one of the two text genres under investigation.

Mathematical discourse is constructed along the same lines as other discourse types and develops at the interface of formal and informal knowledge. A number of studies illustrate this point. English (1998) found that third graders were better able to create more verbal mathematical problems when numerical questions were contextualized in stories, such as Noah's Ark. Another example of the efficacy of different genres in the development of scientific discourse comes from studies about the concept of speed (Druyan, 1995, 2001). Druyan found that a joint activity bringing together same-age children with differing levels of comprehension or adult–child dyads was effective in promoting comprehension of speed. She explains that what brings about the consolidation of this skill is the integration of formal and intuitive strategies in an active discussion between interlocutors, leading to the construction of connections between pieces of knowledge, in turn leading to the development of conceptual knowledge (Hiebert & Lefevre, 1986). There is no doubt that conceptual knowledge is critical for such understanding. If a student is familiar with some mathematical technique but does not know how to apply it in solving a new problem, she has clearly not understood the concept underlying the technique (Silver, 1987). For example, some children can multiply but do not recognize a multiplication problem as such when they encounter it. A comparison of Korean and American grade schoolers' mathematics achievements (Grow-Maienza, Hahn, & Joo, 2001) reveals interesting findings concerning the importance of verbal conceptualization and class discussion: The emphasis on understanding and producing mathematical discourse in the classroom seems to underlie Korean students' top achievements in international mathematics tests. The protocols presented in the study demonstrate how the lively discussion of the different strategies applied to the same problem underscores the relevant concepts, leading to improvement in mathematical performance accompanied by upgraded mathematical discourse.

The domain of verbal mathematical problems offers a promising testing ground for the examination of the relationship between language proficiency in expository and mathematical discourse. The knowledge required to solve mathematical problems consists of knowing how to combine its components into a coherent semantic structure (problem schema), knowledge about the mathematical procedure involved, and strategic knowledge for planning how to solve the problem. Under this theory, certain problem schemas are activated by the semantic structure of mathematical problems. Once activated, the schemas invoke associated strategies, such as finding differences between sets (Riley, Greeno, & Heller, 1983). Gifted children are particularly able to make use of their linguistic abilities to motivate and explain their mathematical problem solving (Krutetskii, 1976), whereas others might find these linguistic requirements challenging. Spanos et al. (1988) point at a number of linguistic areas that might hinder mathematical problem solving, including the use of passive voice and prepositions, mismatch of numerals and words, mathematical jargon, and the ability to make inferences based on text cohesion.

Producing mathematical problems is particularly relevant to our research question since it enables us to assess linguistic components in mathematical discourse, reflecting mathematical thought (Brown, 1981; Silver & Cai, 1996). In generating mathematical problems, children rely on their prior procedural and conceptual knowledge in mathematics, tapping into a reservoir of basic facts, procedures, generalizations, and algorithms; general world knowledge; and domain-specific knowledge, such as knowledge about quantities (Silver, 1987). Analysis of problems created by children thus constitutes a window on their mathematical understanding (English, 1998; Mills, Whitin, & O'Keefe, 1993; Van Den Brink, 1987). Silver and Cai's (1996) study of sixth and seventh graders demonstrates the suitability of problem production to our investigation. Participants who were better at solving mathematical problems were also better at generating a greater number of mathematically more complex problems, and at the same time they were better at correctly comprehending mathematical problems. Finally, a case study of a 12-year-old with dyscalculia shows how language processes factor into the development of the concept flexibility necessary for success in mathematics (Montis, 2000).

## THE STUDY

The study presented in this chapter aimed to explore the relationship between language abilities as expressed in expository and mathematical discourse in Hebrew-speaking fourth and seventh graders. From a theoretical point of view, such a relationship might be assumed to derive from a core domain-general ability to think abstractly, such as Karmiloff-Smith's higher levels of redescription, which might underlie both mathematical prowess with verbal problems and the ability to generate informational language generally. This relationship was explored by (a) examining the linguistic complexity of written expository discourse and of mathematical problems produced by the same participants and (b) determining whether and to what extent measures of linguistic complexity in the two discourse genres correlate.

We expected to find (a) greater linguistic complexity in texts produced by the older age/schooling level compared with the younger level and (b) correlations between measures of linguistic complexity in the two discourse genres.

## Method

**Participants**    The population consisted of 67 boys and girls, all Hebrew speakers (almost all monolingual) from middle socioeconomic status, attending schools in the center of Israel. None of them had been diagnosed with language or other learning disabilities. Four of the participants had not been born in Israel, having immigrated to it between the ages of 1 year, 6 months, to 5 years, 0 months. Their level of Hebrew was assessed to be on par with the other, native-born participants. Of these, 39 participants (14 boys and 25 girls, mean age 9 years, 7 months; age range 9 years, 1 month–10 years, 5 months) attended fourth grade, and 28 (9 boys and 19 girls, mean age 12 years, 9 months; age range 12 years, 3 months–13 years, 4 months) attended seventh grade.

**Tasks**    Both groups were administered two types of tasks: expository writing and a mathematical task.

*Expository text production*    Participants were asked to write an expository text about the notion of "friendship." The instructions they received were as follows: *Tell us what you think of friendship, what is your opinion of friendship. Discuss the topic, do not write a story.* This task was based on similar though not identical tasks developed by Berman and Ravid (2008). Examples of expositions written by participants appear in Appendix 6.A.

*Mathematical problem posing*    The mathematical task analyzed in this chapter was based on the idea that creating verbal mathematical problems requires mathematical knowledge and ability. Participants were asked to produce two sets of five mathematical problems based on short and concise ("telegraphic") numerical information in the form of two brief "story problems" (originally defined in Silver & Cai, 1996). Specifically, participants were asked *to pose questions that could be answered using this given information.* Before the participants embarked on the task, it was explained to them in detail. As training, they were given an example of numerical information in the form of a "story problem," with examples of several possible mathematical problems that could be posed in response to it. After training, participants were given the two task story problems and were then asked to produce their own problems using this numerical information. To ensure comparability, the two age-groups received the same task, with one difference: one of the training problems was more complex in the seventh graders. Appendix 6.B presents the two sets of numerical information in the form of story problems used to elicit mathematical problems from our fourth- and seventh-grade populations. Appendix 6.C presents examples of mathematical problems elicited from our participants.

## Scoring and Analyses

**Constructing study measures**    Measures of linguistic complexity examined in the expository texts were as follows:

1. *Language productivity measures*, consisting of number of words, number of clauses, and mean clause length measured by number of words per clause—These criteria yielded the general *text score* and were also useful for creating the basis for text-length normalization for other measures as against number of words or number of clauses.
2. *Lexical measures*, consisting of the content word categories: number of nouns (including abstract derived nouns), lexical (i.e., not grammatical) verbs, and adjectives (including high-register denominal adjectives) and proportional measures of these categories to neutralize text length and to yield lexical density of clause and text—These criteria yielded the general *lexical complexity and density scores*. Because of our interest in the interface between lexical and syntactic measures, these lexical measures are included in the correlation analysis (described later), but, unlike productivity and syntactic complexity measures, they are not directly compared for frequency across the expository and mathematical texts.
3. *Syntactic complexity*—For the purposes of the study described in this chapter, we focused on subordination constructions from two perspectives: *number of subordinations* and *different types of subordinated constructions*, such as conditionals and relative clauses, which require higher-order thinking and are typical of expository writing. The analysis of subordination measure yielded a *general syntactic score* reflecting syntactic depth, which consisted of the number of subordination nodes as well as the complexity hierarchy involved in the sense of how many subordinations each one controlled. As an example of syntactic depth, consider this sentence: *friendship requires two people who understand the needs that different people have*. This sentence has an noun phrase node with two nested relative clauses.

Linguistic complexity was measured in the mathematical problems using a restricted set of the measures applied across expository texts, including number of words and clauses, number of question marks, and subordination indices. These yielded together the *general language score* for mathematical problems.

**Analyses**    For the purposes of this chapter, two kinds of analyses were undertaken across the two age-groups based on the measures described previously: (a) *comparing linguistic complexity* in the two genres, using language productivity and syntactic complexity measures, and (b) *correlating* measures of linguistic complexity across the two discourse genres (expository texts and mathematical problems) produced by the same participants, using productivity, lexical complexity, and syntactic complexity measures.

## RESULTS: COMPARING LINGUISTIC COMPLEXITY ACROSS GENRES

Comparisons of linguistic complexity across the two genres focused mostly on syntax. We first present language productivity measures, followed by syntactic analyses.

### Language Productivity Measures

Language productivity measures relate to text and clause size (Berman & Ravid, 2008; Ravid, 2004; Ravid & Zilberbuch, 2003a). Text length was measured using two units: (a) number of words—where, given different language typologies and orthographies, a "word" is specified as any element separated by spaces in print, and (b) number of clauses, where the clause is a basic unit of syntax, defined as "any unit that contains a unified predicate expressing a single situation" (Berman & Slobin, 1994, p. 660).* Since text size may vary across different age-groups and individual writers, we assessed linguistic complexity in developing text construction through the derived measure of mean clause length, defined as the number of words per clause (Berman & Nir-Sagiv, 2007; Ravid, 2004; Ravid & Zilberbuch, 2003b). In the mathematical discourse, these measures were calculated across all the mathematical problems produced by each participant.

The findings presented in Table 6.1 indicate that all language productivity measures fall within the range of values determined for children of similar ages in previous research (Ravid, 2004) and provide interesting information about the development of discourse production in early adolescence. Regarding text size in *words* and *clauses* averaged across the five mathematical problems and the expository texts, we found no difference between genres (averaging 50.21 and 53.51 words and 12.09 and 11.02 clauses in expository and mathematical discourse, respectively). However, the mean number of words, averaged across both discourse genres, increased with age from 41.49 in fourth graders to 62.23 in seventh graders ($F[1, 65] = 15.46, p < .001$), and the mean number of clauses, again averaged across genres, increased from 9.76 to 13.36 ($F[1, 65] = 9.63, p < .004$), with no interactions. Mean clause length, a measure of lexical and syntactic complexity, was sensitive enough to discern that for the two age levels combined, mathematical problems had higher linguistic complexity, averaging 4.77 words per clause, compared with

---

* The clause is similar to the simple sentence of traditional grammar; it is semantically and syntactically readily identifiable and has served as a robust unit of analysis for both oral and written narrative and expository texts across a wide range of languages (Berman & Verhoeven, 2002).

**Table 6.1** Means and Standard Deviations of Language Productivity Measures across Genres and Age-Groups

| Age-Group | Fourth Graders Ages 9–10 | | Seventh Graders Ages 12–13 | |
| --- | --- | --- | --- | --- |
| Discourse Genre | Expository Texts | Mathematical Problems | Expository Texts | Mathematical Problems |
| Number of words per text | 39.64 (25.28) | 43.33 (17.8) | 60.79 (42.67) | 63.68 (24.42) |
| Number of clauses per text | 10.0 (6.1) | 9.51 (3.55) | 14.18 (9.7) | 12.54 (4.5) |
| Mean clause length in words | 4.15 (1.0) | 4.5 (0.69) | 4.27 (0.66) | 5.05 (0.6) |
| % Subordinated clauses | 39.02 (20.12) | 4.32 (0.64) | 32.55 (10.9) | 15.57 (8.33) |

expositories, averaging 4.21 words per clause ($F[1, 65] = 19.5, p < .001$). Mean clause length increased across the two genres from 4.32 words in fourth grade to 4.66 in seventh grade ($F[1, 65] = 5.61, p < .03$).

## Syntactic Complexity

To assess syntactic complexity across the two genres, we carried out a number of analyses on comparable measures involving syntactic complexity.

**Subordination**  To assess syntactic depth (see the section "Linguistic Complexity" earlier in this chapter), we first compared the percentage of subordinate clauses out of all clauses in the expositories and the mathematics problems produced by the children (as shown in Table 6.1). We did not find any change with age—subordinated clauses averaged 21.67% in fourth graders and 24.06% in seventh graders; however, genre yielded a significant result, with four times as many subordinated clauses in the expository discourse ($M = 35.78\%$) than in the mathematical problems ($M = 9.95\%$) ($F[1, 65] = 87.27, p < .001$). But the most interesting and informative result was the age-group × genre interaction ($F[1, 65] = 10.25, p < .003$), presented in Figure 6.1. This showed that syntactic depth did not increase in expository texts and in fact decreased somewhat between fourth grade ($M = 39.02\%, SD = 18.43$) and seventh grade ($M = 32.55\%, SD = 14.01$). The dramatic change in subordination occurred in the mathematical problems, where their ratio increased more than threefold from a mean of 4.32% ($SD = 13.02$) to 15.57% ($SD = 13.34$).

**Subordination types**  Our next analyses focused on two types of subordination constructions especially relevant to later language development and to the discourse genres under investigation: relative clauses and conditional constructions.

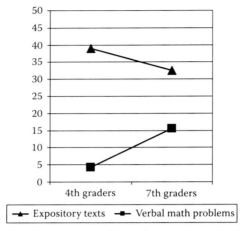

**Figure 6.1**    Interaction of age-group and genre in percentage of subordinated clauses.

*Relative Clauses*    Relative clauses (RCs) are subordinated to noun phrases (NPs), involve insight into their structure, and have a critical role in their expansion, for example, *The question (which) you asked (the question) today was important* (RC underlined). We looked at RCs from three perspectives—in terms of mean number per text and as percentages out of all subordinated clauses and out of all clauses (see Table 6.2).

None of the analyses revealed effects for age, though visual inspection showed that in most cases, there were more RCs in seventh graders than in fourth graders. Two of the three measures clearly showed, however, that expository texts had more RCs than did the mathematical problems: in mean number per text (0. 84 vs. 0.29, $F[1, 65] = 6.26$, $p < .02$) and as percentage out of all clauses (6.57% vs. 1.93%, $F[1, 65] = 9.06$, $p < .005$). A third though

**Table 6.2**    Relative Clause Means and Standard Deviations across Age-Groups and Discourse Genres

| Age-Group | Fourth Graders Ages 9–10 | | Seventh Graders Ages 12–13 | |
|---|---|---|---|---|
| Discourse Genre | Expository Texts | Mathematical Problems | Expository Texts | Mathematical Problems |
| Mean number of relative clauses in the text | 0.54 (0.88) | 0.18 (0.85) | 1.14 (2.16) | 0.39 (0.88) |
| % Relative clauses out of all subordinated clauses | 16.03 (12.97) | 5.0 (7.07) | 11.1 (10.38) | 2.37 (4.31) |
| % Relative clauses out of all clauses | 5.83 (10.37) | 1.37 (6.15) | 7.31 (9.58) | 2.49 (5.93) |

not significant finding is discussed in the section "Relative Clauses" later in this chapter.

    *Conditional Constructions*    If–then structures loom large in mathematical discourse, where they not only relate motive to outcome but also point to the procedure for solution (Byrnes, 1991). Given this role of conditional structures, they were our obvious choice for analysis. Again, we looked at them from three perspectives—in terms of mean number per text and as percentages out of all subordinated clauses and out of all clauses (see Table 6.3).

    Here, the picture is more complex yet consistent. Only the measure of mean number of conditional clauses reveals an increase with age ($F[1, 65] = 5.88$, $p < .02$) from 0.5 in fourth grade to 1.09 in seventh grade. Even more interesting, an interaction of age-group and genre (Figure 6.2) shows that the mean number of conditional clauses per text actually goes down in expository texts, while it increases more than tenfold in seventh graders' mathematical problems. These results indicate that the general increase in conditionals is not merely an artifact of longer text size in older participants.

    The two derived proportional measures support and enhance the claim that the occurrence of conditionals is genre related. We thus see that conditionals constitute 57.42% of all subordinated clauses in the mathematical problems but only 12.9% in the expository texts ($F[1, 21] = 17.84$, $p < .001$). The interaction of age-group and genre ($F[1, 21] = 4.7$, $p < .05$) shown in Figure 6.3 presents a decline in conditionals in expositories and a sharp increase in mathematical problems from fourth to seventh grade. Finally, when measured as a percentage out of all clauses, we see only an interaction ($F[1, 65] = 25.51$, $p < .001$), depicted in Figure 6.4, with the same results.

## Correlations Between Linguistic and Mathematical Discourse

Our second analysis consisted of examining how various measures of linguistic complexity correlate in the two genres under consideration. We went one step

**Table 6.3**   Conditional Clause Means and Standard Deviations across Age-Groups and Discourse Genres

| Age-Group | Fourth Graders Ages 9–10 | | Seventh Graders Ages 12–13 | |
| --- | --- | --- | --- | --- |
| Discourse Genre | Expository Texts | Mathematical Problems | Expository Texts | Mathematical Problems |
| Mean number of conditional clauses in the text | 0.85 (1.35) | 0.15 (0.71) | 0.39 (0.79) | 1.79 (2.23) |
| % Conditional clauses out of all subordinated clauses | 18.33 (26.61) | 40.0 (54.77) | 7.46 (13.76) | 74.85 (37.64) |
| % Conditional clauses out of all clauses | 6.84 (10.1) | 1.25 (5.52) | 1.84 (3.71) | 11.61 (12.5) |

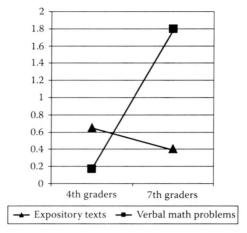

**Figure 6.2**    Interaction of age-group and genre in mean number of conditional clauses per text.

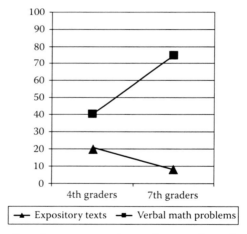

**Figure 6.3**    Interaction of age-group and genre in percentage of conditional clauses out of all subordinated clauses.

further to examine to what extent linguistic measures were correlated across the two texts produced by each participant. We report those linguistic measures (lexical, syntactic, and general) that correlate with the productivity and syntax variables reported in Tables 6.1 through 6.3. We present Pearson correlations in each age-group separately. All correlations reported here are significant at the .05 level, marked by*; those significant at the .01 level are marked by **.

Starting with fourth grade, we first present Pearson correlations between linguistic measures in the expository text with linguistic measures in the

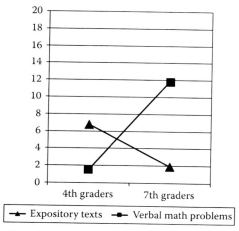

**Figure 6.4**   Interaction of age-group and genre in percentage of conditional clauses out of all clauses.

**Table 6.4**   Fourth Graders: Pearson Correlations between Linguistic Measures in the Expository Texts and the Verbal Mathematical Problems

| Linguistic Measures in the Expository Texts | Linguistic Measures in the Mathematical Problems |
|---|---|
| Number of words | % Conditional clauses/clauses .356* |
| Number of nouns | % Subordinate clauses .367* |
| | General language score 374* |
| | % Conditional clauses/clauses .407* |
| % Nouns/words | % RCs/total clauses .328* |
| Nouns/clauses | % RCs/total clauses .417* |
| % Lexical verbs/content words | Number of words −.397* |
| General syntactic score | Number of RCs .375* |
| Number of RCs | % Subordinate clauses .402* |
| % RCs/subordinate clauses | General language score .331* |
| Number of conditional clauses | % Conditional clauses/clauses .350* |
| Number of temporal clauses | Number of clauses .389* |
| Number of subject clauses | Number of words .388* |
| | Number of clauses .409** |
| General text score | % Conditional clauses/clauses .354* |

problems (Table 6.4). There is an increase in the number of significant correlations from fourth to seventh grade (see Table 6.5). The contribution of these correlations to our understanding of the relationship between verbal and mathematical language is discussed next.

**Table 6.5**   Seventh Graders: Pearson Correlations between Linguistic Measures in the Expository Texts and the Verbal Mathematical Problems

| Linguistic Measures in the Expository Texts | Linguistic Measures in the Mathematical Problems |
| --- | --- |
| Number of clauses | % RCs/total clauses .521** |
| | % RCs/subordinate clauses .563** |
| Number of content words | % RCs/total clauses .559** |
| | % RCs/subordinate clauses .588** |
| Lexical complexity score | % RCs/total clauses* |
| Lexical density—text | Number of question marks .396* |
| Number of nouns | % RCs/subordinate clauses .580** |
| % Nouns/words | Number of question marks .415** |
| % Abstract nouns/words | Mean clause length .377* |
| Number of lexical verbs | % RCs/subordinate clauses .472* |
| | % RCs/clauses .410* |
| Number of adjectives | % RCs/subordinate clauses .490** |
| | % RCs/clauses .580** |
| Adjectives/clauses | Number of question marks .380* |
| Number of subordinate clauses | % RCs/total clauses .412* |
| Number of conditional clauses | % RCs/total clauses .378* |
| Number of purpose clauses | % RCs/total clauses .645** |
| % Predicate clauses/subordinate clauses | % Subordinate clauses .564** |
| | General language score .565** |
| General text score | % RCs/clauses .592** |
| | % RCs/subordinate clauses .638** |

## DISCUSSION

This study investigated the possible relationship between the language of expository and mathematical discourse in groups of Hebrew-speaking grade schoolers and junior high schoolers. Each student produced two texts in writing—the two main tools of our investigation: an expository text on the topic of friendship and a set of mathematical problems posed on the basis of given story problem numerical information (Appendix 6.B). First, measures of syntactic complexity were compared across the two genres. Second, linguistic measures in the expository texts were correlated with linguistic measures assessed in the mathematical problems.

### Syntactic Complexity: The Development of Subordination

One contribution this chapter makes to the study of later language development is to delve deeper into how text-embedded syntactic complexity develops in school-age children and young adolescents and how it is affected by text genre beyond the critical narrative/expository divide. We used one main measure of syntactic complexity in this section—*syntactic depth* or hierarchy, measured by subordination. Subordination links clauses in a hierarchy to create denser clause packages that in turn contribute to the flow of information in the text (Berman & Nir-Sagiv, in press-b; Halliday, 1989). To remove the effect of text length, we used a proportional measure of subordinated clauses in each of the two text genres. First, we found that, overall, a third of the clauses in the expository texts were subordinated, compared with only 10% of the clauses in the mathematical problems. Thus, as demonstrated in previous studies, expository writing fosters linguistic complexity from early on (Ravid, 2004, 2006; Ravid & Zilberbuch, 2003a, 2003b; Ravid et al., 2002). This result indicates that expository discourse is easier for grade schoolers to produce than mathematical problems—in much the same way that narrative discourse is easier for them to produce than expository texts (Berman & Katzenberger, 2004; Berman & Nir-Sagiv, 2007)—perhaps the result of a trade-off due to the cognitive burden placed on students in creating mathematical problems. These results may also be at least partially attributed to the difference in the cognitive templates required by the two very different tasks.

However, from a developmental perspective, our analyses revealed a more interesting picture. We found that expository subordination *decreased* with age and schooling, most likely because of other means of language complexity employed by young adolescents, such as repetitive coordination and NP expansion by nominalization and compounding. In contrast, subordination tripled in mathematical discourse from fourth to seventh grade (Figure 6.1), indicating a growing diversification of syntactic constructions in expressing concepts and processes in expository text on the one hand and increasing awareness of the genre-specific structure of mathematical language on the other.

A qualitative finding is that by junior high school, general cognitive, literacy, and linguistic development enables the formation of denser syntactic clusters in subordinating constructions. For example, a seventh grader produced the following construction, where three subordinated clauses are attached to a single subject (translated from Hebrew; PL = plural): *Close friendship relations (are) that loyalPl to (a) friend, that helpPl him whenever he needs, and also that enjoyPl with him sometimes.* All the verbs in this excerpt are, appropriately, in the subjectless plural mode, indicating a general, impersonal stance typical of expositions (Berman, 2005). Such "deep" subordination in seventh grade is, as we show later, only one of the indications for linguistic development coupled with more coherent relationships with mathematical discourse across adolescence.

Subordination is a label for a general measure, composed of three syntactic relations. *Object complementation* is generally regarded as the least complex or "rich" subordination type in Hebrew since it involves almost linear concatenation with transitive verbs (usually indicating speech acts such as *say*, *announce*, or *explain* or cognitive processes such as *think*, *believe*, or *understand*), using a single complementizer *she*—for example, *dan amar she-hu ra'ev*, "Dan said that-he (was) hungry." Moreover, object complementation is usually part of the transitive argument structure of such verbs and as such is obligatory for creating sentence structure. As a result, complement subordination, which emerges very early in child language (Berman, 1985), was not used as a measure in this study. Note, however, that subject and predicate complementation are a different story altogether, as discussed later.

**Conditional subordination**    A second type of subordination—*adverbial subordination*—is optional, more informative, and more complex in structure and also more diversified in its semantics—such as location, time, reason, purpose, manner, and so on. The most relevant of adverbial subordinations analyzed in this chapter is the modal conditional construction involving the if–then structure. Conditionals are abstract irrealis constructions where the subordinated clause expresses the condition and the matrix clause expresses its expected result and where neither of the clauses indicates the factual occurrence of the event (Comrie, 1986; Palmer, 1986). The basic semantic-pragmatics and structure of conditionals are acquired in Hebrew as in other languages across early childhood and grade school (Au, 1983; Papafragou, 1997; Ravid & Doron-Geller, 2009; Reilly, 1986), but the diversity and complexity of the form, meaning, and functions of conditionals have yet to be investigated in later language development in various communicative functions and especially in textual contexts (Katis, 1998; Shatz & Wilcox, 1991).

Conditionals have a critical function in solving and generating mathematical problems. Note the role of conditions in how eminent mathematician Polya (1957) directs readers to understanding such problems in his best-selling book *How to Solve It* (boldface and italics added):

- First: You have to understand the problem.
- What is the unknown? What are the data? **What is the condition?**
- *Is it possible to satisfy the condition? Is the condition sufficient to* **determine the unknown? Or is it insufficient? Or redundant? Or contradictory?**
- Draw a figure. Introduce suitable notation.
- Separate the various parts of **the condition**. Can you write them down?

What we found across the three analyses described in the "Results" section was, first, that the raw number of conditionals generally increased with age and schooling and, second, that more than half of the subordinated constructions in posed mathematical problems were conditional but that conditionals constitute less than 15% of subordinations in the expositions. The third and most interesting finding across all three measures (Figures 6.3 and 6.4) is the decline in the small number of expository conditionals and the dramatic increase in their number and ratio in the mathematical problems—for example, conditionals constitute three-quarters of all subordinated clauses in seventh-grade problems. This demonstrates that grade schoolers already know that conditionals have a critical role in the syntactic texture of mathematical problems and that seventh graders are able to produce problems whose specific type of syntactic complexity points to genre appropriateness. Expositions do not particularly favor adverbials because of the small number of lexical predicates in expository language in Hebrew, and conditionals have no specific role in them. But posing conditions in mathematical problems is critical and points to understanding the requirements for producing appropriate problems.

A qualitative content analysis highlights the differences between genres and age-groups. Most of the conditionals in the expository texts were open ended and deontic in nature (Byrnes, 1991; Reilly, Jisa, Baruch, & Berman, 2002), for example, the concrete ... *and of course if you are a friend of his, (do not) hit him* (fourth grade) and the more abstract *if we want peace in the world we must maintain friendship and good relations with others* (seventh grade). Some of expository conditionals were counterfactuals about states of relevant affairs in the children's world, for example, *if they hadn't married we wouldn't have been born* (fourth grade) or *if people in the world weren't friends they would be lonely and even sad* (seventh grade). In contrast, some of the conditionals in the mathematical problems were of the type termed *alternative* by Silver (1994)— that is, introducing new constraints and conditions to the original given information and thus raising the level of difficulty of the mathematical question. Other mathematical conditionals not only related motive to outcome but also pointed to the procedure for solution (Byrnes, 1991), for example, *how many pugim will Avi have if Einat gives him 1/4 of her pugim?* (seventh grade). Thus, it seems that our school-aged participants were familiar with and able to produce genre-appropriate conditionals.

Developmentally, both the mathematical and the linguistic quality of the conditional clauses improved with age and schooling. For example, a fourth-grade conditional was *if they bought another package of pugim [metal toys] then how many did they have altogether?*, whereas a problem with conditionals in seventh grade was *How many pugim will Dana have if she gets 5 times as many pugim as Einat?* In fact, less than 1% of the fourth-grade problems using conditionals were mathematically appropriate in that they enabled solving the problem, whereas more than 17% of these in seventh grade were solvable. Finally, problems with conditionals in seventh grade were usually mathematically challenging in using the given information to form new mathematical constraints and to pose alternative problems—while still remaining solvable (Silver, 1994). Thus, while conditional constructions constituted a considerable part of subordination in fourth grade and a majority of subordination constructions in seventh grade, these analyses indicate that, in Karmiloff-Smith's (1992) terms, their representations change inherently from "behavioral mastery" in the younger group to a level of metacognitive abstraction and explicitness in seventh grade.

**Relative clauses**   The third and most difficult subordination type in syntax consists of RCs. Relative clauses participate in hierarchical NP structure, and their construction is the most complex of all Hebrew subordination types, as they copy the higher NP node with the RC and delete it* using the linguistic process of equi-NP deletion, for example, *I liked the question* **(which) you asked today**, where the optional complementizer *which* in the boldface RC in fact represents the copied NP *the question* in the abstract structure *I liked the question [you asked __the question__ today]*. The deleted NP may serve in either subject or nonsubject position in the embedded RC, and, in addition to equi-NP deletion, the RC may be center embedded within the matrix sentence as in the previous example of *The question (which)* __**you asked today**__ *was important*. All these features render RCs the most difficult subordinated clauses to comprehend and produce and the last to emerge across development (Berman, 1997; Biran, 2003; Friedmann & Novogrodsky, 2004), and their presence in monologic texts contributes to the informational richness and syntactic complexity of the NP (Ravid & Berman, 2009).

Although RCs were more numerous in seventh grade than in fourth grade, this difference was not significant. The major finding regarding this type of subordination was genre related, with expositories outstripping mathematical problems by far in amount of RCs. The reason for that is the fact that RCs often participate in creating large and complex NPs (Berman & Ravid, 2008; Ravid, 2006), a typical property of written expository texts (Berman, 2005; Ravid & Cahana Amitay, 2005; chapter 5 in this volume), indicating that speaker-writers rely on (mostly) lexical NPs as a frame of content for anchoring their generalizations (Ravid et al., 2002).

The proportion of relative subordination out of all subordinating constructions did not yield any significant results since only five of the fourth graders (about 12.5%) produced RCs in both genres, compared with 18 seventh graders (about 64%). This by itself is a fascinating result, a developmental yardstick of how RCs increase in number in actual written usage. In those participants who did produce RCs across both genres, fourth graders had 20% in expositories and 40% in mathematical problems, whereas seventh graders had only 18% and 15%, respectively, in expositories and mathematical problems. The concomitant is probably a greater variety of other subordination types—complementation and adverbial subordination—in the higher age-group. The correlation analysis we show next elaborates on the types of complex syntactic constructions employed by our participants across age-groups and genres.

---

* Grammatical Hebrew RC constructions actually differ in omitting the copied NP (*zot ha-xavera she-azra li*, "this is the friend who helped me"), in optionally retaining it (*zot ha-xavera she-ahavti [ota]*, "this is the friend that I-loved [her]"), or in obligatorily keeping it as pronominal inflection on prepositions (*zot ha-xavera she-azrti la*, "this is the friend that I-helped her = whom I helped").

## Expository and Mathematical Discourse Across Development

The second part of our analysis focused on correlations between language complexity and measures of mathematical knowledge in tasks carried out by the same participants. Correlations *across* language measures in the expository text and a smaller set of these measures in the posed problems are reported (Table 6.4), presenting a picture of the interface of linguistic proficiency in expository and mathematical discourse across late childhood and early adolescence.

In fourth graders, language productivity measures and lexical, morphosyntactic, and syntactic measures are correlated across expositories and mathematical problems. However, Table 6.4 indicates that not all the categories and constructions we investigated in the expository texts (known to develop in the school years in Hebrew speaker-writers) yielded correlations with language measures in the mathematical problems. For example, various noun measures in expositories were correlated with subordination and specifically with RCs in the mathematical problems, testifying to the importance of nouns in underlying Hebrew lexical and syntactic development in the school years, yet none of the later-developing lexical classes, such as derived nominals or adjectives, yielded correlations. Moreover, some of the correlations, especially with number of words, were negative—yielding an unclear picture. What we do see in fourth graders is a diversification of subordination constructions expressing various logical relations (conditionals, temporals, and reason subordinations)—together constituting the syntactic architecture of written Hebrew expositions (Berman & Nir-Sagiv, 2007; Ravid & Zilberbuch, 2003a). These are correlated with some language measures in mathematical discourse, such as number of words and clauses, and with several syntactic measures—mostly with RCs and conditionals, as discussed previously. Fourth graders' ability to use genre-appropriate complex syntax in constructing mathematical problems is an indication of some relationship between general language proficiency and the "language" of mathematics. We interpret this finding as further support for Berman's (2004) "dichotomy to divergence" model, which, together with Karmiloff-Smith's (1992) model of metalinguistic development, points at separate domains of knowledge in childhood coalescing into a coherent and more accessible system in adolescence, leading to higher thinking capabilities.

These patterns evolve in seventh graders. According to Table 6.5, there are many more, more diverse, and stronger correlations between expository discourse and mathematical discourse. Moreover, the overwhelming majority of these correlations are positive. Fewer correlations are found, paradoxically, among actual language measures between exposition and problem posing than in fourth grade—pointing perhaps at a differential later language organization in young adolescents: new linguistic items and constructions now appear in the expository texts, such as abstract nouns and adjectives, and a greater diversity of subordinate clause types, such as predicate and subject clauses. Moreover, more general and less isolated language measures now participate in the correlation tables, such as the general language, general text, and general syntactic scores, and the correlation between language measures is often stronger, at the .01 level. We interpret this picture to convey the changing nature of linguistic architecture in the older age-group—more integrated, relating more language domains, and highlighting new acquisition such as denominal adjectives.

This evolving picture of statistical correlations in seventh graders may hail the growth of two abilities in tandem: the *language of literacy* as manifested in expository discourse and the *linguistic proficiencies* described by Mestre (1988) as necessary for tackling mathematical problems—understanding the symbolic language of mathematics and its jargon and being able to move flexibly between the different usages of items and constructions in language and mathematical discourse.

An interesting measure that is similar across both age-groups is the negative correlation between lexical verbs in expository texts and linguistic measures in mathematical problem posing (Tables 6.4 and 6.5). Lexical verbs are the majority of verbs in the Hebrew lexicon, consisting of those nongrammatical, nonauxiliary verbs that carry independent meaning and are composed of a root and a verb pattern. Such verbs are more rare in expository texts, which rely more heavily on copular constructions, such as *friendship is ...* and on present-tense verbless constructions to express general, detached, and nondynamic discourse stances (Berman, 1980, 2005; Ravid & Cahana-Amitay, 2005). This negative correlation thus indicates an early consolidation of intergenre differentiation and the ability to construct genre-appropriate discourse by the middle of grade school.

## CONCLUSION

The results of the comparison between the distributions of "advanced" linguistic structures in the two writing tasks revealed that the utilization of such late-emerging linguistic forms is constrained by the nature of the specific task. While we documented increases over time in the use of advanced forms in both genres, we also reported that in each genre, participants manifested unique distribution of specific structures. Thus, relative clauses were far more prevalent in the expository texts, whereas conditionals proliferated in the mathematical problems. Our study results also clearly indicate that the relationship between linguistic proficiency in the two genres is mediated by age and schooling. While the linguistic abilities of fourth graders may not manifest in math activities, strong links were found in seventh graders between the use of linguistic forms in expository text and in mathematical problems. Qualitative analyses provided support to our observation that the use of advanced linguistic forms not only is related to linguistic growth but may be explained by the increase in cognitive processing. The data on Hebrew-speaking school-age students thus support the claim that the mathematical genre is extremely interesting for exploring domain-specific similarities and differences and that it highlights the importance of language in teaching and learning mathematics. Our results indicate the need for further testing of the relationship between mathematical performance and linguistic abilities.

## REFERENCES

Anglin, J. M. (1993). Vocabulary development: A morphological analysis. *Monographs of the Society for Research in Child Development, 58*(10, Serial No. 238), 1–165.

Au, T. K-F. (1983). Chinese and English counterfactuals: The Sapir-Whorf hypothesis revisited. *Cognition, 15,* 155–187.

Berman, R. A. (1980). The case of an (S)VO language: Subjectless constructions in Modern Hebrew. *Language, 56,* 759–776.

Berman, R. A. (1985). *The acquisition of Hebrew.* Hillsdale, NJ: Lawrence Erlbaum Associates.

Berman, R. A. (1997). Preliterate knowledge of language. In C. Portecovo (Ed.), *Writing development: An interdisciplinary view* (pp. 61–71). Amsterdam: Benjamins.

Berman, R. A. (2004). Between emergence and mastery: The long developmental route of language acquisition. In R. A. Berman (Ed.), *Language development across childhood and adolescence* (pp. 9–34). Amsterdam: Benjamins.

Berman, R. A. (2005). Introduction: Developing discourse stance in different text types and languages. *Journal of Pragmatics, 37,* 105–124.

Berman, R. A. (2007). Developing language knowledge and language use across adolescence. In E. Hoff & M. Shatz (Eds.), *Handbook of language development* (pp. 346–367). London: Blackwell.

Berman, R. A., & Katzenberger, I. (2004). Form and function in introducing narrative and expository texts: A developmental perspective. *Discourse Processes, 38,* 57–94.

Berman, R. A., & Nir, B. (2004). Linguistic indicators of inter-genre differentiation in later language development. *Journal of Child Language, 31,* 339–380.

Berman, R. A., & Nir-Sagiv, B. (2007). Comparing narrative and expository text construction across adolescence: A developmental paradox. *Discourse Processes, 43,* 79–120.

Berman, R. A., & Nir-Sagiv, B. (2009a). Clause-packaging in narratives: A cross-linguistic developmental study. In J. Guo, E. Lieven, S. Ervin-Tripp, N. Budwig, S. Özçalişkan, & K. Nakamura (Eds.), *Cross-linguistic approaches to the psychology of language: Research in the tradition of Dan I. Sloblin* (pp. 119–126). Mahwah, NJ: Lawrence Erlbaum Associates.

Berman, R. A., & Nir-Sagiv, B. (2009b) Cognitive and linguistic factors in evaluating expository text quality: Global versus local? In V. Evans, & S. Pourcel (Eds.), *New directions in cognitive linguistics* (pp. 149–162). Amsterdam: Benjamins.

Berman, R. A., & Ravid, D. (2008). Becoming a literate language user: Oral and written text construction across adolescence. In D. R. Olson & N. Torrance (Eds.), *Cambridge handbook of literacy* (pp. 92–111). Cambridge: Cambridge University Press.

Berman, R. A., & Slobin, D. I. (1994). *Relating events in narrative*. Hillsdale, NJ: Lawrence Erlbaum Associates.

Berman, R. A.,& Verhoeven, L. (2002). Developing text production abilities in speech and writing: Aims and methodology. *Written Language and Literacy, 5*(1), 1–43.

Best, R., Dockrell, J., & Braisby, N. (2006). Lexical acquisition in elementary science classes. *Journal of Educational Psychology, 98,* 824–838.

Biber, D. (1988). *Variation across speech and writing*. Cambridge: Cambridge University Press.

Biran, R. (2003). *Acquisition of relative clauses by typically developing children and children with SLI*. Unpublished master's thesis, Tel Aviv University, Tel Aviv, Israel.

Britton, B. K. (1994). Understanding expository text: building mental structure to induce insights. *Handbook of psycholinguistics* (pp. 641–674). New York: Academic Press.

Brown, M. (1981). Number operations. In K. M. Hart (Ed.), *Children's understanding of mathematics* (pp. 23–47). London: Murra.

Bruner, J. (1986). *Actual minds, possible worlds*. Cambridge, MA: Harvard University Press.

Byrnes, P. J. (1991). Acquisition and development of *if* and *because*: Conceptual and linguistic aspects. In S. A. Gelman & P. J. Byrnes (Eds.), *Perspectives on language and thought* (pp. 354–389). Cambridge: Cambridge University Press.

Cahana-Amitay, D., & Ravid, D. (2000). Optional bound morphology in the development of text production. In S. C. Howell, S. A. Fish, & T. Keith-Lucas (Eds.), *Proceedings of the 24th Annual Boston University Conference on Language Development* (Vol. 1, pp. 176–184). Somerville, MA: Cascadilla Press.

Carlisle, J. F. (2000). Awareness of the structure and meaning of morphologically complex words: Impact on reading. *Reading and Writing, 12,* 169–190.

Comrie, B. (1986). Conditionals: A typology. In E. C. Traugott, A. T. Meulen, J. S. Reilly, & C. H. Ferguson (Eds.), *On conditionals* (pp. 77–99). Cambridge: Cambridge University Press.

Dehaene, S., Spelke, L., Pinel, P., Stanescu, R., & Tsivkin, S. (1999). Sources of mathematical thinking: Behavioral and brain-imaging evidence. *Science, 284,* 970–974.

Delazer, M., Girelli, L., Semenza, C., & Denes, G. (1999). Numerical skills and aphasia. *Journal of the International Neuropsychological Society, 5,* 213–221.

Druyan, S. (1995). The effect of reciprocal socio-cognitive activities on scientific thinking: The conceptualization of speed. *Megamot, 36,* 405–428. [in Hebrew]

Druyan, S. (2001). A comparison of four types of cognitive conflict and their effect on cognitive development. *International Journal of Behavioral Development, 25,* 226–236.

English, D. L. (1998). Children's problem posing within formal and informal contexts. *Journal for Research in Mathematics Education, 29,* 83–106.

Fazio, B. B. (1996). Mathematical abilities of children with specific language impairment: A 2-year follow-up. *Journal of Speech and Hearing Research, 39,* 839–849.

Fazio, B. B. (1999). Arithmetic calculation, short-term memory, and language performance in children with specific language impairment: A 5-year follow-up. *Journal of Speech, Language and Hearing Research, 42,* 420–431.

Friedmann, N., & Novogrodsky, R. (2004). The acquisition of relative clause comprehension in Hebrew: A study of SLI and normal development. *Journal of Child Language, 31,* 661–681.

Giora, R. (1985). A text-based analysis of non-narrative texts. *Theoretical Linguistics, 12,* 115–135.

Grow-Maienza, J., Hahn, D. D., & Joo, C. A. (2001). Mathematics instruction in Korean primary schools: Structures, processes and a linguistic analysis of questioning. *Journal of Education Psychology, 93,* 363–376.

Halliday, M. A. K. (1989). *Spoken and written language.* Oxford: Oxford University Press.

Hiebert, J., & Lefevre, P. (1986). Conceptual and procedural knowledge in mathematics: An introductory analysis. In J. Hiebert (Ed.), *Conceptual and procedural knowledge: The case of mathematics* (pp. 1–23). Hillsdale, NJ: Lawrence Erlbaum Associates.

Kaplan, D. (2008). *The connection between reading comprehension and linguistic abilities in later language development.* Unpublished doctoral dissertation, Tel Aviv University, Tel Aviv, Israel.

Karmiloff-Smith, A. (1992). *Beyond modularity: A developmental perspective on cognitive science.* Cambridge, MA: MIT Press.

Katis, D. (1998). The emergence of conditionals in child language: Are they really so late? In A. Athanasiadou & R. Dirven (Eds.), *On conditionals again* (pp. 355–386). Amsterdam: Benjamins.

Krutetskii, V. A. (1976). *The psychology of mathematical abilities in schoolchildren* (J. Teller, Trans.). Chicago: University of Chicago Press.

Levin, I., Ravid, D., & Rappaport, S. (2001). Morphology and spelling among Hebrew-speaking children: From kindergarten to first grade. *Journal of Child Language, 28,* 741–769.

MacGregor, M., & Price, E. (1999). An exploration of aspects of language proficiency and algebra learning. *Journal for Research in Mathematics Education, 30,* 449–467.

Matthiessen, C., & Thompson, S. A. (1988). The structure of discourse and "subordination." In J. Haiman & S. A. Thompson (Eds.), *Clause combining in grammar and discourse* (pp. 275–329). Amsterdam: Benjamins.

Mestre, J. P. (1988). The role of language comprehension in mathematics and problem solving. In R. R. Cocking & P. J. Mestre (Eds.), *Linguistics and cultural influences on learning mathematics* (pp. 201–219). Hillsdale, NJ: Lawrence Erlbaum Associates.

Mills, H., Whitin, D., & O'Keefe, T. (1993). Teaching math concepts in K-1 class does not have to be like pulling teeth- but maybe it should be! *Young Children, 48,* 17–20.

Montis, K. (2000). Language development and concept flexibility in dyscalculia: A case study. *Journal for Research in Mathematics Education, 31,* 541–556.

Mosenthal, P. B. (1985). Defining the expository discourse continuum. *Poetics, 14,* 387–414.

Nippold, M. A. (2002). Lexical learning in school-age children, adolescents, and adults: A process where language and literacy converge. *Journal of Child Language, 29,* 474–478.

Nippold, M. A. (2007). *Later language development: School-age children, adolescents, and young adults* (3rd ed.). Austin, TX: PRO-ED.

Nir-Sagiv, B., Bar-Ilan, L., & Berman, R. A. (2008). Vocabulary development across adolescence: Text-based analyses. In I. Kupferberg & A. Stavans (Eds.), *Studies in language and language education: Essays in honor of Elite Olshtai* (pp. 47–74). Jerusalem: Magnes Press.

Palmer, F. R. (1986). *Mood and modality.* Cambridge: Cambridge University Press.

Paltridge, B. (1997). *Genre, frames, and writing in research settings.* Amsterdam: Benjamins.

Papafragou, A. (1997). Modality in language development: A reconsideration of the evidence. *UCL Working Papers in Linguistics, 9,* 1–31.

Polya, G. (1957). *How to solve it* (2nd ed.). Princeton, NJ: Princeton University Press.

Ravid, D. (2004). Emergence of linguistic complexity in written expository texts: Evidence from later language acquisition. In D. Ravid & H. Bat-Zeev Shyldkrot (Eds.), *Perspectives on language and language development* (pp. 337–355). Dordrecht: Kluwer.

Ravid, D. (2006). Semantic development in textual contexts during the school years: Noun scale analyses. *Journal of Child Language, 33,* 791–821.

Ravid, D., & Avidor, A. (1998). Acquisition of derived nominals in Hebrew: Developmental and linguistic principles. *Journal of Child Language, 25,* 229–266.

Ravid, D., & Berman, R. A. (2006). Information density in the development of spoken and written narratives in English and Hebrew. *Discourse Processes, 41,* 117–149.

Ravid, D., & Berman, R. (2009). Noun phrase structure and content in later language development: Text-embedded cross-linguistic analyses. *First Language.*

Ravid, D., & Cahana-Amitay, D. (2005). Verbal and nominal expression in narrating conflict situations in Hebrew. *Journal of Pragmatics, 37,* 157–183.

Ravid, D., & Doron-Geller, D. (2009). Development of conditional sentences in Hebrew child language: an experimental study. *Literacy and Language (Oryanut Ve-Safa).* (in Hebrew)

Ravid, D., & Saban, R. (2008). Syntactic and meta-syntactic skills in the school years: A developmental study in Hebrew. In I. Kupferberg & A. Stavans (Eds.), *Language education in Israel: Papers in honor of Elite Olshtain* (pp. 75–110). Jerusalem: Magnes Press.

Ravid, D., & Tolchinsky, L. (2002). Developing linguistic literacy: A comprehensive model. *Journal of Child Language, 29,* 419–448.

Ravid, D., van Hell, J., Rosado, E., & Zamora, A. (2002). Subject NP patterning in the development of text production: Speech and writing. *Written Language and Literacy, 5,* 69–94.

Ravid, D., & Zilberbuch, S. (2003a). The development of complex nominals in expert and non-expert writing: A comparative study. *Pragmatics and Cognition, 11,* 267–297.

Ravid, D., & Zilberbuch, S. (2003b). Morpho-syntactic constructs in the development of spoken and written Hebrew text production. *Journal of Child Language, 30,* 395–418.

Reilly, J. S. (1986). The acquisition of temporals and conditionals. In E. C. Traugott, A. T. Meulen, J. S. Reilly, & C. H. Ferguson (Eds.), *On conditionals* (pp. 309–331). Cambridge: Cambridge University Press.

Reilly, J. S., Jisa, H., Baruch, E., & Berman, R. (2002). Propositional attitudes in written and spoken language. *Written Language and Literacy, 5,* 183–219.

Reilly, J. S., Zamora A., & McGivern, R. F. (2005). Acquiring perspective in English: The development of stance. *Journal of Pragmatics, 37,* 185–208.

Richards, B. J., & Malvern, D. D. (1997). *Quantifying lexical diversity in the study of language development.* Reading: University of Reading.

Riley, M. S., Greeno, J. G., & Heller, J. I. (1983). The development of children's problem-solving ability in arithmetic. In P. H. Ginsburg (Ed.), *The development of mathematical thinking* (pp. 153–171). New York: Academic Press.

Rittle-Johnson, B., & Siegler, R. S. (1998). The relation between conceptual and procedural knowledge in learning mathematics: A review. In C. Donlan (Ed.), *The development of mathematical skills* (pp. 75–110). East Sussex: Psychology Press.

Scott, C. M. (2004). Syntactic ability in children and adolescents with language and learning disabilities. In R. A. Berman (Ed.), *Language development across childhood and adolescence* (pp. 111–133). Amsterdam: Benjamins.

Scott, C. M., & Windsor, J. (2000). General language performance measures in spoken and written narrative and expository discourse of school-age children with language learning disabilities. *Journal of Speech, Language, and Hearing Research, 43,* 324–339.

Seroussi, B. (2004). Hebrew derived nouns in context: A developmental perspective. *Phoniatrica et Logopaedica, 56,* 273–290.

Sfard, A. (2002, January 24). *There is more to discourse than meets the ears: Looking at thinking as communicating to learn about mathematical learning.* Plenary address at MADIF 3, Norrkoping, Sweden.

Shatz, M., & Wilcox, S. A. (1991). Constraints on the acquisition of English modals. In S. A. Gelman & J. P. Byrnes (Eds.), *Perspectives on language and thought* (pp. 319–353). Cambridge: Cambridge University Press.

Silver, E. A. (1987). Foundations of cognitive theory and research for mathematics problem-solving instruction. In H. A. Schoenfeld (Ed.), *Cognitive science and mathematics education* (pp. 33–60). Hillsdale, NJ: Lawrence Erlbaum Associates.

Silver, E. A. (1994). On mathematical problem posing. *For the Learning of Mathematics, 14,* 19–27.

Silver, E. A., & Cai, J. (1996). An analysis of arithmetic problem posing by middle school students. *Journal for Research in Mathematics Education, 27,* 521–539.

Spanos, G., Rhodes, C. N., & Corasaniti Dale, T. (1988). Linguistic features of mathematical problem solving: Insights and applications. In R. R. Cocking & P. J. Mestre (Eds.), *Linguistics and cultural influences on learning mathematics* (pp. 221–239). Hillsdale, NJ: Lawrence Erlbaum Associates.

Steen, G. (1999). Genres of discourse and the definition of literature. *Discourse Processes, 28,* 109–120.

Strömqvist, S., Johansson, V., Kriz, S., Ragnarsdóttir, H., Aisenman, R., & Ravid, D. (2002). Toward a cross-linguistic comparison of lexical quanta in speech and writing. *Written Language and Literacy, 5,* 45–68.

Tolchinsky, L., & Rosado, E. (2005). The effect of literacy, text type, and modality on the use of grammatical means for agency alternation in Spanish. *Journal of Pragmatics, 37,* 209–238.

Van Den Brink, J. (1987). Children as arithmetic book authors. *For the Learning of Mathematics, 7,* 44–47.

## APPENDIX 6.A: EXAMPLES OF EXPOSITORY TEXTS ON FRIENDSHIP WRITTEN BY STUDY PARTICIPANTS

**Note:** These are almost literal translations from Hebrew, giving the precise information presented in the original Hebrew texts, including syntactic errors. Spelling and morphological errors are not represented in this translation. These were numerous in the fourth-grade text and few in the seventh-grade text.

### Fourth-Grade Text

*Friends for me are something that determines the future. Without friends no one could live. My opinion about friendship is that friendship determines our future. Without friendship none of us would live. If there was no friendship in the world none of us would live. Because friendship connected our parents and if there was no friendship then our parents wouldn't have birthed us and so we would not have been born.*

*And then non one would have existed. Because our parents' parents (grandfather, grandmother) wouldn't have been friends then they wouldn't have birthed our parents and then they wouldn't have been born and then we wouldn't have been born.*

### Seventh-Grade Text

*I think that friendly relations are something really nice. When you are in good relations with someone you talk to that person, he's a friend of yours, but there is not much more beyond this connection (I think Plato would call this a Platonic relationship). I can define friendship in this way: it is the middle section on the axis of relationships (I have made this up). When you are not yet somebody's friend (there is still time) you don't not talk to him. It's this part: [drawing of axis appears under this line]. Not talking to someone at all, not knowing him, being friends, being in the middle of the road, being his friend, being his world—friendship in my opinion is something that is found in early ages between a boy and a girl. Also in general between people of the same gender (especially boys). It's an immediate connection because we have the same topics etc. It's the connection with the axis.*

## APPENDIX 6.B: INSTRUCTIONS TO PARTICIPANTS REGARDING THE POSING OF VERBAL PROBLEMS

Now please help us make up arithmetical problems that will be appropriate for fourth graders/seventh graders. Here is some information in two sets of "story problems." Make up five arithmetical problems that can be solved using each of these story problems.

1. Avi, Einat, and Sa'ar collect *pugim* (small metal discs for playing). Sa'ar has 80 more *pugim* than Einat. Einat has twice as many *pugim* as Avi. Avi has 40 *pugim*.
2. Ron, Noa, and Tamar read books. Tamar has read half as many books as Noa. Noa has read 19 more books than Ron. Ron has read 25 books.

## APPENDIX 6.C: EXAMPLES OF MATHEMATICAL PROBLEMS POSED BY STUDY PARTICIPANTS

### Problems Posed by Fourth Graders

How many *pugim* did Einat collect?
How many did Einat and Sa'ar collect together?
How many books did Tamar read?
How many did Ron and Tamar read together [sic]
If we take away 14 books from Ron, how many will be left?
Who read twice as many books?
Who has the most fewest *pugim* [sic]

## Problems Posed by Seventh Graders

How many *pugim* will Sa'ar have if he gets half the number of Avi's *pugim* and half of Einat's?

How many *pugim* did they all collect together?

Who read the most books?

How many books did Tamar read if she read twice as few books than Noa?

After all of the *pugim* were put together, they were given out equally. How many did each kid receive?

What is the difference between the number of books that Ron read and the number that Tamar read?

How many *pugim* do they still have to collect to get to 180?

Who has read the fewest books?

What would be the difference between Sa'ar and Einat if Einat gets 20% of the *pugim* Avi has?

## STUDY GUIDE QUESTIONS

1. Cognitive changes during adolescence include
   a. the ability to reason concretely.
   b. the development of executive control systems.
   c. a decline in the explicitness of domain knowledge.
   d. mechanisms that trigger lengthening reaction times.
2. Later language development is characterized by
   a. greater productivity of words and clauses.
   b. a decline in metalinguistic behavior.
   c. greater use of explicit concrete terms.
   d. restricted use of morphologically complex words.
3. For many school-age children, difficulties with mathematics stem from limitations in the ability to
   a. write quantitative symbols appropriately.
   b. count discrete objects accurately.
   c. understand how people talk about mathematics problems.
   d. infer meaning from observing size relationships of nearby objects.
4. When adolescents are able to verbalize original mathematical problems that are complex yet clear, this provides insight into their
   a. level of cooperation and willingness to please their teachers.
   b. subconscious interest in science, literature, and history.
   c. potential for careers as artists, musicians, and filmmakers.
   d. domain knowledge and linguistic proficiency.

5. In the study by Ravid et al. reported in this chapter, the use of conditional (if–then) subordinate clauses increased between fourth and seventh grades in
   a.  narrative discourse.
   b.  expository discourse.
   c.  mathematical discourse.
   d.  conversational discourse.

## CHAPTER 7

# Expository Discourse in School-Age Children and Adolescents with Language Disorders: Nature of the Problem

*Jeannene M. Ward-Lonergan*

Expository discourse refers to academic, informational language that is typically found in textbooks, classroom lectures, technical papers, and other factual documents. It is critical that speech-language pathologists, special education teachers, general education teachers, and other professionals involved in the education of school-age children and adolescents with language disorders gain a thorough understanding of expository discourse strengths and weaknesses in this population. This knowledge base will greatly enhance their ability to support these students as they strive to master this complex "language of the curriculum." The primary purpose of this chapter is to present a detailed description and analysis of what is currently known about expository text comprehension and production in school-age children and adolescents with language disorders. Information pertaining to spoken expository discourse abilities (i.e., listening comprehension and verbal production) will be reported in the first section of the chapter (on the next page), followed by a section on "Written Expository

Discourse Abilities in Children and Adolescents with Language Impairments." An in-depth discussion of the specific features of expository discourse that are impaired in children and adolescents with language disorders with respect to semantic, syntactic, morphological, and pragmatic abilities is included for both spoken and written expository discourse.

## SPOKEN EXPOSITORY DISCOURSE ABILITIES IN CHILDREN AND ADOLESCENTS WITH LANGUAGE IMPAIRMENTS

### Listening Comprehension and Verbal Production Abilities

Young children begin communicating through conversational discourse, which tends to be relatively informal and unstructured (i.e., connected language beyond the sentence level). During the late preschool through elementary school years (particularly during the primary grades), a great deal of emphasis is typically placed on listening to and telling stories (i.e., narrative discourse). Children in the primary grades often cannot read independently, and most classroom instruction at this level necessarily involves a heavy emphasis on listening-speaking activities (oral presentation and oral responses) (Danner, 1976). During the elementary school years, children are increasingly expected to read and write stories independently in school settings. Narrative discourse is a genre that has been well studied, and it is often analyzed and taught according to its somewhat predictable organizational structure (i.e., story grammar). As a result, narrative discourse helps to form a bridge from highly contextualized, conversational discourse to highly decontextualized, expository discourse.

Expository discourse conveys factual or technical information such as descriptions, procedural directions, or cause-and-effect explanations (Hadley, 1998). Longacre (1983) pointed out two basic differences between narrative and expository discourse that help to explain the syntactic characteristics of each type. Whereas narratives are agent focused (i.e., about people doing things) and chronologically based (temporally organized), expository discourse is not agent focused. Rather, it is focused on objects and ideas and is logically based (organizational structures of several types including problem-solution, cause and effect, and compare and contrast) (Longacre, 1983; Scott, 1995). Narratives typically mirror reality for children in terms of personal event, time-based experiences, while expository discourse expresses very different types of cognitive structures (Scott, 1995). Despite these structural differences, several researchers have noted that even emerging readers can recognize expository language and recall the content from expository textbooks after listening to an adult read a text to them (Duke, 2000; Moss, 1997; Pappas, 1993). Duke (2000) emphasized the importance of providing younger children with more exposure to expository texts in order to enhance their already existing abilities and to help prepare them for their academic work in later grades.

For older children and adolescents, expository discourse is the "language of the curriculum" (Ward-Lonergan, 2001). Indeed, these students are confronted with this type of discourse on a daily basis, particularly in classes such as history, science, geography, and mathematics where a large amount of academic content is typically conveyed. The ability to understand and create elaborate and specific expository texts is critical for academic success in the upper elementary and secondary grades (Gillam, Pena, & Miller, 1999). Since the majority of content area material taught to middle school and high school students is presented in lecture format, it is critical for speech-language pathologists and other educators to become well versed in the area of expository discourse so that they can facilitate academic success to the greatest extent possible. The primary purpose of this section is to summarize research on the ability of students with language and learning disorders to comprehend and produce spoken expository discourse.

**Listening comprehension and recall of expository lectures** Although numerous studies have examined the ability of children and adolescents with language impairments, learning disabilities, and language-learning disabilities (LLD) to read and write expository discourse, very few have examined listening comprehension and verbal production of expository discourse. As previously noted, this is a critical area of investigation in light of the fact that school-age children and adolescents are required to comprehend and produce expository discourse on a daily basis in order to achieve academic success in their school settings.

Ward-Lonergan, Liles, and Anderson (1998) were the first researchers to examine listening comprehension and recall abilities in adolescents with and without LLD. In their investigation, 20 adolescent males with LLD and 29 adolescent males with normal language, ages 12:5 to 14:7 (years:months), viewed two videotaped social studies lectures about an imaginary country. One of the expository lectures had a comparison discourse structure, and the other lecture had a causation (cause and effect) discourse structure. After viewing each lecture, each participant verbally responded to 20 literal and 20 inferential comprehension questions about the lecture. The results indicated a significant main effect for group. Regardless of lecture type, comparison, or causation (cause and effect) or question type (literal or inferential), the group with LLD performed significantly more poorly than did the group with normal language with respect to their response accuracy for the comprehension questions. However, even the group with normal language experienced difficulty with the listening comprehension task (i.e., they responded accurately to only one-half or less of the comprehension questions on average), despite the fact that the listening difficulty level and number of unfamiliar words were controlled for in both lectures. Given that this brief task was found to be difficult for all of the students, use of a solely auditory presentation modality, without opportunity for note taking or discussion, appears to be an ineffective lecture format for facilitating informational comprehension and recall in adolescents.

A significant interaction between question type and lecture type was found, with both groups demonstrating significantly greater accuracy in their responses to literal as opposed to inferential questions pertaining to the comparison lecture. This interaction was also partially accounted for by the comparison of the inferential questions across the two lecture types. Both groups responded accurately to significantly more inferential questions for the causation lecture over the comparison lecture. However, an unexpected finding was that there were no significant differences for either group in their responses to the literal and inferential questions for the causation lecture. In addition, neither group demonstrated a significant difference in their response accuracy for the literal questions across lecture types. There was no significant group × lecture type interaction, group × question type interaction, or three-way group × lecture type × question type interaction. This study offered some preliminary evidence that social studies lectures organized according to a causation discourse structure may be easier to comprehend at an inferential level than those reflecting a comparison structure. The authors concluded that adolescents with LLD are at a distinct disadvantage, as compared to their typically developing peers, with regard to their ability to comprehend and recall social studies lectures and thus for achieving academic success.

Subsequently, verbal retelling abilities for social studies lectures were examined in 20 adolescent males with LLD and 29 males without disabilities, ages 12:5 to 14:7 (Ward-Lonergan, Liles, & Anderson, 1999). Participants viewed one videotaped social studies lecture with a comparison discourse structure and one videotaped lecture with a causation structure. Following each lecture, each participant was instructed to pretend to retell the lecture to a friend who had never viewed it before, using his own words or words from the lecture. Results indicated that the group with LLD produced a significantly smaller number of T-units, subordinate clauses, subordinate clauses per T-unit, T-units per second, lecture components per second, and percentage of lecture components in their retellings, as compared to the group without disabilities, regardless of lecture type. Both groups produced a significantly greater number of T-units and subordinate clauses for the comparison lecture. In contrast, both groups recalled a significantly greater number of lecture components per T-unit and per second for the causation lecture. The authors concluded that the comparison discourse structure facilitated more substantive and elaborate retellings, whereas the causation discourse structure facilitated more efficient, concise retellings in both groups. Depending on the demands of a given situation, one type of discourse structure may be preferable over the other. Further research is warranted to provide additional evidence that type of expository discourse structure is causally related to recall and retelling abilities in lecture situations.

Wynn-Dancy (2001) designed a study to investigate the effects that assistance with data-driven processing (i.e., teachers' use of a slowed presentation rate) and conceptually driven processing (i.e., activation of prior knowledge) would have on the working memory of adolescents for expository lectures. Three groups of adolescents, ages 13:0 to 15:0, served as participants. Ten adolescents with LLD, 10 reading-matched controls, and nine age-matched controls viewed four videotaped history lessons pertaining to the great trading empires of Africa (i.e., Ghana, Mali, Songhai, and Kanem-Bornu). These lectures were presented with both normal and slow speaking rates. Prior to viewing some of the lessons, students were instructed to complete some tasks designed to activate their background knowledge about the topics presented. After viewing these lessons, the students completed a sentence recognition task and were asked to retell as much of the lessons as they could recall. No significant group differences were found on the sentence recognition task. However, all the participants displayed greater sentence recognition accuracy when the lectures were presented at a slow rate, but, surprisingly, activation of prior knowledge did not facilitate sentence recognition. There was no significant rate × group interaction, rate × text sequence interaction or rate × group × text sequence interaction for sentence recognition. In addition, there were no significant interactions involving activation of prior knowledge, group, or text sequence for the sentence recognition task.

With regard to recall of the expository content, the adolescents with LLD remembered fewer propositions than both their reading- and age-matched peers. This finding is in agreement with previously reported results (Ward-Lonergan et al., 1998, 1999). The Ghana expository text followed by the Mali expository text consistently resulted in the highest number of propositions as compared to all other text sequences. There was a significant three-way interaction of activation, text sequence, and rate for the free recall task. All the participants generally exhibited the greatest recall when activation of prior knowledge was paired with slowed presentation rate for both easier and more difficult expository texts. There was no significant rate × group interaction, rate × text sequence interaction, or rate × group × text sequence interaction for the free recall task. The author concluded that mental operations required for sentence recognition were well within the ability of students with LLD, whereas the free recall and expression of information was more challenging. This finding was corroborated by additional test data showing that students with LLD had difficulty generating grammatical sentences when given various subordinate conjunctions (e.g., "until," "unless"), as well as difficulty keeping specified words active in working memory while simultaneously judging the truthfulness of verbally presented sentences on a test that taps verbal working memory.

In summary, adolescents with LLD have been found to perform significantly more poorly than their reading- and age-matched peers with normal language on listening comprehension and recall tasks for social studies lectures. As noted in these studies, tasks that are difficult for students with LLD also tend to be difficult for those with normal language, and there are seldom interactions between group and task or text variables. Since students with

LLD perform more poorly than their typically developing peers on both listening comprehension tasks that require not only short verbal responses to comprehension questions but also free recall of expository content, it is quite possible that both comprehension deficits and working memory deficits combined play a role in these observed performance discrepancies. In addition, preliminary evidence suggests that the comparison and causation discourse structures may result in different performance patterns in adolescents with and without LLD with respect to their responses to literal and inferential comprehension questions and their style of retellings. Lecture recall may also be facilitated by pairing the activation of prior knowledge with a slowed presentation rate for all adolescents. In the next section, syntactic production in descriptive expository discourse is discussed. Given the importance of this area of research, the limited number of existing studies is a significant concern that should be addressed.

**Syntactic abilities in the context of descriptive expository discourse**
Scott (1995) presented a detailed description of the various types of syntactic deficits that are frequently observed in school-age children with language impairments. She noted that many of the same types of problems observed in preschool children with language impairments continue to persist into the school-age and adolescent years. Higher-level syntactic structures that tend to appear less frequently in the spoken and written language of children with language impairments, as compared to their typically developing peers, include complex sentences (i.e., a sentence that contains an independent clause and at least one dependent clause) and noun phrase and verb phrase expansions (Fletcher, 1992; Gillam & Johnston, 1992; Skarakis-Doyle & Mentis, 1991; Tyack, 1981). In addition, the language produced by students with language impairments is generally characterized as having more errors, particularly when they attempt to produce complex sentences orally or in writing (Gillam & Johnston, 1992). Although the majority of information to date related to syntactic abilities in school-age children and adolescents with language impairments pertains to syntactic complexity in narrative discourse, Tyack (1981) presented a case study of a 10-year-old girl with a language impairment who verbally produced a 100-utterance expository picture description language sample in which 28% of her sentences were complex in structure. However, when Scott (1995) analyzed the same material, she noted that many of these sentences were not grammatically correct. For example, there were only two instances of relative clauses, and her use of adverbial clauses was restricted to the word "because." Moreover, this child confused the words "because" and "so," resulting in some semantic difficulties as well. It is clear that further research is needed to examine syntactic abilities in the context of descriptive spoken expository discourse as well as other types of expository discourse with groups of children and adolescents with and without language impairments. Some researchers have investigated expository discourse production in children with language impairments by conducting

cross-genre studies. Studies comparing expository and narrative discourse are presented in the next section.

**Comparison of expository and narrative discourse abilities** To date, a limited number of investigations have directly compared expository and narrative discourse abilities. Copmann and Griffith (1994) conducted one such study that investigated the ability of children with specific learning disabilities, children with language impairments, and children with normal achievement to recall the events and story structures of a narrative text and an expository text that were orally presented to them. Sixty students (20 in each group) ranging in age from 8.33 to 13.92 years who were matched for verbal age served as participants. Unlike the children with language impairments who received intensive speech/language services, the children in the specific learning disabilities group had a learning disability that was not primarily characterized by language difficulties (i.e., Verbal IQ scores were higher than Performance IQ scores on the Wechsler Intelligence Scale for Children–Revised [Wechsler, 1974] and classroom performance, indicating that language difficulties were not their primary problem), and, therefore, they did not receive speech/language services. Both passages contained the same content (i.e., a girl trying to get her cat down from a tree), with one written as a narrative passage and the other written as an expository passage. Participants were told to listen to each passage and then to verbally retell it to a "friend" who had not heard it before. The results of this study indicated that the students with language impairments remembered significantly fewer events correctly and omitted more events than either the group with specific learning disabilities or the normally achieving group, with no significant difference between these latter two groups. This finding is in accordance with the results of Wynn-Dancy's (2001) and Ward-Lonergan et al.'s (1999, 2000) studies related to listening comprehension and recall of expository discourse. Regardless of disability, the participants in the high-verbal age-groups recalled more events correctly as compared to the children in the low-verbal age-groups. In addition, children in all three groups recalled more events correctly from the narrative passage and omitted more events when recalling the expository passage. As discussed previously, children are typically more familiar with narrative discourse than expository discourse, so this was not an unexpected finding. However, across groups, more events were recalled inaccurately for whichever text was presented second. It is possible that students did not include as much information in their second retelling since the listener already had heard some of the needed information in their first retelling, given that the content was so similar. Settings, attempts, and outcomes were recalled significantly more often in the narrative passage than they were in the expository passage. In contrast, more goals (i.e., a plan formulated by the protagonist to deal with events as they occur) were correctly recalled by all groups for the expository passage as opposed to the narrative passage. The authors emphasized the need for additional research studies aimed at examining how children with language impairments process narrative and expository discourse to facilitate the development of specific intervention techniques to match a child's individual processing abilities.

Scott and Windsor (2000) evaluated the degree to which 10 general language performance measures differentiated school-age children with LLD (mean age = 11:5) from their chronological-age (CA) (mean age = 11:6), and language-age (LA) (mean age = 8:11) peers. They compared narrative and expository texts in both spoken and written modalities. Sixty students (20 in each group) viewed two educational videotapes (i.e., one with a narrative discourse structure and one with an expository discourse structure). They then produced spoken and written summaries of these videotapes. In general, the students with LLD performed more poorly than their CA peers and were similar to their LA peers, although their mean scores were usually lower than the mean scores obtained by the LA group. In all four summaries, the participants with LLD performed significantly more poorly than their CA peers with respect to linguistic productivity, including total T-units, total words, and words per minute, supporting the findings of Ward-Lonergan et al. (1999). Grammatical complexity as measured by the number of words produced per T-unit was also found to be significantly lower for the children with LLD; however, there was no significant difference among the three groups on the clauses per T-unit variable. No significant differences were found with regard to fluency (percent of T-units with mazes) or lexical diversity (number of different words produced) across the three groups of children. There was only one measure that distinguished children with LLD from both their CA and LA peers, namely, the extent of grammatical error (i.e., error rate), and this resulted in a trend in spoken summaries and a significant difference in written summaries with poorer performance exhibited by the children with LLD. These results are in agreement with research discussed previously (Gillam & Johnston, 1992; Scott, 1995). The researchers concluded that it is unlikely that children with LLD "will close the gap" with respect to grammatical errors.

Across groups, spoken expository summaries were shorter, less fluent in the spoken versions, more complex (more words per T-unit), and more error prone as compared to narrative summaries. These productivity and fluency differences were predicted on the basis of children's level of experience with these types of discourse genres and topic familiarity (Applebee, Langer, Mullis, Latham, & Gentile, 1994). No significant difference was found with respect to grammatical complexity, as measured by words per T-unit, in spoken and written summaries. Expository writing was found to be extremely difficult for the participants with LLD, lending support to the idea that these children are likely to experience great difficulty meeting the underlying language demands of an essentially "expository" curriculum.

To conclude, all groups of children were found to recall significantly more events correctly when summarizing narrative passages as compared to expository passages across the studies described previously. In addition, expository summaries were found to be shorter, less fluent, more error prone, yet more complex than narrative summaries. Written summaries were shorter and contained more errors than spoken summaries for both narrative and expository passages. Children with LLD and language impairments also recalled significantly fewer events, exhibited poorer linguistic productivity and grammatical complexity, and had a higher grammatical error rate than their peers with normal language for both narrative and expository passages. However, no significant differences were noted with regard to fluency or lexical diversity in the spoken summaries across these groups of children.

**Summary**   School-age children and adolescents are confronted with the challenge of comprehending and producing expository discourse on a daily basis as they attempt to navigate their way through the demands of the curriculum. Research indicates that students with language impairments, learning disabilities, and LLD are at great risk for failing to master the "language of the curriculum" as compared to their typically developing peers with normal language. This section has described some of the specific deficits noted in their comprehension and recall of expository lectures and verbally presented text as compared to their typically developing peers. These include the following: poorer response accuracy for literal and inferential comprehension questions, shorter retellings characterized by reduced linguistic productivity and syntactic complexity on a number of different measures, a higher rate of grammatical errors, and recall of fewer propositions and important events. Based on the available information, research is warranted to investigate further the specific deficits exhibited by these students and to develop effective intervention techniques and approaches to improve their spoken expository discourse abilities to the greatest extent possible. The next section delineates expository discourse abilities in the written language mode.

## WRITTEN EXPOSITORY DISCOURSE ABILITIES IN CHILDREN AND ADOLESCENTS WITH LANGUAGE IMPAIRMENTS

### Reading

In recent years, there has been increased attention among educators, legislators, and parents on the need to improve literacy skills in school-age children and adolescents. One striking finding is that more than 30% of all readers at the fourth-grade level do not meet established standards for reading (National Center for Education Statistics, 2001) and therefore are at significant risk for academic failure. It is estimated that a very large proportion of students with learning disabilities, perhaps over 70%, are at risk for academic failure in mastering the general education curriculum because of a lack of basic, foundational literacy skills (Mason, Meadan, Hedin, & Corso, 2006). The reading comprehension problems that these students experience have been found to be even more severe than those that occur in their peers without disabilities who struggle with reading (Mason et al., 2006).

Struggling readers and those with reading disabilities are at a much greater risk for not being able to comprehend the texts used in their content area classrooms and thus are at greater risk for academic failure as compared to their typically developing peers (Denti & Guerin, 1999; Hall, 2004; Saenz & Fuchs, 2002). In Hall's (2004) article summarizing the results from the limited number of studies that have explicitly attempted to increase expository text comprehension in these types of students, she reported that these students also have difficulty generalizing and applying comprehension skills successfully to expository texts across content areas (Anderson & Roit, 1993). Likewise, they may not understand how, when, and why they would want to apply comprehension strategies to expository texts (Brown & Day, 1983). Hall (2004) also found that the majority of the work in this area has used social studies texts, with very few published studies that have used science or mathematics texts. She also noted that many of the existing studies used texts that were written at students' frustration levels as opposed to their instructional levels. As a result, students with language disorders and reading disabilities are confronted with numerous challenges when attempting to comprehend expository textbooks, as described next.

**Challenges encountered in reading expository discourse**    Comprehending expository text is often challenging for students, particularly those with language impairments, for a variety of reasons. One reason is that while many young children enter elementary school with an awareness of narrative text structure, few possess an awareness of expository text structure (Williams, Hall, & Lauer, 2004). Likewise, elementary school students in the primary grades continue to receive limited exposure to expository text (Duke, Bennett-Armistead, & Roberts, 2002; Duke & Pearson, 2002). Because of this lack of exposure, students in the primary grades often remain unprepared for the reading comprehension demands that await them in the upper elementary school grades (Bernhardt, Destino, Kamil, & Rodriguez-Munoz, 1995). The importance of exposing children to a variety of text structures at earlier ages is a theme that has become increasingly visible in the education and speech/language pathology literature (Newkirk, 1987; Scott, 1995). Expository text generally contains sentences that are lengthier and more complex in structure as compared to sentences found in narrative text (Francis & Kucera, 1982; Scott, 1995), and thus this type of text is particularly challenging for children, especially those with language impairments.

Because of this lack of awareness of expository text structure and the fact that expository discourse is the "language of the curriculum," children should be provided with sufficient opportunities to listen to expository discourse as well as narrative discourse, they should be encouraged to read books and materials other than stories, and they should be expected to use several different types of discourse in their speaking and writing (Neville, 1988).

Neville (1988) conducted a large, cross-sectional study of Scottish school-age children, ages 8 to 9, 10 to 11, and 13 and 14 years, that involved spoken and written narrative and expository discourse. The findings indicated that across age levels, spoken expository discourse was more difficult than spoken narrative discourse in a recount task as measured by ratings of content and language/style. Expository text was difficult for children at all age levels but particularly so at the ages of 8 to 9 years. It was also found that recalling expository discourse was more difficult than recalling other types of text regardless of whether the children heard or read the material or whether they spoke or wrote their responses.

Another reason why expository discourse is particularly challenging is that the relationships among ideas presented in expository text tend to represent abstract logical relations (Stein & Trabasso, 1981) rather than a simple sequence of familiar events more commonly found in narratives. Often times, authors of expository textbooks present the content in such a way that important connections and relationships are not made explicit (Armbruster & Anderson, 1988; Beck, McKeown, Hamilton, & Kucan, 1998). Expository texts also contain content-specific or technical vocabulary that may be unfamiliar to readers, and these texts often fail to provide sufficient background information that would enable readers to comprehend the new vocabulary and content that they encounter (Beck, McKeown, Sinatra, & Loxterman, 1991; Engelmann, Carnine, & Steely, 1991; Graesser, Leon, & Otero, 2002). In addition, Hall (2004) pointed out that authors of mathematics texts tend to introduce new concepts too quickly (Engelmann et al., 1991), whereas authors of science and social studies texts may include irrelevant events and/or information that may detract from students' ability to focus on and recall the main ideas and important details (Beck et al., 1991; Graesser et al., 2002).

To summarize, expository text has been found to be more difficult to read and comprehend than narrative text for various reasons. One reason is that expository text is often characterized by abstract, logical relations, and important connections and relationships are often not made explicit. In addition, expository text generally contains a substantial amount of content words or technical vocabulary, yet limited background information is typically provided that would help children comprehend this new vocabulary and content. Furthermore, new concepts may be introduced too rapidly. These problems are further exacerbated by the fact that few children enter elementary school with an awareness of expository text structure and thus are often unprepared to meet the reading comprehension demands encountered in the upper elementary grades. Therefore, it stands to reason that young children need sufficient opportunities to listen to and read a variety of expository text structures in order to be successful in school. In the following paragraphs, various types of expository discourse structures and their effect on the performance of students with language impairments and LLD are explored.

**Types of expository discourse structures**   As previously discussed, one of the primary reasons why expository discourse is so challenging for students, especially those with language impairments and LLD, to comprehend and produce is that there are numerous different organizational structures (e.g., comparison, problem-solution, cause and effect, description) (Burke, 2000; Ward-Lonergan et al., 1998, 1999) as compared to one fairly predictable story grammar structure that characterizes narrative discourse. Likewise, other expository text features, including more complex/technical vocabulary, graphics, and inferences, contribute to reading comprehension difficulties (Mason et al., 2006). Thus, comprehending expository text is typically more challenging and complex for students with language impairments than comprehending narrative text, and these difficulties begin to surface during the elementary school years (Saenz & Fuchs, 2002).

Even adolescents with normal language development experience some difficulty comprehending expository text structures (Daniels & Zemelman, 2004; Ivey, 1999). These varied expository discourse structures are used to answer different questions (Armbruster & Anderson, 1982), and sensitivity to these structures can affect students' comprehension and composition (Raphael, Englert, & Kirschner, 1986; Raphael & Kirschner, 1985). For example, Williams, Taylor, and deCani (1984) found that seventh graders were not sensitive to how the presence of anomalous information might modify an expository text's main idea, which would likely contribute to reading comprehension difficulties.

Table 7.1 illustrates many of the different types of expository discourse structures (Anderson & Armbruster, 1984; Meyer, Brandt, & Bluth, 1980; Meyer et al., 2002) as well as commonly found corresponding key signal cohesive words/phrases that are used to organize these discourse structures. These discourse structures and key signal words/phrases are those that school-age children and adolescents typically encounter in classroom lectures and textbooks and are required to use in school assignments.

Proficient readers are typically able to recognize these types of key signal words/phrases as well as use titles or headings to help determine the overall organization of an expository text. Even when there are no surface cues that can be used to identify a text's structure, good readers generally have a sense that these structures exist (Williams et al., 2004). In contrast, children who have language impairments or LLD often lack knowledge about text structure and corresponding key signal words/phrases. As a result, they encounter great difficulty when attempting to read and comprehend expository text (Oakhill & Yuill, 1996; Williams et al., 2004). Expository text is challenging for readers of all ability levels (Daniels & Zemelman, 2004; Ivey, 1999), but it is particularly difficult for students who struggle with reading (Hall, 2004).

In conclusion, we have seen that numerous different structures are used to organize expository text as compared to one more predictable narrative text structure (i.e., story grammar). As a result, expository text tends to be more challenging for students to read and comprehend than narrative text. While

**Table 7.1.** Sample Key Cohesive Signal Words/Phrases for Expository Discourse Structures

---

- **Causation (Explanation, Cause/Effect)** (as a result, because, thus, consequently, so, therefore, for this reason, if, then, reason, affected, influenced, resulted in, since, hence, cause, effect)
- **Collection/Description** (defined as, called, labeled, refers to, is someone who, is something that, means, can be interpreted as, describes)
- **Comparison** (in contrast, nevertheless, on the other hand, on the contrary, by comparison, whereas, similarly, same, different, but, yet, although, in spite of)
- **Enumeration (Definition-Example)** (for example, such as, that is, namely, to illustrate, for instance, another, an example of, next, finally)
- **Problem/Solution** (one problem, the problem is, the issues are, a solution[s] is [are])
- **Procedural (Temporal Sequence)** (next, first, second, then, finally, before, earlier, later, after, following, then, meanwhile, soon, until, since, beginning, during, still, eventually)

---

*Source:* From Ward-Lonergan, J. M., *Curriculum-based language intervention for older children and adolescents*, paper presented at the California Speech-Language-Hearing Association annual convention, Monterey, CA, April 2001 (original adapted from Halliday and Hasan [1976], Irwin and Baker [1989], Meyer and Freedle [1984], and Westby [1991]).

proficient readers generally can recognize the key signal words/phrases used to organize expository text as well as use titles/headings to help determine the overall text structure, children with language impairments and LLD lack knowledge about these expository text structures and their corresponding key signal words/phrases. This lack of awareness of the varied expository text structures negatively impacts their reading comprehension and composition performance. The focus now shifts more specifically to the comprehension and recall of main ideas in expository text.

**Comprehension and recall of main ideas in expository discourse**    The earliest studies pertaining to reading comprehension in children with learning disabilities for expository text addressed the question of how well these students were able to comprehend the main ideas expressed. Hansen (1978) discovered that students with learning disabilities did not recall as much main idea information as did normally achieving students, although both groups recalled comparable amounts of detail information after reading expository texts. Wong (1980) found similar results, but she also found that the two groups performed equally well when prompting questions were provided. She concluded that students with learning disabilities have particular difficulty organizing information independently.

Day and Zajakowski (1991) compared the performance of 28 fifth graders (14 average readers, ages 9.67–13 years, and 14 children with learning disabilities, ages 10.8–13 years, who were 1–2 years below grade level in reading) using a reading comprehension task that required them to state the main idea in expository paragraphs. Some of the main ideas were explicitly stated with the topic sentence appearing as either the first or the last sentence in the text, while other main ideas were implicit in texts lacking a topic sentence. During pre- and posttesting, the participants were given six single-paragraph expository texts and two long (i.e., six- to eight-paragraph) texts about common topics (e.g., colors, music) and were instructed to write a sentence stating the main idea contained in these texts.

Following the pretest, the children received individual instruction aimed at teaching them to find the main ideas in one- and two-paragraph length texts and on improving their metacognitive skills (e.g., checking their statement of the main idea with the text). Both groups of children exhibited improvement from prettest to posttest measures on both the single paragraphs and the longer texts; however, all the children had difficulty stating the main idea in the longer texts. Both groups performed significantly better when the topic sentence was the first sentence in a paragraph as opposed to the last sentence and significantly better when the topic sentence was the last sentence as opposed to being implicit in the text (i.e., topic sentence missing). Although the two groups did not differ significantly on pretest/posttest measures, the children with learning disabilities required substantially more instruction than average readers to reach mastery criterion when the topic sentence was last or implicit. The investigators concluded that some of the comprehension difficulties experienced by poor readers might be addressed through explicit instruction and extensive practice in finding the main idea in nonideal text forms. However, their sample size was fairly small, and the texts were written at the fifth-grade level despite the fact that the students with learning disabilities were at the third- and fourth-grade reading levels. These limitations may have affected the results obtained.

To summarize, students with learning disabilities have been found to exhibit significantly more difficulty recalling main idea information after reading expository passages as compared to their typically developing peers. In contrast, preliminary evidence suggests that these groups of students do not differ with respect to the amount of detail information recalled. When prompting questions were provided to assist in identifying the main idea, both groups of students were found to perform equally well in one study. Both groups of students were also found to benefit from treatment aimed at improving their ability to find the main idea, yet both groups continued to exhibit a substantial amount of difficulty in stating the main idea in longer texts. In the subsequent paragraphs, the importance of comprehension monitoring and awareness of expository text structure is emphasized.

**Comprehension monitoring and awareness of expository text structure**
Another critical area of investigation in reading expository text pertains to comprehension monitoring and awareness of text structure. Bos and Filip (1984) investigated the comprehension monitoring skills of 20 seventh graders who were "average" achievers (mean age = 12:10) and 20 seventh graders with

learning disabilities (mean age = 13:1). The participants were required to read two expository passages with text inconsistencies (i.e., one on the topic about ants and the other about homing pigeons, with implicit inconsistencies related to how they find their way home) under a standard condition and a cued condition. Ten progressively leading probes were developed for each passage (e.g., ranging from "What do you think of the essay?" to "Did everything make sense?"). In the standard condition, each participant was told that he or she would be asked if the essay made sense, to suggest any changes that would make it easier to understand, and to rate the essay as "good," "average," or "poor." Each participant read the essay silently and then read it again aloud. Following the second reading, the participants were asked the probe questions. Each participant was then asked to read the second passage under a cued condition in which he or she was cued that something in the passage did not make sense. The same procedure used in the standard condition was then followed. Unlike the average achievers, the seventh graders with learning disabilities did not activate comprehension monitoring in the standard condition, supporting Torgesen's (1980) conceptualization of students with learning disabilities as being inactive learners. However, under the cued condition, the students with learning disabilities were able to activate these strategies and detect the text inconsistency after being directed to use their comprehension monitoring strategies, and there was no significant difference between their performance and that of the average achievers. These results indicate that the students with learning disabilities did not have a deficit in their comprehension monitoring for the expository texts but, rather, were unable to apply these comprehension-monitoring strategies spontaneously. In contrast, the average-achieving students engaged in comprehension monitoring automatically and were able to evaluate texts for inconsistencies without being cued to do so. The researchers concluded that intervention aimed at activating comprehension monitoring may be beneficial for improving reading comprehension abilities in adolescents with learning disabilities.

Subsequently, Englert and Thomas (1987) compared third and fourth graders with sixth and seventh graders in three groups (normally achieving, low achieving, and students with learning disabilities) in their ability to recognize and produce related details that were consistent with a given text structure. Each participant was presented with stimulus paragraph stems representing four types of text structures (i.e., description, enumeration, sequence, and comparison/contrast). Each paragraph stem consisted of two sentences that indicated the topic of the paragraph and signaled a specific type of text structure (e.g., "Birds build their nests in several steps" for a sequence structure) and an exemplar detail sentence that met topic and text structure requirements. The participants then had to rate four sentences (i.e., two target sentences and two distracter sentences) according to their degree of fit with the topic sentences in the paragraph stems. Older students in all three groups exhibited greater sensitivity to expository text structure, suggesting that awareness of text structure is developmental. The normally achieving students identified more inconsistencies (i.e., distractor sentences) in expository text than did the low-achieving students, who identified more inconsistencies than the students with learning disabilities. The readers with learning disabilities were less able to recognize the signal word cues (e.g., "first," "finally," "in contrast," "similarly") in expository text and less capable of making hypotheses about relevant details based on interrelationships indicated through text structure than the other two groups of students. These findings also support those of Bos and Filip (1984) related to comprehension monitoring. It was concluded that poor readers could not use the interrelations in text to guide their comprehension and were not sensitive to their comprehension failures because they did not demonstrate any self-monitoring of their comprehension (e.g., rereading the text).

There is also some evidence that students appear to have more awareness of certain types of expository discourse than others. For example, Richgels, McGee, Lomax, and Sheard (1987) found that sixth graders had sensitivity and awareness of text structure that varied as a function of structure type. Across five awareness and recall tasks, students were more consistently aware of a compare-and-contrast structure than a causation structure. According to Englert et al. (1989), research has suggested that readers' sensitivity to organizational patterns was positively related to reading comprehension. Less successful readers have been found to be less sensitive to the organizational patterns in expository texts than more successful readers, and this insensitivity negatively affects the quality and structure of their recall of information (Richgels et al., 1987; Taylor, 1980; Taylor & Samuels, 1983).

In conclusion, students with learning disabilities have been found to be less sensitive to expository text inconsistencies and less able to spontaneously activate comprehension-monitoring strategies than normally achieving and language-matched students. This insensitivity to text structure negatively affects the quality and structure of their recall of expository content. Similarly, students with learning disabilities have also been found to be less capable of recognizing key signal word cues and of producing related details consistent with a given expository text structure when presented with paragraph stems. Awareness of expository text structure and the ability to use cues in well-structured text were found to be developmental across all three groups of students regardless of text structure type. However, awareness of text structure was found to vary according to expository structure type in one study (i.e., greater awareness of comparison than causation structures) across a range of awareness and recall tasks. It is clear that there is much work that needs to be done to develop effective intervention techniques and instructional modifications for increasing awareness of expository text structure that would make academic success attainable for students with learning disabilities. To this end, the influence of textbook organization on reading comprehension must be considered and is discussed next.

**Organization of textbooks**   It has been suggested that the way in which expository textbooks are organized can substantially affect reading comprehension. Dull and van Garderen (2005) report that many at-risk students and students with learning problems struggle to understand social studies textbooks. Many textbooks have been described as being "inconsiderate" of their readers because they often lack adequate structure, coherence, and audience appropriateness, features that prevent them from being read and understood with relative ease (Armbruster & Anderson, 1988). These expository textbooks often do not make important connections and relationships explicit. Armbruster and Anderson (1988) presented ways that textbooks might be improved by offering examples from Ghanaian textbooks. These authors also suggested strategies that teachers might use to "bring back the story" in social studies. Similarly, Beck et al. (1991) modified passages from history textbooks so that they followed a narrative sequence (problem–action–effect) as opposed to the commonly found expository sequence (action–effect–problem). In doing so, they found that fourth- and fifth-grade students who read the revised texts recalled significantly more idea units and answered more questions correctly than did those who read the original textbook passages. Dickson, Simmons, and Kameenui (1998) reviewed 17 studies that focused on the relationship between text organization and comprehension and concluded that knowledge of text organization affects comprehension, especially with respect to the identification and recall of the most important information in text.

Lauer (2002) followed up on Beck et al.'s (1991) finding that fourth- and sixth-grade students understood revised texts that followed a narrative sequence (problem–action–effect) better than they understood the typical expository textbook sequence (action–effect–problem). These two sequences were compared to determine whether second graders who were at risk for academic failure were also sensitive to text structure variations. Texts were used that included both actions and events that typically and rarely occur in children's daily lives. The effectiveness of text structure and content familiarity was also examined to see if this differed for children who were proficient in reading comprehension as opposed to those who were not. After reading each text, students were asked to summarize the text, and then they were asked four text structure questions that were related to the important information in the text (i.e., Who is the paragraph about?, What was wrong?, What did the character do?, and What happened?). The participants were then asked to summarize the text again and to respond to detail and content questions related to important information.

The results of Lauer's (2002) study indicated that all three variables (text structure, content familiarity, and reading comprehension ability) affected performance. High reading comprehension ability led to better performance on all tasks, and content familiarity helped students answer questions concerning important content only. Text structure helped with regard to their responses to important content questions as well as on the summarization and resummarization tasks. In other words, the narrative text structure helped the students select important information to be included in their summaries with texts containing both familiar and unfamiliar content. As expected, students understood texts about familiar events better than texts about unfamiliar events. It was concluded that young second-grade readers, including both high and low comprehenders, are sensitive to expository text structure, and instruction in text structure awareness may be beneficial in elementary school.

Based on the results discussed previously, it is clear that textbook organization can significantly affect reading comprehension performance. There is substantial evidence that knowledge of text organization affects reading comprehension, with good readers being more capable of using this type of knowledge than poor readers. Many expository textbooks lack adequate structure, coherence, and audience appropriateness, factors that contribute to comprehension difficulties. Studies have shown that children understand textbooks that have been revised to follow a narrative sequence better than those with a traditional expository sequence.

**Summary**  Children and adolescents with language impairments and LLD exhibit significant deficits in their ability to read and comprehend expository discourse for a variety of reasons. Some of their specific areas of difficulty include lack of awareness of expository text structures, poor identification and recall of main ideas, and limited ability to self-monitor comprehension. The organization of textbooks is another factor that often contributes to comprehension difficulties. All these factors that affect reading comprehension have a direct negative impact on school performance. Therefore, these limitations need to be addressed in order to facilitate academic success in students with language impairments and LLD.

## Writing

Skilled expository writing becomes increasingly important to all students in the secondary grades, yet it can be particularly demanding for students with learning disabilities (Sturm & Rankin-Erickson, 2002) at both transcription (e.g., spelling and mechanics) and composition (e.g., organization and generation of content) levels (Sturm & Rankin-Erickson, 2002). These students also have difficulty choosing an appropriate text structure to organize their writing, and they exhibit language difficulties that include gaps in vocabulary and weak word, phrase, sentence, and discourse structures (Ehren, 1994). Collectively, these difficulties contribute to a persistent pattern of academic failure and a negative attitude toward writing (Sturm & Rankin-Erickson, 2002). The next section of the chapter focuses on the many challenges that students encounter during expository writing tasks.

**Challenges posed by expository writing tasks**  According to Scott (1995), a debate exists related to the onset and status of children's expository writing abilities. Some researchers have reported use of relatively sophisticated expository writing at earlier ages than others, with considerable use of hierarchical text structure by third grade (Langer, 1985, 1986; Newkirk, 1987). The ability to successfully produce this type of informational writing is believed to typically lag behind proficient narrative writing ability (Scott, 1989, 1994). Studies reviewed by Scott (1995) also support the finding by Scarborough and Dobrich (1990) of "illusory recovery" in children with language impairments at 5 to 7 years of age. By the age of 5 years, such children often have acquired enough basic language skills that enable them to communicate adequately, and thus their language deficits are not very apparent. However, recovery is shown to be illusory, as language problems frequently surface again when these children encounter the curriculum demands of the mid-elementary school years that emphasize comprehension and production of more extended, complex informational discourse. The literature contains occasional comparisons of narrative and expository writing from the same child that appear to support the notion that narrative writing skills develop earlier than expository writing skills (Scott, 1995). However, few investigations have directly compared these two genres in children with language impairments (Scott & Windsor, 2000; Windsor, Scott, & Street, 2000).

Wong (2000) described five specific aspects of writing in which students with learning disabilities differ significantly from their peers with normal language: the ability to express their ideas in writing; their conception of good writing; their tendency to use an unproductive strategy to compensate for their limited vocabularies (e.g., substituting another word when unable to retrieve or spell a desired word); their tendency to make more errors in spelling, punctuation, and grammar; and their need for more practice in writing in order to achieve mastery of a writing strategy. Regarding expository writing specifically, students with learning disabilities typically exhibit two related problems. First, they seem to have no notion of the structure of a paragraph (i.e., that it contains a topic sentence, supporting detail sentences, and a concluding sentence). Second, they seem unaware of the need to organize written sentences in some logical order within a paragraph (Wong, 2000).

Thus, the written composition abilities of students with learning disabilities have been found to differ from their peers with normal language in several respects. In the area of expository writing, they have no notion of the structure and organization of a paragraph. Although there is some debate over the age of onset of expository writing abilities, this type of writing has been found to develop later than narrative writing. Additional research that compares expository and narrative writing ability in students with language impairments and learning disabilities is needed to identify similarities and differences that may in turn guide assessment and treatment. One specific aspect of expository writing performance to be discussed next pertains to syntactic and morphological abilities in students with language impairments and learning disabilities.

**Syntactic and morphological deficits in expository writing**    Newcomer and Barenbaum (1991) conducted a review of the published literature from 1980 to 1990 that pertained to the written composing ability of children with learning disabilities. They reviewed 30 articles (15 narrative and 15 expository) that were either research studies or discussions of research-based instructional procedures involving school-age children and college students with learning disabilities. The authors presented an analysis of the story-composing ability of children with learning disabilities, the expository writing ability of individuals with learning disabilities, and the response of students with learning disabilities to writing training and practice. Seven of the expository discourse studies (Blair & Crump, 1984; Gajar, 1989; Houck & Billingsley, 1989; Moran, 1981; Morris & Crump, 1982; Vogel, 1985; Vogel & Moran, 1982) examined the syntactic maturity of essays produced by students with learning disabilities who ranged in age from 9 years to college age. A frequent finding across these studies was a higher rate of spelling, grammatical, and punctuation errors for students with learning disabilities. The persistence and frequency of punctuation errors in children with language impairments and LLD may also signify problems at a deeper linguistic level than what is implied when punctuation difficulties are described as problems with surface "mechanics" (Scott, 1995). In the three studies that examined fluency and vocabulary usage (Gajar, 1989; Houck & Billingsley, 1989; Morris & Crump, 1982), students with learning disabilities were found to be deficient on various criteria used to measure these aspects of writing (e.g., number of different words, number of sentences, number of words with seven letters). Espin and Sindelar (1988) found that middle school students with learning disabilities were less able to correct syntactic errors in an expository essay under two conditions (i.e., reading the essay and listening to it being read) than their reading-matched peers and their normally achieving peers.

Although the literature examining syntactic abilities in the expository writing of children with language impairments is somewhat sparse, Scott (1995) concluded that the syntactic problems encountered by school-age children with language impairments appear to be problems of degree rather than kind. For example, Wong, Wong, and Blenkinsop (1989) found that students with learning disabilities wrote expository essays that were less interesting and less clear, contained fewer well-chosen words, and contained more mechanical errors (particularly spelling) as compared to their typically developing peers. Sentence complexity via embedding and subordination is a particularly vulnerable syntactic area in school-age children with language impairments (Scott, 1995). When errors occur, they tend to occur more frequently in complex sentences, and they are even more significant in the written mode.

Results reported by Scott and Klutsenbaker (1989) also support the idea that writing places an extra burden on children with language impairments when producing complex sentences. They compared spoken and written versions of four narrative and informational summaries (two of each type), produced by an 11-year-old child with a language impairment and an age-matched control. In three of their four comparisons, written summaries produced by the child with the language impairment contained proportionally fewer complex sentences as compared to the child's spoken summaries. In contrast, in three of four comparisons produced by the age-matched control, the written version contained a higher percentage of complex sentences than the spoken version. In the fourth comparison, a narrative written text was found to be less complex than a spoken text. Scott (1995) noted, however, that written language may be more complex than spoken language for some children with language impairments.

Inflectional morphology also remains problematic for school-age writers (Rubin, Patterson, & Kantor, 1991; Windsor et al., 2000). Windsor et al. (2000) investigated the use of verb and noun morphology in school-age children's written language. Twenty 10- to 12-year-old children with LLD, 20 CA-matched peers, and 20 7- to 10-year-old LA-matched peers produced two written language samples as well as two spoken samples with one narrative and one expository sample (i.e., descriptive text structure) in each modality. The language samples were summaries of two 15- to 20-minute educational videotapes: the narrative video was about a boy who wanted to be a fisherman, and the expository video was a description of animal and plant life in the desert. A comparison was made between the children's accuracy in using morphemes that mark verb finiteness (regular past tense, third-person singular present tense, copula, and auxiliary BE) and their accuracy in using noun morphology (regular plural, possessive, articles). Results indicated that the CA children had mastered the verb and noun morphology in both the spoken and the written samples, while the children with LLD mastered these only in the spoken samples. These children had considerable difficulty in the written samples with the regular past tense as well as difficulty with the regular plural, and all errors were omissions of these morphemes. However, it is important to note that data from both the expository and the narrative discourse samples were combined because of the low error rate, so it is not possible to determine if there were differences in grammatical skill across these discourse contexts. There is a clear need to evaluate children's written language skills since it was the written language samples that differentiated performance in children with and without LLD, and the consequences of persisting grammatical errors in writing should not be underestimated.

In short, essays written by students with language impairments and LLD are characterized by a higher rate of spelling, grammatical, and punctuation errors as compared to those written by their typically developing peers. Students with learning disabilities exhibit significant deficits in the areas of fluency and vocabulary usage, and they tend to be less able to correct syntactic errors in written essays. Their expository essays are less clear and interesting and contain fewer well-chosen words as compared to those written by their typically developing peers. Likewise, children with LLD have higher error rates in verb and noun morphology in written narrative and expository summaries. Writing has been found to place an extra burden on children with language impairments in their production of complex sentences as compared to their spoken language. Furthermore, written language samples appear to differentiate syntactic and morphological abilities in children with and without LLD to a much greater extent than spoken samples. The use of expository text structures in written compositions is discussed next.

**Use of text structures in expository writing**    Newcomer and Barenbaum (1991) described several studies by a group of cooperating authors (Englert, Raphael, Fear, & Anderson, 1988; Englert & Thomas, 1987; Englert et al., 1989; Thomas, Englert, & Gregg, 1987) that examined the use of text structures in expository writing. In the Englert and Thomas (1987) study, difficulties with using text structure when writing, as well as problems comprehending material, were evident in their participants with learning disabilities (grades 3–4 and 6–7). The Englert et al. (1989) study expanded on these results by demonstrating that a relationship existed between the poor comprehension and production of expository text structures by students with learning disabilities (grades 4–5) and their metacognitive knowledge about the writing process.

Thomas et al. (1987) stressed the importance of expository writing in upper elementary, middle school, and high school classrooms. They noted that successful expository writing requires sensitivity to informational text structures and an ability to predict or organize ideas on the basis of one's knowledge of the topic. These investigators described three specific difficulties inherent in expository discourse for young writers: (a) the structures of expository discourse are often unfamiliar, variable, or poorly defined; (b) the writer must demonstrate a knowledge of various types of expository discourse structures and have facility in signaling text structure and relationships through the use of key signal words and phrases (Meyer et al., 1980); and (c) the writer is required to continually hold in memory at least two chunks of information (i.e., memory of the text structure and the intention of the whole text and memory of the preceding utterance) in order to prevent various types of writing problems (Bereiter & Scardamalia, 1984). Children as young as 5 or 6 years can produce sustained and coherent narratives (Bereiter & Scardamalia, 1984), yet they have been found to have a working memory capacity to store only one chunk of information while carrying out another mental operation (Case, 1974). Based on this fact, these researchers inferred that it must be possible to meet the minimal demands of narrative discourse with only this amount of processing capacity, although they acknowledge that exactly how this is possible is not clear.

Thomas et al. (1987) examined the expository writing errors of three groups of students. The groups consisted of (a) 36 students with learning disabilities (grades 3–4 and 6–7), (b) 36 regular education students who were matched to the students with learning disabilities according to IQ and reading ability but had not been referred for special education services, and (c) 36 students who were normally achieving. All the students with learning disabilities also exhibited receptive or expressive language abilities below mental age expectations. Half these students with learning disabilities were third and fourth graders, while the other half were sixth and seventh graders. Errors were categorized according to various types of text structure difficulties (e.g., redundancies, early terminations, irrelevancies, key words) as well as according to general mechanical or syntactic difficulties. A writing measure was used that consisted of eight paragraph stimulus stems with two stems for each of four text structures (i.e., description, sequence, comparison, and enumeration). Paragraph stems consisted of two sentences that indicated the topic of the paragraph, signaled a specific type of text structure, and provided an exemplar detail sentence that fulfilled topic and text structure requirements (see Table 7.2). Topics were selected from elementary school science and social studies materials. The participants were told that they would be given the beginnings of paragraphs and needed to finish the paragraphs by writing at least two sentences closely related to the topic indicated.

Results indicated that students with learning disabilities did exhibit quantitatively and qualitatively different writing performances than normally achieving students and, to a lesser extent, the regular education students matched for IQ and reading ability. The students with learning disabilities

**Table 7.2**   Sample Paragraph Stems for Expository Text Types

| Text Type | Examples |
|---|---|
| Description | a.  Elephants are found in Africa and India. Elephants are large animals that can weigh over 1 ton. |
|  | b.  Mosquitoes are pesky, funny-looking bugs. Mosquitoes are small, less than half an inch in length. |
| Sequence | a.  To make a sandwich, you have to complete several steps. First, you buy the food. |
|  | b.  Birds build nests in several steps. First, they locate a place for a nest. |
| Comparison | a.  Babies are different from adults. Babies can't feed themselves, while adults eat with knives and spoons. |
|  | b.  Dogs look very different from birds. Dogs have noses; birds have beaks. |
| Enumeration | a.  Animals are used in many different ways. People who live in the desert use camels for transportation. |
|  | b.  There are many ways to travel across town. One girl used her bike to get to school. |

*Source:* Modified from Thomas, C. C., Englert, C. S., & Gregg, S., *Remedial and Special Education, 8,* 21–30, 1987.

produced a greater number of four types of errors (redundancies, irrelevancies, early terminations, and mechanical errors) than the normally achieving students, and they produced more early terminations and mechanical errors than the regular education students matched for IQ and reading ability. They found that the students with learning disabilities tended to approach writing as more of a question-and-answer task and either used a "knowledge telling strategy" (i.e., pouring out any information that comes to mind without concern for its relevance) (Bereiter & Scardamalia, 1984; Brown, Day, & Jones, 1983) through their early terminations or responded with short, choppy phrases with mechanical errors that answered the question but did not result in a well-formed composition. The types of errors made by students varied according to text structure (e.g., errors in using key words and redundancies occurred more often with compare/contrast writing, and irrelevancies and early termination occurred more frequently with enumeration writing). The compare/contrast discourse structure tended to be the most difficult for the students, supporting the results of previous investigations (Englert & Hiebert, 1984; Raphael et al., 1986). Likewise, Ward-Lonergan et al. (1998) found that expository lectures organized according to a causation discourse structure were easier to comprehend at an inferential level than those organized according to a compare/contrast structure.

However, in contrast to the findings of the studies cited previously, the compare/contrast text structure was most closely related to better overall performance, as compared to the explanation text structure, for all participants in the Englert et al. (1989) study. In this study, a total of 138 students in fourth and fifth grades (i.e., 46 high-achieving, 46 low-achieving, and 46 with a learning disability) wrote two compositions organized according to a comparison/contrast text structure (i.e., compare and contrast two different people, places, or things that they knew about) and an explanation text structure (i.e., explain how to do something they were familiar with or knew about). These researchers found that the compare/contrast text structure resulted in better organized compositions, whereas the explanation text structure resulted in greater written productivity. Likewise, Richgels et al. (1987) also found that the compare/contrast text structure was related to better written composition abilities than the causation structure. Therefore, results are mixed regarding how various types of text structures support or hinder language performance, and thus specific instructional goals (e.g., improving organization vs. improving linguistic productivity) may be facilitated by using certain types of expository text structures more than others.

In short, several investigations have demonstrated that successful expository writing depends on sensitivity to informational text structures and an ability to predict or organize ideas on the basis of one's knowledge of the topic. Expository writing is particularly challenging for young writers for a variety of reasons as compared to narrative writing. Students with learning disabilities have been found to produce a greater number of errors, including redundancies, irrelevancies, early terminations, and mechanical errors, as compared to their peers with average achievement. Likewise, students with learning disabilities rely on an ineffective "knowledge-telling strategy" in their expository writing. Various expository text structures have also been found to be related to specific types of errors. Furthermore, results are mixed related to the level of difficulty of the compare/contrast structure versus the causation structure in composition writing. The effect of metacognitive knowledge about expository writing on students' performance is discussed in the next section.

**Metacognitive knowledge of expository writing**   Englert et al. (1988) examined the relationship between metacognitive knowledge about expository writing and writing performance in fourth- and fifth-grade students with learning disabilities, high-achieving students, and low-achieving students. Thirty students (10 in each group) served as participants. The students with learning disabilities had receptive or expressive language abilities below mental age expectations. All the students were interviewed regarding their knowledge about the expository writing process (planning, drafting, monitoring, editing, and revising text) and the role of text organization (e.g., processes related to categorizing ideas and those associated with text structure). The participants were interviewed through the use of three vignettes concerning the writing problems of three hypothetical children and were asked to give these children advice. In addition, all the participants were instructed to write two types of expository essays (i.e., compare/contrast and explanation). Results indicated that the students with learning disabilities were less aware of modeled writing strategies, steps in the writing process, strategies for presenting expository ideas, and procedures for selecting and integrating information from multiple sources than the high-achieving students. Across groups, the strongest relationship was found to exist between writing performance and the following metacognitive variables: awareness of modeled writing strategies, knowledge of processes related to monitoring the completeness of text, and categorizing abilities. The authors concluded that writing instruction should focus on developing students' metacognitive knowledge of the writing process and increasing their ability to generate, organize, and monitor their expository writing. Further research related to the relationship between metacognitive knowledge and expository writing is clearly needed to provide additional information involving different age-groups and expository discourse structures. In the next section, the importance of concept mapping in expository writing tasks is discussed.

**Effects of the use of concept mapping on expository writing performance**   Sturm and Rankin-Erickson (2002) conducted a treatment study that was designed to examine the effects of the use of two forms of "concept mapping" (also known as cognitive mapping, flowcharting, semantic mapping, semantic webbing, and graphic organizers), hand drawn and computer generated, on the descriptive essay writing performance of 12 eighth-grade students with learning disabilities. All these students had deficits in written expression, and eight had also been diagnosed with a speech/language impairment. Prior to writing instruction, all students wrote two baseline essays. Hand-drawn concept mapping was then taught during the first week of instruction in five 50-minute sessions, and computer mapping was taught in the second week in five 50-minute sessions to all students. The instructional procedures used in both conditions included strategy description, discussion of goals and purposes, modeling of the strategy, student mastery of strategy steps, and guided practice and feedback. On completion of the instructional program, students composed two descriptive essays (i.e., one essay each week for 6 weeks) when provided with written prompts (e.g., "Describe your dream home") under each of three conditions (i.e., a total of six essays per student): no-mapping support (no concept map provided), hand-mapping support (a hand-drawn, paper-and-pencil, concept map), and computer-mapping support (a computer-generated concept map created with Inspiration 4.0 software (Inspiration Software, 1988–1993). The essays were compared on four measures: number of words, syntactic maturity, number of T-units, and holistic writing scores.

Results indicated that student descriptive essays produced in the hand- and computer-mapping conditions demonstrated significant increases above baseline writing samples with regard to the number of words produced, the number of T-units produced, and the holistic scores of writing quality but not in the syntactic complexity of their sentence structures. However, students who participated in all three writing conditions wrote essays that were longer and of higher quality than they did prior to mapping instruction. The researchers stated that this improvement under the no-mapping condition may have been due to the constant questioning of students and the encouragement to expand ideas that all students received throughout the instructional program. The researchers noted that prior to instruction, the students tended to use the "knowledge-telling strategy" previously discussed. They also noted that their results support other research demonstrating that use of concept mapping as a prewriting strategy results in higher levels of text organization for typically developing students (Kaminski, 1993) and significant gains in the quality of writing for middle school students with learning disabilities (Zipprich, 1995). Generalization effects were observed in the no-mapping condition, which indicated that students may have acquired writing skills that carried over into their essay writing when not using maps. In addition, students' attitudes toward writing were found to be significantly more positive in the computer-mapping condition as compared to the no-mapping and hand-mapping conditions. It was concluded that strategy instruction paired with concept mapping as a prewriting strategy appears to be beneficial for middle school students with learning disabilities.

**Summary**  Expository writing is a challenging task for all students, but it is extremely challenging for students who have language impairments or LLD. Numerous specific difficulties have been revealed in their expository writing, including their lack of awareness of the structure of an expository paragraph, syntactic and morphological deficits, limited use of organizational text structures, and lack of metacognitive knowledge about the expository writing process. In reviewing these deficits, it becomes quite evident that these students will encounter difficulty when faced with expository writing tasks. The final section of this chapter summarizes the results of studies that have examined both expository reading and writing performance in these populations.

## Reading and Writing

**Metacognitive knowledge and use of expository text structure**
Metacognitive knowledge about text structures is an important phenomenon that can underlie and influence expository comprehension and composition (Gordon & Braun, 1985). However, research related to examining the performance of students with learning disabilities when instructed to both read and write expository text, as well as the potential impact of their metacognitive awareness of the types of information contained in expository text on reading/writing performance, is limited to date. Englert et al. (1989) investigated the extent to which students with and without learning disabilities adhered to text structures during composition and comprehension of expository text. These researchers examined expository reading and writing performance in 138 fourth- and fifth-grade students who were equally divided among three ability groups of high-achieving students, low-achieving students, and students with learning disabilities. All the students with learning disabilities were also described as having receptive or expressive language abilities below mental age expectations, which would be indicative of LLD. Three performance tasks were used that required students to (a) compose two types of expository texts (e.g., comparison/contrast, explanation), (b) read and recall these types of texts, and (c) write summaries using information from multiple sources. In addition, a subset of students was interviewed about their metacognitive knowledge of the organization of expository texts.

Although direct comparisons were not made between reading and writing measures, similar patterns of performance with no notable differences across these modalities were found for the students with learning disabilities. Specifically, the compositions of the students with learning disabilities were significantly less organized and contained fewer ideas than those written by the low- and the high-achieving students. The comprehension recalls of students with learning disabilities were also significantly less organized than the high-achieving students, and their recalls contained fewer ideas than those of both the low- and the high-achieving students. Examination of students' summaries of information from multiple sources suggested that students with learning disabilities produced significantly less well-organized summaries with fewer ideas than both the low- and the high-achieving students and that they also possessed less metacognitive knowledge about the expository writing process. In addition, students with learning disabilities performed significantly more poorly than other ability groups when they attempted to apply an organizational pattern to their own textual ideas in compositions or tried to construct an organizational pattern for summarizing information from multiple sources. They also generated fewer ideas on free writing measures when they wrote about their own chosen topics. These findings were consistent with other studies of written productivity and fluency in students with learning disabilities (Englert et al., 1988; Myklebust, 1973; Poplin, Gray, Larsen, Banikoski, & Mehring, 1980). On the other hand, students with learning disabilities performed more like low-achieving students (albeit poorly) when they were asked to recall textual ideas in well-organized and structured texts.

Another important finding pertained to the relative difficulty of the expository text structures in reading and writing tasks. Although some previous research has suggested that comparison/contrast was one of the more difficult text structures to comprehend and produce (Englert & Hiebert, 1984; Raphael et al., 1986), the Englert et al. (1989) study suggested that the comparison/contrast text structure resulted in the best-organized compositions and written recalls. This finding also supports previous research by Richgels et al. (1987). However, students produced significantly more ideas in their explanation compositions than they did in their comparison/contrast essays. The researchers concluded that if written productivity is the major instructional goal, then the explanation text structure might be easier for students to learn and produce than the comparison/contrast structure. On the other hand, if text organization is the major instructional goal, then the comparison/contrast text structure might be easier for the students to produce.

## CONCLUDING REMARKS

In conclusion, students with language impairments exhibit significant difficulty when required to listen to, verbally produce, read, and write expository discourse as compared to their typically developing peers. The serious negative consequences that result from these deficits cannot be underscored enough. This chapter presented a detailed, comprehensive picture of the nature of these expository discourse problems as demonstrated through the existing research in this area of investigation. Teachers and speech-language pathologists need to be keenly aware of these difficulties and strive to provide effective intervention aimed at addressing these deficits through direct instruction and the teaching of compensatory strategies. Through such efforts, students with language impairments will have a much greater likelihood of mastering the language of the curriculum, which is essential for achieving academic success.

# REFERENCES

Anderson, V., & Roit, M. (1993). Planning and implementing collaborative strategy instruction for delayed readers in grades 6–10. *Elementary School Journal, 94,* 121–137.

Applebee, A., Langer, J., Mullis, I., Latham, A., & Gentile, C. (1994). *NAEP, 1992 writing report card* (Report No. 23-W01). Washington, DC: Office of Educational Research Improvement, U.S. Department of Education.

Armbruster, B. B., & Anderson, T. H. (1982). *Producing considerate expository texts; or easy reading is damned hard writing* (Reading Education Report No. 46). Urbana: University of Illinois, Center for the Study of Reading.

Armbruster, B. B., & Anderson, T. H. (1988). On selecting "considerate" content area textbooks. *Remedial and Special Education, 9*(1), 47–52.

Beck, I. L., McKeown, M. G., Hamilton, R., & Kucan, L. (1998). Getting at the meaning: How to help students unpack difficult text. *American Educator, 22*(1 & 2), 66–71, 85.

Beck, I. L., McKeown, M. G., Sinatra, G. M., & Loxterman, J. A. (1991). Revising social studies text from a text-processing perspective: Evidence of improved comprehensibility. *Reading Research Quarterly, 26,* 251–276.

Bereiter, C., & Scardamalia, M. (1984, April). *Reconstruction of cognitive skills.* Paper presented at the annual meeting of the American Educational Research Association, New Orleans.

Bernhardt, E., Destino, T., Kamil, M., & Rodriguez-Munoz, M. (1995). Assessing science knowledge in an English-Spanish bilingual elementary school. *Cognosos, 4,* 4–6.

Blair, T., & Crump, D. (1984). Effects of discourse mode on the syntactic complexity of learning disabled students' written expression. *Learning Disability Quarterly, 7,* 19–29.

Bos, C. S., & Filip, D. (1984). Comprehension monitoring in learning disabled and average students. *Journal of Learning Disabilities, 17*(4), 229–233.

Brown, A. L., & Day, J. D. (1983). Macro rules for summarizing texts: The development of expertise. *Journal of Verbal Learning and Verbal Behavior, 22,* 1–14.

Brown, A. L., Day, J. D., & Jones, R. S. (1983). The development of plans for summarizing texts. *Child Development, 54,* 968–989.

Burke, J. (2000). *Reading reminders: Tools, tips, and techniques.* Portsmouth, NH: Boynton/Cook.

Case, R. (1974). Structures and strictures: Some functional limitations on the course of cognitive growth. *Cognitive Psychology, 6,* 544–573.

Copmann, K. S. P., & Griffith, P. L. (1994). Event and story structure recall by children with specific learning disabilities, language impairments, and normally achieving children. *Journal of Psycholinguistic Research, 23,* 231–248.

Daniels, S., & Zemelman, H. (2004). *Subjects matter: Every teacher's guide to content area reading.* Portsmouth, NH: Heinemann.

Danner, F. W. (1976). Children's understanding of intersentence organization in the recall of short descriptive passage. *Journal of Educational Psychology, 68,* 174–183.

Day, J. D., & Zajakowski, A. (1991). Comparisons of learning ease and transfer propensity in poor and average readers. *Journal of Learning Disabilities, 24*(7), 421–426, 433.

Denti, L., & Guerin, G. (1999). Dropout prevention: A case for enhanced early literacy efforts. *Clearing House, 72,* 231–235.

Dickson, S., Simmons, D. C., & & Kameenui, E. J. (1998). Text organization: Research bases. In D. C. Simmons & E. J. Kameenui (Eds.), *What reading research tells us about children with diverse learning needs* (pp. 239–277). Mahwah, NJ: Lawrence Erlbaum Associates.

Duke, N. K. (2000). 3.6 minutes per day: The scarcity of informational texts in first grade. *Reading Research Quarterly, 35,* 202–224.

Duke, N. K., Bennett-Armistead, V. S., & Roberts, E. M. (2002). Incorporating informational text in the primary grades. In C. M. Roller (Ed.), *Comprehensive reading instruction across grade levels: A collection of papers from Reading Research 2001 Conference* (pp. 40–54). Newark, DE: International Reading Association.

Duke, N. K., & Pearson, P. D. (2002). Effective practices for developing reading comprehension. In A. E. Farstrup & S. J. Samuels (Eds.), *What research has to say about reading instruction* (3rd ed., pp. 205–242). Newark, DE: International Reading Association.

Dull, L. J., & van Garderen, D. (2005). Bringing the story back into history: Teaching social studies to children with learning disabilities. *Preventing School Failure, 49*(3), 27–31.

Ehren, B. J. (1994). New directions for meeting the academic needs of adolescents with language learning disabilities. In G. P. Wallach & K. Butler (Eds.), *Language learning disabilities in school age children: Some principles and applications* (pp. 393–417). New York: Macmillan.

Engelmann, S., Carnine, D., & Steely, D. G. (1991). Making connections in mathematics. *Journal of Learning Disabilities, 24,* 292–303.

Englert, C. S., & Hiebert, E. H. (1984). Children's developing awareness of text structures in expository materials. *Journal of Educational Psychology, 76*(1), 65–74.

Englert, C. S., Raphael, T. E., Anderson, L. M., Gregg, S. L., & Anthony, H. M. (1989). Exposition: Reading, writing, and the metacognitive knowledge of learning disabled students. *Learning Disabilities Research, 5*(1), 5–24.

Englert, C. S., Raphael, T. E., Fear, K. L., & Anderson, L. M. (1988). Students' metacognitive knowledge about how to write informational reports. *Learning Disability Quarterly, 11,* 18–46.

Englert, C. S., & Thomas, C. C. (1987). Sensitivity to text structure in reading and learning: A comparison between learning disabled and non-learning disabled students. *Learning Disability Quarterly, 71,* 279–320.

Espin, C., & Sindelar, P. (1988). Auditory feedback and writing: Learning disabled and non-disabled students. *Exceptional Children, 55,* 45–51.

Fletcher, P. (1992). Sub-groups in school-age language impaired children. In P. Fletcher (Ed.), *Specific speech and language disorders in children* (pp. 152–182). San Diego, CA: Singular.

Francis, W., & Kucera, H. (1982). *Frequency of analysis of English usage: Lexicon and grammar.* Newton, MA: Allyn & Bacon.

Gajar, A. (1989). A computer analysis of written language variables and a comparison of compositions written by university students with and without learning disabilities. *Journal of Learning Disabilities, 22,* 125–130.

Gillam, R., & Johnston, J. (1992). Spoken and written language relationships in language/learning impaired and normally achieving school-age children. *Journal of Speech and Hearing Research, 35,* 1303–1315.

Gillam, R. B., Pena, E. D., & Miller, L. (1999). Dynamic assessment of narrative and expository discourse. *Topics in Language Disorders, 20*(1), 33–47.

Gordon, C. J., & Braun, C. (1985). Metacognitive processes: Reading and writing narrative discourse. In D. L. Forrest-Pressley, G. E. MacKinnon, & T. G. Waller (Eds.),

*Metacognitive, cognition, and human performance* (Vol. 2, pp. 1–75). New York: Academic Press.

Graesser, A., Leon, J. A., & Otero, J. (2002). *The psychology of science text comprehension.* Mahwah, NJ: Lawrence Erlbaum Associates.

Hadley, P. A. (1998). Language sampling protocols for eliciting text-level discourse. *Language, Speech and Hearing Services in Schools, 29,* 132–147.

Hall, L. A. (2004). Comprehending expository text: Promising strategies for struggling readers and students with reading disabilities? *Reading Research and Instruction, 44*(2), 75–95.

Halliday, M. A. K., & Hasan, R. (1976). *Cohesion in English.* London: Longman.

Hansen, C. L. (1978). Story retelling used with average and learning disabled readers as a measure of reading comprehension. *Learning Disability Quarterly, 1,* 62–69.

Houck, C., & Billingsley, B. (1989). Written expression of students with and without learning disabilities: Differences across the grades. *Journal of Learning Disabilities, 22,* 561–572.

Inspiration Software. (1988–1993). *Inspiration* (Ver. 4.0). Portland, OR: Author.

Irwin, J. W., & Baker, I. (1989). *Promoting active reading comprehension strategies.* Englewood Cliffs, NJ: Prentice Hall.

Ivey, G. (1999). A multicase study in middle school: Complexities among young adolescent readers. *Reading Research Quarterly, 34,* 172–192.

Kaminski, R. A., Lazar, M. K., & Bean, R. M. (1993, December). *Students' ability to apply and reflect on organizational structures used in composing.* Paper presented at the annual meeting of the National Reading Conference, Charleston, SC.

Langer, S. (1985). Children's sense of genre: A study of performance on parallel reading and writing tasks. *Written Communication, 3,* 157–187.

Langer, S. (1986). Reading, writing, and understanding: An analysis of the construction of meaning. *Written Communication, 3,* 219–267.

Lauer, K. D. (2002). *The effect of text structure, content familiarity, and reading ability on second-graders' comprehension of text.* Unpublished doctoral dissertation, Columbia University, New York.

Longacre, R. E. (1983). *The grammar of discourse.* New York: Plenum.

Mason, L. H., Meadan, H., Hedin, L., & Corso, L. (2006). Self-regulated strategy development instruction for expository text comprehension. *Teaching Exceptional Children, 38*(4), 47–52.

Meyer, B. J. F., Brandt, D. M., & Bluth, G. J. (1980). Use of top-level structure in text: Key for reading comprehension of ninth-grade students. *Reading Research Quarterly, 16,* 72–103.

Meyer, B. J. F., & Freedle, R. O. (1984). Effects of discourse type on recall. *American Educational Research Journal, 21,* 121–143.

Meyer, B. J. F., Theodorou, E., Brezenski, K. L., Middlemiss, W., McDougall, J., & Bartlett, B. J. (2002). Effects of structure strategy instruction delivered to fifth-grade children using the Internet with and without the aid of older adult tutors. *Journal of Educational Psychology, 94,* 486–519.

Moran, M. (1981). Performance of learning disabled and low achieving secondary students on formal features of a paragraph-writing task. *Learning Disability Quarterly, 4,* 271–280.

Morris, N., & Crump, W. D. (1982). Syntactic and vocabulary development in the written language of learning disabled and non-learning disabled students at four age levels. *Learning Disability Quarterly, 5,* 163–172.

Moss, B. (1997). A qualitative assessment of first graders' retelling of expository text. *Reading Research and Instruction, 37,* 1–13.

Myklebust, H. R. (1973). *Development and disorders of written language: Vol. 2. Studies of normal and exceptional children*. New York: Grune & Stratton.

National Center for Education Statistics. (2001, April). *The Nation's Report Card: Fourth-Grade Reading 2000*. Retrieved August 20, 2009 from http://nces.ed.gov/nations reportcard/pubs/main2000/2001499.asp

Neville, M. (1988). *Assessing and teaching language: Literacy and oracy in schools*. London: Macmillan Education.

Newcomer, P., & Barenbaum, E. (1991). The written composing ability of children with learning disabilities: A review of the literature from 1980 to 1990. *Journal of Learning Disabilities, 24,* 578–593.

Newkirk, T. (1987). The non-narrative writing of young children. *Research in the Teaching of English, 21,* 121–144.

Oakhill, J., & Yuill, N. (1996). Higher order factors in comprehension disability: Processes and remediation. In C. Cornoldi & J. Oakhill (Eds.), *Reading comprehension difficulties* (pp. 69–92). Mahwah, NJ: Lawrence Erlbaum Associates.

Pappas, C. C. (1993). Is narrative "primary"? Some insights from kindergarteners' pretend readings of stories and informational books. *Journal of Reading Behavior, 25,* 97–129.

Poplin, M. S., Gray, R., Larsen, S., Banikoski, A., & Mehring, T. (1980). A comparison of components of written expression abilities in learning disabled and non-learning disabled students at three grade levels. *Learning Disability Quarterly, 3,* 46–53.

Raphael, T. S., Englert, C. S., & Kirschner, B. W. (1986). *The impact of text structure instruction and social context on students' comprehension and production of expository text* (Research Series No. 177). East Lansing: Michigan State University, Institute for Research on Teaching.

Raphael, T. E., & Kirschner, B. M. (1985). *The effects of instruction in comparison/contrast text structure on sixth-grade students' reading comprehension and writing products* (Research Series No. 161). East Lansing, MI: Institute for Research on Teaching.

Richgels, D. J., McGee, L. M., Lomax, R. G., & Sheard, C. (1987). Awareness of four text structures: Effects on recall of expository text. *Reading Research Quarterly, 22,* 177–196.

Rubin, H., Patterson, P., & Kantor, M. (1991). Morphological development and writing ability in children and adults. *Language, Speech, and Hearing Services in Schools, 22,* 228–235.

Saenz, L. M., & Fuchs, L. S. (2002). Examining the reading difficulty of secondary students with learning disabilities: Expository versus narrative text. *Remedial and Special Education, 23,* 31–41.

Scarborough, H. S., & Dobrich, W. (1990). Development of children with early language delay. *Journal of Speech and Hearing Research, 33,* 70–83.

Scott, C. (1988). Learning to write: Context, form, and process. In M. Nippold (Ed.), *Later language development: Ages nine through nineteen* (pp. 49–95). San Diego, CA: College Hill Press.

Scott, C. (1994). A discourse continuum for school-age students: Impact of modality and genre. In G. Wallach & K. Butler (Eds.), *Language learning disabilities in school-age children and adolescents: Some underlying principles and applications* (pp. 219–252). Columbus, OH: Merrill/Macmillan.

Scott, C. M. (1995). Syntax for school-age children: A discourse perspective. In M. F. Fey & J. Windsor (Eds.), *Language intervention: Preschool through the elementary years* (pp. 107–143). Baltimore: Paul H. Brookes.

Scott, C., & Klutsenbaker, K. (1989, November). *Comparing spoken and written summaries: Text structure and surface form.* Paper presented at the annual convention of the American Speech-Language-Hearing Association, St. Louis, MO.

Scott, C. M., & Windsor, J. (2000). General language performance measures in spoken and written narrative and expository discourse of school-age children with language learning disabilities. *Journal of Speech, Language, and Hearing Research, 43,* 324–339.

Skarakis-Doyle, E., & Mentis, M. (1991). A discourse approach to language disorders: Investigating complex sentence production. In T. M. Gallagher (Ed.), *Pragmatics of language: Clinical practice issues* (pp. 283–305). San Diego, CA: Singular.

Stein, N. L., & Trabasso, T. (1981). What's in a story: An approach to comprehension and instruction. In R. Glaser (Ed.), *Advances in instructional psychology* (Vol. 2, pp. 213–267). Hillsdale, NJ: Lawrence Erlbaum Associates.

Sturm, J. M., & Rankin-Erickson, J. L. (2002). Effects of hand-drawn and computer-generated concept mapping on the expository writing of middle school students with learning disabilities. *Learning Disabilities Research & Practice, 17*(2), 124–139.

Taylor, B. M. (1980). Children's memory for expository text after reading. *Reading Research Quarterly, 15*(3), 399–411.

Taylor, B. M., & Samuels, S. J. (1983). Children's use of text structure in the recall of expository materials. *American Educational Research Journal, 20*(4), 517–528.

Thomas, C. C., Englert, C. S., & Gregg, S. (1987). An analysis of errors and strategies in the expository writing of learning disabled students. *Remedial and Special Education, 8,* 21–30.

Torgesen, J. (1980). Conceptual and educational implications of the use of efficient task strategies by learning disabled children. *Journal of Learning Disabilities, 13,* 364–371.

Tyack, D. (1981). Teaching complex sentences. *Language, Speech, and Hearing Services in Schools, 12,* 49–56.

Vogel, S. (1985). Syntactic complexity in written expression of LD college writers. *Annals of Dyslexia, 35,* 137–157.

Vogel, S. A., & Moran, M. (1982). Written language disorders in learning disabled college students: A preliminary report. In W. Cruickshank & J. Lerner (Eds.), *Coming of age: The best of ACLD* (Vol. 3, pp. 137–157). Syracuse, NY: Syracuse University Press.

Ward-Lonergan, J. M. (2001, April). *Curriculum-based language intervention for older children and adolescents.* Paper presented at the annual convention of the California Speech-Language-Hearing Association, Monterey, CA.

Ward-Lonergan, J. M., Liles, B. Z., & Anderson, A. M. (1998). Listening comprehension and recall abilities in adolescents with language-learning disabilities and without disabilities for social studies lectures. *Journal of Communication Disorders, 1,* 1–32.

Ward-Lonergan, J. M., Liles, B. Z., & Anderson, A. M. (1999). Verbal retelling abilities in adolescents with and without language-learning disabilities for social studies lectures. *Journal of Learning Disabilities, 32*(3), 213–223.

Wechsler, D. (1974). *Wechsler Intelligence Scale for Children—Revised.* New York: The Psychological Corporation.

Westby, C. (1991). *Steps to developing and achieving language-based curriculum in the classroom.* Rockville, MD: American Speech-Language-Hearing Association.

Williams, J. P., Hall, K. M., & Lauer, K. D. (2004). Teaching expository text structure to young at-risk learners: Building the basics of comprehension instruction. *Exceptionality, 12*(3), 129–144.

Williams, J. P., & Taylor, M. B., & deCani, J. S. (1984). Constructing macrostructure for expository text. *Journal of Educational Psychology, 76,* 1065–1075.

Windsor, J., Scott, C. M., & Street, C. K. (2000). Verb and noun morphology in the spoken and written language of children with language learning disabilities. *Journal of Speech, Language, and Hearing Research, 43,* 1322–1336.

Wong, B. Y. L. (1980). Activating the inactive learner: Use of questions/prompts to enhance comprehension and retention of implied information in learning disabled children. *Learning Disability Quarterly, 3,* 29–37.

Wong, B. Y. L. (2000). Writing strategies instruction for expository essays for adolescents with and without learning disabilities. *Topics in Language Disorders, 20*(4), 29–44.

Wong, B., Wong, R., & Blenkinsop, J. (1989). Cognitive and metacognitive aspects of learning disabled adolescents' composing problems. *Learning Disability Quarterly, 12,* 300–322.

Wynn-Dancy, M. L. (2001). *Working memory in adolescents with language-learning disabilities: The effects of prior knowledge and presentation rate on the recognition and recall of expository text.* Unpublished doctoral dissertation, University of Texas, Austin.

Zipprich, M. A. (1995). Teaching web making as a guided planning tool to improve student narrative writing. *Remedial and Special Education, 16*(1), 3–15.

## STUDY GUIDE QUESTIONS

1. With respect to listening comprehension and verbal production of expository discourse, school-age children and adolescents with language-learning disabilities typically
   a. exhibit adequate listening comprehension but inadequate verbal production of expository discourse.
   b. exhibit adequate verbal production but inadequate listening comprehension of expository discourse.
   c. produce expository retellings that are shorter and less complex than those produced by their typically developing peers.
   d. produce expository retellings that are longer but less complex as compared to those produced by their typically developing peers.
2. Some of the specific deficits that have been found in reading comprehension of expository text in school-age children and adolescents with language-learning disabilities include
   a. difficulty with phonemic awareness and poor phonics skills.
   b. lack of understanding of basic episode structure and poor narrative abilities.
   c. lack of familiarity with content-specific or technical vocabulary and difficulty applying reading comprehension strategies appropriately.
   d. poor visual discrimination and visual memory skills.

3. One of the major reasons why expository writing is particularly challenging for students with language-learning disabilities is due to
   a. their limited knowledge of various types of expository discourse structures and key signal words/phrases.
   b. their limited knowledge of the story grammar discourse structure.
   c. their difficulty using time-based experiences as the primary tool for organizing expository writing.
   d. their difficulty interpreting motivations of characters accurately.
4. Emerging readers typically
   a. have no awareness of expository discourse after listening to a textbook passage read to them.
   b. have some awareness of expository discourse but cannot recall content from a textbook passage read to them.
   c. have some awareness of expository discourse and can recall content from a textbook passage read to them.
   d. have no exposure to expository texts in their school settings and to recall expository content after listening to a textbook passage.
5. Some of the key cohesive signal words/phrases for the causation (cause-and-effect) expository discourse structure include
   a. "in contrast," "nevertheless," and "whereas."
   b. "for example," "such as," and "to illustrate."
   c. "first," "next," and "finally."
   d. "as a result," "because," and "consequently."

## CHAPTER 8

# Assessing Expository Texts Produced by School-Age Children and Adolescents
## *Cheryl M. Scott*

Expository text is pervasive throughout the school day of children and adolescents. Informational text[*] is heard, read, spoken, and written on most school days by most students. Expository writing is the most common type of writing in elementary and secondary curricula (Graham & Perin, 2007). The chief commodity in school is information, the content embodied in expository text. As students learn about history, science, geography, or government, they are being educated about the natural world we inhabit and the institutions that form the social fabric of life. These informational transactions occur seamlessly across modalities where connections are the rule rather than the exception. Thus, students are commonly asked to summarize in writing information that they have heard or read, and after doing so, it may be apparent that they need to search for additional material to read. Expository discourse is also prominent in home and social contexts outside of school in discussions of sports, social relationships, likes and dislikes, and analyses of events; in these contexts, informational discourse and personal narratives are

---

[*] The terms *informational* and *expository* are used synonymously throughout this chapter. The terms *text* and *discourse* are also used as synonyms to mean a unit of language composed of more than one sentence where the content coheres across sentences.

often seamlessly interwoven (Berman & Nir-Sagiv, 2007). It is not surprising, then, that the topic of assessing how well (or poorly) expository text is comprehended and produced by students is of great interest and relevance for language clinicians, teachers, special educators, parents, and district/state/federal bodies charged with assessing student learning.

This chapter explores the assessment of expository text with an emphasis on production (speaking and writing). The distinction between production and comprehension is somewhat artificial because production by nature reflects comprehension, and indeed writing is frequently used as a *test of comprehension* (Moffett, 1988). With that caveat, the emphasis on production here is also in part a reflection of the production emphasis in the extant literature. In all probability, this imbalance reflects the practical reality that production processes are more easily captured in a written product compared to comprehension processes, which are less transparent.

In the first section, expository writing assessed as part of national- and state-level writing assessments is examined. Regrettably, assessments of oral expository text production have not been instantiated at the national or state level, even though state educational standards in the area of language arts typically address all modalities (reading, writing, listening, and speaking). Student writers are commonly asked to produce several samples of writing, one of which is informational (the others are typically narrative and persuasive). In the second section, "Expository Test Assessment in Individuals and Small Groups," tests and protocols used with children and adolescents who struggle with spoken and/or written language as well as commonly used measures in developmental research are explored. Following a review of the limited ways of testing expository writing in norm-referenced tests, the topic turns to the use of language samples as a means of exploring expository speaking/writing, including the types of tasks that have been used and the measures calculated from these samples. A variety of measures at word (lexical), sentence, and discourse levels are described and also examined for what they do and do not reveal about expository skills.

## EXPOSITORY TEXT ASSESSMENT AT THE NATIONAL AND STATE LEVELS

In countries and states that have large-scale writing assessments in place, more than one type of writing is usually evaluated. Expository writing is almost always one (of three or four) type of text assessed.* This section is organized around two topics. To illustrate the structure of these types of tests generally and expository writing assessment specifically, writing is explored in the National Assessment

---

* Although the concern in this chapter is limited to expository writing and the specific examples are restricted accordingly, obviously the broader structure of these assessments applies to the other types of writing assessed (usually narrative and persuasive), as does the discussion of reliability and validity issues surrounding these assessments.

of Educational Progress (NAEP), the major national-level assessment of writing in the United States. Then state-level writing assessments are discussed. Often these are similar to the NAEP system, but several important differences across states are addressed. Given the time and monetary resources required for such large-scale testing programs, it comes as no surprise that there is a hearty debate in scholarly, professional, and lay public circles about the structure, function, and effects of such assessments.

## Expository Writing Assessment on the NAEP

Writing capabilities of elementary and secondary students have been assessed periodically at the national level in the United States since the establishment in 1969 of the NAEP, also called the Nation's Report Card, under the auspices of the U.S. Department of Education. Broadly described, the writing assessment is one of several domains assessed at regular intervals; others include reading, mathematics, science, history, geography, civics, economics, foreign languages, and the arts. The implementation of national assessments was in response to widespread debate about the state of education in the United States in light of declining performance on college entrance exams as well as unfavorable comparisons with students from other developed countries. Although reading and mathematics are assessed at least every other year, writing has been assessed less frequently; in the past 15 years, writing was assessed in 1992, 1998, 2002, and 2007. The sample size is substantial. In 2002, more than 270,000 students in 44 states were assessed for writing ability. In 2007, another 167,900 students (only eighth and twelfth graders) took the writing test (National Center for Education Statistics, 2008).

Three general types of writing (narrative, informative, persuasive) are assessed on the NAEP at grades 4, 8, and 12 in impromptu, or *on-demand*, writing formats.[*] The intent is that the exam is broadly experiential rather than narrowly content based. Students are not able nor are they expected to prepare in a specific content domain; rather, they are expected to compose material "on the spot," drawing from their experiences. For example, in 2002, one 12th-grade informative writing prompt asked students to write an essay discussing a book they would choose to save for future generations. The setup for this prompt was a science fiction scenario where people are not allowed to read books and some take it on themselves to memorize a book so that it can be preserved for future generations. An example of a fourth-grade informative writing prompt in 1998 was one in which students learned that a televised educational series for teenagers was being planned. Given a choice of several topics (e.g., women in history, great cities of the world), the writer was to choose one of the listed topics and compose a letter to the network president describing the proposed content of an episode. Formats for informational

---

[*] In the 2011 writing framework document (National Assessment Governing Board, 2007), the term used to capture the impromptu nature of the task is "on-demand" writing.

writing have included letters, reports, and reviews. Prompts could include visual (charts, graphs, photographs) as well as verbal input. Students are given 25 minutes to plan and write a piece, and each student writes two (of the three) tasks (e.g., informative and narrative). The fact that informational writing prompts are *not* tied to any specific content domain is, of course, at the heart of the debate about their validity, as is shown later.

Trained readers assign a holistic score on a 6-point scale (only one score for each text) based on rubrics that address content, organization, and language parameters. Based on established cutoff criteria, the text is placed into one of four achievement categories: below basic, basic, proficient, and advanced. The NAEP reports results separately by state, gender, and race/ethnicity but does not disaggregate data for genre. For the 2002 assessment, the NAEP reported that only 24% of 12th graders wrote at or above a proficient level; comparable numbers for eighth and fourth graders were 31% and 28%, respectively (Persky, Daane, & Jim, 2003). The NAEP provides examples of student informational writing with associated scores and critiques.

The National Assessment Governing Board (NAGB) of the NAEP assumes responsibility for the content and design of the NAEP writing assessment. A document detailing the framework adopted by the NAGB is published several years in advance of a scheduled assessment year. The framework for the next scheduled writing assessment in 2011 details several major changes on the horizon (NAGB, 2007). These include the following:

- Eighth- and 12th-grade students will write on computers rather than paper and pencil. They may use commonly available word processing tools. This change reflects the reality that a large majority of individuals use computers for writing in secondary schools, higher education, and the workplace and that the technology used to write becomes an integral part of the writing process.
- Changes in prompts and instructions are planned that "encourage writers to move beyond prescriptive or formulaic approaches in their writing" (NAGB, 2007, p. 9) and to take on more responsibility for making rhetorical choices when writing to a specific audience. Students will get to choose the format (e.g., a letter *or* an essay) that they think would be most effective for the assigned audience and scenario. The new format is motivated by the desire to provide students with prompts that are more motivating and transparent with respect to real-world writing situations. Again, three types of writing prompts will be used, but two of the three use different labels: to persuade, to explain (formerly "informative"), and to convey experience (formerly "narrative"). Specific to our interest in exposition, writing to explain is defined as that which presents "information and ideas to others in a manner that aids understanding of the topic" (NAGB, 2007, p. 30). What the writer is asked to explain will vary with age. In fourth grade,

students might be asked to explain a domain of personal knowledge (e.g., write a letter for a new student explaining what your school is like). A possible prompt for eighth graders might be to write a piece for a time capsule predicting what life might be like (students are given examples of possible trends) or to compare two events or ideas. Identifying the causes of a problem or explaining a concept could be assigned to a 12th-grade writer (e.g., explain what elements make a good community).

- Another major change slated for 2011 is that analytic as well as holistic results will be reported. A subset of student writing will be examined at a deeper level that includes how students actually develop ideas, rhetorical flexibility offered by the prompts, style choices, and level of language complexity, including word choice and sentence length (NAGB, 2007). One anticipated outcome is the ability to more closely link the content and form characteristics of writing to overall quality ratings provided in holistic scores.

## Expository Writing Assessment at the State Level

Although the origins of state writing assessments differ, some based on educational policy and others mandated by state legislatures, the ostensible purpose of writing assessment in most states is to test how well writing standards are being met. In the 49 states with established writing standards, there is considerable variation in specificity. Some states describe broad standards that cross grades and content areas, while others have numerous standards at each grade (Isaacson, 2004). As a result, it should not be surprising to find considerable variability in assessment protocols. With funding from the Spencer Foundation, George Hillocks and colleagues set out to capture the variation in state-mandated writing assessments and the consequent effects on the teaching of writing (Hillocks, 2002). He studied writing assessment protocols in five states, chosen because they offered some variation across several key parameters and also for their geographic diversity. The states were Texas, Kentucky, Illinois, Oregon, and New York.

State testing programs have frequently been called "high-stakes" tests because of significant penalties for individual students, teachers, schools, and districts that can result from low scores. Hillocks found differences among the states in terms of how high the stakes actually were. Thus, in Texas and New York, writing assessments can affect the graduation status of a student, but this is not the case in Illinois, where, instead, schools with low scores are put on a watch list. The five states had substantially different variations of on-demand writing. The most impromptu of the protocols was in Illinois, which allotted 40 minutes for the writer to respond to a prompt. In contrast, Oregon students wrote over the course of 3 days, and New York writers composed three essays, one of which was in response to literature read outside of class. Oregon was in the process of adding a portfolio assessment component to its system when Hillocks published his results; Kentucky already had a well-developed portfolio component where student essays over the course of a year were assessed. Of interest, expository writing, compared to other genres, received the most emphasis in New York.

Assessment protocols followed by the states for scoring essays, particularly for on-demand texts, were typically similar to that used in the NAEP. For example, the ISAT Writing Rubric, used for evaluating expository writing in fifth grade in Illinois (Illinois State Board of Education, 2008), requires the evaluator to assign a score from 1 (lowest) to 6 (highest) in each of five parameters: focus, support, organization, integration, and conventions. As may be obvious from these labels, discourse-level content, elaboration, and text structure features are emphasized in this system, and word- and sentence-level features receive less attention. At the highest level (a score of 6), these five parameters are described using 23 bulleted points, only four of which address word- and sentence-level features, as follows:

- Word choice enhances specificity (under Support).
- Varied sentence structure produces cohesion (under Organization).
- Minor errors in usage and sentence formulation may occur (under Conventions).
- A variety of sentences is evident (under Conventions).

Educational assessments serve as a measure of educational accountability and have frequently been a source of controversy in political as well as educational arenas. Writing assessments are no exception. Of note, it is only within the past several decades that large-scale assessments have measured writing directly in the sense that students are asked to actually write at the text level (i.e., in units of language larger than a sentence). Such assessments have been promoted as a more valid way of assessing writing without sacrificing reliability. In addition, text-level assessments are purported to align more directly with writing standards and, it is hoped, with the teaching of writing and the critical thinking at its core (Ketter & Poole, 2001). In light of these high expectations and the considerable resources involved in collecting and evaluating thousands of texts, it is understandable that researchers have been interested in validity issues.

Hillocks (2002) went beyond describing variability in his five-state survey and asked whether and how the assessments actually aligned with writing standards and how the assessment protocol adopted affected the teaching of writing. To answer these questions, he interviewed 390 teachers and examined assessment rubrics as well as examples of "benchmark" writing texts used in training evaluators. The results of his analyses would not assuage the fears of those who question the content validity of these assessments. According to Hillocks, only two states (Oregon and Kentucky) assessed writing in a way that was consistent with their writing standards and in ways that went beyond form to encompass content and critical thinking. Other states employed rubrics that failed to address the consistency, logic, or relevancy of bits of information offered as "evidence." When "teaching to" the rubrics becomes a major focus of classroom writing instruction, "vacuous" writing can result (p. 114). Hillocks was also distressed about assessment systems where texts were shipped cross-country to firms whose evaluators must meet stringent speed requirements (sometimes only 1 minute per essay). At the risk of oversimplifying Hillocks's research, the cumulative picture he paints is that impromptu, on-demand writing assessments fall short of being a true partner with standards for good writing and best practices in the teaching of writing. If, like Hillocks, we view the process of producing an expository text as a process of inquiry, thinking, "mulling" something over, and having sufficient knowledge of a topic to be able to analyze it critically before being able to explain it to someone else (see chapter 3 in this volume), research into the validity of impromptu assessments should continue.

Transitioning from a discussion of expository writing assessment at the state and national levels to assessment of individuals and smaller groups, it is necessary to point out a fundamental difference in approach. As shown previously in the example from Illinois, large-scale assessments typically score texts on four to six dimensions or scales, the majority of which capture global content and organization features. By comparison, assessment protocols for developmental research and for clinical uses with individuals have concentrated on the linguistic characteristics of texts rather than content (for a discussion of the distinction between *local* linguistic usage on the one hand and thematic content and *global* discourse organization on the other, see chapter 5 in this volume). The sheer numbers of texts that must be evaluated in large-scale assessments, in the thousands, has undoubtedly influenced the development of scoring rubrics in terms of choices of scales and features described under each scale. Perhaps content-related characteristics of texts lend themselves to holistic decisions/rating more than structural (linguistic form) features. It may be easier to form a holistic impression of how an essay "provides sufficient support for the main premise" than for its "use of appropriate connectives for explicit signaling of logical relations."

## EXPOSITORY TEXT ASSESSMENT IN INDIVIDUALS AND SMALL GROUPS

When the focus is on how well an individual or a small group of speaker/writers manage expository text, other assessment options are available. In this section, expository writing is approached from the perspective of the clinician or teacher interested in assessing a particular student to see how well the individual compares with age peers or classmates. The discussion should also be valuable for researchers studying groups of children or adolescents. One approach is to compare a student to age or grade peers on a norm-referenced test. A more common assessment strategy is descriptive analysis of language samples. When the focus is on one student or a classroom or a group of research participants, there is more time to pursue finer-grained quantitative and/or qualitative analyses of the resulting texts.

## Expository Assessment in Norm-Referenced Tests

Norm-referenced tests, by definition, are instruments that compare an individual to age peers. In the development stage, such tests are administered to large numbers of individuals followed by item analyses and calculations of reliability and validity. Some tests are designed to be comprehensive in the sense that there are multiple subtests that address several components of language (e.g., vocabulary and grammar) in both comprehension (receptive) and production (expressive) modalities. Other tests are specific to a single domain or component of language, for example, listening comprehension for sentences or spelling. Taking into consideration both types of language tests (general or specific) commonly used with school-age children and adolescents, discourse-level language features are rarely assessed (compared to word- and sentence-level features), writing is rarely assessed (compared to reading, listening, or speaking), and expository text is rarely assessed (compared to narrative text).

To illustrate, on the Clinical Evaluation of Language Fundamentals (4th ed.) (Semel, Wiig, & Secord, 2003), which tests oral but not written language, only one subtest (of 13) contains discourse-level language. On this subtest (Understanding Spoken Paragraphs), examinees listen to a short passage (four to six sentences) and answer questions about content. Of 11 different passages, 10 are short narratives, and only one is informational. To this author's knowledge, there is only one comprehensive language test that prompts expository discourse production. The Written Expression Scale of the Oral and Written Language Scales (Carrow-Woolfolk, 1996) contains six items that require writing in units longer than one sentence. There are three such items for examinees between the ages of 12 and 14 and three additional prompts at ages 15 to 21, as follows:

1. In two sentences, state reasons for a preference of a dog or cat (expository writing)
2. Summarize a historical story about a scout being lost (story retelling)
3. Write a note to a parent explaining how a cup was broken (functional writing)
4. Describe what a famous quotation means and whether you agree or disagree, using examples (descriptive writing)
5. Describe a new cartoon character (animal, machine, or person) that you have created for a contest (descriptive writing)
6. Write a paragraph based on information in table form about monthly book reading by fifth- and ninth-grade boys and girls (functional writing)

All prompts except in item 2 would seem to elicit a form of expository writing (the terminology shown in parentheses are labels in the test manual). Texts written in response to these prompts are not expected to be long (one prompt says to write two sentences), but if texts shown in the manual as scoring illustrations are representative, they are typically five sentences or slightly longer. Responses are assigned points (0, 1, and in some cases 2) for conventions (e.g., capitalization and punctuation), linguistics (e.g., modifiers, complex sentences), and content (meaningful content, supporting ideas, coherence).

Two domain-specific tests prompt language at the discourse level, but both elicit narratives. On the Test of Written Language (3rd ed.) (TOWL-3; Hammill & Larsen, 1996), children are given 15 minutes to write a story in response to a scene picture (e.g., people in spacesuits exploring an extraterrestrial terrain). A recently published discourse-level test, the Test of Narrative Language (Gillam & Pearson, 2003) asks children to demonstrate both listening comprehension and oral production of narrative text built around the scenario of action in a fast-food restaurant.

Although word- and sentence-level tasks on norm-referenced tests do not address expository text capabilities directly, it is probable that an individual's performance on at least some subtests that require manipulation of complex sentences would be positively related (Scott & Stokes, 1995). One sentence-level task, sentence combining, is such a candidate. Comprehending or producing expository discourse requires drawing logical connections between propositions in the form of offering reasons, making comparisons, stating exceptions, and so forth. To express such meanings, clauses are "packaged" (combined) together to form longer, complex sentences. Several norm-referenced tests have sentence-combining subtests that ask individuals to combine short sentences (from two to six) into one longer sentence. The TOWL-3 and the Test of Adolescent and Adult Language (3rd ed.) (Hammill, Brown, Larsen, & Wiederholt, 1994) are two examples of tests with sentence-combining subtests. Recent research reported that sentence combining is a linguistic/grammatical skill that shows developmental growth across the school-age years, relates to general language ability, and correlates significantly with sentence complexity in naturalistic text-level narrative writing (Scott, Nelson, Andersen, & Zielinski, 2006). The fact that a recent meta-analysis of common writing interventions showed positive effects of sentence-combining training on writing outcomes (Graham & Perin, 2007) provides additional evidence of an association with expository text production. This is one example of ways in which clinicians and researchers could pursue connections between a variety of linguistic skills assumed to be important in expository discourse, even when these skills are not tested in situ.

To date, then, with the few exceptions noted previously, expository text capabilities are not typically included in either comprehensive or more domain-specific, norm-referenced tests of language commonly use in education, clinical, or research settings. Language sample analysis, on the other hand, enjoys a long history of use in child language disorders as input that contributes important information for both diagnosis and intervention. The evaluation of expository language samples is addressed in the next section.

## Expository Assessment in Naturalistic Language Samples

Clinicians interested in comparing a naturalistic language sample, spoken or written, of a child or adolescent to developmental benchmarks can find a rich database summarized in the literature (e.g., Nippold, 2007; Scott, 1988, 2005; see also chapter 3 in this volume). Much of this information, however, is derived from adult–child interviews, as in Loban's (1976) early work on spoken language, or from narrative tasks (e.g., making up a story to go along with a wordless picture book). Similarly, the benchmark data provided with the widely used Systematic Analysis of Language Samples (SALT) (Miller & Iglesias, 2006), a software package for the analysis of naturalistic language samples, are based on conversation or narration. The underrepresentation of expository text in the developmental literature (this volume excepted) and the lack of expository benchmark data in language analysis software is troublesome for several reasons. The first is that by the mid-elementary years and beyond, as emphasized throughout this volume, expository text carries the load of informational content that consumes most of the school day. Another reason—but one not as well known—is the diagnostic sensitivity of expository text and written expository text in particular. As children with language impairments mature, they may appear to have acquired discourse skills on par with their age peers who are typically developing if engaged in an informal conversation, for example, a chat about their pets or friends or a recent experience. These types of texts do not require the complex language that is more characteristic of expository genres, as discussed in chapter 3 of this volume. Further evidence comes from direct comparisons of narrative and expository texts produced by children with and without language impairments (Scott & Lane, 2008; Scott & Windsor, 2000). In a comparison of four language samples that included narrative speaking, narrative writing, expository speaking, and expository writing, children with language impairments were least like their age peers on measures of sentence complexity when asked to write expository texts. Expository discourse, then, because of the conceptual and linguistic requirements entailed, is a good place to look for language impairments in children and adolescents.

**Effect of task and topic**    This relative neglect of informational language in the language disorder assessment literature creates challenges for clinicians and educators interested in developing assessment protocols for expository speaking and writing. The best preparation is a thorough understanding of the local (linguistic) and global (thematic and organizational) characteristics of expository texts, the subject of several chapters in this volume as well as this author's larger body of work in this area. The task is complicated, however, by the fact that informational language encompasses such a wide array of variation (e.g., descriptions, procedural instructions, editorials, critiques). Although it is possible to capture some general features of exposition at both local and global levels, the finer details will vary from one task/topic to another. To illustrate, if clinicians use the task of asking a child how to play a favorite game, as described in chapter 3, they will see a larger number of *if–then* adverbial clauses signaling the conditional nature of playing games (i.e., *if* [this] happens, then you need to …). Or, if the task is to discuss one's opinions about interpersonal conflict, as described in chapter 5, analysts would find many examples of modal auxiliary verbs (*can, may, might, should, will*) used along with timeless present forms of verbs (e.g., *may lead to, can negotiate*), indicating that a particular way of behaving in these situations of conflict may lead to alternative (perhaps better) outcomes. Other tasks and topics would show other semantic/syntactic propensities. This inherent variety in informational language should be taken into account when deciding on the task/topic for a language sample and, just as important, when interpreting results.

**Word-level assessments in expository text**   When evaluating expository texts, we are interested in whether vocabulary is sufficiently diverse, topic specific, and developmentally appropriate. Word-level measures can be quantitative or qualitative. One of the most widely used quantitative lexical measures in the development and disorders child literature is *lexical diversity*. The notion of lexical diversity relates to whether the speaker/writer uses a sufficient "store" of *different* words or, alternatively, are the same words used repeatedly. Lexical diversity has been operationalized in either of two measures: (a) number of different words (NDW: a count of the number of different words, usually word roots, in a sample) and (b) type–token ratio (TTR: a ratio of different words, or types, divided by total words, or tokens). Both measures are easily calculated by language analysis software. A major caveat in the use of either measure centers on the effects of sample size. NDW increases as sample size increases, so when comparing NDW of a particular sample with developmental data, sample size must be strictly controlled; otherwise, the comparison is spurious. TTR varies in the opposite direction. As sample size increases, TTR decreases because of the cumulative repetition of frequent, closed-class words (e.g., *a, the, this*). Genre and modality effects on lexical diversity are unclear. Scott and Windsor (2000) did not find differences in NDW when comparing narrative versus expository spoken and written language samples produced by school-age children, but their comparison samples were relatively short at 100 words, which may have decreased chances for finding differences. In my own clinical experience, it is not uncommon to find that narrative samples generated by children with language impairments differ significantly from comparisons with average data from same-age peers in the SALT reference database (Miller & Iglesias, 2006).* However, findings regarding the sensitivity of lexical diversity

---

* When comparing NDW in a sample of a particular child to reference database values for children of the same age, the program allows for the control of sample size (in either number of words or number of utterances).

measures for distinguishing children with/without language impairments or learning disabilities in several studies that have compared either narrative or expository texts or both are equivocal. For a more detailed analysis of the evidence for writing, see Scott (2009).

Qualitative observations about the lexical sophistication in an expository language sample can also be made reliably and are frequently revealing. A favorite exercise in my university classes about child language disorders is to ask students to circle any/all words in a language sample that they consider to be "higher level." The only definition provided of higher level is that such words are "more adult-like" and usually occur less frequently in the language. Without fail, class consensus is very high. Examples of such words are shown in Figure 8.1, which contains sentences excerpted from expository texts in a study by Scott and Windsor (2000) that compared narrative and expository writing and speaking in children with and without language impairments.* The age and language status of the speaker/writer, whether typically developing or specific language impairment (SLI), is shown for each sentence. Sentences with similar content have been grouped together. The italicized words are those that university students routinely circle as "higher level." The examples illustrate a paucity of higher-level words in sentences produced by children with SLI. *Water* in (1b) and (1c) is *moisture* in (1a), and *bite* in (1b) and (1c) is expressed as *steal* in (1a). The writer of (1b) uses the lower-frequency contrastive connective *regardless*. In (2a), the terminology *barren region* is a *hot and dry place* in (2b), and *shelter* in (3a) is expressed as *hole* in (3b). Further examples of the use of higher-level lexical items are italicized in the spoken expository texts reproduced in Figure 8.3 (also an informational summary of desert conditions and life).

In addition to searching for higher-level words that are specific to a particular topic, expository texts contain types of words that define the genre in a more general way. As described elsewhere in this volume, such texts deal with conceptual topics (facts, ideas, opinions about states of affairs). A thesis or topic is stated as a generalization, followed by qualifications, elaborations, or examples. Propositions are related logically by connections that signal

---

* These and subsequent examples used to illustrate assessment measures are drawn from a database of expository speaking and writing of elementary schoolchildren with and without specific language impairment (Scott & Windsor, 2000). Children were asked to summarize narrative and expository (descriptive) educational videos in both spoken and written form. Children with specific language impairment ($N$ = 20, mean age = 11 years, 5 months) were matched with children without the diagnosis ($N$ = 20, mean age = 11 years, 6 months) and with children at the same general language level who were younger ($N$ = 20; mean age = 8 years, 11 months). For purposes of clarity, spelling and punctuation errors have been corrected in written samples, and mazes (filled pauses, repetitions, and reformulations) have been eliminated from spoken samples. Work on this database is ongoing (Scott & Lane, 2008).

1a.  The plants *protect* themselves so animals don't *steal* the *moisture* from them. (TD, age 13 years, 2 months, spoken)
1b.  The reason they are *prickly* is to *protect* the water from thirsty animals/ but some animals bite through *regardless*. (TD, age 12 years, 1 month, written)
1c.  And on the cactuses they have spikes so that an animal would not come up and bite it to try and get its water out of the *ribs*. (SLI, age 12 years, 3 months, spoken)
2a.  The desert is a very *barren region*. (TD, age 13 years, 1 month, written)
2b.  The desert is a hot and dry place. (SLI, age 13 years, 6 months, written)
3a.  The animals have to hunt at night and stay in *shelter* or shade from the sun during the day. *Otherwise* they'll loose an *unnecessary* amount of water and *moisture*. (TD, age 13 years, 2 months, spoken)
3b.  But when it gets that hot they have to go in holes and stuff and like that. (SLI, age 13 years, 6 months, spoken)

**Figure 8.1**  Comparisons of lexical characteristics in excerpts from expository texts produced by children with and without language impairments. Words in italics are those identified as higher-level vocabulary by university students. TD, typically developing; SLI, specific language impairment. (From Scott, C., & Windsor, J., *Journal of Speech, Language, and Hearing Research, 43*, 324–339, 2000.)

condition, contrast, result, reason, and so forth. Sentences shown in Figures 8.1 through 8.4 contain many examples of such genre-specific vocabulary:

- Qualification, elaboration, comparison, illustration: *some* (animals), *many* (scenes), *most* (plants); *quite* (rare); *most of the time, sometimes, usually*; (animals) *like* (snakes)
- Adverbial connectives: *so* (that), *otherwise, regardless, but when, even though, unless*
- Explicit terms: (need thorns) *for many reasons, the reason* (they are prickly is)

Another feature of words in expository texts, no doubt related to the fundamentally different content, is their greater abstractness. Using a four-place ranking system, Berman and Nir-Sagiv (2007) demonstrated that nouns in expository texts are ranked at a higher level of abstractness (nonimageable, rare, low frequency) than those in narratives (concrete, imageable, specific people and objects). Sentences in Figures 8.1 through 8.4 include many words at higher levels of abstraction, including nonimageable words (e.g., *reason, amount, lives, variety, beginning*), words for higher categories (e.g., *vegetation, region, climate, ecosystem, herbivores*), and words for processes and events (*erosion, rainstorms, feast*).

Finally, beyond qualitative descriptions, there are several quantitative ways to capture higher-level vocabulary in expository texts. The connection between word length and word frequency is an inverse one. As length increases, frequency of use in the language decreases (Zipf, 1932). The length of words, then, operationalized as either the number of syllables or the number of characters (letters), is a good barometer of the use of higher-level vocabulary. Word processing applications typically calculate average characters per word in a text. Another approach is to use an online word frequency text profiler (e.g., Word Frequency Text Profiler [Edict, 2008]) that can be used to indicate words in a text that are/are not found in various word frequency lists, such as the 1,000 (or 2,000) most frequent words.

**Sentence-level assessments in expository text**   Because the sentence is a unit defined by grammatical rules, syntax is the main focus of sentence-level assessment; however, it is assumed that syntax is only the framework for semantic meanings encoded by words and groups of words and that these meanings should always be central in terms of what speaker/writers *do* with syntax. Hence, if syntax is a weakness for a child, meaning will automatically be a weakness as well. Syntactic units that operate at the following levels are all of interest:

- Word level (inflectional or derivational morphemes)
- Phrase level (noun phrase or verb phrase structure rules)
- Clause level (rules governing the types and order of clausal elements, e.g., subject–verb–object)
- Sentence level (rules for combining clauses in complex sentences)

Although none of these systems are unique to expository text, just as there are certain word-level propensities or preferences in expository text, the same is true at the sentence level. The sentence is also the "carrier" of grammatical cohesion systems that "make a text a text," for example, pronominal reference and ellipsis.

By the time students are routinely speaking and writing in expository formats (e.g., giving oral reports in school, answering essay questions on tests, offering opinions on controversial topics, providing explanations, summarizing information), they have typically mastered basic word, phrase, and clausal syntax. Morphosyntax is in place with correct obligatory markers for tense, aspect, agreement, and number. Basic clause structure is in place with verbs and obligatory arguments (subjects, objects) included. Clauses are being expanded with optional adverbial elements. At the sentence level, by the mid-elementary years, children are routinely combining clauses into complex sentences, and by the age of 10, writing has "caught up" with speaking in the sense that written sentences are generally as long, complex, and grammatically correct as those produced orally. By this age, children's writing even begins to take on a grammatical flavor that is different from spoken language (as summarized in Scott, 1988, 2005). Thus, by the time that a child is expected to produce expository discourse regularly, particularly in school, a major question is whether general sentence complexity has advanced to a level to support such texts.

Sentence complexity has been operationalized in child language literature in two ways. One measure is *average sentence length in words* (or mean length of T-unit [MLTU]),* a simple measure reflecting the fact that sentences become longer when syntactic elements are expanded or added. Thus, as pre- and postmodifiers are added to the head noun of a noun phrase (e.g., the head noun *game* in the noun phrase *the very last game of the season against Westside was …*), as clause elements such as optional adverbials are added (e.g., <u>yesterday</u> *the play opened* <u>to a full house</u> <u>in the restored theater</u>), and as clauses are combined, sentences obviously become longer. The other way to measure sentence complexity, *clause density*, focuses on clause combining and is a measure of the average number of clauses per sentence (this metric is also called the *subordination index*). Although average sentence length is easily calculated in language analysis software, clause density is usually coded manually.† Developmental benchmarks are provided for both measures in the SALT reference database but again only for conversational and narrative discourse. Both measures are featured in research reviewed in this volume (see chapters 3 and 7).

As with word-level measures, caveats also apply to the use of sentence complexity measures. Although developmental data show slow, steady increases in MLTU and clause density into young adulthood, both measures increase slowly, and standard deviations are large for age or language ability groups in cross-sectional studies. As a result, when interpreting the significance of either measure for an individual child or adolescent, one would need to be conservative about conclusions. Another problem is that both measures vary considerably depending on the genre. Typically, and of interest here, when compared with conversational discourse (Nippold, Hesketh, Duthie, & Mansfield, 2005) or narrative discourse (Scott & Windsor, 2000), sentences produced by school-age children and adolescents in expository texts are longer. A student may produce sentences of adequate length and complexity in conversational or narrative discourse, but this does not ensure competence in expository discourse. Further, by their very nature as global indexes, neither measure is transparent with regard to the specific structures that contributed to the sentence complexity. Two children could achieve the same value but in a different manner. To illustrate, one child could produce many nonfinite object complement clauses (e.g., he started *to gather his belongings*), and another could produce many relative clauses (e.g., the boy *who saw the accident* called the police). Both types of clauses would contribute equally to the clause density

---

* A T-unit stands for "terminable unit," defined as an independent clause with any attached dependent clauses. There is a methodological advantage of using T-units when segmenting monologic text into utterances, particularly when there is a tendency for clauses to begin with the word *and* (more common in narrative discourse). In the definition of a T-unit, clauses beginning with *and* (or other coordinating conjunctions) start a new T-unit, and the transcriber does not have to make (sometimes) arbitrary decisions about combining clauses into "compound" sentences. The T-unit was originally defined by Hunt (1965).

† Although automatic grammatical tagging programs have been used in child language analysis, accuracy is problematic at the complexity level needed for older children (Channell, 2003).

measure, but relative clauses are generally considered to be later developing and more indicative of a literate register (Diessel, 2004).

The lack of detail about sentence complexity provided by global measures has encouraged finer-grained analyses of the nature of clause combinations that are frequent in expository texts (Scott, 2004; Scott & Lane, 2008; Verhoeven et al., 2002; chapter 5 in this volume). There is consensus across these works that types of clausal subordination and embedding favored in expository discourse include adverbial clauses (particularly conditionals with *if* in the interpersonal conflict texts analyzed by Berman and colleagues), relative clauses, and nonfinite participial clauses.

Recently, Scott and Lane (2008) reported on structural features of sentences with three or more clauses in expository and narrative texts produced by school-age children. As children and adolescents develop their informational knowledge base and their interests (as with the chess players described in chapter 3), sentences used to communicate about these topics also expand. This type of clause-combining fluency requires multiple depths of subordination and coordination where some clauses are subordinate to clauses that are themselves subordinate clauses. In these types of complex sentences, the hierarchical, truly recursive nature of clause packaging is highlighted. Figure 8.2 illustrates this phenomenon

---

1. It <u>tells</u> about the quiet community that the deserts <u>have</u> even though, if you <u>visited</u> there you <u>wouldn't see</u> anything that well unless you <u>were examining</u> the holes in the ground or other stuff. (TD, age 12 years, 8 months, written)
   5 clauses, 2 levels of subordination
   - Matrix clause verb: TELLS
   - Level 1 verbs: HAVE (relative clause); WOULDN'T SEE (adverbial clause)
   - Level 2 verbs: VISITED (adverbial clause; WERE EXAMINING (adverbial clause)
2. It <u>ended</u> sort of <u>saying</u> that even though it <u>may look</u> like there <u>was</u> nothing <u>living</u> or moving around, there <u>were</u> animals that <u>could survive</u> living in a desert even though it <u>was</u> extremely hot and humid with not enough water sometimes. (TD, age 12 years, 8 months, written)
   10 clauses, 5 levels of subordination
   - Matrix clause verb: ENDED
   - Level 1 verb: SAYING (nonfinite participial, adverbial)
   - Level 2 verb: WERE (object complement)
   - Level 3 verbs: MAY LOOK (adverbial); COULD SURVIVE (relative)
   - Level 4 verbs: WAS (adverbial); LIVING (nonfinite object complement)
   - Level 5 verbs: LIVING (nonfinite object complement); MOVING (nonfinite object complement); WAS (adverbial)
   - Level 5 verbs: LIVING (relative, nonfinite); MOVING ABOUT (coordinated relative, nonfinite)

---

**Figure 8.2**  Two examples of complex sentences in excerpts from expository texts produced by a child with typical language development. Levels (depths) of subordination are shown for each example. (From Scott, C., & Windsor, J., *Journal of Speech, Language, and Hearing Research, 43*, 324–339, 2000.)

in two sentences excerpted from expository texts in this study (Scott & Lane, 2008). The first sentence combines five clauses (one matrix clause and four subordinate clauses), and there are two levels of subordination. The second example combines 10 clauses (one matrix clauses and nine subordinate clauses) and has five levels of subordination. These types of multiclausal sentences are common in adult informational texts where the *average* sentence has almost three clauses (Francis & Kucera, 1982). Clause combinatorial fluency of this type, if observed in an individual child or adolescent, would be another sign that sentence complexity needed for expository discourse is developing.

**Text-level assessments in expository text**    A recurring theme in this volume is that exposition is a broad term that includes many subgenres. Consequently, although one organizational template will not apply to all expository texts, the prototypical feature of expository text is its hierarchical, logical organization accomplished via a central, "core" proposition with subsequent elaboration by way of examples, counterexamples, delimiting features, and so forth. Developing the ability to produce this type of "thesis/support for thesis" text takes time; many researchers have shown that children tell (and write) well-structured narratives before they show comparable skills in exposition. Indeed, when young children (second grade or younger) do attempt to write informational text, it may be more like a "list" of sentences that could be rearranged without much if any impact on the meaning (Scott, 2005). In later elementary school years, however, children improve in their ability to express a central theme or point. Sentences that state a generalization, or a type of "true-for-all-time" proposition, occur at several points in the spoken text reproduced in Figure 8.3, notably at the beginning (1) and end (26) but also at several points in between in various degrees (4, 10, 14, 15, 16, 25). Clinicians may be interested in the fact that children with SLI produced significantly fewer such generalizations than age peers who were typically developing (Scott & Jennings, 2004). As illustrated in these examples, the ability to generalize with appropriate elaboration and support is a core text-level feature to evaluate in expository discourse.

Another text feature that is easily assessed is cohesion. An informational text written by a 9-year-old (Figure 8.4) contains an example of cohesion— either lexical cohesion, ellipsis, or conjunction—in almost every sentence (Halliday & Hasan, 1976). This child is very skilled in grammatical cohesion, which contributes to the overall coherence of his text.

A final line of inquiry is to ask whether the text meets basic productivity requirements. Did the individual say/write *enough* text to meet the requirements of the task, or was the text too short? Productivity can be quantified as a measure of total words or total utterances/sentences for the text, but the decision regarding adequacy is basically a judgment. Of note, productivity is one of the most robust traits that distinguishes texts produced by school-age children and adolescents with and without language impairments (Scott &

Example 1 (TD, age 13 years, 1 month, spoken)
The desert is an *ecosystem* where all animals and plants *rely* on each other.

Example 2 (TD, age 10 years, 2 months, spoken)
The desert is home to all kinds of plants and animals.

Example 3 (TD, age 12 years, 10 months, written)
1. The video I watched was about desert *vegetation* and desert animals.
2. It talks about *vegetation* first.
3. The saguaro cactus gets its water easier by its *wideness*.
4. In the desert it doesn't rain a lot so plants have to *adapt* to the weather just like the mesquite cactus does.
5. Its long root system can reach 30 meters down in the ground to reach that little bit of water.
6. The cactuses in the desert need thorns for many reasons.
7. One is that so animals that are *herbivores* don't come along and eat the plants.
8. But the plants are friends to some animals such as some birds.
9. It can make nests in the cactus to protect its eggs from animals like snakes that eat birds' eggs.
10. In the desert there is some water.
11. It is usually located in canyons.
12. There also *underground* water that are called oases.
13. You can tell where there is an oasis by a *variety* of plants in that area also by how many plants there are.
14. The desert may look *scarce*.
15. but it is home to many animals, such as, spiders, some birds, raccoons, pumas, snakes and insects.
16. All of these have to adapt to the *harsh* weather in the desert.
17. Some insects can blend in great with cactuses and other desert plants.
18. Spiders make webs and make holes in the ground for shade.
19. Many *predators* dig in the ground and look in *unusual* places in the ground.
20. Pumas find shade under big rocks.
21. Most plants in the desert have different ways of *surviving*.
22. One plant blooms when it becomes dry.
23. Some birds dig holes on the sides of cactuses for *shelter*.
24. The desert plants are *usually* very spread out so they can all *absorb* as much water as possible.
25. The desert is very hot.
26. but plants and animals can and do *adapt* to the strange climate.

**Figure 8.3**  Examples of statements classified as generalizations in excerpts from expository texts produced by children with and without language impairments. (From Scott, C., & Jennings, M., Paper presented at the annual meeting of the American Speech Language Hearing Association, Philadelphia, PA, November 2004.)

Windsor, 2000). Expository text is challenging for many students, particularly in the academic contexts where one of the most frequent assignments is to summarize what has been learned about a topic (Moffett, 1988). If, in addition to limited knowledge or understanding of a topic, a student lacks linguistic facility with the word-, sentence-, and text-level features of expository text described in this section, it is highly unlikely that he or she will produce a text that satisfies productivity expectations.

| | |
|---|---|
| 1. The sand, wind, and terrible heat make the desert's beginning. | |
| 2. As the heat increases, many lives of plants are scarce. | Lexical cohesion: *heat* (from previous T-unit) |
| | Conjunction: via adverbial connective *as* |
| 3. And as for the landscape, the desert might be one of the most spectacular scenes. | Conjunction: via adverbial connective *as for* |
| 4. Many scenes are created by erosion. | Lexical cohesion: *scenes* |
| 5. Some may be created by wind, or even water! | Ellipsis: *some [scenes] may ...* |
| 6. Even though the erosion may take place very slow, even unnoticed, it still has an effect. | Conjunction: *even though* |
| | Lexical cohesion: *erosion* |
| 7. Water is quite rare. | |
| 8. But most is underground. | Conjunction: *but* |
| | Ellipsis: *most [water] is ...* |
| 9. Still rainstorms are still here, and still give water. | Conjunction: *still, and* |
| | Ellipsis: *and [rainstorms] still give ...* |
| | Lexical cohesion: *water* |
| 10. But most of the time the rain gives out water in short but very large bursts. | Conjunction: but |
| | Lexical cohesion: *rain, water* |
| 11. Now with a fresh supply of water, life goes on. | Conjunction: *now* |
| | Lexical cohesion: *water* |
| 12. With enough water, plants bloom. | Lexical cohesion: *water* |
| 13. Animals now enjoy a small but rare feast. | Conjunction: *now* |

**Figure 8.4** Examples and description of cohesion in a written expository text (summary of a video film about the desert) from the author's files. The writer (age 9 years, 6 months) is in a program for gifted children at his school. The first 13 T-units are shown here; the text continues for another 20 T-units.

**A general note on age and language ability benchmarks for expository text** Interpretation of the significance of all these measures and observations, for any one student, requires that we consult a developmental research base. There is no doubt that a classroom teacher, with years of experience reading informational papers of students, would have developed valuable insights. Clinicians and educators should also consult the developmental language literature; regrettably, compared to the developmental literature on narrative discourse, there is a paucity of research on the range and details of expository discourse development. However, the collective works of two groups of researchers, Berman and her colleagues and Nippold and her colleagues, much of it reviewed in this volume, provide us with a rich store of data to build on.

Of note, both research groups have reported on a developmental range that spans the years between late elementary school through young adults. Their data confirm that the span of growth in expository text production is wide, beginning in the early elementary years and continuing into young adulthood. Even young elementary schoolchildren provide evidence of intergenre differentiation when narratives are compared to expository texts

(Berman & Nir-Sagiv, 2004, 2007). Further, cross-linguistic research from the project described in chapter 5 has shown that the developmental growth curves of various features of expository text are not all linear across the entire age span under study. For example, age effects for lexical diversity, length, and density were significant for the comparison of students at ages 13 and 17 but not at 10 and 13 years or at age 17 and young adults (Strömqvist et al., 2002). Another indication of the fact that there may be developmental windows for various measures was reported recently by Scott and Lane (2008), who found that clause density at ages 11 to 12 was greater for narratives than for expository text. This finding may reflect the greater overall combinatorial fluency for narrative discourse *at this age*; the comparative advantage on this measure is unlikely to hold at older ages.

To bring this discussion to a close, consider once more the case of the student with specific language impairment. Even if granted an accommodation of more time to produce an on-demand informational essay, it is unlikely that this student's informational writing would be highly rated in either a state or a national large-scale assessment. Scott and Windsor (2000) included a group that was matched on general language ability in addition to age-matched controls in their study of expository and narrative discourse in school-age children with SLI. The average age of participants with SLI was 11 years, 6 months. On almost every word, sentence, and text measure, these children were indistinguishable from the children who served as language-matched controls who were, on average 2 years, 5 months, younger. Will students with SLI be able to close this gap over time? Will the gap widen even further? We now appreciate that the developmental growth period for expository text is a long one for all individuals and that expository discourse is a language domain with greater sensitivity for distinguishing levels of language ability. As assessment tools discussed here enjoy wider use among clinicians, educators, and researchers, our ability to facilitate positive growth in expository discourse for individuals who struggle to inform, explain, and generalize about the world will, it is hoped, benefit as well.

## REFERENCES

Berman, R. A., & Nir-Sagiv, B. (2004). Linguistic indicators of inter-genre differentiation in later language development. *Journal of Child Language, 31,* 339–380.
Berman, R. A., & Nir-Sagiv, B. (2007). Comparing narrative and expository text construction across adolescence: A developmental perspective. *Discourse Processes, 43*(2), 79–120.
Carrow-Woolfolk, E. (1996). *Oral and Written Language Scales.* Circle Pines, MN: American Guidance Service.
Channell, R. (2003). Automated Development Sentence Scoring using Computerized Profiling Software. *American Journal of Speech Language Pathology, 12,* 369–375.
Diessel, H. (2004). *The acquisition of complex sentences.* Cambridge: Cambridge University Press.

Edict. (2008). *Word Frequency Text Profiler*. Retrieved July 3, 2008, from http://www.edict.com.hk/textanalyser

Francis, W., & Kucera, H. (1982). *Frequency analysis of English usage: Lexicon and grammar*. Boston: Houghton Mifflin.

Gillam, R. B., & Pearson, N. (2004). *Test of narrative language*. Austin, TX: PRO-ED.

Graham, S., & Perin, D. (2007). A meta-analysis of writing instruction for adolescent students. *Journal of Educational Psychology, 99*(3), 445–476.

Halliday, M. A. K., & Hasan, R. (1976). *Cohesion in English*. London: Longman.

Hammill, D., Brown, V., Larsen, S., & Wiederholt, J. (1994). *Test of Adolescent and Adult Language* (3rd ed.). Austin, TX: PRO-ED.

Hammill, D., & Larsen, S. (1996). *Test of Written Language* (3rd ed.). Austin, TX: PRO-ED.

Hillocks, G. (2002). *The testing trap: How state writing assessments control learning*. New York: Teachers College Press.

Hunt, K. (1965). *Grammatical structures written at three grade levels* (Research Report No. 3). Champaign, IL: National Council of Teachers of English.

Illinois State Board of Education. (2008). *ISAT Writing Rubric—Grade 5 Expository*. Retrieved June 23, 2008, from http://www.isbe.state.il.us/assessment/pdfs/Grade_5_Expository_Rubric.pdf

Isaacson, S. (2004). Instruction that helps students meet state standards in writing. *Exceptionality, 12*(1), 39–54.

Ketter, J., & Poole, J. (2001). Exploring the impact of high-stakes direct writing assessment in two high school classrooms. *Research in the Teaching of English, 25*, 344–393.

Loban, W. (1976). *Language development: Kindergarten through grade twelve*. Urbana, IL: National Council of Teachers of English.

Miller, J., & Iglesias, A. (2006). Systematic Analysis of Language Transcripts (SALT), English and Spanish (Version 9) [Computer software]. Madison: University of Wisconsin, Language Analysis Lab.

Moffett, J. (1988). *Coming on center: Essays in English education* (2nd ed.). Portsmouth, NH: Heinemann.

National Assessment Governing Board. (2007). *Writing framework for the 2011 National Assessment of Educational Progress, pre-publication edition*. Retrieved February 19, 2008, from http://www.nagb.org/publications/frameworks/2011naep-writing-framework.doc

National Center for Education Statistics. (2007). The nation's report card: Writing 2007. Retrieved August 16, 2009, from http://nces.ed.gov/nationsreportcard/pdf/main2007/2008468.pdf

Nippold, M. (2007). *Later language development: School-age children, adolescents, and young adults* (3rd ed.). Austin, TX: PRO-ED.

Nippold, M. A., Hesketh, L. J., Duthie, J. K., & Mansfield, T. C. (2005). Conversational versus expository discourse: A study of syntactic development in children, adolescents, and adults. *Journal of Speech, Language, and Hearing Research, 48*, 1048–1064.

Persky, H., Daane, H., & Jin, Y. (2003). *The nation's report card: Writing 2002*. Washington, DC: U.S. Department of Education.

Scott, C. (1988). Spoken and written syntax. In M. Nippold (Ed.), *Later language development: Ages 9 through 19* (pp. 45–95). San Diego, CA: College Hill Press.

Scott, C. (2004). Syntactic ability in children and adolescents with language and learning disabilities. In R. Berman (Ed.), *Language development across childhood and adolescence* (pp. 111–134). Philadelphia: Benjamins.

Scott, C. (2005). Learning to write. In H. Catts & A. Kamhi (Eds.), *Language and reading disabilities* (2nd ed. pp. 233–273). Boston: Pearson.

Scott, C. (2009). Language-based assessment of written expression. In G. Troia (Ed.), *Writing instruction and assessment for struggling writers: From theory to evidenced-based principles* (pp. 358–385). New York: Guilford Press.

Scott, C., & Jennings, M. (2004, November). *Expository discourse in children with LLD: Text level analysis.* Paper presented at the annual meeting of the American Speech Language Hearing Association, Philadelphia, PA.

Scott, C., & Lane, S. (2008, June). *Capturing sentence complexity in school-age children with language impairments.* Paper presented at the annual meeting of the Society for Research in Child Language Disorders, Madison, WI.

Scott, C., Nelson, N., Andersen, S., Zielinski, K. (2006, November). *Development of written sentence combining skills in school-age children.* Paper presented at the annual meeting of the American Speech Language Hearing Association, Miami, FL.

Scott, C., & Stokes, S. E. (1995). An analysis of syntax norms for school-age children and adolescents. *Language, Speech, and Hearing Services in Schools, 25,* 309–319.

Scott, C., & Windsor, J. (2000). General language performance measures in spoken and written narrative and expository discourse in school-age children with language learning disabilities. *Journal of Speech, Language, and Hearing Research, 43,* 324–339.

Semel, E., Wiig, E., & Secord, W. (2003). *Clinical Evaluation of Language Fundamentals* (4th ed.). San Antonio, TX: Harcourt Assessment.

Strömqvist, S., Johansson, V., Kriz, S., Ragnarsdóttir, H., Aisenman, R., & Ravid, D. (2002). Toward a cross-linguistic comparison of lexical quanta in speech and writing, *Written Language and Literacy, 5*(1), 45–68.

Verhoeven, L., Aparici, M., Cahana-Amitay, D., van Hell, J., Kriz, S., & Viguié-Simon, A. (2002). Clause packaging in writing and speech: A cross-linguistic developmental analysis. *Written Language and Literacy 5*(2), 135–162.

Zipf, G. (1932). *Selected studies of the principle of relative frequency in language.* Cambridge, MA: Harvard University Press.

## STUDY GUIDE QUESTIONS

1. The expository writing task used most frequently by state and national student writing assessments is
   a. judging which of several essays is the best example of expository writing.
   b. writing a "how-to" (procedural) essay about a topic where the student has real expertise.
   c. writing several drafts of an essay about a topic covered in the school curriculum.
   d. writing for a limited time in response to a prompt that does not require mastery of specific content.
2. State and national writing assessments use trained evaluators who
   a. assign rating to several general traits, such as organization, conventions, and so on.
   b. assign one holistic rating to the essay as a whole.

    c.  measure particular features, such as sentence complexity in a quantitative manner.

    d.  assign a grade-level equivalent

3. The representation of comprehension and/or production of expository text in norm-referenced language tests highlighted in the chapter is best described as

    a.  substantially represented in comprehensive language tests.

    b.  represented in a few domain-specific tests.

    c.  comprehension being well-represented but production not.

    d.  writing production having limited representation on one comprehensive test.

4. Based on developmental benchmarks, clinicians and teachers should expect to see some degree of sentence complexity, advanced vocabulary, and grammatical form specific to expository text by

    a.  the early elementary years.

    b.  the late elementary years.

    c.  middle school.

    d.  high school.

5. Assessment of expository speaking or writing at the text level is complicated because there are several organizational schemes. Even so, the following textual feature is characteristic of most expository discourse:

    a.  Presence of setting statements

    b.  Presence of generalizations

    c.  Presence of a clear resolution

    d.  Presence of complex sentences

## CHAPTER 9

# Reading Comprehension and Expository Text Structure: Direction for Intervention with Adolescents

*Barbara J. Ehren*

Comprehension of expository text involves a complex set of processes. Recognizing many other factors that affect comprehension, Dickson, Simmons, and Kameenui (1998b) emphasized the importance of attending to text organization for students they called "diverse learners," whom they defined as "students, who because of their instructional, experiential, sociolinguistic, linguistic, physiological, or cognitive backgrounds, differ in their instructional, and curricular requirements" (p. 241). Following their lead, this chapter focuses on teaching various aspects of expository text structure, including its strategic use by adolescents, as a productive direction for improving comprehension in struggling students. In an attempt to provide "considerate" text (see subsequent section for what this means), this introduction lists the questions that are addressed, along with the heading for that section of the chapter:

- Why is expository text comprehension so important to adolescents? ("Rationale")
- What components should intervention in expository text comprehension include? ("Direction for Intervention")

- What elements of text structure should be taught explicitly ("Teaching Text Structure Explicitly")
- How do practitioners teach adolescents to analyze text? ("Teaching Text Analysis")
- How do practitioners teach adolescents to use text analysis strategically? ("Teaching Strategic Use of Text Analysis")
- How should practitioners address differences in clarity of text presentation? ("Identifying and Structuring Inconsiderate Text" [Inconsiderate text is discourse that lacks organizational clarity.])

Note that we address the internal aspects of text and not external elements, such as figures, diagrams, text boxes, maps, charts, tables, and pictures, that might also assist comprehension.

## RATIONALE

Comprehension of expository text is an important focus for practitioners concerned about literacy acquisition and academic achievement in struggling adolescents for two major reasons: It is essential to school success, and it is difficult. Regarding its importance, reading expository text is the typical access route for subject area knowledge in middle and high schools. While reading narrative text in the form of stories is the mainstay of instruction in the primary grades, a shift occurs in fourth grade, where greater emphasis is placed on science and social studies learning (Barton, 1997; Hudson, Lignugaris-Kraft, & Miller, 1993; Lapp, Flood, & Farnan, 1989). An even greater demand is placed on students in middle and high school, where secondary teachers rely heavily on textbooks to teach content and where high-stakes tests to demonstrate mastery of standards increasingly focus on expository text. For example, the progression of focus on informational text can be seen on the reading portion of the Florida Comprehensive Achievement Test (FCAT) (Ehren, Lenz, & Deshler, 2004). In sixth grade, 50% of the reading is informational, rising to 60 % in seventh and eighth grades and to 70% in ninth and 10th grades. Correspondingly, on the FCAT writing test in eighth grade, students have to write to explain, and in 10th grade, they must write to convince, both requiring expository text structures (Florida Department of Education, 2005). Therefore, it is easy to see how students who struggle with comprehension of expository text fall further and further behind academically as they progress through the grades.

Regarding the difficulty of expository text for all students, several factors are relevant. Unfamiliarity is one. Students usually do not come to school with knowledge of expository texts, unlike narrative texts. Narratives are based on shared experiences and more familiar world knowledge, such as is involved with familiar oral stories, television programs, and movie formats (Graesser, Golding, & Long, 1991). Exposure to expository text occurs primarily during formal schooling. Unless students have been explicitly taught to process expository text, it is possible for them to reach secondary grades and still not know how to construct meaning successfully to meet their classroom learning demands.

Another factor is that expository texts are more varied across and within disciplines. Although discipline-specific texts share some similarities, they can differ in substantive ways (Grossman & Stodolsky, 1995). Therefore, students have to learn specific types of discourse for each of the academic disciplines, requiring great flexibility within a school day to comprehend what they read in all their classes. This demand is difficult enough for typically achieving students; imagine the burden on adolescents who struggle with reading. It is also true that any given textbook within a discipline may feature many different types of expository texts within the same chapter (Bakken, Mastropieri, & Scruggs, 1997). So, even within a single subject area, readers will have to deal with a variety of structures that may be difficult for them, frequently switching orientation to text while reading.

Complexity is another issue. Most secondary textbooks involve reading long passages (Bereiter & Scardamalia, 1987) with more complicated organizational patterns that represent differing relationships between important information, for example, general to particular relationships, as in definitions; object to object relationships, as in comparisons; and object to part relationships, as in cause and effect (Weaver & Kintsch, 1991). They are more demanding because they often are impersonal, deal with unfamiliar or abstract content, and are organized along logical rather than temporal dimensions (Culatta, Horn, & Merritt, 1998); in contrast, narrative text deals with event sequences that occur in everyday life (Graesser et al., 1991). Further, some discipline specific discourse demands might be more difficult than others (Graesser, Mills, & Zwan, 1997). For example, science text is loaded with technical terms, deals with complex mechanisms with multiple components, often relies on a mathematical language, and defies visualization without distorting the integrity of the content (Graesser, Leon, & Leon, 2002).

Another problem is that authors of textbooks tend to be experts in their respective fields and assume prior knowledge that novices typically do not have (Best, Rowe, Ozuru, & McNamara, 2005). This adds to the inferencing burden that students face. In general, inferencing is a key element to expository text comprehension. At best, even considerate texts (defined as those that are written and presented in ways to facilitate comprehension) do not state all the relevant information the reader will need to understand the text. However, when textbook authors assume more knowledge than is typical of the reader, inferencing demands escalate.

The conceptual density of expository text also makes it more difficult than narrative text (Taylor & Samuels, 1983). Consider the following sentence and note the number of important concepts it contains: "Stoichiometry is the branch of chemistry concerned with the ratios by atoms of the elements in compounds or with the ratios by formula units of the substances in chemical reactions" (Team 3659 ThinkQuest Contest, 1996). In order to make any sense of the definition of stoichiometry, one has to know "chemistry," "ratios," "atoms," "elements," "compounds," "formula units," "substances," and "chemical reactions." In addition to its conceptual density, this sentence contains unfamiliar combinations of vocabulary and phraseology—"ratios by atoms" and "ratios by formula units."

Closely tied to conceptual density is the issue of knowledge of technical vocabulary needed for comprehension, words that adolescents are unlikely to have encountered in nonacademic milieus, for example "quadratic" and "tessellation" in math, "colloidal" and "cytokinesis" in science, and "brink-manship" and "federalist" in social studies. Adding to the vocabulary problem is the tendency for unknown words to be multisyllabic and more difficult to decode (Armbruster & Nagy, 1993; Bryant, Ugel, Thompson, & Hamff, 1999), for example, "thermodynamics," "Pythagorean," and "manorialism."

As difficult as expository texts are for all students, they pose special problems for students with learning disabilities. Researchers have identified myriad difficulties students have when reading content area texts. For example, they exhibit difficulty distinguishing between relevant and irrelevant information, identifying main ideas, recognizing the interrelationships between main ideas, organizing information, and memorizing and retaining facts (Seidenberg, 1989). Negative consequences of these problems include (a) not learning the required content, (b) failure to pass high-stakes tests, (c) low self-efficacy, and (d) behavior problems (Hall, 2004).

## DIRECTION FOR INTERVENTION

Although researchers have paid much more attention to narrative than expository text, a growing body of literature points to promising practices in addressing the thorny issues involved in helping adolescents comprehend expository text. In a recent research synthesis, Gajria, Jitendra, Sood, and Sacks (2007) summarized findings of studies related to comprehension of expository text by students with learning disabilities. Although most of the studies included in their review involved middle school students and some high school students, they did not parse out results for adolescents specifically. They grouped interventions into two categories: those related to content enhancements (i.e., approaches used by teachers to support students' mastery of content presented in text) and those targeting cognitive strategy instruction (i.e., approaches that teach students to employ various methods to promote their independent comprehension of text). The 11 studies that met their criteria for inclusion in the review provided strong support for the use of content enhancements to aid comprehension of text, including use of various visual representations of key ideas and their relationships as well as mnemonic illustrations. It is important to note, however, that long-term outcomes were documented in only three studies. The results of 10 studies related to single cognitive strategies and eight studies involving multiple strategies provided evidence of the effectiveness of systematic strategy instruction.

Effective single interventions included text structure, cognitive mapping, identifying main ideas, paraphrasing, summarization, and self-questioning, among other strategies. Combined strategies included summarization with self-monitoring, identifying main ideas with self-monitoring, reciprocal teaching with other strategies, and collaborative strategic reading. Roughly one-third of the cognitive strategy studies in the Gajria et al. review assessed maintenance beyond posttest results and one-fifth addressed transfer. In their conclusions, they echoed the suggestion by Gersten, Fuchs, Williams, and Baker (2001) in their descriptive review of reading comprehension instruction for students with learning disabilities: While reading strategy instruction has demonstrable effects on comprehension, maintenance and transfer effects require further study. An important point regarding their findings is the limitation of content enhancement approaches. Although content enhancements do support content acquisition, their major drawback is the degree to which they foster dependence on the teacher; contrastively, the cognitive strategy approaches foster student independence in text processing.

The complexity of comprehension processes requires multifaceted intervention. Practitioners might consider the following targets, gleaned from oft-repeated recommendations in the comprehension instruction literature, to guide the building of adolescents' competencies in this area:

1. Make sure adolescents have strategies for decoding and understanding the meaning of discipline-specific vocabulary words. Also make sure they know more familiar words that teachers will presume they know from common knowledge, for example, "investigate" in science, "revolution" in history, and "parallel" in math.
2. Help adolescents activate prior knowledge in an efficient and effective way and to connect prior knowledge to new learning. Take inventory and remedy gaps in foundational concepts and principles on which new learning must be built.
3. Work specifically on identifying and formulating main ideas and separating essential from nonessential details, as these skills are foundational to any comprehension task.
4. Teach the process of inferencing as it relates to specific types of inferencing common to discipline-specific texts.
5. Teach adolescents expository text structure elements explicitly: macrostructures and accompanying frames, signaling devices, cohesive ties, and complex sentence structures to express relationships.
6. Teach adolescents how to analyze text on the basis of their knowledge of text structure.
7. Teach adolescents to use their knowledge of text structure strategically to improve their comprehension of expository text that may pose difficulty for them. Introduce structure to assist with comprehension and later teach them how to do that for themselves.

As important as all these elements are, it would be impossible to address intervention in all of them within this chapter. Therefore, we focus on the last four targets, involving text structure, that is, teaching expository text structure explicitly, teaching text analysis, teaching strategic use of text structure, and identifying and structuring inconsiderate text.

## TEACHING TEXT STRUCTURES EXPLICITLY

There is strong empirical evidence that readers' awareness of text structure is highly related to reading comprehension (Armbruster & Anderson, 1984; Block, 1993; Dickson et al., 1998b; Meyer, 1975; Slater, Graves & Piche, 1985; Taylor & Beach, 1984). Effective readers appear to use strategies linked to expository text structure awareness to process text information (Englert & Hiebert, 1984; Hiebert, Englert, & Brennan, 1983; Taylor & Beach, 1984). Students who are familiar with the way texts are typically organized can use that knowledge to understand and remember information (Pearson & Camperell, 1994; Williams, Brown, Silverstein, & deCani, 1994).

Research also suggests that many students with reading disabilities lack text structure awareness and have difficulty using textual cues (Englert & Thomas, 1987; Meyer, Brandt, & Bluth, 1980; Montague, Maddux, & Dereshiwsky, 1990; Wong & Wilson, 1984). They have difficulty using the author's organizational framework to guide and structure their attempts at comprehension. These problems affect their ability to use the interrelationships in text to predict forthcoming, relevant details based on the text structure and to extract essential from nonessential information. Students who have trouble with expository text are described by Blachowicz (1994) as "fact accumulators" because they try to remember every fact and detail without using structure to help them organize and find coherence.

What features of expository text do students need to know? There are many different categorization frameworks to address the teaching of organizational text patterns. We address content, macrostructure, signaling devices, cohesive ties, and sentence-level factors; that is, advice to practitioners is that it is important to teach students to understand content differences, to identify macrostructures, to pay attention to signaling devices, to utilize cohesive devices, and to attend to sentence-level factors in analyzing text.

## Content

Different text genres deal with different kinds of information, or content. Understanding the nature of the genre can help students understand the topics, themes, and levels of meaning of the material. For example, in a biology textbook, students can safely predict that they will be reading about anatomy and physiology, not causes of World War II. Another point about content is that information across genres may exist on a continuum of concrete to abstract. Concrete concepts represent objects or actions that have clear referents within the realm of personal experience. Abstract concepts are those that refer to ideas that are not perceptible or have not been experienced. Because the purpose of textbooks is to teach unknown content, one would expect them to be more abstract for students. To address content issues in texts, Culatta and Merritt (1998) suggest the following:

1. Make selections about which concepts will be highlighted and taught, which will be defined, and which will be bypassed. For example, in the selection shown in Figure 9.1 on global warming, a teacher might decide to highlight and teach the concepts of global warming and the greenhouse effect without focusing on how measurements in surface temperatures are taken.
2. Substitute familiar terms for abstract ones. For example, the first sentence in Figure 9.1 contains a definition of global warming in simple terms, that is, "the worldwide rise in surface temperatures." However, for some students, depending on their age and grade levels, the term "surface temperature" may have to be explained.
3. Explore the meanings of terms with simpler vocabulary. For example, "surface temperature" may be explained as "how hot or cold it is on the top of land or oceans."
4. Provide familiar, personalized examples of unfamiliar terms. Thus, a teacher might elaborate on the "rapid retreat of glaciers" by showing pictures of glaciers from a trip to Alaska.

---

In the simplest terms, global warming is just what it sounds like: the worldwide rise in surface temperatures. The National Academy of Science has put the rise at 1 degree F over the course of the 20th century, but measurements from satellites of both land and sea surfaces are showing that the rate of warming is increasing sharply.

It's more than just surface temperatures that are going up, however. Much research into temperature changes in the upper layers of the atmosphere, as well as the deep oceans, is showing warming. Then, there are the more obvious signs: the rapid retreat of glaciers in Greenland, Alaska, the Himalaya, the Antarctic Peninsula and on high tropical mountains; the thinning and disappearance of sea ice in the Arctic Ocean during summer; the melting of permafrost in Canada, Alaska and Siberia; and the rise of sea level and an increase in extreme weather.

The cause of global warming is what's called the "greenhouse effect." That is shorthand for the ability of gases in the atmosphere to slow down the release of heat into space at night. Some gases are better at this than others. Carbon dioxide, methane and nitrous oxide are the top three "greenhouse gases." They are very good at absorbing sunlight and converting that energy into heat – rather like a rock does just sitting in the sun. (O'Hanlon, n.d.)

---

**Figure 9.1.** Global warming text.

## Macrostructure

The top-level organizational pattern of text is often called a macrostructure, or text grammar. It involves the more global aspects of structure and reflects the shape of a text unit, such as a chapter. Westby's (1994) list provides a useful guide to teach students the specific text grammars that they will encounter in their textbooks:

1. Description: texts that tell the attributes or features of something
2. Enumeration: texts that give a list related to a topic
3. Sequence/procedure: texts that tell what happened or how to do something
4. Comparison/contrast: texts that show how two or more things are the same or different
5. Cause and effect: texts that give reasons for why something happened
6. Problem/solution: texts that state a dilemma and offer a remedy or remedies
7. Argumentation/persuasion: texts that take a position on some issue and justify it

Students need to know the structures of these patterns and how to recognize them. This is not an easy task. Even if the reader has prior knowledge of content covered in an expository text, that schema does not help one know the text grammar. For example, if you read the title "The Truth about Our Schools" in a newspaper editorial, even though you may be very familiar with education in your community, you would not know from your background knowledge what to expect from this newspaper article. It might describe a scandal, compare your educational system with another, or persuade you to support a school referendum in an upcoming election. Until you engage in reading it, insufficient cues may be present regarding the text grammar. Teaching students how to deal with macrostructures is addressed in the next two sections of this chapter.

## Signaling Devices

Signaling devices are text structures that clue the reader to the macrostructure and relationships among specific ideas. Evidence exists that making students aware of these patterns assists with comprehension (Seidenberg, 1989). Several different kinds of visual cues may be used in well-presented text as signaling devices. The first kind is an introductory paragraph organizer that cues the reader about a forthcoming pattern of information. An example of this device is this opening section of an online resource for biology students: "In this chapter, you will read about how seed plants reproduce. You will also read about the asexual reproduction of plants and how people have been able to produce and manipulate plants for practical uses" (Miller & Levine, 2006). Interestingly, this text does not appear in the print version of the text. Another example is the opening paragraph of this chapter.

The second kind of visual cue is the location of the topic sentence in a paragraph. It is common for it to appear first, as in this example from a history text:

> Relations between Indians and Europeans during the sixteenth and seventeenth centuries ran the spectrum from cooperation and accommodation to bitter conflict. Where the number of colonists was fewest, relationships were based on trade, and the Indians viewed the Europeans as potential allies, relations were friendliest. Where European numbers were greatest and their primary objective was Indian land or labor, relations were least friendly. By the early eighteenth century, however, it was already clear that friendly relations and cooperation would be the exception, since in areas as diverse as New Mexico, New England, Pennsylvania, and the Chesapeake Bay region of Virginia and Maryland, European colonizers were encroaching on Indian lands and radically disrupting the Indian ways of life.
>
> **Mintz, 2007**

The fact that the topic sentence is the first sentence orients you to what is to follow. It describes relations between Indians and Europeans as varied from cooperation to conflict. Subsequent sentences provide the details of relations and the conditions associated with the different types. Students who recognize the topic sentence can begin to relate the other information to it. However, students have to learn that a topic sentence will not always appear at the beginning of a paragraph and may be absent entirely.

Other signaling devices are headings and subheadings offset with a different font style. For example, if you were to read a subheading titled "Causes of Water Pollution," you would expect a cause-and-effect pattern. Other visual cues are signal words typically used with certain text grammars; for example, the macrostructure of enumeration often has phrases like "some examples are," "there are several," and "for instance." In a sequence/procedure pattern, signal words such as "first," "then," and "next" would be typical. Other examples of signal words are conjunctions used to link ideas; for example, words like "because" and "so" denote a causal relationship. Words that are underlined, in italics, or in boldface type present a visual cue in textbooks that they are important words in a chapter, often part of a targeted vocabulary list. Students need to be taught to note those cues and to act on them.

Also germane to expository genres is the use of authors' direct statements about the importance of an idea, like the following statement: "In order to understand the history of civil rights in the United States, you need to appreciate the role played by the ratification of the 14th Amendment." Students need to recognize that that kind of statement signals them to pay attention to that event as they continue to study.

## Cohesive Ties

Cohesive ties are linguistic devices that link structures so that ideas hang together. Text cohesion is built both within and between sentences. Cohesive ties can be chained in a sequence of immediate ties, or they can be remote, separated by one or more sentences. Conjunctions serve as cohesive ties as well as signal words. There are also other devices that provide cohesion. Examples include the following:

1. Reiteration, that is, saying the same words for clarity, for instance, "Jane couldn't take Sally with her because Jane had other plans." If we had not repeated "Jane" and used the word "she" instead, we would not have known whether "she" referred to Jane or Sally.
2. Collocation, or placing words in close proximity; for instance in the sentence, "The men worked with the dogs that were well-behaved," the fact that the clause "that were well-behaved" is positioned next to "dogs" indicates that the dogs and not the men were well behaved.
3. Reference, or correct use of pronouns, for instance, "he" in the sentence "Don got to the airport late, so he missed his plane."
4. Substitution, where the substitute word can point backward or ahead to new information, for example, "In dormancy the growth of a seed is suspended. This state allows a seed to survive for very long periods of time." The phrase "this state" refers back to dormancy.
5. Ellipsis, which is omission of one or more words presupposed from information in the preceding text, as in "The basketball game was a sellout. Some fans did not get to see the game." The word "basketball" is omitted as a modifier in the second sentence and presupposed from the previous sentence.

Understanding relations between sentences that have cohesive devices are among the higher-level linguistic and problem-solving skills required for text comprehension (Roth & Spekman, 1989). At the paragraph level, text can be made more or less cohesive by arranging and rearranging clauses and sentences. For example, in the Global Warming selection (see Figure 9.1) if the sentence "It's more than just surface temperatures that are going up, however" were to be moved (minus "however") to come after the sentence "A lot of research into temperature changes in the upper layers of the atmosphere, as well as the deep oceans, is showing warming," cohesion would be lost because the tie to the immediately preceding paragraph about surface temperature would be broken. It would read, "A lot of research into temperature changes in the upper layers of the atmosphere, as well as the deep oceans, is showing warming. It's more than just surface temperatures that are going up." The text flows better and makes much more sense with the first sentence order (as shown in Figure 9.1).

Teaching students to recognize and use cohesive ties can help with processing text. Specifically, cohesion assists with inferencing. If students can tie text together, they can apply text they have read to interpret text they are reading. For example, if a student reads in her biology book, "Meiosis... begins with a diploid cell but produces four haploid (N) cells. These cells are generally different from the diploid cell and from one another" (Miller & Levine, 2006, p. 278), she might be thinking, "I don't know what a diploid cell is." She will have to go back three pages in the book to find "A cell that contains both sets of homologous chromosomes is said to be **diploid**, which means 'two sets'" (Miller & Levine, 2006, p. 278). The fact that "diploid" was in boldface print will help her find that key word. Now she is also probably wondering what "homologous" means and may have to hunt for that meaning as well.

Most of the research on cohesive ties has focused on the effect of adding cohesive devices on comprehension, and, indeed, that technique does improve text understanding (Beck, McKeown, Sinatra, & Loxterman, 1991; Lehman & Schraw, 2002; Linderholm, et al., 2000). However, with students who may not recognize that cohesive devices exist, it seems prudent to teach them explicitly about these devices, to recognize them in text, and to manipulate meaning relying on them.

## Sentence-Level Factors

In addition to the cohesive ties that may occur at the sentence level, there are other sentence-level factors affecting reading comprehension. The complexity of individual sentences affects comprehension and recall (Bisanz, Das, Vanahagen, & Henderson, 1992). Processing difficulty increases as the propositions, or ideas within a sentence, increase, requiring higher-level syntactic forms (Bashir, Conte, & Heerde, 1998). Consider this example: "In the late 1950s, the Soviets successfully tested long-range rockets known as intercontinental ballistic missiles, or ICBMs, which for the first time could target locations in the United States" (Farah & Karls, 1997, p. 873). Similar to the approach noted previously with cohesive ties, research has addressed altering the semantic/syntactic complexity of sentences to improve comprehension. For example, Abrahamsen and Shelton (1989) found that simplifying sentences semantically and syntactically greatly improved comprehension of social studies text for adolescents with learning disabilities. However, an argument against such an approach in intervention is that the volume of reading materials in secondary schools would make simplifying text undoable. Further, it is possible that such simplification would distort the meaning of complex ideas (Otero, Leon, & Graesser, 2002).

Borrowing from Bulgren, Lenz, Marquis, Schumaker, and Deshler (2002), who taught adolescents to "unpack" questions to aid with in-depth comprehension of the information being requested, teaching students how to unpack the structures in a sentence, like the previous mentioned one, would seem to be a wise intervention target, especially for those with syntactic limitations. For example, a teacher or support professional might work with students to identify the kernel ideas conveyed by the syntactic structures in the previously mentioned sentence above: (a) the Soviets tested long-range rockets, (b) those rockets are also known as intercontinental ballistic missiles,

(c) intercontinental ballistic missiles are referred to as ICBMs, and (d) these rockets could hit places in the United States.

## TEACHING TEXT ANALYSIS

For proficient readers, text grammar serves as a frame or guide to help them identify important information and logical connections among ideas. Students need to learn to use the organizational structure of text as the basis for strategies to enhance reading (Dickson, Simmons, & Kameenui, 1998a). Students with learning disabilities need to be taught explicitly how to analyze text and later to use this analysis strategically to assist with reading comprehension. Specifically, they can be taught to detect the organizational frame of a reading and to use that information to decipher meanings and relationships (Bakken et al., 1997; Dimino, Taylor, & Gersten, 1995; Newby, Caldwell, & Recht, 1989).

### General Considerations

In comparison to teaching narrative text, teaching expository text grammars is a considerably harder task because of the variety of text grammars for these genres. Because students must become competent with all these different text structures, a variety of genres should be included in reading instruction, even for students experiencing reading difficulty. The danger for students who are at lower reading levels is that their reading will be limited to the narrative genres of simpler reading materials. For students who have difficulty reading specific genres, interventionists should be sure to use read alouds and shared reading for text the students cannot read independently.

An overall instructional approach suggested by Culatta and Merritt (1998) is to do the following:

- Call attention to the author's purpose: describe or label the organization of the text
- Conduct discussion with students along an organizational framework
- Make connections among major and minor topics
- Highlight or add devices that signal organization
- Make the connections between sentences clear

Another practice is to have students engage in writing activities using the genre they are working to understand (Seidenberg, 1989; Dickson, Simmons, & Kameenui, 1998b). For example, if you are helping students to understand the macrostructure of a descriptive expository text, have them write descriptive essays using a visual depiction of that macrostructure as an aid. In addition, as Nelson (1993) suggests, learning to read and write expository texts should involve opportunities to talk about expository texts, to ask and answer questions about them, and to take notes from written and oral presentations.

In working with macrostructures, include the following elements:

1. Teach visual depictions (see the following discussion) to go with frames
2. Identify a particular text structure pattern and use it to organize reading and studying
3. Teach the components unique to the different structure types, for example, signal words
4. Provide students with top-level information before they read (Dickson et al., 1998a; McGee & Richgels, 1985)

In deciphering macrostructures, work with visual and structural cues from the physical presentation of text when available. For example, use headings and subheadings to help students identify macrostructure. Regarding this last point, it will be necessary to work with students on analyzing considerate text before they will be able to create macrostructures with inconsiderate text.

## Use of Visual Depictions

Visual depictions include a variety of graphic structures, from simple time lines to complex matrices the purpose of which is to organize information in a manner that makes the information easier to learn (Crank & Bulgren, 1993). Their value is to make concepts more concrete, depict relationships, serve as an aid to memory, and use context to enhance learning. Webs, maps, diagrams, flowcharts, matrices, conceptual frames, time lines, and networks are examples of visual depictions, sometimes called graphic organizers. Common features include the use of connective lines, symbols, or spatial arrangement of items.

Work with macrostructures can be enhanced by using these devices to help students visualize and organize content into a structured format (Dickson et al., 1998b; Pearson & Fielding, 1991). Although more research has been done with story grammar and struggling readers, promising results in reading comprehension and expository texts have been obtained by using expository frames. Low-performing students especially seem to benefit from the creation of visual devices. For example, in one study, eighth-grade students with learning disabilities learned, applied, and transferred complex strategies on the basis of text structure (Bakken et al., 1997). There is also evidence to suggest that instruction for struggling readers in using graphic organizers is effective regardless of content or grade level (Boyle, 1996; Horton, Lovitt, & Bergerud, 1990).

Visual depictions should help specifically with clarifying relationships among ideas (Gajria et al., 2007). Each macrostructure may be depicted by a different visual organizer. The general structures are called "frames" and the content categories "slots" (Armbruster & Anderson, 1984). See Westby (1994) for frames for each of the expository text grammars.

Another technique is to use note sheets with written prompts to provide a framework in which to analyze text (Englert & Thomas, 1987). The Survey Routine (Schumaker, Deshler, & McKnight, 1989) described later utilizes such a device, called the TRIMS Worksheet.

Visual devices can be teacher or student generated. There is evidence that both types work with students with learning disabilities. Boyle and Weishaar (1997) found that students with learning disabilities who were trained either to use an expert-generated organizer or to generate their own cognitive organizer performed significantly better than controls on measures of literal comprehension.

In the example shown in Figures 9.2 and 9.3, one can see how an instructor uses a text grammar frame to help students understand a passage. Note as well how she takes the opportunity to assist students with inconsiderate text by dealing explicitly with a label ("LBJ") and an expression ("In the White House") for which the textbook author assumed prior knowledge, thereby requiring inferencing on the part of the reader.

## Order of Teaching

Although the goal is to teach adolescents how to analyze expository text, it may be advisable to have students work with narrative text first and then introduce expository text grammars. Nelson (1993) suggests using favorite

---

Class, I want you to turn to page 802 in your history book.[*] You will notice at the bottom of the page there's a heading in red that says "LBJ's Path to the White House." We know from what we have been reading that when President Kennedy was assassinated Lyndon Johnson took over as president. So when we come to this section of the textbook, we can guess that LBJ stands for Lyndon Johnson because we know he was "in the White House," which is an expression that means he was president. We can suspect from this heading that the author is going to tell us how Johnson got to be president because a "path" gets you from one place to another.

I want to show you how to use a frame for analyzing this text to make it easier for you to understand the content. You know about frames like this because we have used them before. Take a look at the frame that I've written on the board. It will help us understand the sequence of events in Johnson's career that led to the presidency. In the oval we write the topic—"LBJ's Path to White House." In the ovals underneath we will write the path he took. We will write what happened in the order that it occurred. As we read this text we're going to think about this structure and we're going to look for the things to write in those places.

---

**Figure 9.2**   Teacher instruction in text analysis, using a sequence frame. (© Student Success Initiatives, Inc., Barbara J. Ehren. With permission.)
[*] Cayton, Perry, Reed, & Winkler (2000)

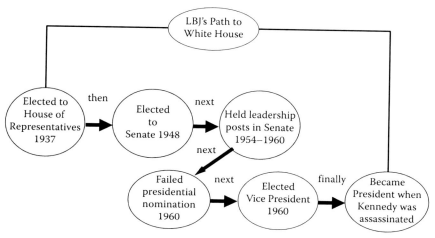

**Figure 9.3**   Sequence frame in history. (© Student Success Initiatives, Inc., Barbara J. Ehren. With permission.)

narrative stories rewritten as expository texts for those students having difficulties learning expository macrostructures.

The order of teaching expository text grammar should also be addressed. First, start with considerate texts that would support comprehension and recall and that have a familiar and discernible organization, frequent and salient signaling devices, few major topic shifts, and clear, cohesive ties (Culatta et al., 1998). Ultimately, students have to be able to identify text structure in the absence of clear signaling devices, but it would not be appropriate to begin by having students analyze inconsiderate texts. Second, since research has identified some text grammars to be easier to decipher than others, it would make sense to teach the easier ones first. Sequence/procedure text appears to be the easiest, followed by enumeration and description. Next, comparison/contrast seems easier than cause and effect (Englert & Thomas, 1987).

## Identifying Main Ideas

Deciphering overall text organization can assist students in identifying main ideas as well as the relationships among ideas. However, additional work with main ideas may be needed. It may help to focus on headings and subheadings as well as identification of topic sentences in paragraphs.

When main idea statements are not located at the beginning of the paragraph, students with reading disabilities need to be taught to look at the end of the paragraph and then elsewhere. If there is no main idea statement (or topic sentence), that is, if one has to be inferred, then students need to construct one. Without the ability to identify main ideas, students are unable to use a main idea strategy to understand or recall information from content area textbooks (Seidenberg, 1989). The following strategy steps have been useful in identifying the main idea at the paragraph level whether it is explicitly stated in the first sentence of the paragraph, embedded in the paragraph, or missing: (a) test the first sentence as a main idea sentence, (b) test the sentences following the first sentence to see if they are relevant to the probable main idea, and (c) if the sentences do not fit the probable main idea, revise the main idea to one that the sentences will fit (Kieras, 1981). With regard to integrating several ideas, work should include systematic attention to clauses that signal how authors relate ideas to one another (Seidenberg, 1989).

### Use of "the Survey Routine"

An example of a packaged text analysis approach is the chapter survey routine developed by researchers at the University of Kansas Center for Research on Learning to help teachers prepare students to analyze text (Schumaker et al., 1989). The elements of the Survey Routine are signaled by the acronym TRIMS, which stands for the following: (a) title, (b) relationship, (c) introduction, (d) main parts, and (e) summary. These elements are used by the teacher to prepare for a lesson and as a guide for analyzing the text for useful organizers and cues embedded within the text. If, however, these organizers are not present in the text, the teacher can then use the TRIMS process as a guide to enhancing the inconsiderate text.

A key part of the process presented in TRIMS involves the identification of common idea relationship structures and the signal words associated with them. These organizational patterns or relationship structures become advance organizers for the reading assignment. Common structures include the following: (a) simple listing, (b) comparison/contrast, (c) temporal sequence, (d) cause and effect, (e) problem/solution, (f) general/specific, and (g) related concept or category. These structures are organized on a teaching device called the TRIMS Worksheet, and specific procedures are used by the teacher to help students do a "TRIMS" of the chapter. For further information about this teaching routine, go to http://www.kucrl.org.

## TEACHING STRATEGIC USE OF TEXT ANALYSIS

Once struggling students have knowledge of expository text structures and the skills to analyze text elements, they need to be taught explicitly to use their knowledge and skills strategically (Gersten et al., 2001). In order to use text structure strategically to aid comprehension, students have to activate their metacognitive resources and ask themselves some key questions about text structure. These questions might include the following: What kind of text is this—narrative or expository? What visual clues are there to help me figure out the organizational pattern—headings, subheadings, signal words, topic sentences, and introductory paragraphs? What seems to be the overall organizational pattern? How can I figure out the most important ideas? What devices in the text help me figure out how the ideas are connected? (Ehren, 2005).

Characteristics of strategic instruction include teaching students how, when, and why to use strategies, modeling the use of strategies, guided practice, independent practice in different texts and contexts, systematic feedback, and shifting responsibility for learning from the teacher to the learner (Borkowski, Weyhing, & Carr, 1988; Gersten et al., 2001; Graham & Harris, 1989; Graham, Harris, & Troia, 2000; Mastropieri & Scruggs, 1997; Peterson, Caverly, Nicholson, O'Neal, & Cusenbary, 2000; Paris, Lipson, & Wixson, 1994; Pressley, Symons, Snyder, & Cariglia-Bull, 1989). Further, in the teaching of strategies, it is essential to attend specifically to generalization as part of the overall instructional approach, not as an afterthought at the end of instruction (Ellis, Lenz, & Sabornie, 1987a, 1987b). For example, at the beginning stages of strategy instruction when a teacher is introducing a strategy, he would provide a rationale for learning the strategy that addresses its use, thereby setting the stage for generalization. Specifically, he might say to the students, "The idea of learning this strategy is that you will use it in your history class when your teacher gives you a reading assignment. Where else might you use it?" As strategy instruction progresses, the teacher might utilize reading materials from the student's textbook or other class reading materials, taking time to make the point that the whole point of learning a strategy is to use it in other settings.

To facilitate this strategic use of text structure, here are some things to keep in mind:

- Adolescents can apply strategically only knowledge and skills that they have. Therefore, ample time must be spent on teaching the text structures themselves as well as identification of structural elements. Remember also that students with learning disabilities often need a greater level of instructional intensity than that required by other students.
- Dickson et al. (1998a) summarize the key elements of explicit instruction in the area of strategic teaching for struggling students.
  1. Explain how to use text structure awareness strategically to assist with comprehension
  2. Tell the importance of the strategy
  3. Model how, when, and where to use the strategy and how to evaluate the effectiveness of its use by including think alouds
  4. Provide guided and independent practice in strategic use of text analysis

    5. Teach for transfer and evaluation by making sure that you have students independently apply new strategies while reading their required textbooks

- After initial teaching, use judicious review frequently with short, varying tasks and incorporate previously taught information (Dickson et al., 1998a). Closely spaced, shorter reviews are more effective than single, long reviews (Dempster, 1991). Effective review is also cumulative with skills and strategies integrated over longer periods of time (Dixon, Carnine, & Kameenui, 1992).

- Prompt students to use text analysis strategically. For example, you might say to students taking an Earth science course, "How might you understand your Earth science textbook more easily by using what you know about how textbooks are written?" Then ask the Earth science teacher to prompt the students to use text structure strategically when they read the textbook.

- Even though you may have taught students more complex text grammars, when it comes to teaching students to use them strategically, you will want to teach the metacognitive processes with simpler expository passages and progress to more difficult expository text. When you introduce strategic use of text grammar to students, you will want to start with narrative text and story grammar (Nelson, 1993; Westby, 1999).

See Figure 9.4 for a summary of intervention targets.

## IDENTIFYING AND STRUCTURING INCONSIDERATE TEXT

An important aspect of working with students and expository text organization is the clarity of text presentation. A text is described as "considerate" or "well presented" when it is organized in a way that is easier to understand (Dickson et al., 1998b). Considerate text would use the structural and visual cues we discussed in the section "Signaling Devices" to make the organization clear, for example, placing a topic sentence at the beginning of a paragraph to make identification of the main idea easier (Lorch & Lorch, 1985).

    Inconsiderate text, on the other hand, lacks organizational clarity and is more difficult for students to understand. Unfortunately, students too frequently encounter inconsiderate text in materials they read in school (Armbruster & Anderson, 1988). However, even with inconsiderate text, students are expected to use them as a primary source of information (Dickson et al., 1998b). For example, science textbooks provide extensive coverage but little opportunity for in-depth practice of important concepts. They often fail to present information in a way that would help students organize facts into a coherent whole (Scruggs & Mastropieri, 1993).

| What to Teach: | Text Structure |
|---|---|
| Content Awareness | The nature of expository text, its predictable information, distinguishing it from narrative |
| Pattern Awareness | The various expository text grammars and typical signaling devices: description, enumeration, sequence/procedure, comparison/contrast, cause/effect, problem/solution, argumentation/persuasion |
| Cohesion Structures | Knowledge of within sentence and across sentence cohesive ties to assist with inferencing |
| Sentence Structures | Understanding a variety of syntactic patterns |
| **What to Teach:** | **Text Analysis** |
| Identification of Macrostructure | Figuring out text grammar from a passage; using signaling devices |
| Use of Cohesive Ties | Applying knowledge of cohesion to make inferences |
| Sentence Level Analysis | Working with the syntax of sentences to derive meaning |
| Use of Visual Device | Using graphic organizers or prompt sheets to do text analysis |
| **What to Teach:** | **Strategic Use of Text Analysis** |
| Rationale | Why to use text analysis strategically |
| Process | How to use text analysis strategically (a step-by-step process) |
| Timing | When to use text analysis strategically |
| Independent Use | Strategic use of text analysis without external prompting |
| Generalization | Strategic use of text analysis in a variety of settings with different texts |

**Figure 9.4** Summary of intervention targets related to text structure. (© Student Success Initiatives, Inc., Barbara J. Ehren. With permission.)

Poorly organized textbooks may play a part in the comprehension difficulties of poor readers, especially those who have difficulty recalling content, organizing information, identifying main ideas, and discriminating between relevant and irrelevant information. With inconsiderate text, educators will have to create a cogent organizational framework to assist students in understanding information, basically imposing structure where one is lacking. Using visual depictions will support this effort.

A related factor is that well structured or considerate text can help build fluency but does not help a struggling reader move beyond literal levels of understanding (McNamara & Kintsch, 1996; McNamara, Kintsch, Songer, & Kintsch, 1996; Peterson et al., 2000). Therefore, students need opportunities to engage with more complicated text along with support in how to use background knowledge and text structure to determine relationships among ideas and draw conclusions (Peterson et al., 2000).

## CONCLUSION

In this chapter, we focused on working with text structure to assist adolescents in comprehending the expository text they read. Because secondary school instruction relies heavily on textbooks and because expository text poses a number of problems to adolescent readers, work in this area should help practitioners facilitate academic achievement for these students. Although intervention in expository text comprehension involves multiple and complex processes, this chapter did not attempt to cover them all. Emphasis was placed on the internal text structures that should be taught explicitly, teaching adolescents to perform text analysis and to use text analysis knowledge and skills strategically to improve their comprehension. Practitioners involved with struggling adolescent readers have to be sure to also address vocabulary and prior knowledge (establishing and activating it) requirements as well. Other areas typically in need of much attention are identifying main ideas, distinguishing them from details, and inferencing. Although "main idea" was addressed in the section "Teaching Text Analysis," the focus of that section was limited to how understanding text organization can assist with identifying the main idea.

Further, an important consideration is that it is difficult and ill-advised to separate the comprehension of expository text in specific disciplines from effective teaching in those subject areas. The critical role of background knowledge in comprehension demands that educators address in substantive ways the interconnectedness of knowledge in a subject area and reading comprehension in that area. Classroom teachers, special education teachers, reading specialists, and speech-language pathologists should work collaboratively to deliver instruction/intervention to adolescents that will meld content mastery with content literacy to promote academic achievement.

# REFERENCES

Abrahamsen, E. P., & Shelton, K. C. (1989). Reading comprehension in adolescents with learning disabilities: Semantic and syntactic effects. *Journal of Learning Disabilities, 22,* 569–572.

Armbruster, B. B., & Anderson, T. H. (1984). Studying. In P. D. Pearson, R. Barr, L. Kamil, & P. B. Mosenthal (Eds.), *Handbook of reading research* (Vol. 1, pp. 657–679). New York: Longman.

Armbruster, B. B., & Anderson, T. H. (1988). On selecting "considerate" content area textbooks. *Remedial and Special Education, 9*(1), 47–52.

Armbruster, B. B., & Nagy, W. E. (1993). Vocabulary in content area lessons. *The Reading Teacher, 7,* 550–551.

Bakken, J. P., Mastropieri, M. A., & Scruggs, T. E. (1997). Reading comprehension of expository science material and students with learning disabilities: A comparison of strategies. *Journal of Special Education, 31*(3), 300–314.

Barton, M. L. (1997). Addressing the literacy crisis: Teaching reading in the content areas. *National Association of Secondary School Principals, 81*(587), 2–30.

Bashir, A. S., Conte, B. M., & Heerde, S. M. (1998). Language and school success: Collaborative challenges and choices. In D. D. Merritt & B. Cullatta (Eds.), *Language intervention in the classroom* (pp. 1–36). San Diego, CA: Singular.

Beck, I. L., McKeown, M. G., Sinatra, G. M., & Loxterman, J. A. (1991). Revising social studies text from a text-processing perspective: Evidence of improved comprehensibility. *Reading Research Quarterly, 26,* 251–276.

Bereiter, C., & Scardamalia, M. (1987). *The psychology of written composition.* New York: Lawrence Erlbaum Associates.

Best, R. M., Rowe, M., Ozuru, Y., & McNamara, D. S. (2005). Deep-level comprehension of science texts. *Topics in Language Disorders, 25*(1), 65–83.

Bisanz, G. L., Das, J. P., Vanahagen, C., & Henderson, H. (1992). Structural components or reading time and recall for sentences in narratives: Exploring chances with age and reading ability. *Journal of Educational Psychology, 84*(1), 103–115.

Blachowicz, C. L. Z. (1994). Problem-solving strategies for academic success. In G. P. Wallach & K. G. Butler (Eds.), *Language learning disabilities in school-age children and adolescents* (pp. 304–322). New York: Macmillan.

Block, C. (1993). Strategy instruction in a literature-based reading program. *Elementary School Journal, 94*(2), 139–151.

Borkowski, J. G., Weyhing, T. M., & Carr, M. (1988). Effects of attributional retraining on strategy-based reading comprehension in learning-disabled students. *Journal of Educational Psychology, 80,* 46–53.

Boyle, J. R. (1996). The effects of a cognitive mapping strategy on the literal and inferential comprehension of students with mild disabilities. *Learning Disability Quarterly, 19,* 86–93.

Boyle, J. R., & Weishaar, M. (1997). The effects of expert-generated versus student-generated cognitive organizers on the reading comprehension of students with learning disabilities. *Learning Disabilities Research and Practice, 12*(4), 228–235.

Bryant, D. P., Ugel, N., Thomson, S., & Hamff, A. (1999). Instructional strategies for content-area reading instruction. *Intervention in School and Clinic, 34,* 293–302.

Bulgren, J., Lenz, B. K., Marquis, J., Schumaker, J. B., & Deshler, D. D. (2002). *The effects of the use of the Question Exploration Routine on student performance in secondary content classrooms* (Research Report). Lawrence: University of Kansas Center for Research on Learning,

Cayton, A., Perry, E., Reed, L., & Winkler, A. (2000). *America: Pathways to the present.* Needham, MA: Prentice Hall.

Crank, J. N., & Bulgren, J. A. (1993). Visual depictions as information organizers for enhancing achievement of students with learning disabilities. *Learning Disabilities Research and Practice, 8*(3), 140–147.

Culatta, B., Horn, D. G., & Merritt, D. D. (1998). Expository text: Facilitating comprehension. In D. Merritt & B. Culatta (Eds.), *Language intervention in the classroom* (pp. 215–276). San Diego, CA: Singular.

Culatta, B., & Merritt, D. D. (1998). Enhancing comprehension of discourse. In D. Merritt & B. Culatta (Eds.), *Language intervention in the classroom* (pp. 175–214). San Diego, CA: Singular.

Dempster, R. N. (1991). Synthesis of research on reviews and tests. *Educational Leadership, 71,* 71–76.

Dickson, S. V., Simmons, D. C., & Kameenui, E. J. (1998a). Text organization: Instructional and curricular basics and implications. In D. C. Simmons & E. J. Kameenui (Eds.), *What reading research tells us about children with diverse learning needs* (pp. 279–294). Mahwah, NJ: Lawrence Erlbaum Associates.

Dickson, S. V., Simmons, D. C., & Kameenui, E. J. (1998b). Text organization: Research bases. In D. C. Simmons & E. J. Kameenui (Eds.), *What reading research tells us about children with diverse learning needs* (pp. 239–277). Mahwah, NJ: Lawrence Erlbaum Associates.

Dimino, J. A., Taylor, R. M., & Gersten, R. M. (1995). Synthesis of the research on story grammar as a means to increase comprehension. *Reading and Writing Quarterly: Overcoming Learning Difficulties, 11,* 53–71.

Dixon, R., Carnine, D., & Kameenui, E. J. (1992). *Curriculum guidelines for diverse learners* (Monograph for the National Center to Improve the Tools of Educators). Eugene: University of Oregon.

Ehren, B. J. (2005). Looking for evidence-based practice in reading comprehension. *Topics in Language Disorders, 25*(4), 312–326.

Ehren, B. J., Lenz, B. K., & Deshler, D. D. (2004). Enhancing literacy proficiency with adolescents and young adults. In A. Stone, E. Siliman, B. Ehren, & K. Apel (Eds.), *Handbook of language and literacy* (pp. 681–701). New York: Guilford Press.

Ellis, E. S., Lenz, B. K., & Sabornie, E. J. (1987a). Generalization and adaptation of learning strategies to natural environment: Part 1: Critical agents. *Remedial and Special Education, 8*(1), 6–20.

Ellis, E. S., Lenz, B. K., & Sabornie, E. J. (1987b). Generalization and adaptation of learning strategies to natural environment: Part 1: Research into practice. *Remedial and Special Education, 8*(2), 6–23.

Englert, C. S., & Hiebert, E. H. (1984). Children's developing awareness of text structures in expository material. *Journal of Educational Psychology, 76,* 65–75.

Englert, C. S., & Thomas, C. C. (1987). Sensitivity to text structure in reading and writing: A comparison between learning disabled and non-learning disabled students. *Learning Disability Quarterly, 10,* 93–105.

Farah, M. A., & Karls, A. B. (1997). *World history: The human experience.* New York: Glencoe.

Florida Department of Education. (2005). *Florida Comprehensive Assessment Test: Summary of tests and design.* Retrieved December 15, 2007, from http://fcat.fldoe.org/pdf/fc05designsummary.pdf

Gajria, M., Jitendra, A. K., Sood, S., & Sacks, G. (2007). Improving comprehension of expository text in students with LD: A research synthesis. *Journal of Learning Disabilities, 40*(3), 210–225.

Gersten, R., Fuchs, L. S., Williams, J. P., & Baker, S. (2001). Teaching reading comprehension strategies to students with learning disabilities: A review of research. *Review of Educational Research, 71,* 279–320.

Graesser, A., Golding, J. M., & Long, D. L. (1991). Narrative representation and comprehension. In R. Barr, M. L. Kamil, P. Mosenthal, & P. D. Pearson (Eds.), *Handbook of reading research* (Vol. 2, pp. 171–204). White Plains, NY: Longman.

Graesser, A., Leon, J. A., & Leon, J. (2002). Introduction to the psychology of science text comprehension. In J. Otero, J. A. Leon, & A. C. Graesser (Eds.), *The psychology of science text comprehension* (pp. 1–15). Mahwah, NJ: Lawrence Erlbaum Associates.

Graesser, A. C., Millis, K. K., & Zwan, R. A. (1997). Discourse comprehension. *Annual Review of Psychology, 48,* 163–189.

Graham, S. & Harris, K. (1989). Components analysis of cognitive strategy instruction: Effects on learning disabled student's composition and self-efficacy. *Journal of Educational Psychology, 81*(33): 353–361.

Graham, S., Harris, K., & Troia, G. (2000). Self-regulated strategy development revisited: Teaching writing strategies to struggling writers. *Topics in Language Disorders, 20*(4), 1–14.

Grossman, P. L., & Stodolsky, S. S. (1995). Content as context: The role of school subjects in secondary school teaching. *Educational Researcher, 4*(8), 5–11.

Hall, L. A. (2004). Comprehending expository text: Promising strategies for struggling readers and students with reading disabilities? *Reading Research and Instruction, 44*(2), 75–95.

Heibert, E. H., Englert, C. S., & Brennan, S. (1983). Awareness of text structure in recognition and production of expository discourse. *Journal of Reading Behavior, 15*(4), 63–79.

Horton, S. V., Lovitt, T. C., & Bergerud, D. (1990). The effectiveness of graphic organizers for three classifications of secondary students in content area classes. *Journal of Learning Disabilities, 23,* 335–342, 348.

Hudson, P., Lignugaris-Kraft, B., & Miller, T. (1993) Using content enhancements to improve the performance of adolescents with learning disabilities in content classes. *Learning Disabilities Research and Practice, 8,* 106–126.

Kieras, D. E. (1981). Topicalization effects in cued recall of technical prose. *Memory and Cognition, 9,* 541–549.

Lapp, D., Flood, J., & Farnan, N. (1989). *Content area reading and learning: Instructional strategies.* Englewood Cliffs, NJ: Prentice Hall.

Lehman, S., & Schraw, G. (2002). Effects of coherence and relevance on shallow and deep text processing. *Journal of Educational Psychology, 94,* 738–750.

Linderholm, T., Everson, M., vandenBroek, P., Mischinski, M., Critenden, A., & Samuels, J. (2000). Effects of causal text revisions on more- and less-skilled readers' comprehension of easy and difficult texts. *Cognition and Instruction, 18,* 525–556.

Lorch, R. F., & Lorch, E. P. (1985). Topic structure representation and text recall. *Journal of Educational Psychology, 77,* 137–148.

Mastropieri, M. A., & Scruggs, T. E. (1997). Best practices in promoting reading comprehension in students with learning disabilities: 1976 to 1996. *Remedial and Special Education, 18*(4), 197–213.

McGee, L. M., & Richgels, D. J. (1985). Teaching expository text structure to elementary students. *The Reading Teacher, 38,* 739–748.

McNamara, D. S., & Kintsch, W. (1996). Learning from texts: Effects of prior knowledge and text coherence. *Discourse Processes, 22*(3), 247–288.

McNamara, D. S., Kintsch, E., Songer, N. B., & Kintsch, W. (1996). Are good texts always better? Interactions of text coherence, background knowledge, and levels of understanding in learning from text. *Cognition and Instruction, 14*(1), 1–43.

Meyer, B. J. R. (1975). The organization of prose and its effects on memory. Amsterdam: North-Holland.

Meyer, B. J. R., Brandt, D. M., & Bluth, G. J. (1980). Use of top-level structure in text: Key for reading comprehension on ninth-grade students. *Reading Research Quarterly, 16,* 72–103.

Miller, K., & Levine, J. (2006). *Biology.* Upper Saddle River, NJ: Prentice Hall.

Mintz, S. (2007). *Native American voices.* Retrieved December 15, 2007, from http://www.digitalhistory.uh.edu/native_voices/nav2.html

Montague, M., Maddux, C. D., & Dereshiwsky, M. I. (1990). Story grammar and comprehension and production of narrative prose by students with learning disabilities. *Journal of Learning Disabilities, 23,* 190–197.

Nelson, N. W. (1993). *Childhood language disorders in context: Infancy through adolescence.* New York: Macmillan.

Newby, R. F., Caldwell, J., & Recht, D. R. (1989). Improving the reading comprehension of children with dysphonetic and dyseidetic dyslexia using story grammar. *Journal of Learning Disabilities, 22*(6), 373–380.

O'Hanlon, L. (n.d.). *Global warming: A primer.* Retrieved June 12, 2008, from http://dsc.discovery.com/convergence/globalwarming/primer/primer.html

Otero, J., Leon, J. A., & Graesser, A. C. (Eds.). (2002). *The psychology of science text comprehension.* Mahwah, NJ: Lawrence Erlbaum Associates.

Paris, S., Lipson, M., & Wixson, K. (1994). Becoming a strategic reader. In R. B. Ruddell, M. R. Ruddell, & H. Singer (Eds.), *Theoretical models and processes of reading* (pp. 788–810). Newark, DE: International Reading Association.

Pearson, P. D., & Camperell, K. (1994). Comprehension of text structures. In R. B. Ruddell, M. R. Ruddell, & H. Singer (Eds.), *Theoretical models and processes of reading* (pp. 448–468). Newark, DE: International Reading Association.

Pearson, P. D., & Fielding, L. (1991). Comprehension instruction. In R. Barr, M. L. Kamil, P. Mosenthal, & P. D. Pearson (Eds.), *Handbook of reading research* (Vol. 2, pp. 815–860). White Plains, NY: Longman.

Peterson, C. L., Caverly, D. C., Nicholson, S. A., O'Neal, S., & Cusenbary, S. (2000). *Building reading proficiency at the secondary level: A guide to resources.* Austin, TX: Southwest Educational Development Laboratory.

Pressley, M., Symons, S., Snyder, B. L., & Cariglia-Bull, T. (1989). Strategy instruction research comes of age. *Learning Disabilities Quarterly, 86,* 360–406.

Roth, F., & Spekman, N. (1989). Higher-order language processes and reading disabilities. In A. G. Kamhi & H. W. Catts (Eds.), *Reading disabilities: A developmental language perspective* (pp. 159–197). Boston: College Hill Press.

Schumaker, J., Deshler, D., & McKnight, P. (1989). *The survey routine.* Lawrence: University of Kansas.

Scruggs, T. E., & Mastropieri, M. A. (1993). Current approaches to science education: Implications for mainstream education of students with disabilities. *Remedial and Special Education, 14,* 15–24.

Seidenberg, P. L. (1989). Relating text-processing research to reading and writing instruction for learning disabled students. *Learning Disabilities Focus, 5*(1), 4–12.

Slater, W. H., Graves, M. F., & Piche, G. L. (1985). Effects of structural organizers on ninth-grade students' comprehension and recall of four patterns of expository text. *Reading Research Quarterly 20,* 189–202.

Taylor, B. M., & Beach, R. W. (1984). The effects of text structure instruction on middle-grade students' comprehension and production of expository text. *Reading Research Quarterly, 19,* 114–146.

Taylor, B. M., & Samuels, S. J. (1983). Children's use of text structures in the recall of expository material. *American Educational Research Journal, 20,* 517–528.

Taylor, B. M., & Beach, R. W. (1984). The effects of text structure instruction on middle-grade students' comprehension and production of expository text. *Reading Research Quarterly, 19,* 134–146.

Team 3659 ThinkQuest Contest. (1996). *CHEMystery: An interactive guide to chemistry* Retrieved January 5, 2008, from http://library.thinkquest.org/3659/

Weaver, C. A., & Kintsch, W. (1991). Expository text. In R. Barr, M. L. Kamil, P. Mosenthal, & P. D. Pearson (Eds.), *Handbook of reading research* (Vol. 2, pp. 230–244). White Plains, NY: Longman.

Westby, C. E. (1994). The effects of culture on genre, structure and style or oral and written texts. In G. P. Wallach & K. G. Butler (Eds.), *Language learning disabilities in school-age children and adolescents* (pp. 181–218). New York: Macmillan.

Westby, C. E. (1999). Assessing and facilitating text comprehension problems. In H. W. Catts & A. G. Kamhi (Eds.), *Language and reading disabilities* (pp. 154–223). Boston: Allyn & Bacon.

Williams, J. P., Brown, L. G., Silverstein, A. K., & deCani, J. S. (1994). An instructional program in comprehension of narrative themes for adolescents with learning disabilities. *Learning Disability Quarterly, 17,* 205–221.

Wong, B. Y. L. & Wilson, M. (1984). Investigating awareness of and teaching passage organization in learning disabled children. *Journal of Learning Disabilities, 17,* 477–482.

## STUDY GUIDE QUESTIONS

1. Leroy is an eighth grader who is having great difficulty understanding his science text. He has no knowledge of expository text grammars. The first thing you should consider doing is to
   a. teach the concept of text structure and text analysis using narratives.
   b. teach him a strategy for text analysis.
   c. teach the concept of text structure and text analysis using descriptive text grammar.
   d. focus on sentence-level syntactic patterns because that knowledge will transfer to the discourse/text level.

2. Sandra struggles with comprehension of information in her ninth-grade algebra textbook. She does well with the literature she reads for English. An appropriate course of action to improve her algebra comprehension is to
   a. be patient; in time, she will figure out how to apply what she knows about reading narratives to reading expository texts.
   b. give her a graphic organizer and have her fill it out.
   c. teach expository text structure explicitly using her algebra book.
   d. have her do word problems.

3. Billy is an adolescent with a learning disability who has learned the seven expository text structures named in this chapter. He can also read a passage and identify the macrostructure. As an interventionist you would
   a. breathe a sigh of relief; your work is done.
   b. still have to teach him explicitly how to use that knowledge strategically.
   c. give him a written test to make sure he can name the text grammars.
   d. give him additional practice opportunities to identify macrostructures.

4. Mr. Sanchez, a high school social studies teacher, is very concerned about his struggling students who cannot adequately comprehend information from their textbook. He has read this chapter and knows

he should address text structure. He has checked with the English teacher, who has the same students in her class. She assures Mr. Sanchez that the students know story grammar. Based on what he has learned about expository text structure, he decides to begin his instruction with

   a.  comparison/contrast.
   b.  cause and effect.
   c.  description.
   d.  sequence/procedure.

5. Kim, a seventh grader with reading disabilities, has been learning expository text structure. She is now working with recognizing cause-and-effect structure in her science book but has not mastered this target. A good idea for intervention at this point is to

   a.  have her write cause-and-effect paragraphs.
   b.  switch to her social studies book.
   c.  use the newspaper to work on inferencing.
   d.  have her write the answers to the questions at the end of the science chapters.

## CHAPTER 10

# Expository Discourse Intervention: Helping School-Age Children and Adolescents with Language Disorders Master the Language of the Curriculum

*Jeannene M. Ward-Lonergan*

As discussed in chapter 7, students with language impairments exhibit significant difficulty when required to listen to, verbally produce, read, and write expository discourse as compared to students with normal language abilities. Therefore, intervention focused on improving expository discourse abilities is essential for facilitating academic success in school-age children and adolescents with language impairments. The primary purpose of this chapter is to present a comprehensive review of research findings that have clinical implications for the treatment of expository discourse abilities in students with language impairments. The first section addresses reading comprehension, and the second section addresses written expression. The intent is to provide information on language intervention that attempts to help this population master the "language of the curriculum" (i.e., expository discourse) in order to achieve academic success.

## READING INTERVENTION

### Rationale for Intervention to Improve Reading Comprehension of Expository Text in Children and Adolescents with Language Disorders

In the upper elementary grades and beyond, reading comprehension of a variety of texts can be the key to academic success (Mason, Meadan, Hedin, & Corso, 2006). In spite of the difficulties that students have with comprehending expository text, especially those students with language impairments and learning disabilities, teachers in grades 4 through 12 typically do not instruct students in the reading comprehension process (DiCecco & Gleason, 2002). Unfortunately, many upper elementary, middle school, and high school teachers assume that their students have mastered the fundamentals of reading and often do not provide explicit instruction in strategic practices that provide the basic foundation needed for good reading comprehension (Durkin, 1978–1979; Moody, Vaughn, Hughes, & Fischer, 2000; Vaughn, Moody, & Schumm, 1998). Students are generally assigned chapters to read and comprehension questions to answer, with little instruction on how to decipher text structure and interpret information (Beck, McKeown, Hamilton, & Kucan, 1998; Durkin, 1978–1979; Gillespie & Rasinski, 1989). Instruction in text structures has been found to positively affect students' knowledge about the expository writing process as well as improve their reading comprehension and composition performance levels, although changes in performance have varied across different text structures and the various types of instruction received (Englert, Raphael, Anderson, Gregg, & Anthony, 1989; Raphael, Englert, & Kirschner, 1986). However, the research to date has tended to focus on high-achieving students. Extension of such instruction to students with learning disabilities may be desirable, but further examination of the differences and the needs of students with language impairments and learning disabilities is needed before the most effective instruction can be designed and implemented (Newcomer & Nodine, 1988; Englert et al., 1989).

### Direct Instruction versus Strategic Instruction

Direct instruction is an intervention approach that provides clear, explicit skill instruction through systematic steps that offer multiple opportunities for learning (Carnine, Silbert, & Kameenui, 1990). A distinctive feature of direct instruction is its focus on teaching prerequisite subskills, such as letter sounds or linguistic elements (e.g., what is typically used in phonological awareness intervention) prior to teaching more complex skills. The goal is to fine-tune a subskill, hopefully to the level of automaticity, so that students' processing in working memory can be freed up for higher-level thinking.

When word recognition is automatic, students can more rapidly attend to and comprehend the meaning of the new information being presented during reading. Considering that one goal of direct instruction is automatic processing of particular subskills, this approach is often used to support data-driven (i.e., bottom-up) processing.

In contrast, strategy instruction is a more global intervention approach. It is a "big-picture" type of intervention (Gillam, Hoffman, Marler, & Wynn-Dancy, 2002). Although it may utilize a graduated sequence of steps, the ultimate goal is to create independent learners who are able to communicate more effectively in spoken and written language modalities. Learning strategies are defined as "techniques, principles, or rules that will facilitate the acquisition, manipulation, integration, storage, and retrieval of information across situations and settings" (Alley & Deshler, 1979, p. 13). The primary focus of a learning strategies approach is on teaching students *how* to learn (i.e., a process) rather than *what* to learn (i.e., a product or specific content) and on how to effectively use what has been learned (Schumaker & Sheldon, 1999). Another important purpose of strategy instruction is an emphasis on improving metacognitive skills. For example, understanding why a strategy is needed, selecting a strategy, and determining whether a selected strategy is successful or unsuccessful are integral components. Intervention aimed at improving conceptually driven (top-down) language processing must focus on helping students connect their prior knowledge with the content being presented for the purpose of facilitating effective information processing in expository, conversational, or narrative discourse (Gillam et al., 2002). Speech-language pathologists (SLPs) and teachers who provide strategic instruction are teaching students with language impairments and language-learning disabilities some specific language-learning strategies that will allow them to achieve success in mastering the language of the curriculum across content areas (Ward-Lonergan, 2002).

## Improving Reading Comprehension through Information Processing/Language Intervention

Gillam et al. (2002) proposed that since language and information processing are dynamically related, good language intervention is also good information processing intervention. They stated that the primary focus of language intervention should relate to encouraging form, meaning, and use interactions in pragmatically relevant contexts. Many SLPs use book discussions as the primary context for intervention with school-age children since this type of discourse activity commonly occurs in elementary school classrooms. In this approach, activities that facilitate semantics, syntax, morphology, narration, and phonological awareness are centered on a common theme. Gillam and colleagues further stated that intervention that combines direct instruction and strategic instruction holds great promise for providing effective language intervention within an information processing framework. They also suggested that this type of intervention model may be highly effective for addressing language impairments that may entail both data-driven and conceptually driven processing deficits.

Gillam et al. (2002) described a number of language intervention techniques that SLPs can use to facilitate information processing in students with language impairments while incorporating either direct instruction or strategy instruction approaches into their treatment sessions. While these techniques may easily be incorporated into treatment designed to improve reading comprehension, they may also be used to facilitate listening comprehension in students with language impairments and include the following:

- Focus students' attention. SLPs explain the purpose and rationale of the lesson. During a lesson, SLPs ask students to discuss what new information they are learning, explain its importance, and state how they can apply this new information.
- Reduce rate of speech. SLPs should speak slower, with greater stress placed on critical information, to provide extra processing time.
- Strengthen knowledge bases. SLPs can ask children about their prior knowledge of the topic of a lesson. Students can then gradually add to their knowledge base by frequently having the opportunity to rephrase their prior knowledge and integrate it with their newly acquired knowledge.
- Create mental maps. SLPs can coconstruct schematic maps with children by listing key words for important concepts and using lines to connect these key words to help students visualize connections between preexisting and newly acquired knowledge.
- Facilitate cue integration. SLPs can present minilessons to improve cue integration abilities by demonstrating how to attend to various types of cues. SLPs can do this by writing sets of "cloze" sentences where each sentence provides increasingly more information than the preceding sentence. As each individual sentence is uncovered, the students brainstorm possible answers on the basis of the cues provided, and the SLP writes down this list. Following the presentation of each sentence, the students discuss which words are not possibilities any longer given the cues provided. Once the last sentence has been displayed, the author's target word is revealed.
- Implement mediated teaching. SLPs can apply the steps of mediated teaching to various intervention targets (e.g., state the goal of the lesson, explain the rationale for the goal, use modeling and strategies, discuss alternative strategies and responses, provide generalization opportunities, encourage students to self-evaluate their learning, and discuss application of newly learned information to outside settings) (Miller, Gillam, & Pena, 2000).

## Teaching Expository Reading Comprehension Strategies to Struggling Readers

A number of researchers have presented specific language-learning strategies that may be useful for improving expository discourse abilities. For example, Gajria and Salvia (1992) examined the effectiveness of a summarization strategy for increasing comprehension of expository prose in students with learning disabilities. These authors concluded that direct instruction in this summarization strategy significantly increased reading comprehension in their experimental group. Coutant and Perchemlides (2005) also discussed strategies for adolescents who are struggling readers. These strategies help teach adolescents "how to read" as opposed to "what to read," and they can be generalized across settings and applied to any piece of expository text that they may encounter.

Students need to learn genre-specific comprehension strategies for decoding and comprehending expository texts that differ from those that they employ when reading narrative texts. This becomes particularly critical since the demand for middle and high school students to read expository materials such as textbooks, essays, lab reports, and newspaper articles dramatically increases from what was required of them during their elementary school years (Coutant & Perchemlides, 2005). Students who have language-learning disabilities that affect their reading skills typically use simpler, less efficient strategies and fail to implement what strategies they do know in a smooth, effective manner as compared to students with normal language development (Mason, 2004).

Coutant and Perchemlides (2005) offered suggestions to help struggling readers comprehend expository texts that can be used before, during, and after reading a textbook or article. Prior to reading a text, teachers or SLPs can discuss the subject of the text with the students and explain how the text is organized. They can also draw students' attention to key words/phrases that signal a particular type of expository discourse structure and discuss the meaning.

Prior to reading, students can also be encouraged to prepare a standard outline or fill-in-the-blank notes for listing the main idea and supporting details that they can complete as they are reading a text. For example, students can copy the headings and subheadings from a textbook directly into their notebooks, leaving space to fill in important information. While reading, they write in details under each heading or subheading, such as the people and places discussed, dates, and definitions. When students read a text that does not include standard headings or subheadings, they can create their own set of notes using the familiar "wh-" questions: who, what, when, where, why, and how (Coutant & Perchemlides, 2005).

During the reading process, students can also be encouraged to use a pencil to mark portions of a text that they find to be confusing, surprising, or important with specific symbols (e.g., question marks, exclamation points, and asterisks), and they can also be encouraged to circle key signal words/phrases and words that they do not understand. Students can also underline important content words that occur repeatedly in a text (Coutant & Perchemlides, 2005). This can help provide students with a purpose for reading as well as help them focus on details that relate to main ideas, improve their recall of important facts, and help them draw conclusions on the basis of evidence found in the text (Connecticut Teachers, 2004). As students are reading, they can also be encouraged to pause and write a very short summary of what they have read in the margin after reading a given paragraph or section of the text. This practice helps students solidify their understanding of the main ideas discussed and helps them identify the stated or implied thesis of the text (Coutant & Perchemlides, 2005).

After reading an expository text, students can be encouraged to reorganize the essential facts and information from their reading that they listed on their preconstructed outlines. SLPs and teachers can facilitate formal or informal discussions among students using questions that they have posed about the text in order to further promote their reading comprehension, help them draw new conclusions about what they have read, and provide them with an opportunity to use evidence to support their opinions in writing (Coutant & Perchemlides, 2005). They can also be encouraged to engage in discussions with their peers using questions that they had raised while reading the text. These authors concluded that by sacrificing a little academic content for additional strategic instruction, it is possible to create a generation of readers who can generalize what they have learned by applying these types of strategies to any piece of expository text that they encounter.

Various instructional programs have been developed to teach language-learning strategies to low-achieving students and students with learning disabilities (Deshler & Lenz, 1989). Single-approach strategies (e.g., RAP for main ideas and details; Ellis & Graves, 1990) and multiapproach strategies (e.g., POSSE for acquisition and retention of curricular material; Englert & Mariage, 1991) have been developed for teaching students how to obtain meaning from text. Researchers at the University of Kansas Center for Research on Learning have been developing and expanding on their Learning Strategies Curriculum for nearly 30 years. Currently, the Learning Strategies Curriculum is comprised of approximately 15 different learning strategies that are organized according to four major strands (i.e., Reading, Storing and Remembering Information, Expressing Information, and Demonstrating Competence). The following eight-stage instructional sequence is used to teach these strategies: pretest and make commitments, describe, model, verbal practice, controlled practice and feedback, advanced practice/posttest and feedback, make commitments for generalization, and generalization. According to Schumaker and Sheldon (1999), research has shown that 98% of low-achieving students who have been taught learning strategies have mastered them if this eight-stage instructional sequence described in the instructor's manual is followed carefully.

The Paraphrasing Strategy (Schumaker, Denton, & Deshler, 1984) is one of the learning strategies in the Reading strand that is designed to facilitate reading comprehension in struggling readers by teaching them to paraphrase the main idea and important details in each paragraph of a passage. The mnemonic device RAP (i.e., Read a paragraph; Ask yourself, "What were the main ideas and details in this paragraph?; Put main ideas and details into your own words) is used to remember the strategy steps. This strategy helps students focus on the most important information in a passage. Research results indicate that students performed at a 48% comprehension rate on grade-level materials prior to learning the strategy and comprehended 84% of the material on the posttest used following instruction in this strategy. Another learning strategy from the Reading strand that has been found to be beneficial for improving reading comprehension is the Self-Questioning Strategy (Schumaker, Deshler, Nolan, & Alley, 1994). This strategy is designed to help students create their own motivation for reading by creating questions in their minds about information that has not been initially divulged by the author, predicting the answers to those questions, searching for the answers to those questions as they read, and paraphrasing the answers. Research results indicated average gains of 40 percentage points in reading comprehension for grade-level materials following instruction in this strategy. Both of these strategies can be used to increase reading comprehension for expository text in students with language impairments, learning disabilities, and language-learning disabilities.

Another strategy, TWA (Think before reading, think While reading, think After reading) (Mason et al., 2006), combines previously validated reading comprehension strategies into a nine-step, multiple-strategy expository reading package. Research that has investigated the use of TWA taught within the Self-Regulated Strategy Development (SRSD) (Graham & Harris, 2003) instructional approach has yielded excellent results and demonstrated improvement in reading comprehension for struggling readers with and without learning disabilities (Mason, 2004; Mason & Bentz, 2004; Mason, Hickey Snyder, Jones, & Kedem, 2006). The nine-step TWA strategy is used before, during, and after reading an expository passage. Before beginning to read, students are taught to activate their prior knowledge by thinking about the author's purpose, what they already know about the topic, and what they would like to learn about the topic (Ogle, 1989). During the reading process, students are instructed to consider their reading speed, linking their prior knowledge to what they are reading, and rereading confusing parts of the text (Graves & Levin, 1989; Hansen & Pearson, 1983).

After reading, students are first taught to develop main ideas using a version of the RAP strategy (Ellis & Graves, 1990). Next, students are encouraged to use Brown and Day's (1983) summarization strategy (i.e., delete trivial information, delete redundant information, substitute superordinate terms for a list of terms or actions, select a topic sentence, and invent a topic sentence). Finally, students are provided with the opportunity to practice verbally retelling the information contained in the passage, with support provided from the teacher as needed to those students who have an expressive language impairment or short-term memory difficulties.

Mason et al. (2006) suggested facilitating expository reading comprehension with science and social studies texts by teaching TWA within the SRSD instructional framework. This framework is designed to foster metacognition, maintenance, and generalization. The SRSD instructional approach includes the following components: preskill development, discussion of strategy usage and how it helps with reading, teacher cognitive modeling, strategy step memorization, student and teacher collaborative practice, partner practice, and independent practice. Student application of self-regulation skills, including goal setting, self-monitoring, self-instruction, and self-reinforcement to improve reading comprehension, is also explicitly taught through this approach to help promote students' independence in strategy usage across outside settings and situations. This approach can be implemented with a whole class, with a small group, or during individualized instruction.

The SQ3R strategy (Cheek & Cheek, 1983; Just & Carpenter, 1987; Robinson, 1970; Schumaker et al., 1982) is a five-step strategy that students can use to help increase their reading comprehension of expository text. The following steps make up this strategy:

1. Survey. Get a general idea of what text is about by skimming chapter titles, headings, subheadings, illustrations, graphs, chapter introduction, and chapter summary
2. Question. Read any study questions in the text or given by the teacher or create your own questions by turning titles and headings into questions
3. Read. Read the text, keep study questions in mind, and keep track of main ideas
4. Recite. After reading, recite answers to study questions and write a few notes to help remember important ideas
5. Review. Look back at study questions and try to answer them without using notes and, finally, study notes to remember the content later on

The POSSE Strategy (Englert & Mariage, 1991) mentioned previously in this section is similar to the SQ3R strategy for increasing reading comprehension and retention of expository text. This strategy involves the following sequence of steps:

1. Predict. Scan text for headings, boldface print, pictures, and so forth, and for information that can be used to develop a preparatory set, activate background information, and generate prereading questions

2. Organize. Brainstorm prereading questions into a set of categories of information that the passage will contain, possibly through the use of a semantic map or graphic organizer
3. Search. Read the passage while keeping prereading questions and organizer in mind
4. Summarize. Give an oral summary of the passage, including the main idea, supporting ideas, and most important details and ask additional questions
5. Evaluate. Identify gaps in understanding and compare what has been learned with predictions, clarify misunderstandings encountered, and predict the topic of the next section of the passage

In summary, a number of different research-validated strategies have been developed to improve expository reading comprehension abilities in struggling readers and in those with reading disabilities. It is important for SLPs and other educators to become well versed in these strategies so that they can provide effective written language intervention to facilitate comprehension of expository text in their students. The results of several research studies specifically related to improving expository reading comprehension of mathematics, science, and social studies texts are discussed next.

## Research Related to Improving Reading Comprehension of Expository Text

Gersten, Fuchs, Williams, and Baker (2001) published a very comprehensive review of the existing literature on reading comprehension instruction for students with learning disabilities with respect to both narrative and expository text. The majority of the expository text studies in their review pertained to the use of single-strategy interventions, including the following: (a) reorganizing expository text (Wong & Wilson, 1984), (b) a self-questioning strategy (Chan, 1991; Mastropieri et al., 1996; Wong & Jones, 1982), (c) a cognitive mapping strategy (Boyle, 1996; Swanson, Kozleski, & Stegink, 1987), (d) detecting invalid arguments (Darch & Kameenui, 1987), (e) the SQ3R strategy (McCormick & Cooper, 1991), (f) a summarization strategy (Gajria & Salvia, 1992; Nelson, Smith, & Dodd, 1992), and (g) the Question/Answer Relationships Strategy (i.e., students are taught three types of comprehension questions: "right there," "think and search," and "on my own"; Simmonds, 1992). Gersten et al. (2001) concluded that this limited number of studies lend support to the idea that careful teacher modeling as well as monitoring of strategy use appear to be potentially important factors in improving reading comprehension in students with learning disabilities. However, these authors caution that the achievement of maintenance or transfer effects has not yet been convincingly demonstrated through use of these single-strategy interventions.

Gersten et al. (2001) also reviewed published studies that examined the use of multiple comprehension strategies that included the following:

(a) a combination of summarization with self-monitoring training (Graves, 1986; Jitendra, Cole, Hoppes, & Wilson, 1998; Jitendra, Hoppes, & Xin, 2000; Malone & Mastropieri, 1992), (b) use of the Multipass strategy (i.e., requires three passes—survey, size up, sort out—through expository passages; Schumaker et al., 1984), and (c) use of peer mediation to transfer control of a multiple-component strategy from the teacher to the students (Englert & Mariage, 1991; Klingner, Vaughn, & Schumm, 1998; Labercane & Battle, 1987). Again, it was concluded that effective teacher modeling, extensive student feedback, and consistent monitoring of strategy use are essential for ensuring that students with learning disabilities master and apply reading comprehension strategies for expository text. The authors also concluded that longer interventions may be necessary to achieve desired outcomes, but instruction in multiple strategies appears to facilitate generalization to a greater extent than single-strategy interventions for expository text comprehension.

Hall (2004) also conducted a comprehensive review of the existing research studies that have attempted to help increase comprehension of expository text for students who are struggling readers (i.e., those with average to above-average intelligence who have reading skills that are 2 or more years below their intellectual level but have not been identified as having a learning disability) (Gambrell & Bales, 1986; Gardner & Ransom, 1986; Zecker & Zinner, 1987) and/or those who have reading disabilities (i.e., those with a discrepancy between their intellectual abilities and academic achievements who read 3 to 7 years below grade level) (Bakken, Mastropieri, & Scruggs, 1997; Bos, Anders, Filip, & Jaffe 1989). Consequently, these students are at great risk for failing to comprehend the expository texts used in their content area classes. She found very few of these studies (i.e., 11 studies, with four that included only struggling readers, four that included only students with reading disabilities, and three that included both struggling readers and students with reading disabilities) despite the fact that teachers have been encouraged for decades to incorporate reading instruction into their content area courses. Although there was some overlap among the studies cited in Hall's (2004) and Gersten et al.'s (2001) reviews, there were also several studies, that were cited in only one or the other of these two articles. This may be due, at least in part, to differences in inclusion criteria. For example, Hall's (2004) review was restricted to studies with students who specifically had been diagnosed with a reading disability or were struggling readers, whereas Gersten et al.'s (2001) review used the more general learning disability diagnosis as criteria for inclusion.

In Hall's (2004) review, she described a variety of intervention approaches as follows: (a) revising texts (Le Sourd, 1985; Weiss, 1983), (b) using study guides (Horton, Boone, & Lovitt, 1990; Horton, Lovitt, Givens, & Nelson, 1989), (c) presentation of text (Montali & Lewandowski, 1996), (d) teaching vocabulary (Bos et al., 1989; Lyda & Duncan, 1967), (e) teaching comprehension skills (Bakken et al., 1997; Klingner et al., 1998; Spence, Yore, & Williams,

1999), and (f) using reciprocal teaching (Klingner et al., 1998; Lederer, 2000). Hall (2004) noted that the information that we have about which intervention techniques are most effective for these students is still very limited because of the small number of students who have been studied and the grade levels and content areas where the research was conducted. She also noted that with the exception of a study by Montali and Lewandowski (1996), the studies that she reviewed required both struggling readers and students with reading disabilities to read texts that were at or above their grade level despite the fact that they were primarily reading at least 2 years below grade level. Montali and Lewandowski (1996) found that struggling readers performed better when they read text written 2 years below their grade level.

Two studies (Le Sourd, 1985; Weiss, 1983) reviewed by Hall (2004) examined how struggling readers' comprehension of social studies text could be increased when they were allowed to read revised texts. In the Le Sourd (1985) study, a group of ninth-grade struggling readers were given a revised passage about politics that was adapted from the grade-level curriculum, while a second group read the text in its original form. The revised text included the name of the concept being studied, its definition, a list of the concepts' attributes, and an explanation of irrelevant attributes as well as two examples of the one concept and one nonexample. In general, struggling readers who read the revised text had a slightly higher mean comprehension score than those who read the text as it was originally written. However, given the small differences in these mean scores, the author concluded that struggling readers did not significantly benefit from the revised text. In contrast, in the Weiss (1983) study, struggling readers in fourth and seventh grades were found to benefit from reading revised social studies text. One group read text that was structured according to Johnson's (1970) "pausal phrase format" (i.e., text was broken into segments where 50% of a sampled adult population would pause when reading it out loud), a second group read text that was revised according to LeFevre's (1964) "syntactic phrase format" (i.e., text was segmented into separate noun phrases, verb phrases, and pattern completers), and a third group read the text in its original form. It was concluded that when struggling readers read passages that were written in either of the revised formats, their reading comprehension was comparable to students who were average readers. However, these studies had limitations in that neither study stated how many struggling readers were included in their samples, and neither study required students to take a pretest, nor did they require students to read original and revised texts for purposes of comparison.

Two other studies (Horton et al., 1989, 1990) reviewed by Hall (2004) examined how study guides can be used to help improve reading comprehension abilities. Horton et al. (1989) studied two groups of struggling readers and students with reading disabilities. In the first group, nine students with reading disabilities and 10 struggling readers read two passages from their social studies textbook on a computer at their own pace. They were then expected to complete two multiple-choice study guides related to the passages on the computer. At the end of the session, each student was given a hard copy of the study guide along with the correct answers. In the second group, eight struggling readers and four students with reading disabilities were instructed to read the same passages directly from their textbook. Rather than completing a study guide, students in the second group were informed that they could take notes on the text. However, these students did not receive specific feedback that might have contributed to their understanding of the text as did the students in the first group. Afterward, all participants were given a written test about the passages. Those students who were allowed to complete computerized study guides comprehended and retained information better than students who only took notes from their textbook. However, these findings need to be interpreted cautiously because the number of students studied within these contexts was relatively small across both studies and also because both studies examined only students who were at the high school level in a social studies class. In addition, the note-taking group was not given instruction in how to complete this process.

Montali and Lewandowski (1996) revealed that the way in which text was presented could increase comprehension of science and social studies material for eighth- and ninth-grade struggling readers (Hall, 2004). In this study, two struggling readers and 16 students with reading disabilities were instructed to learn from text that was presented in three different formats: (a) silently as it was presented on a screen, (b) silently as the words on the screen were read out loud to them, and (c) by listening to a voice read an unseen passage to them. Students who followed a passage on a screen as it was simultaneously being read out loud to them showed the most significant increase in comprehension of science and social studies text. Students who were instructed to read text on a computer screen silently to themselves did not make significant improvement. Likewise, students who were instructed to listen as the unseen passage was read out loud to them did not make any improvement in their comprehension.

Two studies reviewed by Hall (2004) were conducted to examine if teaching the vocabulary found in expository texts would help increase reading comprehension (Bos et al., 1989; Lyda & Duncan, 1967). Each study suggested that struggling readers and students with reading disabilities could increase their comprehension of math and social studies texts if they were presented with new words and corresponding definitions prior to reading a text. In the Lyda and Duncan (1967) study, a second-grade teacher presented 178 mathematical vocabulary words to her class over an 8-week period by providing an explanation of the words being discussed each day and an explanation of the meaning of the words. Then she had the students complete a set of vocabulary exercises related to the target words. Results indicated that this approach resulted in improvement in the second-grade struggling readers' mathematical computation skills and in their ability to comprehend mathematics text. However, Hall (2004) noted that these researchers did not directly state how they arrived at these conclusions, and no control group was included.

In the Bos et al. (1989) study, it was found that vocabulary instruction could result in significantly improved reading comprehension of social studies texts for high school students with reading disabilities. Twenty-five students were provided with a list of vocabulary words. They were instructed to locate the definition of each word by using a dictionary and then to use each word in a sentence. The other 25 students participated in a semantic feature analysis condition where they were given a chart with two columns (i.e., one column with related vocabulary terms and a second column with important ideas students would be reading about in the text) prior to reading the text. Definitions were provided for each term by either the students themselves or one of the researchers. Students were then asked to predict if the vocabulary words and the important ideas would be positively or negatively related, have no relationship, or have an unknown relationship. Later, they confirmed or revised these predictions as they read the text. Students who participated in the semantic feature analysis condition were found to exhibit a higher level of comprehension than students who read the same text but were required to look up the meaning of vocabulary words in a dictionary. Furthermore, the students in the semantic feature analysis group performed better on a follow-up test given 6 months later. While both of these studies demonstrated the success that specific types of vocabulary instruction had on students' comprehension of expository text, the studies were limited in that the Lyda and Duncan (1967) study did not state how many struggling readers participated, and the Bos et al. (1989) study did not include any struggling readers (Hall, 2004).

Students with reading disabilities and struggling readers may benefit from specific, explicit instruction aimed at teaching them how to apply comprehension strategies to expository texts. According to Hall (2004), the majority of work that has been done in this area suggests that teaching students how to preview texts, monitor their comprehension, locate and state main ideas, and summarize what they have read can result in increased comprehension of both science and social studies text (Bakken et al. 1997; Spence et al., 1999). The results of the Bakken et al. (1997) study indicated that explicit teaching of comprehension strategies can increase comprehension of science text for eighth-grade students with reading disabilities.

In the Bakken et al. (1997) study, 54 students with reading disabilities were assigned to one of three conditions (i.e., text structure–based strategy, paragraph restatement strategy, or traditional instruction strategy conditions). In the text structure–based strategy condition, students were first taught the different ways that science passages were organized, how to identify the main idea in a science passage, how to locate the supporting evidence for the main idea, and how to write this information down in their own words. On the second day, they were given a "list" passage and explicitly taught how to locate the topic and subtopics of the passage as well as how to record this information in their own words. On the last day of instruction, all the skills taught were reviewed, and students read a list passage that described a sequence of events. Students were taught how to locate the topic of the passage and sequence the stories. Students in the paragraph restatement strategy condition were provided with a narrative passage and then taught how to write a statement about that passage in their own words. During the next 2 days of instruction, days 2 and 3, this same procedure was followed with list and order passages. Students in the traditional instruction strategy condition were provided with an explanation of the difference between leisure and scientific reading and were subsequently taught how to read a scientific passage and answer comprehension questions about that passage. This same procedure was used during the next 2 days of instruction with list and order passages. Results indicated that students who were in the text structure–based strategy condition were able to recall more ideas from the text that they had read than the students in the other two conditions. The students in the paragraph restatement condition performed better than those who had been in the traditional instruction group, and the students in the traditional group did not exhibit any significant improvement in their reading comprehension abilities.

Spence et al. (1999) found similar results with seventh-grade struggling readers. Their study involved 27 students enrolled in one science class, 11 of whom were struggling readers. All the students were either taught a new comprehension strategy or reviewed a previously learned strategy each day over a 22-week period. The students were then instructed to read science texts, and they were expected to apply the strategies they had learned. At the end of the study, the researchers concluded that the struggling readers demonstrated improvement with respect to both their comprehension of science text and their metacognitive awareness.

Two studies (Klingner et al., 1998; Lederer, 2000) reviewed by Hall (2004) examined the effects of reciprocal teaching (Palincsar & Brown, 1984) on students' abilities to comprehend expository texts. In the Lederer (2000) study, 15 fourth-through-sixth-grade students with reading disabilities were taught to use the reciprocal teaching method, with 10 additional students serving as controls. The 15 students who received instruction displayed improvement in their ability to write summaries of the text they had read. However, they did not exhibit significant increases in their comprehension of the social studies texts. The researcher concluded that the improvement noted in the students' written summaries may have been due to the fact that students in the reciprocal teaching group were given more time to discuss what they had read.

In contrast, Klingner et al. (1998) found that comprehension of social studies text can be increased through the use of the reciprocal teaching method. The participants in this study were fourth graders in a heterogeneous classroom that included students with and without reading disabilities. All the participants were assigned to either a treatment group or a control group. The students in the treatment group were initially provided with explicit instruction from a researcher regarding how to use four comprehension strategies over a 3-day period. Following this phase of instruction, the students were given opportunities to try out these new strategies with the researchers offering support. Finally, the students were placed into small groups and given a text that they were expected to read and learn from. Results indicated that the students in the experimental group performed better than the students in the control group with respect to both comprehension of text and content knowledge. However, the students with reading disabilities who participated in the treatment group did not make significant improvement in these areas. According to Hall (2004), neither the Lederer (2000) study nor the Klingner et al. (1998) study helped students with reading disabilities to make significant gains in their comprehension of social studies text; however, they did show some improvement in the Klingner et al. study, suggesting that reciprocal teaching may be beneficial for students with reading difficulties.

To conclude, the results of several research studies have demonstrated that there are a number of intervention techniques and approaches that may be used to improve expository reading comprehension abilities in struggling readers and in students with reading disabilities. On the basis of the results of these studies, it was concluded that students with learning disabilities benefit from strong teacher modeling, extensive feedback, and consistent modeling of strategy use. In addition, students with reading disabilities have been shown to increase their reading comprehension significantly when they are provided with definitions of vocabulary words prior to reading social studies text and are given the opportunity to predict how these words are related to concepts in the text. Struggling readers were also found to increase their comprehension significantly when they (a) read science and social studies texts that were presented to them on a screen while simultaneously being read out loud and (b) were provided with definitions of mathematical vocabulary words prior to reading. Both struggling readers and students with reading disabilities increased their comprehension significantly when they (a) used study guides with social studies text and (b) were explicitly taught how to apply comprehension skills to science and social studies text. Studies related to revising texts have provided conflicting evidence regarding how well this strategy helps struggling readers comprehend social studies text. Studies on reciprocal teaching also provide conflicting evidence about how successful this strategy is with students with reading disabilities who are reading social studies texts. Additional research is needed that includes larger sample sizes, more detailed research designs that would allow for easier replication, and students from a wider age range. Next, the use of graphic organizers for improving reading comprehension of expository text is considered.

## Use of Graphic Organizers for Improving Reading Comprehension of Expository Text

Students with language-learning disabilities, as well as other students who struggle to understand relationships among critical concepts, need instruction that explicitly demonstrates how content is related in domain knowledge (Alexander, Schallert, & Hare, 1991; Prawat, 1989). It is insufficient for students to acquire factual knowledge; they must also learn how concepts are connected or related to each other. However, many students with learning disabilities experience difficulties with extracting relationships from expository text, especially if those relationships are implicit. Results from numerous studies with K–12 participants have been inconclusive regarding the efficacy of the graphic organizer as a comprehension tool, although the results have been more positive in recent studies.

A graphic organizer refers to a visual portrayal or illustration that depicts relationships among the key concepts involved in a learning task (Hudson, Lignugaris-Kraft, & Miller, 1993; Moore & Readence, 1984). The interrelationships of superordinate and subordinate ideas are typically visually depicted by using spatial arrangements, geometric shapes, lines, and arrows to portray content structure and to demonstrate key relationships among concepts (Darch, Carnine, & Kameenui, 1986). Graphic organizers are used to identify salient details and to eliminate extraneous information that frequently distracts students with learning disabilities from the most important content (DiCecco & Gleason, 2002). They are also used to highlight high-level knowledge embedded in a text, to provide a foundation for comprehending the text (Bernard, 1990), and to help students plan and organize their spoken and written discourse (Ward-Lonergan, 2002). However, the appeal of graphic organizers and the intuitive sense that they should be beneficial, as evidenced by the vast number of curriculum materials that include this technique (Bromley, Irwin-De Vitas, & Modlo, 1995; Hyerle, 1996; Lenz, Bulgren, Schumaker, Deshler, & Boudah, 1994), has often overshadowed the question of their true effectiveness.

According to DiCecco and Gleason (2002), three major research reviews and critiques of using graphic organizers with K–12 students appeared in the literature between 1992 and 2002 (Dunston, 1992; Griffin & Tulbert, 1995; Rice, 1994). These studies addressed the issue of where the graphic organizer was used in the instructional sequence, whether the graphic organizer was teacher constructed, and whether participants with a learning disability differed from typical learners. Few of the earlier graphic organizer studies used students with learning disabilities as participants. In addition, the earlier studies that were conducted with students with learning disabilities employed short treatment periods (2–12 days), and no studies prior to DiCecco and Gleason's (2002) study examined whether graphic organizers enhanced relational knowledge since they used multiple-choice tests. According to DiCecco and Gleason (2002), these earlier studies did not appear to closely align the content of the text with the content of the graphic organizers or the content of the teachers' wording that accompanied the use of the graphic organizers.

Kim, Vaughn, Wanzek, and Wei (2004) conducted an extensive synthesis of the 21 experimental research studies (single-subject design studies were excluded) published between 1963 and 2001 that did specifically examine the effects of the use of graphic organizers on the reading comprehension of students with learning disabilities. It is important to note that only three of these studies were published between 1994 and 2004. Of the 21 studies reviewed, six included high school students, six included junior high school students, and five included elementary school students as participants. The authors concluded that the use of graphic organizers was found to be beneficial overall with respect to improving the reading comprehension of students with learning disabilities across these studies, and larger effect sizes were associated with the use of researcher-developed comprehension measures as opposed to standardized reading assessments. Furthermore, the use of semantic organizers, cognitive maps with and without mnemonic devices, and framed outlines were found to be specific types of graphic organizers that yielded positive outcomes.

Subsequently, DiCecco and Gleason (2002) conducted a study designed to address some of the concerns with graphic organizer research previously noted. This study examined the effects of using graphic organizers with 24 middle school students with learning disabilities. These researchers used graphic organizers to convey and cue relational knowledge, implemented a longer intervention period, and obtained written essays to assess the students' attainment of relational knowledge. A pretest/posttest control group design was used to examine the effects of a combination of explicit instruction and the use of graphic organizers on students' ability to gain and apply relational knowledge from social studies texts. Participants received instruction for a period of 4 weeks through 40-minute lessons. These lessons focused on the direct teaching of word meanings and difficult-to-decode words, strategy instruction for writing summaries, and carefully structured scaffolding for reading text and answering comprehension questions. The graphic organizer group and the "no graphic organizer" group were taught in separate classrooms that were familiar to the students. The content used was selected from a middle school social studies textbook. Graphic organizers were developed for each unit of thought, which contained content that was centered on a single theme, concept, or focal idea (Tindal & Marston, 1990), and each lesson was limited to the facts, concepts, and relationships for one unit of thought. A total of five graphic organizers were introduced to help make implied relationships more explicit and to cue relational knowledge. Instructional scripts were used to ensure consistency across groups. Every opportunity was afforded to the control group to learn the content and relational knowledge that would be tested throughout the study, with the exception of using graphic organizers or any other visual display of relational knowledge.

Results supported the idea of using graphic organizers with students with learning disabilities to gain relational knowledge from expository textbooks. There were no significant differences found between the treatment and control groups with regard to their ability to display factual knowledge on multiple-choice tests and quizzes. These results also supported the findings from previous graphic organizer studies in that both groups demonstrated attainment of facts and concepts. However, when relational knowledge was assessed, the two groups responded differentially. Students with learning disabilities also benefited from a longer treatment period than had previously been used as well as from treatment that was more intensive and more explicitly aligned than treatments used in previous studies (DiCecco & Gleason, 2002). Interestingly, the retrieval of specific domain knowledge for the no graphic organizer group of students did not seem to be cued despite their participation in a hands-on activity (being part of an assembly line) and in a discussion about the assembly line, mass production, and cars becoming cheaper to buy. The researchers emphasized that the conclusions of this study must be interpreted with caution, and they also emphasized that merely showing students a graphic organizer on an overhead projector without the accompanying teacher modeling, guided practice, and review on subsequent days is not likely to achieve the desirable results observed in this study. They also noted that instruction in summary writing may be a necessary component to ensure graphic organizer efficacy. They concluded that their study clearly demonstrated that students with learning disabilities benefited from the combination of graphic organizers, intensive instruction, and summary writing. Studies aimed at increasing comprehension of different types of expository text structures are discussed in the next main section.

## Reading Comprehension Strategies for Various Types of Expository Text Structures

Bakken (1997) described treatment strategies that may be used to facilitate reading comprehension of five different types of expository passages: main idea, list, order, classification, and compare/contrast. These strategies are presented in Table 10.1.

## Summary

A substantial number of treatment techniques and approaches have been advocated for improving expository reading comprehension abilities in school-age children and adolescents with language impairments. However, it is important to note that additional research with a larger number of students from diverse backgrounds is needed. Furthermore, an examination of the effectiveness of proposed treatment techniques and approaches across a wider range of grade levels and content areas is necessary before definitive conclusions can be drawn regarding the efficacy of many of these intervention suggestions. In the final portion of this chapter, language intervention designed to improve expository writing abilities is considered.

**Table 10.1**  Treatment Strategies for Comprehending Five Different Types of Expository Passages

| Paragraph Type | Treatment Strategy |
| --- | --- |
| Main Idea | Step 1: Underline the main idea |
| | Step 2: Write down the main idea and other important information in your own words |
| List | Step 1: Underline the general topic |
| | Step 2: Write down the general topic and subtopics in your own words |
| Order | Step 1: Underline the topic of the passage |
| | Step 2: Write down what is different from one step to the next |
| Classification | Step 1: Underline the general topic |
| | Step 2: Write down categories and related information in columns |
| Compare/contrast | Step 1: Underline the general topics |
| | Step 2: Write down general topics and what is similar and/or different between them |

*Source:* Modified from Bakken, J. P., Mastropieri, M. A., & Scruggs, T. E., *Journal of Special Education, 31,* 300–324, 1997.

## WRITTEN EXPRESSION INTERVENTION

### Teaching Expository Writing Strategies

Gersten and Baker (2001) conducted a meta-analysis of writing interventions for students with learning disabilities. These researchers reviewed seven published studies that attempted to improve expository writing abilities in students with learning disabilities (Englert, Raphael, Anderson, Anthony, & Stevens, 1991; Englert et al., 1995; MacArthur, Graham, Schwartz, & Schafer, 1995; Reynolds, 1986; Welch, 1992; Wong, Butler, Ficzere, & Kuperis, 1996; Wong, Butler, Ficzere, Kuperis, Corden, & Zelmer, 1994). They also reviewed six narrative writing studies and three creative writing studies. The results of this meta-analysis revealed that all the interventions resulted in positive outcomes for the students with learning disabilities. Specifically, strong effects were found related to the quality of students' writing, their sense of efficacy about their writing abilities, and their understanding of the writing process. Treatment effects were consistent across genres as well as across assessment measures (i.e., global quality ratings and scoring rubrics). Based on the results of these studies, the authors concluded that there are three essential components to an effective writing program for students with learning disabilities: explicit teaching of the writing process, awareness of text structures, and extensive teacher and/or peer feedback. The need for additional research aimed at promoting generalization of writing strategies was also noted.

Thomas, Englert, and Gregg (1987) suggested that successful writing programs for students with learning disabilities need to foster their confidence in their written expression abilities and to provide them with opportunities to engage in sustained writing as opposed to just having them complete sentence-writing or worksheet activities. These researchers also stressed that students with learning disabilities need to be made aware of the purposes of writing and that they also need more specific instruction in writing strategies with less emphasis on the mechanics of the writing process. For example, Sheinker and Sheinker (1989) presented the following eight-step strategy for writing a summary paragraph that students may be taught to apply whenever they need to write a paragraph:

1. Read the passage.
2. List the key points.
3. Combine related points that could be written as single statements.
4. Eliminate the least important points by crossing them out.
5. Reread the list.
6. Combine and cross out additional points to condense the list further.
7. Renumber points in a logical order.
8. Write listed points into a paragraph in the numbered order.

Writing strategy instruction typically involves (a) modeling of cognitive strategies through the think-aloud technique (Bereiter & Scardamalia, 1984; Scardamalia & Bereiter, 1983), (b) an interactive instructional sequence in which teachers and students engage in the cognitive process and dialogue interactively (Brown, Palincsar, & Armbruster, 1984; Palincsar, 1985; Palincsar & Brown, 1984), (c) development of inner speech or metacognitive skills through self-instruction focusing on the coordination of behavior and strategies during the writing stages (Wong & Jones, 1982; Wong & Sawatsky 1984), and (d) an emphasis on "what" the writing strategy is, "how" and "when" it should be used, and "why" it is important (Brown, Campione, & Day, 1981; Brown & Palincsar, 1982; Roehler, Duffy, & Meloth, 1986).

Englert et al. (1991) noted that few studies have examined the effects of intervention designed to increase expository writing abilities and students' ability to generalize their knowledge to write expository texts using novel text structures. These researchers conducted a study with 183 fourth and fifth graders that attempted to increase students' expository writing abilities through an instructional program (Cognitive Strategy Instruction in Writing [CSIW]) that emphasized teacher and student dialogues about expository writing strategies, provided scaffolded instruction, and transformed solitary writing into a collaborative activity. Of these students, 128 were regular education students, and 55 were students with learning disabilities (33 in the CSIW group and 22 in the control group) who also had receptive or expressive language abilities below mental age expectations. The CSIW program was developed to increase students' knowledge of the writing process and the role of expository text structures. The CSIW curriculum materials included "think-sheets" that were designed to make the strategies, self-talk, and text structures for performing the writing process visible to students. The acronym POWER (plan, organize, write, edit/editor, and revise), was used to refer to the entire set of strategies. Instruction in CSIW occurred over a 6- to 7-month period and consisted of four phases for each text structure taught: text analysis, modeling of the writing process, guided practice, and independent use of strategies (Raphael & Englert, 1990).

Results strongly supported the use of CSIW for improving the overall quality of expository writing. Students in the experimental group produced compositions that were significantly more organized than those produced by students in the control group. In addition, students who participated in the CSIW intervention were successful in generalizing their knowledge to less structured writing situations in which they wrote about topics of personal interest to them and used text structures of their own choice. Finally, students displayed increased sensitivity to their audience and greater ownership of the writing process. Of particular interest was that the students with learning disabilities were found to perform much more poorly on all writing variables across the three types of text (explanation, comparison/contrast, and expert) on pretest measures than the students without disabilities. However, the students with learning disabilities did not perform significantly different on any writing variable on the posttest. This indicated that preintervention differences that existed prior to the CSIW instruction tended to be eliminated by the time the students with learning disabilities completed the instructional program. It was concluded that CSIW was an effective writing program for students with and without learning disabilities that combined the best features of strategy instruction within a curriculum that fostered the development of students' knowledge of the writing process and text structures. They also noted that the data from their study suggested that instruction in the writing process and expository text structures can be effective when they are embedded in an instructional framework emphasizing teacher modeling, scaffolding, procedure facilitation, peer collaboration, and encouragement of the development of an inner language and vocabulary for talking about writing.

Williams and Ward-Lonergan (2009) presented research related to the use of a referential communication strategy to improve written expression skills in school-age children with learning disabilities. Five dyads, each consisting of one child with a learning disability and one typically developing child, served as participants. Four of the participants were third graders, and six were fourth graders. The children with learning disabilities had a reported history of writing difficulties. A pretest, treatment, posttest design was used in this study. The pretest/posttest measure involved each dyad being physically separated as they wrote instructions for their communication partner to complete a construction paper design depicting hieroglyphics (see Figure 10.1) (e.g., a totem pole, a shield, hieroglyphics, a blanket). After writing the directions, the children in each dyad exchanged papers. Each child was given the individual pieces of construction paper needed to complete the construction paper design. The children subsequently read the directions their partner had written and used them to complete their own design. No feedback was provided to the participants regarding their written instructions.

During treatment sessions conducted on 4 consecutive days, the same procedure described previously was followed using other designs (i.e., a totem pole, a shield, a blanket). However, during the treatment sessions, the children in each dyad met to compare their designs with the original models immediately after completing them. The members of each dyad then orally gave their partner feedback about the effectiveness of the written message. With verbal guidance from the investigator, the children told their partner what worked, what did not work, and what would have made the written instructions clearer and easier to follow. The investigator then verbally reiterated the main points of the partner's feedback.

The results of this study indicated that four of the five children with learning disabilities demonstrated substantial improvement in their overall writing scores from the pretest to the posttest measure. However, these scores were not statistically significantly different, primarily because of the small sample size and the lack of change for one participant. Figure 10.1 illustrates the pretest/posttest sample design and specific improvements made by one child with a learning disability from his pretest to his posttest writing sample. Across participants, increases were noted in the use of position terms that were necessary for the communication partner to place the individual items more accurately. A slight increase in specificity of label use was also observed, and some children demonstrated use of visual organizers, such as numbering each step. A decrease in spelling errors was also found for the children with learning disabilities. However, no significant improvement was observed in mechanical writing skills (i.e., capitalization and punctuation). Results suggest that a referential communication task may be a potentially efficacious treatment paradigm for improving the content of the writing of children with learning disabilities, although further research with a larger sample is warranted.

Researchers from the University of Kansas Center for Research on Learning (KU-CRL) have developed four detailed strategies (i.e., sentences, paragraphs, error monitoring, and themes) designed to improve written expression skills as part of the Expressing Information strand in their Learning Strategies Curriculum (http://www.ku-crl.org). It is recommended that these strategies be taught in this order unless the student has already mastered some of these, in which case instruction should begin with the

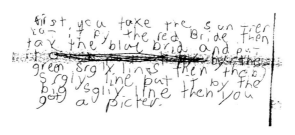

first, you take the sun tren
tak it by the red bride then
tak the blue brid and put
it green srgly lines then by the
srgiy line but then the big
big sgliy line then by the you
got a picter.

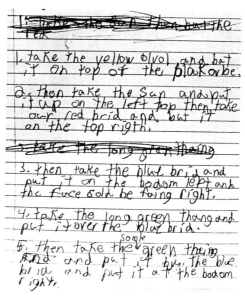

1. take the yellow oval and bat
it on top of the black orbe.

2. then take the san and put
it up on the left top then take
our red brid and but it
on the top rigth.

3. then take the blue brid and
put it on the bodom left anb
the face cold be faing right.

4. take the long green thang and
put it over the blue brid.

5. then take the some green thing
and and put it by the blue
brid and put it at the bodom
right.

**Figure 10.1** Pretest/posttest stimulus, pretest writing sample, and posttest writing sample.

next strategy in the sequence. These strategies may be applied across various genres of writing, including expository writing. Teachers and SLPs who wish to obtain copies of these strategy manuals to instruct their students need to attend a training workshop offered by a certified KU-CRL professional developer. The sentence writing strategy has a basic, developmental version designed to teach students how to write simple sentences known as Fundamentals in the Sentence Writing Strategy (Schumaker & Sheldon, 1998) as well as a more advanced version designed to teach students to use 14 different formulas for writing a variety of simple, compound, complex, and compound-complex sentences known as the Proficiency in the Sentence Writing Strategy (Schumaker & Sheldon, 1999). Research results have shown that students wrote an average of 65% complete sentences on the pretest measure and an average of 88% complete sentences on the posttest measure following instruction in this strategy.

The Error Monitoring Strategy (Schumaker, Nolan, & Deshler, 1985) is designed to teach students to systematically detect and correct errors in their written products in order to improve the overall quality of their written work. Students are taught to proofread their writing for both content and mechanical errors and then to eliminate these errors prior to submitting their final written products. Research results indicated that students who have mastered this strategy have dramatically increased their ability to detect and correct errors in their written work (i.e., making approximately one error in every four words prior to instruction and making approximately one error in every 20 words following instruction).

The Paragraph Writing Strategy (Schumaker & Lyerla, 1993) is a comprehensive strategy that enables students to write well-organized, cohesive paragraphs by writing a variety of topic, detail, and clincher sentences, with consistent point of view and verb tense. Research results indicated that students earned an average of 40% of the points available when writing a paragraph on the pretest as compared to an average of 71% of the points available when writing a paragraph on the posttest measure. In the Written Language Program at the University of the Pacific, numerous school-age children and adolescents with language disorders have significantly improved their expository written expression abilities through instruction in the Sentence Writing Strategy and Paragraph Writing Strategy.

Finally, the Fundamentals in the Theme Writing Strategy (Schumaker, 2003) is designed to teach students how to compose themes or essays of at least five paragraphs in length. In one research study, it was found that individuals who received instruction in this strategy earned a significantly higher percentage of available points than a control group following instruction in this strategy, and there were no significant differences between their grades in an "English 101" course and their overall grade-point averages, even though the experimental group had initially entered college with poorer skills than the control group.

The four written expression strategies described previously have been field-tested in a variety of settings with different kinds of students since 1979 (Schumaker & Deshler, 2003). Each strategy involves a mnemonic device that students use to apply the strategy steps. For example, the PENS mnemonic is used in both the Sentence Writing Strategy and the Paragraph Writing Strategy. As it applies to the Proficiency in the Sentence Writing Strategy (Schumaker & Sheldon, 1999), PENS refers to *P* (pick a formula), *E* (explore words to fit the formula), *N* (note the words), and *S* (search and check). According to Schumaker (2003), the results of these field tests have indicated that when the strategies are taught according to the procedures found in the instructor's manuals, significant gains occur in both cognitive and writing skills associated directly with the strategy as well as in general writing competencies (e.g., writing achievement scores). Schumaker (2003) further noted that low-achieving students who use these strategies are able to perform at levels that are comparable to their typically developing peers and are often able to succeed independently in general education classes. Many students who were at risk for dropping out of high school ultimately have earned high school diplomas, and some have proceeded to be successful in community colleges and universities (Schumaker, 2003). In addition to the Learning Strategies Curriculum, researchers at KU-CRL have developed and field-tested a series of Content Enhancement Routines that are designed for the classroom teacher to use during group instruction in middle and high school settings. Some of these routines (e.g., Framing, Order) are aimed at facilitating text exploration and comprehension (for descriptions, see http://www.ku-crl.org).

In short, researchers have developed several different writing strategies and instructional programs that may be used to improve expository writing abilities in students with language disorders. These strategies are comprised of a series of steps that students can be taught to generalize across various writing tasks and situations. The use of strategy description, modeling, interactive instruction, guided practice and feedback, and advanced practice using curriculum-based assignments are important features of strategic instruction. Given that these writing strategies have been research validated, the future holds great promise for improving expository writing skills in these students.

## Schoolwide Instruction Integrating Academic Content and Literacy

Over the past 15 years, researchers at KU-CRL have also developed a schoolwide instructional approach for promoting literacy designed for use in middle and secondary school settings known as the Content Literacy Continuum (CLC) (http://www.ku-crl.org/featured/wholeschool.shtml). The CLC is comprised of five increasingly intensive levels of literacy support that optimally should be in place in every school in order to meet the individual needs of all students. Level 1 of the CLC involves having general education teachers present expository content in learner-friendly ways, and Level 2 involves embedding strategy instruction into core content area classes. In

Level 3, intensive, specialized instruction in learning strategies is provided by someone other than the general education teacher, and reading specialists and special education teachers work collaboratively to provide even more specialized, intensive direct instruction in listening, speaking, reading, and writing skills to those students who need this level of intensity in Level 4. Finally, Level 5 involves SLPs delivering direct curriculum-based language intervention to students with language disorders and providing collaborative and consultative services across all levels of the CLC. The primary goal of Level 5 is facilitating mastery of both the underlying language demands of the curriculum and learning strategies necessary for academic success (Ehren, 2006; Ward-Lonergan, 2006).

## CONCLUDING REMARKS

In summary, intervention aimed at improving expository writing appears to be very beneficial for school-age children and adolescents with language impairments. As previously noted, further research is warranted to provide more definitive support for the use of some of these treatment techniques and approaches with a greater number of diverse students across a wider range of grade levels and content areas. Because of the serious negative consequences that can result from poor expository discourse abilities, treatment aimed at improving these abilities is essential if these students are to master the language of the curriculum and thus achieve academic success. As a field, we are currently at the "tip of the iceberg" with respect to our knowledge about best practices in intervention related to expository discourse abilities, and we need to continue to strive to make a difference in the lives of our students by addressing their needs in the realm of expository discourse. It stands to reason that the future holds great promise for students with language impairments as researchers continue to make advances in this critical area.

## REFERENCES

Alexander, A. A., Schallert, D. L., & Hare, C. H. (1991). Coming to terms: How researchers in learning and literacy talk about knowledge. *Review of Educational Research, 61,* 315–343.

Alley, G., & Deshler, D. (1979). *Teaching the learning disabled adolescent: Strategies and methods.* Denver: Love.

Bakken, J. P. (1997, April). *Teaching students with learning disabilities expository comprehension strategies in a classroom setting.* Paper presented at the annual meeting of the Council for Exceptional Children, Salt Lake City, UT.

Bakken, J. P., Mastropieri, M. A., & Scruggs, T. E. (1997). Reading comprehension of expository science material and students with learning disabilities: A comparison of strategies. *Journal of Special Education, 31,* 300–324.

Beck, I. L., McKeown, M. G., Hamilton, R., & Kucan, L. (1998). Getting at the meaning: How to help students unpack difficult text. *American Educator, 22*(1 & 2), 66–71, 85.

Bereiter, C., & Scardamalia, M. (1984). Information-processing demand of text composition. In H. Mandl, N. L. Stein, & T. Trabasso (Eds.), *Learning and comprehension of text* (pp. 407-428). Hillsdale, NJ: Lawrence Erlbaum Associates.

Bernard, R. M. (1990). Effects of processing instructions on the usefulness of a graphic organizer and structural cueing in text. *Instructional Science, 19*, 207–216.

Bos, C. S., Anders, P. L., Filip, D., & Jaffe, L. E. (1989). The effects of an interactive instructional strategy for enhancing reading comprehension and content area learning for students with learning disabilities. *Journal of Learning Disabilities, 22*, 384–389.

Boyle, J. R. (1996). The effects of a cognitive mapping strategy on the literal and inferential comprehension of students with mild disabilities. *Learning Disabilities Quarterly, 19*, 86–98.

Bromley, K., Irwin-De Vitas, L., & Modlo, M. (1995). *Graphic organizers: Visual strategies for active learning.* New York: Scholastic.

Brown, A. L., Campione, J. C., & Day, J. D. (1981). Learning to learn: On training students to learn from texts. *Educational Researcher, 10*, 14–21.

Brown, A. L., & Day, J. D. (1983). Macro rules for summarizing texts: The development of expertise. *Journal of Verbal Learning and Verbal Behavior, 22*, 1–14.

Brown, A. L., & Palincsar, A. S. (1982). Inducing strategic learning from texts by means of informed, self-control training. *Topics in Learning and Learning Disabilities, 2*, 1–17.

Brown, A. L., Palincsar, A. S., & Armbruster, B. B. (1984). Instruction comprehension-fostering activities in interactive learning situations. In H. Mandl, N. L. Stein, & T. Trabasso (Eds.), *Learning and comprehension of text* (pp. 255–286). Hillsdale, NJ: Lawrence Erlbaum Associates.

Carnine, D., Silbert, J., & Kameenui, E. J. (1990). *Direct instruction reading* (2nd ed.). Columbus, OH: Merrill.

Chan, L. K. S. (1991). Promoting strategy generalization through self-instructional training in students with reading disabilities. *Journal of Learning Disabilities, 24*, 427–433.

Cheek, E., & Cheek, M. (1983). *Reading instruction through content teaching.* Columbus, OH: Merrill.

Connecticut Teachers. (2004). *CAPT reading across the disciplines.* Ridgefield, CT: Webster House.

Coutant, C., & Perchemlides, N. (2005). Strategies for teen readers. *Educational Leadership, 63*, 42–47.

Darch, C., Carnine, D., & Kameenui, E. J. (1986). The role of graphic organizers and social structure in content area instruction. *Journal of Reading Behavior, 28*, 275–294.

Darch, C., & Kameenui, E. J. (1987). Teaching LD students critical reading skills: A systematic replication. *Learning Disability Quarterly, 10*, 82–91.

Deshler, D. D., & Lenz, B. K. (1989). The strategies instructional approach. *International Journal of Disability, Development, and Education, 36*(3), 203–224.

DiCecco, V. M., & Gleason, M. M. (2002). Using graphic organizers to attain relational knowledge from expository text. *Journal of Learning Disabilities, 35*(4), 306–320.

Dunston, P. J. (1992). A critique of graphic organizer research. *Reading Research and Instruction, 32*(2), 57–65.

Durkin, D. (1978–1979). What classroom observations reveal about reading comprehension instruction. *Reading Research Quarterly, 4*, 482–533.

Ehren, B. J. (2006). *Speech-language pathologists and the content literacy continuum.* Unpublished manuscript.

Ellis, E. S., & Graves, A. W. (1990). Teaching rural students with learning disabilities: A paraphrasing strategy to increase comprehension of main ideas. *Rural Special Education Quarterly, 4,* 482–533.

Englert, C. S., Garmon, A., Mariage, T., Rozendal, M., Tarrant, K., & Urba, J. (1995). The early literacy project: Connecting across the literacy curriculum. *Learning Disability Quarterly, 18,* 253–275.

Englert, C. S., & Mariage, T. V. (1991). Making students partners in the comprehension process: Organizing the reading "POSSE." *Learning Disabilities Quarterly, 14,* 123–138.

Englert, C. S., Raphael, T. E., Anderson, L. M., Anthony, H. M., & Stevens, D. D. (1991). Making strategies and self-talk visible: Writing instruction in regular and special education classrooms. *American Educational Research Journal, 28*(2), 337–372.

Englert, C. S., Raphael, T. E., Anderson, L. M., Gregg, S. L., & Anthony, H. M. (1989). Exposition: Reading, writing, and the metacognitive knowledge of learning disabled students. *Learning Disabilities Research, 5*(1), 5–24.

Gajria, M., & Salvia, J. (1992). The effects of summarization instructions on text comprehension of students with learning disabilities. *Exceptional Children, 58*(6), 508–516.

Gambrell, L., & Bales, R. (1986). Mental imagery and the comprehension-monitoring performance of fourth and fifth-grade poor readers. *Reading Research Quarterly, 21,* 454–464.

Gardner, J., & Ransom, G. (1986). Academic reorientation: A counseling approach to struggling readers. *The Reading Teacher, 21,* 529–536, 540.

Gersten, R., & Baker, S. (2001). Teaching expressive writing to students with learning disabilities: A meta-analysis. *Elementary School Journal, 101,* 251–272.

Gersten, R., Fuchs, L. S., Williams, J. P., & Baker, S. (2001). Teaching reading comprehension strategies to students with learning disabilities: A review of research. *Review of Educational Research, 71,* 279–320.

Gillam, R. B., Hoffman, L. M., Marler, J. A., & Wynn-Dancy, M. L. (2002). Sensitivity to increased task demands: Contributions from data-driven and conceptually driven information processing deficits. *Topics in Language Disorders, 22*(3), 30–48.

Gillespie, C., & Rasinski, T. (1989). Content area teachers' attitudes and practices toward reading in the content areas: A review. *Reading Research and Instruction, 28,* 45–67.

Graham, S., & Harris, K. R. (2003). Students with learning disabilities and the process of writing: A meta-analysis of SRSD studies. In H. L. Swanson, K. R. Harris, & S. Graham (Eds.), *Handbook of learning disabilities* (pp. 323–344). New York: Guilford Press.

Graves, A. W. (1986). Effects of direct instruction and metacomprehension training of finding main ideas. *Learning Disabilities Research, 1,* 90–100.

Graves, A. W., & Levin, J. R. (1989). Comparison of monitoring and mnemonic text-processing strategies in learning disabled students. *Learning Disabilities Quarterly, 12,* 232–236.

Griffin, C. C., & Tulbert, B. L. (1995). The effect of graphic organizers on students' comprehension and recall of expository text: A review of the research and implications for practice. *Reading and Writing Quarterly, 11*(1), 73–89.

Hall, L. A. (2004). Comprehending expository text: Promising strategies for struggling readers and students with reading disabilities? *Reading Research and Instruction, 44*(2), 75–95.

Hansen, J., & Pearson, P. D. (1983). An instructional study: Improving the inferential comprehension of good and poor fifth-grade readers. *Journal of Educational Psychology 75,* 821–829.

Horton, S. V., Boone, R., & Lovitt, T. (1990). Teaching social studies to learning disabled high school students: Effects of a hypertext study guide. *British Journal of Educational Technology, 21*(2), 118–131.

Horton, S. V., Lovitt, T. C., Givens, A., & Nelson, R. (1989). Teaching social studies to high school students with academic handicaps in a mainstreamed setting: Effects of a computerized study guide. *Journal of Learning Disabilities, 22,* 102–107.

Hudson, P., Lignugaris-Kraft, B., & Miller, T. (1993). Using content enhancements to improve the performance of adolescents with learning disabilities in content classes. *Learning Disabilities Research and Practice, 8,* 106–126.

Hyerle, D. (1996). *Visual tools for constructing knowledge.* Alexandria, VA: Association for Supervision and Curriculum Development.

Jitendra, A. K., Cole, C., Hoppes, M. K., & Wilson, B. (1998). Effects of a direct instruction main idea summarization program and self-monitoring on reading comprehension of middle school students with learning disabilities. *Reading and Writing Quarterly: Overcoming Learning Difficulties, 14,* 379–396.

Jitendra, A. K., Hoppes, M. K. I., & Xin, Y. P. (2000). Enhancing main idea comprehension for students with learning problems: The role of summarization strategy and self-monitoring instruction. *Journal of Special Education, 34,* 127–139.

Johnson, R. E. (1970). Recall of prose as a function of the structural importance of the linguistic units. *Journal of Verbal Learning and Verbal Behaviour, 9,* 12–20.

Just, M., & Carpenter, P. (1987). *The psychology of reading and language comprehension.* Boston: Allyn & Bacon.

Kim, A., Vaughn, S., Wanzek, J., & Wei, S. (2004). Graphic organizers and their effects on the reading comprehension of students with LD: A synthesis of research. *Journal of Learning Disabilities, 37,* 105–118.

Klingner, J., Vaughn, S., & Schumm, J. (1998). Collaborative strategic reading during social studies in heterogeneous fourth-grade classrooms. *Elementary School Journal, 99*(1), 3–22.

Labercane, G., & Battle, J. (1987). Cognitive processing strategies, self-esteem, and reading comprehension of learning disabled students. *BC Journal of Special Education, 11,* 167–185.

Lederer, J. M. (2000). Reciprocal teaching of social studies in incisive elementary classrooms. *Journal of Learning Disabilities, 33*(1), 91–106.

LeFevre, C. A. (1964). *Linguistics and the teaching of reading.* New York: McGraw-Hill.

Lenz, K., Bulgren, J., Schumaker, J., Deshler, D., & Boudah, D. (1994). *Content enhancement series.* Lawrence, KS: Edge Enterprises.

Le Sourd, S. J. (1985). Using text structure to improve social science concept attainment. *Journal of Social Studies Research, 9*(2), 1–14.

Lyda, W. J., & Duncan, F. M. (1967). Quantitative vocabulary and problem solving. *The Arithmetic Teacher, 14,* 289–291.

MacArthur, C. A., Graham, S., Schwartz, S. S., & Schafer, W. D. (1995). Evaluation of a writing instruction model that integrated a process approach, strategy instruction, and word processing. *Learning Disability Quarterly, 18,* 278–291.

Malone, L. D., & Mastropieri, M. A. (1992). Reading comprehension instruction: Summarization and self-monitoring training for students with learning disabilities. *Exceptional Children, 58,* 270–279.

Mason, L. H. (2004). Explicit self-regulated strategy development versus reciprocal questioning: Effect on expository reading comprehension among struggling readers. *Journal of Educational Psychology, 96,* 283–296.

Mason, L. H., & Bentz, J. (2004, June). *Self-regulating and guiding reading comprehension for 87 students who struggle with expository text.* Paper presented at the 11th annual conference of the Society for the Scientific Study of Reading, Amsterdam, Netherlands.

Mason, L. H., Hickey Snyder, K., Jones, D. P., & Kedem, Y. (2006). Self-regulated strategy development for expository reading comprehension and informative writing: Effects for nine 4th-grade students who struggle with learning. *Exceptional Children, 73,* 69–89.

Mason, L. H., Meadan, H., Hedin, L., & Corso, L. (2006). Self-regulated strategy development instruction for expository text comprehension. *Teaching Exceptional Children, 38*(4), 47–52.

Mastropieri, M. G., Scruggs, T. E., Hamilton, S. L., Wolfe, S., Whedon, C., & Canevaro, A. (1996). Promoting thinking skills of students with learning disabilities: Effects on recall and comprehension of expository prose. *Exceptionality, 6,* 1–11.

McCormick, S., & Cooper, J. O. (1991). Can SW3R facilitate secondary learning disabled students' literal comprehension of expository text? Three experiments. *Reading Psychology: An International Quarterly, 12,* 239–271.

Miller, L., Gillam, R. B., & Pena, E. (2000). *Dynamic assessment and intervention of children's narratives.* Austin, TX: PRO-ED.

Montali, J., & Lewandowski, L. (1996). Bimodal reading: Benefits of a talking computer for average and less skilled readers. *Journal of Learning Disabilities, 29,* 271–279.

Moody, S. W., Vaughn, S., Hughes, M. T., & Fischer, M. (2000). Reading instruction in the resource room: Set up for failure. *Exceptional Children, 66,* 305–316.

Moore, D. W., & Readence, J. E. (1984). A quantitative and qualitative review of graphic organizer research. *Journal of Educational Research, 78*(1), 11–17.

Nelson, J. R., Smith, D. J., & Dodd, J. M. (1992). The effects of a summary skills strategy to students identified as learning disabled on their comprehension of science text. *Education and Treatment of Children, 15,* 228–243.

Newcomer, P., & Nodine, B. F. (1988). Story composition by learning disabled, reading disabled, and normal children. *Learning Disability Quarterly, 8,* 167–181.

Ogle, D. M. (1989). The know, want to know, learn strategy. In K. D. Muth (Ed.), *Children's comprehension of text* (pp. 205–223). Newark, DE: International Reading Association.

Palincsar, A. S. (1985, April). *The unpacking of a multi-component, metacognitive training package.* Paper presented at the annual meeting of the American Educational Research Association, Chicago, IL.

Palincsar, A., & Brown, A. (1984). Reciprocal teaching of comprehension fostering and comprehension monitoring activities. *Cognition and Instruction, 1,* 117–175.

Prawat, R. S. (1989). Promoting access to knowledge, strategy, and disposition in students: A research synthesis. *Review of Educational Research, 59*(1), 1–41.

Raphael, T. E., & Englert, C. S. (1990). Reading and writing: Partners in constructing meaning. *The Reading Teacher, 43,* 388–400.

Raphael, T. S., Englert, C. S., & Kirschner, B. W. (1986). *The impact of text structure instruction and social context on students' comprehension and production of expository text* (Research Series No. 177). East Lansing: Michigan State University, Institute for Research on Teaching.

Reynolds, C. J. (1986). The effects of instruction in cognitive revision strategies on the writing skills of secondary learning disabled students (Doctoral dissertation, Ohio State University, 1985). *Dissertation Abstracts International, 46*(9-A), 2662.

Rice, G. E. (1994). Need for explanations in graphic organizer research. *Reading Psychology: An International Quarterly, 15,* 39–67.

Robinson, F. (1970). *Effective study.* New York: Harper & Row.

Roehler, L., Duffy, G., & Meloth, M. (1986). What to be direct about in direct instruction in reading: Content-only versus process-into-content. In T. E. Raphael (Ed.), *Contexts of school-based literacy* (pp. 76–96). New York: Random House.

Scardamalia, M., & Bereiter, C. (1983). Child as coinvestigator: Helping children gain insight into their own mental processes. In S. G. Paris, G. M. Olson, & H. W. Stevenson (Eds.), *Learning and motivation in the classroom* (pp. 61–82). Hillsdale, NJ: Lawrence Erlbaum Associates.

Schumaker, J. B. (2003). *Learning strategies curriculum: Fundamentals in the theme writing strategy.* Lawrence: University of Kansas, Center for Research on Learning.

Schumaker, J. B., Denton, P. H., & Deshler, D. D. (1984). *Learning strategies curriculum: The paraphrasing strategy.* Lawrence: The University of Kansas, Center for Research on Learning.

Schumaker, J., & Deshler, D. (2003). Can students with LD become competent writers? *Learning Disability Quarterly, 26,* 129–142.

Schumaker, J., Deshler, D., Denton, P., Alley, G., Clark, F., & Nolan, M. (1982). Multipass: A learning strategy for improving reading comprehension. *Learning Disability Quarterly, 5,* 295–304.

Schumaker, J. B., Deshler, D. D., Nolan, S. M., & Alley, G. R. (1994). *Learning strategies curriculum: The self-questioning strategy.* Lawrence: University of Kansas, Center for Research on Learning.

Schumaker, J. B., & Lyerla, K. S. (1993). *Learning strategies curriculum: The paragraph writing strategy.* Lawrence: University of Kansas.

Schumaker, J. B., Nolan, S. M., & Deshler, D. D. (1985). *Learning strategies curriculum: Error monitoring strategy.* Lawrence: University of Kansas.

Schumaker, J. B., & Sheldon, J. B. (1998). *Learning strategies curriculum: Fundamentals in the sentence writing strategy.* Lawrence: University of Kansas.

Schumaker, J. B., & Sheldon, J. B. (1999). *Learning strategies curriculum: Proficiency in the sentence writing strategy.* Lawrence: University of Kansas.

Sheinker, J., & Sheinker, A. (1989). *Metacognitive approach to study strategies.* Gaithersburg, MD: Aspen.

Simmonds, E. P. M. (1992). The effects of teacher training and implementation of two methods of improving the comprehension skills of students with learning disabilities. *Learning Disabilities Research and Practice, 7,* 194–198.

Spence, D., Yore, L., & Williams, R. (1999). The effects of explicit science reading instruction on selected grade seven students: Metacognition and comprehension of specific science text. *Journal of Elementary Science Education, 11*(2), 15–30.

Swanson, H. L., Kozleski, E., & Stegink, P. (1987). Disabled readers' processing of prose: Do any processes change because of intervention? *Psychology in the Schools, 24,* 378–384.

Thomas, C. C., Englert, C. S., & Gregg, S. (1987). An analysis of errors and strategies in the expository writing of learning disabled students. *Remedial and Special Education, 8,* 21–30.

Tindal, G. A., & Marston, D. B. (1990). *Classroom-based assessment: Evaluating instructional outcomes.* Columbus, OH: Merrill.

Vaughn, S., Moody, S. W., & Schumm, J. S. (1998). Broken promises: Reading instruction in resource rooms. *Exceptional Children, 64,* 211–225.

Ward-Lonergan, J. M. (2002, April). *Curriculum-based language intervention for older children and adolescents.* Paper presented at the annual convention of the California Speech-Language-Hearing Association, Monterey, CA.

Ward-Lonergan, J. M. (2006, June). *Content literacy continuum (CLC)—Level 5: The role of the speech-language pathologist.* Paper presented at the annual conference of the California Speech-Language-Hearing Association, Sacramento, CA.

Weiss, D. S. (1983). The effects of text segmentation on children's reading comprehension. *Discourse Processes, 6*(1), 77–89.

Welch, M. (1992). The PLEASE strategy: A meta-cognitive learning strategy for improving the paragraph writing of students with learning disabilities. *Learning Disability Quarterly, 15,* 119–128.

Williams, D. L., & Ward-Lonergan, J. M. (2009). Use of a referential communication task to improve written expression abilities in school-age children with learning disabilities. Manuscript in preparation.

Wong, B. Y. L., Butler, D. L., Ficzere, S. A., & Kuperis, S. (1996). Teaching low achievers and students with learning disabilities to plan, write, and revise opinion essays. *Journal of Learning Disabilities, 20,* 197–212.

Wong, B. Y. L., Butler, D. L., Ficzere, S. A., Kuperis, S., Corden, M., & Zelmer, J. (1994). Teaching problem learners revision skills and sensitivity to audience through two instructional modes: Student-teacher versus student-student interactive dialogues. *Learning Disabilities Research and Practice, 9,* 78–90.

Wong, B. Y. L., & Jones, W. (1982). Increasing metacomprehension in learning disabled and normally achieving students through self-questioning training. *Learning Disability Quarterly, 5,* 228–239.

Wong, B. Y. L., & Sawatsky, D. (1984). Sentence elaboration and retention of good, average, and poor readers. *Learning Disability Quarterly, 7,* 229–236.

Wong, B. Y. L., & Wilson, M. (1984). Investigating awareness of and teaching passage organization in learning disabled children. *Journal of Learning Disabilities, 17,* 477–482.

Zecker, S., & Zinner, T. (1987). Semantic code deficit for reading disabled children on an auditory lexical decision task. *Journal of Reading Behavior, 19,* 177–190.

## STUDY GUIDE QUESTIONS

1. Some of the intervention techniques or strategies that have been found to be beneficial for improving reading comprehension of expository discourse in children and adolescents with language-learning disabilities include
   a. use of specific reading comprehension strategies, such as RAP, POSSE, or TWA.
   b. use of a story grammar strategy.
   c. use of an auditory processing approach.
   d. use of a whole-language approach.

2. Recent research involving use of graphic organizers to improve reading comprehension has suggested that
    a. graphic organizers are not beneficial in facilitating reading comprehension.
    b. students with learning disabilities do not need a longer, more intensive period of intervention using graphic organizers as compared to their typically developing peers.
    c. graphic organizers may be used to help students with learning disabilities gain relational knowledge from expository textbooks.
    d. SLPs and teachers can expect improvement in reading comprehension by simply providing students with graphic organizers without any modeling or guided practice.
3. Strategies for improving reading comprehension of expository discourse
    a. are specific to one particular type of expository discourse structure.
    b. may be generalized across expository reading tasks.
    c. are very limited in number in the existing literature.
    d. have not yet been published in research articles.
4. With respect to expository writing intervention,
    a. there are several published strategies that have been research validated.
    b. there are numerous published strategies specific to each type of expository discourse structure.
    c. there is no need for further validation of existing strategies.
    d. there are no published strategies that have been research validated.
5. Intervention to improve expository writing abilities often involves
    a. increasing storytelling abilities.
    b. increasing the ability to write opinion-based essays.
    c. increasing the ability to write dialogue commonly found in plays and novels.
    d. improving the ability to write descriptive and procedural discourse.

## CHAPTER 11

# Expository Discourse in Older Children and Adolescents with Traumatic Brain Injury

*Catherine Moran and Gail T. Gillon*

Effective communication is vital for social and academic success in older children and adolescents. Communicating with peers is frequently a focal point in an adolescent's life. The rapid cultural change to text messaging and e-mail communication embraced by adolescents in many societies throughout the world provides evidence of their social need for constant peer communication. Academic success also draws heavily on effective communication with many aspects of an advanced education curriculum demanding strong competency in this area.

Older children and adolescents who have suffered a traumatic brain injury (TBI) often experience difficulty in complex communication tasks (Ewing-Cobbs, Brookshire, Scott, & Fletcher, 1998; Jordan, Cremona-Meteyard, & King, 1996). Expository discourse is a challenging form of spoken communication (Snow, Douglas, & Ponsford, 1995) and may therefore prove problematic for individuals with TBI. Consider the following educational and social scenarios that engage adolescents in expository forms of discourse:

## Scenario 1

A student listens to a presentation by the teacher describing the body's digestive system. The student is graded on his or her ability to retell the information in an oral examination.

275

## Scenario 2

A 12-year-old boy listens intently while his older brother explains how to play the latest video game. The boy then attempts to explain the procedures to his friend so that they can play the game together.

## Scenario 3

A parent explains the conditions that will be necessary for an adolescent daughter to host a party in their home. The daughter is required to relate these conditions to her peers whom she invites to her party.

Competency in expository discourse will help facilitate successful outcomes in each of these scenarios, but poor communication may lead to teacher disappointment in the adolescent's underachievement, peer frustration at the lack of a clear explanation of the video game instruction, and parents' distrust in their daughter in not relating party conditions to her friends. Such outcomes may have cumulative negative effects on self-confidence and future language engagement in the older child or adolescent with TBI.

## TBI IN YOUTH: NATURE OF THE DEFICITS

It is estimated that approximately 1.2 million Americans suffer a TBI each year (Langlois, Rutland-Brown, & Thomas, 2006). Young people are particularly susceptible to brain injury (Langlois, Rutland-Brown, & Thomas, 2005), and negative outcomes following TBI are often lifelong (e.g., Jordan & Murdoch, 1994). Repeated injuries, even mild traumas like those sustained in sports activities, can result in cumulative cognitive and health deficits (Iverson, Gaetz, Lovell, & Collins, 2004). For the developing brain, the effects of TBI are compounded. Difficulties with later-emerging communication skills, such as production and comprehension of complex syntax and semantic knowledge, have been described even when there has been relative recovery of previously acquired language skills (e.g., Ewing-Cobbs et al., 1998; Jordan, Cannon, & Murdoch, 1992; Jordan & Murdoch, 1994; Moran & Gillon, 2004). Conflicting results, however, relating to the extent of language impairment are reported in the literature. For instance, Jordan and colleagues (e.g., Jordan & Murdoch, 1990; Jordan, Ozanne, & Murdoch, 1990; Jordan et al., 1992, 1996) found that apart from word-finding difficulties, language deficits persisted in only those children with severe injuries. In contrast, Turkstra (1999) found that adolescents between 13 and 21 years old who had sustained head injuries within 3 years of testing demonstrated difficulty across the linguistic domains of listening, speaking, reading, and writing and required academic assistance to facilitate success in the curriculum. Biddle, McCabe, and Bliss (1996) and Ewing-Cobbs et al. (1998) also described a range of communication deficits in adolescents following head injury, including deficits in pragmatic conversational skills. An obvious reason for the apparently conflicting findings is the language assessment measures employed. It is suggested that children with

TBI tend to score within normal limits on standardized language assessments (Biddle et al., 1996), possibly because the cuing and structure of standardized tests may support these individuals in spite of their impairments.

Evaluation of language using discourse measures is one method of identifying communication difficulties that may not be evidenced in standardized tests. Assessment of discourse allows for the observation of core linguistic skills (e.g., vocabulary and syntax) and may be a more sensitive means of assessing communicative abilities in children with TBI as they are evaluated in context and the cognitive demands of communication are addressed. In addition, discourse continues to develop through adolescence (Chapman, Levin, Wanek, Weyrauch, & Kufera, 1998; Nippold, 2007). Therefore, a childhood TBI may alter the ability to acquire new discourse skills. Researchers have shown that discourse impairments are evident in children with TBI regardless of the age at which the injury was sustained and the stage of recovery (Biddle et al., 1996; Chapman et al., 1992, 1997, 1998; Ewing-Cobbs et al., 1998).

This chapter presents important considerations related to one type of discourse, expository discourse, and TBI. Specifically, the chapter addresses questions that clinicians may ask when evaluating and treating expository discourse. The questions are the following:

1. Why assess expository discourse production in children and adolescents with TBI? Will language samples eliciting expository discourse reveal anything different from other types of samples?
2. How should expository discourse for individuals with TBI be elicited?
3. What analyses and measures of expository samples are informative?
4. When expository discourse production is problematic for an individual with TBI, what intervention methods are indicated?

## QUESTION 1: WHY ASSESS EXPOSITORY DISCOURSE PRODUCTION IN CHILDREN AND ADOLESCENTS WITH TBI?

Assessment of expository discourse should be viewed in the context of a comprehensive assessment battery for older children and adolescents with TBI. As with the evaluation of language impairment in other populations, a comprehensive language assessment for this population should include a variety of measures, such as standardized assessments, criterion-referenced assessments, and behavioral ratings. Assessment of language should evaluate comprehension and production in both spoken and written language modalities and should include measures of syntax and semantics, including "high-level" language functions, such as figurative language, understanding of multiple meanings, and inference comprehension (e.g., Moran & Gillon, 2004, 2005). In addition, measures of cognitive function such as memory, including working memory, that contribute to language performance should be administered. Thus, eliciting oral expository language samples should be viewed as one aspect of the evaluation process.

It is generally agreed that assessment of language at the discourse level is useful for individuals with TBI (e.g., Chapman, 1997; Chapman et al., 1997; Snow, Douglas, & Ponsford, 1997). Although the evaluation of expository discourse for individuals with TBI has received relatively little attention, it is acknowledged that it is important to consider a variety of discourse measures when assessing and treating individuals with TBI (Blosser & DePompei, 2003; Coehlo, 1995; Hay & Moran, 2005). There are a number of reasons why clinicians should include expository discourse specifically as part of their assessment protocol. These reasons include the following:

1. Expository measures can be used to assess performance across developmental stages. One of the difficulties in determining the persistence of language deficits following TBI is that as children develop, the cognitive demands of the tasks they are expected to engage in also change. Discourse measures are effective in measuring change across time. Studies of developmental changes in expository discourse production across age in typically developing, non–brain-injured populations revealed that measurable changes in complex syntax and utterance length were evident (e.g., Moran, Nippold, Mansfield, & Gillon, 2005; Nippold, Hesketh, Duthie, & Mansfield, 2005; Nippold, Mansfield, & Billow, 2007; Nippold, Moran, Mansfield, & Gillon, 2005). Of particular importance in these studies is that the same task was appropriate for children across a wide range of ages. For instance, Nippold, Hesketh, et al. (2005) evaluated expository discourse production in children as young as 7 years old through to adults. All participants were asked to describe their favorite game or sport. Although there were differences in sentence length and complexity across the age-groups, all participants were able to perform the task (see chapter 4). Given that the expository discourse task was appropriate across age-groups and identified differences across groups, it seems a valuable tool for examining language performance in individuals of all ages with TBI.

2. Expository discourse tasks may be better suited to assessing the subtle language difficulties post-TBI. Common difficulties associated with discourse production following TBI are the production of long utterances that have irrelevant content, that drift off topic, and that include false information (Blosser & DePompei, 2003). It has been suggested that expository discourse may make greater demands on an individual's ability to be precise and explicit in conveying information than other forms of discourse such as conversation. (e.g., Ulatowska, Allard, & Chapman, 1990). Expository discourse requires specific factual information that often is required to be presented in a specific

sequence. In addition, "real-world knowledge" often has to be drawn on to support the discourse. Other forms of discourse, such as conversation, allow individuals to compensate for difficulties by talking about what is highly familiar. In addition, in conversation, the conversational partner often takes responsibility for managing the structure of the conversation (Youse & Coehlo, 2005).

3. Expository discourse tasks may provide a more sensitive platform for measuring syntactic errors following TBI than other forms of discourse. Syntax is considered to be less susceptible to disruption following TBI than other linguistic areas, such as semantics (e.g., Chapman, 1997). However, given that developing language is likely to be disrupted following TBI, advanced syntactic forms, such as those produced in expository discourse, are at risk. Since complex syntax is more likely to occur in expository discourse than in other forms of discourse, such as conversation (Nippold, Moran, et al., 2005), it is a valuable tool for evaluating potential difficulties. This was shown by Hay and Moran (2005), who identified reduced syntactic complexity for a group of adolescents with TBI compared to their typically developing peers.

4. Expository discourse tasks are ecologically valid. Conversation, picture description, and narrative language sampling through story generation and story retell are the most common methods of gathering language samples for individuals with TBI (Coehlo, 1995). Although evaluation of children with TBI should continue to include narrative discourse ability, a greater focus on expository discourse is needed. As children develop, a greater emphasis is placed on their ability to use and understand expository discourse in both their social and their academic lives (Stewart, 1985). Expository discourse is used extensively in school as teachers describe how to do something, give instructions, and clarify answers to questions (Gillam, Pena, & Miller, 1999). Students are expected to listen to factual presentations and identify and understand the main points and relevant details from textbooks and lectures (Nelson, 1993). Expository discourse sampling is highly related then to what school-aged children and adolescents are exposed to during their school days.

## QUESTION 2: HOW SHOULD EXPOSITORY DISCOURSE FOR INDIVIDUALS WITH TBI BE ELICITED?

Expository discourse can take a variety of forms. Some examples of expository structures include descriptive (telling what something is), causative (explaining or giving reasons why something happens), comparative (explaining similarities and differences), and procedural (telling how to do or make something) (e.g., Paul, 2007). Methods for eliciting those discourse structures range from

having individuals watch an educational video and retell the information
(e.g., Scott & Windsor, 2000) to simply having individuals explain how a task
is carried out (e.g., how to withdraw money from a bank account; Snow et al.,
1995). Given the variety of methods available for eliciting discourse, clinicians
are faced with the decision of how to best elicit an expository language sample
for children and adolescents with TBI.

In order to assist in that decision-making process, clinicians should
consider the following: (a) What is to be derived from the language sample
(Coehlo, 1995; Snow et al., 1995)? This issue is particularly relevant with
regard to whether the elicited task is a generation task or a retelling task.
(b) Will the language that is elicited reflect the effects of TBI on discourse
production (Snow et al., 1995)? (c) Is the task sensitive to the developmental stage of the child/adolescent being assessed? Using those questions as a
guide, clinicians can determine the most appropriate method of eliciting the
expository language sample.

1. What is to be derived from the language sample? Generation versus retelling tasks: Expository language sampling tasks generally
   fall within two categories: generation tasks and retelling tasks.
   Generation tasks are those that require the child or adolescent to
   generate their own facts and information. Generation tasks can be
   elicited through a question or prompt, for example, "How do you
   make a sandwich?" (Cannito, Hayashi, & Ulatowska, 1989) or "Tell
   me all the steps involved in withdrawing money from a bank account"
   (Snow et al., 1995). In retelling tasks, the child or adolescent listens to
   an expository passage and retells the information that was presented.
   The presentation methods can vary. For instance, the information
   may be presented auditorily (e.g., Hay & Moran, 2005) or auditorily
   with visual support (e.g., Moran et al., 2005; Ward-Lonergan, Liles, &
   Anderson, 1999). Some examples of generation and retelling tasks
   used for eliciting expository discourse in children and adolescents
   are described in Table 11.1.

   Although previous studies have not specifically compared generation and retelling of expository discourse in individuals with TBI,
   generation versus retelling has been examined in other genres and
   with other populations (Coehlo, 2002; Moran, et al., 2005). Coehlo
   (2002) compared language performance of 55 adults with TBI and
   47 non–brain-injured adults on a story generation task versus a
   story retelling task. The story generation task involved presenting
   a Norman Rockwell scene and asking participants to tell a story
   about what was happening in the picture. For the retelling task,
   participants were shown a short silent filmstrip depicting a story,
   and at the conclusion of the film, they were asked to describe the
   story. Story generation resulted in longer, more complex utterances.

**Table 11.1** Description of Expository Generation and Retelling Tasks Used with Children and Adolescents with and without TBI

| Task | Generation or Retelling | Population |
|---|---|---|
| Favorite Game or Sport (FGS) task (Nippold, Hesketh, et al., 2005): The child/adolescent/adult is asked to name his or her favorite game or sport and tell why it is his or her favorite. The clinician then states that he or she is unfamiliar with the game and asks for the game to be explained. Details are prompted (e.g., How do you score goals/points? How many players?). Finally, the clinician asks the individual to summarize the key strategies needed to be good at the game. | Generation | 120 participants with no known language problems ranging in age from 7 to 49 years |
| Dice Game (Turkstra et al., 1995): A novel game is taught to the child or adolescent. The game is not explained; rather, rules for playing the game are modeled. When the child demonstrates understanding of the game, he or she is asked to explain the game into a tape recorder so that someone unfamiliar with the game would understand it. | Generation | Three adolescents with TBI and 36 typically developing high school students aged 15 to 18 years |
| Peer Conflict Resolution (PCR) task (Nippold et al., 2007): For this task, the clinician reads two stories that illustrate a conflict among young people. The participant retells the story, and then the clinician asks six questions related to the conflict presented (e.g., nature of the conflict, how it should be handled, and consequences). | Generation | Three groups of 20 individuals with no known disorders, including children (mean age 11 years, 4 months), adolescents (mean age 17 years, 3 months), and adults (mean age 25 years, 6 months) |
| Lecture Retell Task (Ward-Lonergan et al., 1999): Two videotaped lectures were presented. Both lectures presented information that was previously unfamiliar to the participants. Each lecture was approximately 5 minutes in duration. The lectures varied in expository structure with one using a comparison structure and the other a causation structure. | Retelling | 20 adolescent boys (aged 12 years, 5 months–14 years, 7 months) with language-learning disabilities and 29 age-matched peers |

*continued*

**Table 11.1 (*continued*)**    Description of Expository Generation and Retelling Tasks
Used with Children and Adolescents with and without TBI

| Task | Generation or Retelling | Population |
|------|-------------------------|------------|
| Retelling of information in an educational video (Scott & Windsor, 2000): A 15-minute educational video about the desert was played to the participants, and they were asked to summarize it. The video had a clear expository structure. Summaries were elicited in both spoken and written modalities. | Retelling | 20 students (aged 10 years to 12 years, 6 months) with language-learning disabilities; 20 chronological age–matched peers; and 20 language age–matched children. |
| Retelling of a game or sport (Hay & Moran, 2005; Moran et al., 2005): Participants listened to an expository passage describing a game and/or sport that was unfamiliar to them and then were asked to retell it. The expository passages had a defined expository structure with key elements that were to be included. | Retelling | Nine children and adolescents with TBI and nine age-matched peers |

It was speculated that the restrictive nature of retelling discouraged elaboration and hence resulted in shorter utterances. On the other hand, retelling resulted in more meaningful content; therefore, story structure and story cohesion were more obvious and easier to assess in that condition. Coehlo (2002) concluded that for individuals with TBI, story generation was better for evaluating sentence complexity and overall productivity, while story retelling was better suited for measuring content, cohesive adequacy, and story structure.

A range of variables influence the quality and length of oral language samples in children with language impairment (Westerveld & Gillon, 2001). It may be useful to examine these variables in expository discourse conditions for children with TBI. These variables include whether the listener is familiar with the information to be retold (Liles, 1985; Masterson & Kamhi, 1991), the number of exposures to the material prior to retelling (Gummersall & Strong, 1999), the linguistic complexity of the material presented to the child (Griffith, Ripich, & Dastoli, 1986), and whether pictorial support is available to the child when retelling the information (Masterson & Kamhi, 1991; Schneider, 1996; see chapter 8 for a discussion of the effects of expository task on syntactic structure). To summarize, then, evidence from previous research suggests that, when possible, clinicians should consider including both an expository generation and a retell task in their assessment battery and should carefully consider the language sampling conditions that may influence the quality of the adolescent's discourse.

2. Will the language that is elicited reflect the effects of TBI on discourse production? As noted earlier, expository discourse can take a variety of forms. One type of expository discourse that would be expected to be sensitive to the difficulties associated with TBI is procedural discourse (Snow et al., 1997). Procedural discourse tasks, particularly generation tasks, require individuals to plan what is to be said, to organize the information logically and sequentially, and to take the perspective of the listener (i.e., provide sufficient information so that the listener could carry out the task). All these behaviors have been shown to be impaired following TBI (Snow et al., 1997). Snow et al. (1995) conducted a pilot study to examine whether adults with TBI differed from adults without TBI on a procedural discourse task. Three participants with TBI, ranging in age from 19 to 34 years, and three "closely matched" peers were involved in the study. All participants engaged in three language sampling situations: conversational, procedural (expository), and narrative. For the expository task, participants were asked to "describe all the steps necessary for withdrawing money from a bank account" (Snow et al., 1995, p. 955). Contrary to expectation, there were no obvious differences between the TBI and non-TBI participants on the expository task despite differences being evident on the narrative task.

The failure of Snow et al. (1995) to find a significant difference between adults with TBI and adults without TBI may be due to a variety of factors. First, the study included only a small number of participants. Second, the task used to elicit the procedural discourse may have been overly familiar to both the speaker and the listener. When topics are chosen that express daily routines and that are highly familiar to most people, the speaker may assume that there is shared knowledge; therefore, not all steps in the procedure need to be explicitly stated (Snow et al., 1997). Although the examiners in the Snow et al. (1995) study prompted participants to "tell me as though I have never done it before," the routine nature of the task may have precluded elaboration. A better expository generation task may be one that is familiar to the speaker but less familiar to the listener. For instance, in the Favorite Game or Sport (FGS) task described by Nippold, Hesketh, et al. (2005), the task employed is familiar to the child or adolescent, but the listener is naive or can pretend to know little about the game being described.

Another possible explanation for Snow et al.'s (1995) findings is that the procedure being described by the individuals with TBI (how to withdraw money from a bank account) was not demanding enough to challenge the speaker. The task elicited straightforward sequential steps for carrying out the procedure. It has been shown that simple sequence structures have not identified differences in high- and low-ability college students (Richgels, McGee, Lomax, & Sheard, 1987). In contrast, when an individual is describing something like a game or sport, there may be complex rules and regulations, exceptions to rules, and multifaceted strategies for scoring goals and winning the game. All studies employing the FGS with typically developing children and adolescents (e.g., Moran et al., 2005; Nippold, Hesketh, et al., 2005; Nippold, Moran, et al., 2005) found that the task resulted in long, complex utterances and a greater number of utterances than other forms of discourse.

Although use of the FGS task (Nippold, Hesketh, et al., 2005) has not been reported with individuals with TBI, two studies that have used a similar game or sport description task when examining children and adolescents with TBI have found it to be effective in identifying the deficits associated with TBI (Hay & Moran, 2005; McDonald & Pearce, 1995; Turkstra, McDonald, & Kaufmann, 1995). McDonald and Pearce (1995) administered the Dice Game to 20 adults with TBI and 20 age-matched peers. As described in Table 11.1, the participants in the study learned the Dice Game by playing it. When it was determined that the rules were understood, the participants were asked to describe, in detail, how to play the game. They found that the individuals with TBI included less essential information and more irrelevant information than their age-matched peers.

Turkstra et al. (1995) administered the Dice Game task to three adolescents with TBI as part of a larger test battery that evaluated pragmatics. Two of the three adolescents with TBI performed poorly on the task. They had difficulty abstracting the rules and provided fewer essential elements than their typically developing peers. One participant performed well on the Dice Game, and that was also reflected in his higher overall scores on the other tests of pragmatic functioning.

Hay and Moran (2005) also found that a procedural discourse task describing a game or sport was sensitive to difficulties following TBI. Nine adolescents with TBI were compared with nine typically developing peers on an expository retelling task. The participants listened to two expository discourse passages that described how to play a game or sport that was unfamiliar to them. After listening to the passages, the participants were asked to retell what they had heard in as much detail as possible and to summarize the main objective of the game. The participants with TBI produced fewer words and utterances, and their utterances were less syntactically complex. In addition, they provided less information, and their retellings were less complete and more poorly structured. This suggested that the task was sensitive to discourse problems in children and adolescents with TBI. Although there may be a number of other expository discourse tasks (e.g., problem solution, compare and contrast) that are sensitive to difficulties following TBI, there have been few studies in these areas.

In summary, expository discourse tasks can be used to elicit language that reflects the difficulties typically experienced by children and adolescents following a TBI. Although there have been too few studies on the usefulness of different expository subgenres and tasks to draw definitive conclusions, it does appear that choosing tasks that are highly familiar may not be as effective as more complex tasks. When choosing a method for eliciting expository discourse, then, one type of task that clinicians may utilize is one that describes a game or sport (e.g., Hay & Moran, 2005; McDonald & Pearce, 1995).

3. Is the task sensitive to the developmental stage of the child/adolescent being assessed? Accurate assessment of linguistic deficits in adolescents with TBI necessitates an understanding of typical adolescent language development. It has been shown that individuals with TBI are especially likely to experience disruption in developing language areas (Langlois et al., 2005, 2006). One area of expressive language that continues to develop across childhood and adolescence is syntax (Nippold, 2007). A number of different expository discourse tasks have been shown to elicit complex syntax in typically developing children and adolescents (see also chapter 3 in this volume). Across two studies (Nippold, Hesketh, et al, 2005; Nippold et al., 2007), Nippold and colleagues compared two expository generation tasks, the FGS task and the Peer Conflict Resolution (PCR) task, in children (mean age 11, years, 4 months), adolescents (mean age 17 years, 3 months), and adults (mean age 25 years, 6 months). As described in Table 11.1, during the FGS task, participants were asked to explain the rules of their favorite game or sport (Nippold, Hesketh et al., 2005), while the PCR involved the participants listening to two scenarios that related conflicts between peers either at school or at work. The participants were asked to retell what they had heard and then answer a series of questions related to the nature of the conflict, how it should be handled, and the possible consequences. Although both tasks resulted in the production of complex sentences, participants produced longer and more complex utterances in the PCR task. The authors concluded that the PCR and FGS tasks are useful for eliciting complex syntax in children, adolescents, and adults.

Production of syntactically complex utterances was also investigated by Moran et al. (2005). They compared performance of typically developing children and adolescents, aged 11 and 17 years, on the FGS task (Nippold, Hesketh et al., 2005) and a retelling task that involved description of an unfamiliar game or sport. For the retelling task, participants listened to a passage describing the rules and strategies of an unfamiliar sport. Pictures that depicted what was being heard were also presented. Following a single presentation of the passage, participants were asked to describe the rules of the game as though they were teaching someone else how to play it. Language samples were compared for (a) mean length of utterance in words; (b) number of independent clauses; (c) percentage of subordinate clauses: adverbial, nominal, and relative; and (d) clausal density. They found that although the FGS task resulted in greater production overall, both tasks were effective in eliciting complex syntactic structures in typically developing children and adolescents.

## Summary

In addressing the question of how to elicit expository discourse in an older child or adolescent with TBI, it is recommended that both generation tasks and retelling tasks be used. Retelling tasks that elicit retelling of an unfamiliar game or sport have been shown to be effective not only for eliciting expository discourse but also for identifying differences between typically developing children and children with TBI (Hay & Moran, 2005). When selecting generation tasks, those that are challenging and do not convey overly familiar concepts, such as daily routines (e.g., making a sandwich), are preferred. Generation tasks that have been shown to be appropriate developmentally and to generate descriptions of multifaceted situations that are likely to be of interest to children and adolescents (e.g., Nippold et al., 2007) include (a) description of a favorite game or sport (Nippold, Hesketh, et al., 2005), (b) description of a newly learned game (McDonald & Pearce, 1995), and (c) interpretation of an interpersonal conflict (Nippold et al., 2007).

## QUESTION 3: WHAT ANALYSES AND MEASURES OF EXPOSITORY SAMPLES ARE INFORMATIVE?

The analyses used to examine performance on expository discourse tasks following TBI depend, in part, on what critical aspects are being examined. When producing expository discourse, individuals with TBI have demonstrated difficulty with syntax (e.g., Hay & Moran, 2005), semantics (e.g., Ewing-Cobbs et al., 1998), and pragmatics (amount and organization of content) (e.g., Hay & Moran, 2005; McDonald & Pearce, 1995). Therefore, it is important to evaluate language samples across all those domains. A number of different procedures for analyzing expository discourse have been described in the literature (Chapman et al., 1997, 1998; Hay & Moran, 2005; Nippold, Hesketh et al., 2005; Scott & Windsor, 2000; Windsor, Scott, & Street, 2000). Discourse analyses for individuals with TBI have typically included a variety of core language measures (e.g., syntax and semantics) as well as pragmatic measures (e.g., meaningful content and organizational structure of the discourse) (e.g., Chapman et al., 1997; Coehlo, 1995, 2002; Hartley, 1995). A summary of selected core language and pragmatic measures that have been used for evaluating expository discourse are described next.

## Core Language Measures

1. Productivity: This refers to how many utterances and/or words are produced. When determining productivity, utterances are typically described by T-units. A T-unit is broadly defined as an independent clause and any dependent clauses (Hunt, 1970). Measures of productivity have included total number of words and total number of utterances (e.g., Scott & Windsor, 2000). Children and adolescents with TBI have been shown to have reduced productivity on all productivity measures (e.g., Hay & Moran, 2005; Turkstra et al., 1995). (See chapter 8 for a more extensive discussion and critique of productivity and other measures discussed here.)
2. Syntax: Sentence length and complexity have been used as measures of syntactic production. Use of subordinate clauses reflects not only syntactic development but also the efficiency with which discourse is communicated. Analysis of the percentage of specific types of clauses (adverbial, nominal, relative) has been used. Nippold, Hesketh, et al. (2005) found that mean length of T-unit and the production of relative clauses were two measures that were sensitive to developmental change.
3. Lexical diversity: Lexical diversity reflects the semantic abilities of children and adolescents with TBI and is measured by the number of different words. Children with TBI have been shown to be impaired on a measure of lexical diversity in narrative production (Ewing-Cobbs et al., 1998).

## Pragmatics (Content and Organizational Measures)

Measures of content (information) and organizational structure are relatively common in studies of narrative discourse production (e.g., Coehlo, 2002; Chapman et al., 1997) and have been found to differentiate individuals with TBI from non–brain-injured peers and individuals with language impairment.

1. Number of essential information units generated or recalled: This refers to the key propositions or units of meaning in a passage. A proposition refers to a unit of meaning in a clause or sentence (Crystal, 1987). A single proposition can be expressed in many ways. For instance, in an expository passage on "curling," a statement like "There are four members on a team" would be one proposition or

unit of meaning, but it could also be expressed as "It takes four people to make up a team." Likewise, a single sentence or clause can have more than one proposition (Crystal, 1987). Using the "curling" passage, a statement like "Each of the four members of the team takes turns throwing a stone toward painted rings, called the house" includes three propositions: (a) there are four members on a team, (b) each team member throws a stone, and (c) the painted rings are called "the house." This measure has been shown to be sensitive to the effects of TBI (e.g., Hay & Moran, 2005; McDonald & Pearce, 1995). Hay and Moran found that children and adolescents with TBI produced significantly fewer information units (propositions) overall in an expository retelling task. McDonald and Pearce (1995) noted in their study of adults generating expository discourse that although the amount of information was similar to individuals without TBI, the number of essential information units was decreased. That is, individuals with TBI tended to repeat the same information over and over.

2. Irrelevant or repeated information: In addition to the inclusion of relevant information, measures of irrelevant or repeated information have been evaluated for individuals with TBI (e.g., McDonald & Pearce, 1995; Snow et al., 1997). Both measures have been evident in the expository discourse of individuals with TBI.

3. Organizational structure: This measure reflects how well the child or adolescent with TBI organizes the discourse. For procedural discourse, for instance, the sequential nature of the discourse necessitates that information be presented in a certain order. McDonald and Pearce (1995) generated a score that reflected the sequence with which the key information units were produced. They found it difficult to have strict sequential criteria, however. They concluded that sequential organization may be better evaluated on a case-by-case basis (McDonald & Pearce, 1995). Hay and Moran (2005) evaluated organizational structure by examining completeness rather than sequential order of the key information units. For instance, they evaluated whether there was a clear introduction to the game, key rules identified, and a conclusion. They found that adolescents with TBI had fewer complete episodes than adolescents without TBI.

4. Global understanding or gist: This refers to the ability of the individual to summarize the main points or gist of the discourse. This is evaluated by determining whether the main ideas of the discourse that convey the essential meaning are included (e.g., Chapman et al., 1997; Hay & Moran, 2005). Children and adolescents with TBI were less likely to identify and relay the main ideas of an expository passage than their age-matched peers (Hay & Moran, 2005).

## Summary

Scoring procedures for expository text should include both core language measures and pragmatic measures of content and text structure (e.g., episode structure, theme/aim, relevance). Use of these measures can assist clinicians in identifying potential problems and can assist in directing intervention.

## QUESTION 4: WHEN EXPOSITORY DISCOURSE PRODUCTION IS PROBLEMATIC FOR AN INDIVIDUAL WITH TBI, WHAT INTERVENTION METHODS ARE INDICATED?

Given the importance of expository production in everyday academic and social settings and the difficulties experienced by individuals with TBI when producing expository discourse, it is important to consider intervention. There is a paucity of intervention studies in TBI and few if any specific to expository discourse. Therefore, clinicians have to be guided by general principles of intervention and consider a step-by-step approach to determining an appropriate intervention approach. Some steps clinicians can take when determining an intervention approach are the following:

Step 1: What are the goals? What goals should be targeted first?
Step 2: What approach will achieve those goals?
Step 3: How will intervention effectiveness be determined?
Step 4: What are the next steps?

These considerations are discussed in the following sections, and then a case study is presented to illustrate each concept.

### Step 1: What Are the Goals? What Goals Should Be Targeted First?

In determining what goals or areas to target during intervention, clinicians first have to consider the nature of the problem. Given the description of expository discourse production following TBI discussed earlier in this chapter, emphasis on both language structure and information content should be considered. Table 11.2 details potential intervention goals the clinician could consider.

Although there are a large number of possibilities for approaching expository intervention with a youth with TBI (e.g., Paul, 2007), clinicians need to prioritize goals in terms of what to target first and what will have the greatest impact on communication. Although there are some differences across studies, it is generally agreed that individuals with TBI have difficulties with the content of their discourse. Production of expository discourse for individuals with TBI is characterized by insufficient information (indicated by reduced number of propositions) and disorganized discourse (e.g., incomplete episode structure and presence of irrelevant information) (e.g., Hay &

**Table 11.2**   Language Behaviors and Intervention Strategies for Expository
Discourse in Individuals with TBI

| Domain | Behavior in TBI | Measurement | Potential Intervention Strategy |
|---|---|---|---|
| Syntax | Reduced syntactic complexity; short utterances | Words per T-unit, MLU words, number of dependent clauses divided by total clauses | Improve syntax through direct teaching of complex structures; increase use of subordinating and coordinating conjunctions |
| Semantics | Reduced lexical diversity | Number of different words | Improve expressive vocabulary; improve awareness of semantic relations |
| Pragmatics | Insufficient information | Reduced number of propositions; incomplete episode structure; absence of key global components | Increase recognition of main points; increase sequencing and organization of episodes using schema |
| Pragmatics | Disorganized discourse | Incomplete episode structure; presence of irrelevant information | Improve organization using schema |

Moran, 2005; McDonald & Pearce, 1995). Given this, we would suggest that clinicians begin with targeting the content and structure of the discourse. Once an individual is producing sufficient meaningful content, the clinician can begin targeting syntactic and semantic goals to result in more efficient, sophisticated discourse.

## Step 2: What Approach Will Achieve Those Goals?

Whatever approach a clinician chooses, it should be set within a theoretical framework. A number of theoretical frameworks have been suggested when working with individuals with acquired language disorders, including TBI. For instance, a neuropsychological/impairment approach has been utilized with adults with TBI to target narrative discourse production (Youse & Coehlo, 2005). In this approach, individuals with TBI were trained on an attention program based on the tenet that poor attention is related to poor discourse production. Although there was minimal improvement, the researchers noted that there was enough evidence to suggest that working on underlying deficits was beneficial. However, treatment needed to be modified to facilitate carryover. Another approach worthy of consideration is a working memory approach to intervention. Memory, including working memory, is a persistent problem for individuals with TBI (e.g., Hanten, Levin, & Song, 1999; Hartley, 1995). Working memory has been shown to be related to discourse production (e.g., Hay & Moran, 2005), and manipulations of factors that influence working memory have been shown to affect language comprehension and production of discourse (e.g., Moran & Gillon, 2004).

In order to understand how one would apply a working memory approach to intervention with TBI, it is important to have an understanding of working memory and the factors that facilitate and constrain it. Working memory is an area of both storage and processing of information (Baddeley, 1976). One theory of working memory is that it is a limited capacity system that must continually trade off between processing and storage resources (Just & Carpenter, 1992). That is, as storage demands increase, processing resources are weakened. If working memory is considered a possible explanation for the difficulties evidenced in discourse formulation, then intervention strategies should be aimed at reducing either the storage or the processing load (Hay & Moran, 2004, 2005). There are a number of means of reducing storage and processing load. For instance, Moran and Gillon (2005) presented a group of adolescents with TBI with paragraphs containing an utterance that elicited generation of a predictive inference. Following presentation of the paragraph, the adolescents with TBI were asked to describe what the passage was implying. When the predictive utterance was presented early in the passage, the participants had to store the information over several utterances and subsequently were unable to formulate the inference. However, when the predictive utterance was at the end of the passage, the adolescents with TBI performed like their age-matched peers.

## Step 3: How Will Intervention Effectiveness Be Determined?

One method of evaluating effectiveness is to conduct the intervention within a single-subject design paradigm. There are a number of different ways to design a single-subject experiment to evaluate efficacy, including a multiple baseline design across behaviors and ABA designs (Portney & Watkins, 2002). In the multiple baseline design across behaviors, both the target behavior and a control behavior are sampled. Once intervention is implemented, both behaviors continue to be sampled during the intervention and at the completion of intervention. If the intervention is effective, the target behavior should improve, while the control behavior remains static. The caveat with this design is that seemingly unrelated behaviors may be affected by change in one or the other. For instance, Hay and Moran (2004) found that as the number of propositions increased, so did the number of syntactic errors, although on the surface these measures may have initially seemed unrelated. Therefore, it is important to choose a control behavior that is unlikely to be affected by change in the target behavior. Another method of evaluating effectiveness is to use a pretreatment, treatment, posttreatment design and measure change using a quantitative measure, namely, a two-standard-deviation band method (Portney & Watkins, 2002). This method involves measuring the target behavior a minimum of three times before beginning intervention. A mean and a standard deviation are calculated from that baseline. If at least two consecutive data points in either the intervention or the postintervention phase fall outside the two-standard-deviation band, changes from baseline to intervention or postintervention are considered significant.

## Step 4: What Are the Next Steps?

Given the complex needs of individuals with TBI, it is likely that ongoing intervention will be required. For children and adolescents, this is particularly true because as the child or adolescent ages, school and social demands change, and it could be difficult for an individual with TBI to adapt to those changes. The clinician will need to determine whether more intervention is required and which targets are relevant. In the case of discourse, once the clinician has targeted the information or content portion of discourse, it might be an appropriate time to target linguistic measures, such as improving syntactic complexity or reducing syntactic errors. Likewise, the clinician may work toward improving generalization of the targeted behaviors. Individuals with TBI tend to show very poor generalization. Hence, generalizing the behaviors across situations could be an appropriate goal.

## Case Study

The following case study illustrates the steps of intervention discussed in this chapter. This case study, which highlights one of two participants described by Hay and Moran (2004), evaluates the response of an adolescent with TBI to an intervention designed to improve the participant's expository discourse retelling ability.

**Background**   John was referred to a speech-language pathologist because of language difficulties following a head injury. John sustained a TBI at 7 years of age as a result of a motor vehicle accident. John was verified as having sustained a head injury of moderate severity by both a pediatrician and a neurosurgeon. Despite having no previous history of academic or language difficulties prior to the accident, John presented with pervasive language difficulties since the injury. At the time of intervention, he was in a mainstream classroom with 12.5 hours of teacher aide support per week to assist him in academic subject areas.

**Description of communication**   John was 13 years old at the time this intervention was implemented. John's difficulties were evident in his overall communication abilities as well as on standardized measures of language. An overall description is as follows.

*Standardized testing*   John scored below one standard deviation on all subtests of the Clinical Evaluation of Language Fundamentals (3rd ed.) (Semel, Wiig, & Secord, 1995) and had an overall language score greater than 1.5 standard deviations below the mean. Difficulties in vocabulary were evidenced by poor performance (greater than 1.5 standard deviations below the mean) on the Test of Word Knowledge (Wiig & Secord, 1992) and the Peabody Picture Vocabulary Test (3rd ed.) (Dunn & Dunn, 1997). He scored below the first percentile on the Test of Adolescent/Adult Word Finding (German, 1990). As working memory has been indicated as a factor in retelling and discourse formulation (e.g., Hay & Moran, 2005; Wolfe, 2005), two working memory measures were carried out. John demonstrated significantly reduced working memory as measured by the Nonword Repetition Test (Dollaghan & Campbell, 1998) and the Competing Language Processing Task (Gaulin & Campbell, 1994).

*Discourse production*    John's discourse production was typical of many individuals with TBI. That is, his productions contained little meaningful information (e.g., Coehlo, 2002), and his utterances tended to be repetitive and/or irrelevant. In terms of discourse production on expository discourse passages, this presented as what appeared to be an adequate number of T-units (i.e., John produced an acceptable number of utterances) but with very few propositions or information units. For instance, John would repeat the same information frequently in the passage. In terms of scoring, he was credited only once for including a key piece of information even if he repeated the information over and over. Despite overall language difficulties, John's utterances ranged in complexity, and he had few syntactic errors.

**Step 1: What are the goals, and what should be targeted first?**    Given that John's discourse was characterized primarily by poor performance in terms of content and given what we know about discourse difficulties following TBI (e.g., Hay & Moran, 2005), the following goals were selected:

1. Increase the number of propositions (ideas) John produces in an expository discourse retelling task.
2. Reduce the amount of irrelevant or redundant information that John produces in an expository discourse retelling task. This may be exhibited by a decrease in overall number of T-units and an increase in number of propositions.

**Step 2: What approach to intervention should be considered?**    The intervention that was chosen was based on a working memory theory of impairment following TBI. Hence, the overall aim was to reduce working memory load and, by doing so, to facilitate performance. It has already been shown that reducing storage load/memory load is useful in facilitating comprehension of discourse with adolescents with TBI (e.g., Moran & Gillon, 2004). Therefore, it was decided that an intervention that would reduce the storage load would be implemented for improving retelling of expository discourse (see two examples in the appendix). One means of reducing storage and processing load is to use memory charts or organizational schemas that aid retelling. Visual or graphic organizers have been used by students with language-learning disabilities to improve comprehension of expository discourse (e.g., Westby, 1991) as well as overall length and quality of expository discourse production (Strum & Rankin-Erickson, 2002). In addition, text organization has been found to account for unique variance in recall of expository text (Wolfe, 2005). Therefore, teaching a schema or organizational chart would likely improve performance in expository production, particularly during a retelling.

**Step 3: How should the effectiveness of intervention be evaluated?** In order to evaluate the effect of the intervention across all the variables, a single-subject design using baseline, intervention, and postintervention measurements was employed. A two-standard-deviation band method was used to determine whether there were significant differences during and following intervention. Changes were considered significant if at least two data points during any phase (treatment or posttreatment) were more than two standard deviations above or below the baseline mean (Portney & Watkins, 2000). The baseline, intervention, and postintervention procedures are described next.

**Baseline phase**    The baseline phase took place over three separate sessions within a 1-week period. Three different expository passages, matched for length and complexity, were presented at each baseline session. Each passage described factual information that was unfamiliar to John. The passages took the form of pure descriptive passages. The passages were presented on tape and were repeated to elicit maximum output (Westerveld & Gillon, 2001). John was asked to retell what he had heard in as much detail as possible, as if he were explaining the information to someone who was unfamiliar with it (e.g., Westerveld & Gillon, 2001).

**Treatment phase**    The treatment consisted of 8 hours of individual therapy implemented over four 2-hour sessions held weekly. Given that John's discourse was characterized by reduced information (decreased numbers of propositions) and relevant content, the intervention consisted of teaching John to use an information template to help him remember information presented in the oral expository discourse. As in the baseline measures, the passages were presented on tape. The passages were equal in length, and topics were varied. Examples of topics included "The Earth," "Dinosaurs," and "Woodpeckers." The template consisted of a standard-sized sheet of paper with a box at the top for the title, three boxes below the title box to record the three main points or key components of the discourse, and a box below each of the main idea boxes to record specific details about each main idea. At each teaching session, a new discourse passage was introduced. Modeling and scaffolding techniques (e.g., Larson & McKinley, 1995) were used to teach John how to record information in the template as the examiner presented the expository discourse. The passage was read twice. John was encouraged to fill in the title and main points during the first reading and the specific information during the second reading. At the end of each teaching session, the clinician retold the expository discourse, and John was required to independently use the template to aid his retelling of the information. As in the training, the clinician read the passage twice. John then retold the passage immediately.

***Posttest phase***   The posttest phase was conducted over three sessions within 1 week following treatment. The postphase was carried out in two parts: postphase A and postphase B. In postphase A, the template was withdrawn, and the procedures carried out in the baseline phase were repeated with three new passages. For postphase B, the template was reintroduced in order to determine whether John's performance postintervention differed depending on whether the template was present or absent. Post-Postphase B differed from the treatment phase in that no prompting, modeling, or scaffolding was done to assist John in using it. That is, the clinician presented the template, and John filled in key words during presentation of a novel passage. John then used the information he recorded on the passage to retell the information. Postphase B was added in order to determine whether John could independently use the template for novel passages.

**Outcomes**   The outcomes for the two targeted goals are as follows:

***Goal 1: Improve the amount of information produced***   This would be reflected in the number of propositions or information units produced. Figure 11.1 displays the results for the baseline, treatment, and posttreatment phases for the number of propositions produced. As can be seen in the graph, John produced significantly more propositions when he used the template. All passages that were presented had a minimum of 10 propositions. In Figure 11.1, it can be seen that at baseline there were instances where there were no propositions specific to the passage. For instance, utterances such as "I can't remember much about the Earth. I know we live on the Earth. I know there's stars and stuff. I think there's planets" did not count as propositions related to the passage. Without the template, John produced fewer than

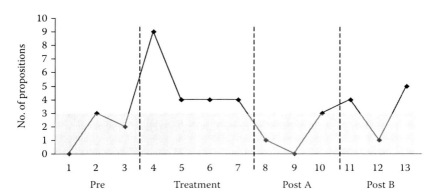

**Figure 11.1**   Number of propositions produced during the pretreatment, treatment, and posttreatment phases. Post A, posttreatment without the template; Post B, posttreatment when the template was reintroduced. The shaded area represents the two-standard-deviation band around the mean where performance is expected to vary without intervention.

half the meaningful propositions; however, with the template, he produced significantly more.

**Goal 2: Reduce the amount of irrelevant information and nonmeaningful content produced**    This may be reflected by a reduced number of T-units overall. Figure 11.2 depicts the number of T-units produced with and without the template. John used significantly fewer T-units using the template, suggesting that he reduced the number of utterances used. This result is interesting when viewed alongside the increase in meaningful content. This suggests that although John produced fewer utterances, the utterances contained meaningful information relevant to the passage he was asked to retell.

Other discourse measures were also monitored during the intervention, including episode structure and syntactic complexity. Despite changes in the number of propositions and the number of T-units, there were no other changes in language or information measures. That leads the clinician to step 4.

**Step 4: What are the next steps?**    Using a visual organizational template to improve discourse production in individuals with TBI showed promising results with John. Once sufficient and relevant information was produced, the next stages for intervention could include increasing complexity of utterances, increasing length of utterances, and improving structure of the discourse.

## CONCLUSIONS

Expository discourse production, like other forms of discourse production, appears to be affected following TBI (e.g., Hay & Moran, 2005). A comprehensive assessment protocol should include assessment of expository discourse.

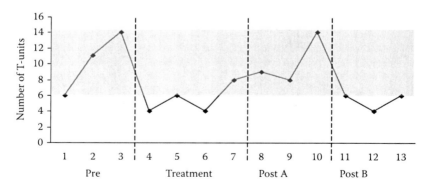

**Figure 11.2**    Number of T-units produced during the pretreatment, treatment, and posttreatment phases. Post A, posttreatment without the template; Post B, posttreatment when the template was reintroduced. The shaded area represents the two-standard-deviation band around the baseline mean where performance is expected to vary without intervention.

Clinicians need to consider how they will elicit and analyze the discourse, as different methods have been shown to produce differing results. Analyses of discourse following TBI should include measures of information/content and language structure. Finally, intervention focusing on improving information/content through the use of a visual organizer has shown some promising results and is a good starting point for clinicians wanting to improve discourse production in individuals with TBI.

## REFERENCES

Baddeley, A. D. (1976). *The psychology of memory*. New York: Basic Books.

Biddle, K. R., McCabe, A., & Bliss, L. S. (1996). Narrative skills following traumatic brain injury in children and adults. *Journal of Communication Disorders, 29*(6), 446–469.

Blosser, J., & DePompei, R. (2003). *Pediatric traumatic brain injury: Proactive intervention*. San Diego, CA: Singular.

Cannito, M. P., Hayashi, M. M., & Ulatowska, H. K. (1989). Discourse in normal and pathologic ageing: Background and assessment strategies. *Seminars in Speech and Language, 9,* 117–134.

Chapman, S. B. (1997). Cognitive-communication abilities in children with closed head injury. *American Journal of Speech-Language Pathology, 6*(2), 50–58.

Chapman, S. B., Culhane, K. A., Levin, H. S., Harward, H., Mendelsohn, D., Ewing-Cobbs, L. (1992). Narrative discourse after closed head-injury in children and adolescents. *Brain and Language, 43*(1), 42–65.

Chapman, S. B., Levin, H. S., Wanek, A., Weyrauch, J., & Kufera, J. (1998). Discourse after closed head injury in young children [Special issue]. *Brain and Language, 61*(3), 420–449.

Chapman, S. B., Watkins, R., Gustafoson, C., Moore, S., Levin, H. S., & Kufera, J. A. (1997). Narrative discourse in children with closed head injury: Children with language impairment and typically developing children. *American Journal of Speech-Language Pathology, 6*(2), 66–76.

Coelho, C. A. (1995). Discourse production deficits following traumatic brain injury: A critical review of the recent literature. *Aphasiology, 9*(5), 409–429.

Coelho, C. A. (2002). Story narratives of adults with closed head injury and non-brain-injured adults: Influence of socioeconomic status, elicitation task, and executive functioning. *Journal of Speech, Language, and Hearing Research, 45*(6), 1232–1248.

Crystal, D. (1987). *The Cambridge encyclopedia of language*. Cambridge: Cambridge University Press.

Dollaghan, C., & Campbell, T. E. (1998). Nonword repetition and child language impairment. *Journal of Speech, Language and Hearing Research, 41*(5), 1136–1147.

Dunn L. M., & Dunn, D. M. (1997). *Peabody Picture Vocabulary Test* (3rd ed.). Circle Pines, MN: American Guidance Service.

Ewing-Cobbs, L., Brookshire, B., Scott, M. A., & Fletcher, J. M. (1998). Children's narratives following traumatic brain injury: Linguistic structure, cohesion, and thematic recall. *Brain and Language, 61,* 395–419.

Gaulin, C. A., & Campbell, T. F. (1994). Procedure for assessing verbal working memory in normal school-age children: Some preliminary data. *Perceptual and Motor Skills, 79,* 55–64.

German, D. (1990). *Test of Adolescent/Adult Word Finding*. Austin, TX: PRO-ED.

Gillam, R. B., Pena, E. D., & Miller, L. (1999). Dynamic assessment of narrative and expository discourse. *Topics in Language Disorders, 20*(1), 33–47.

Griffith, P. L., Ripich, D. N, & Dastoli, S. L. (1986). Story structure, cohesion, and propositions in story recalls by learning-disabled and non-disabled children. *Journal of Psycholinguistic Research, 15,* 539–555.

Gummersall, D., & Strong, C. (1999). Assessment of complex sentence production in narrative context. *Language, Speech, and Hearing Services in the Schools, 30,* 153–164.

Hanten, G., Levin, H. S., & Song, J. X. (1999). Working memory and metacognition in sentence comprehension by severely head-injured children: A preliminary study. *Developmental Neuropsychology, 16*(3), 393–414.

Hartley, L. L. (1995). *Cognitive-communicative abilities following brain injury.* San Diego, CA: Singular.

Hay, E., & Moran, C. (2004). Improving expository discourse in children with traumatic brain injury. *New Zealand Journal of Speech-Language Therapy, 59,* 19–32.

Hay, E., & Moran, C. (2005). Discourse formulation in children with closed head injury. *American Journal of Speech-Language Pathology, 14*(4), 324–336.

Hunt, K. W. (1970). Syntactic maturity in school children and adults. *Monographs for the Society for Research in Child Development, 35*(1, Serial No. 134).

Iverson, G. L., Gaetz, M., Lovell, M. R., & Collins, M. W. (2004). Cumulative effects of concussion in amateur athletes. *Brain Injury, 18,* 433–443.

Jordan, F. M., Cannon, A., & Murdoch, B. E. (1992). Language abilities of mildly closed head injured (CHI) children 10 years post-injury. *Brain Injury, 6*(1), 39–44.

Jordan, F. M., Cremona-Meteyard, S., & King, A. (1996). High-level linguistic disturbances subsequent to closed-head injury in children: A follow-up study. *Brain Injury, 4,* 147–154.

Jordan, F. M., & Murdoch, B. E. (1990). Linguistic status following closed head injury in children: A follow-up study. *Brain Injury, 4*(2), 147–154.

Jordan, F. M., & Murdoch, B. E. (1994). Severe closed head injury in childhood: Linguistic outcomes into adulthood. *Brain Injury, 8*(6), 501–508.

Jordan, F. M., Ozanne, A. E., & Murdoch, B. E. (1990). Performance of closed head-injured children on a naming task. *Brain Injury, 4*(1), 27–32.

Just, M. A., & Carpenter, P. A. (1992). A capacity theory of comprehension: Individual differences in working memory. *Psychological Review, 99*(1), 122–149.

Langlois, J. A., Rutland-Brown, W., & Thomas, K. E. (2005). The incidence of traumatic brain injury among children in the United States: Differences by race. *Journal of Head Trauma Rehabilitation, 20*(3), 229–238.

Langlois, J. A., Rutland-Brown W., & Thomas, K. E. (2006). *Traumatic brain injury in the United States: Emergency department visits, hospitalizations, and deaths.* Atlanta: Centers for Disease Control and Prevention, National Center for Injury Prevention and Control.

Larson, V., & McKinley, N (1995). *Language disorders in older students.* Eau Claire, WI: Thinking Publications.

Liles, B. (1985). Cohesion in the narratives of normal and language-disordered children. *Journal of Speech and Hearing Research, 28,* 123–133.

Masterson, J. J., & Kamhi, A. G. (1991). The effects of sampling conditions on sentence production in normal, reading disabled, and language-learning-disabled children. *Journal of Speech, Language and Hearing Research, 34,* 549–558.

McDonald, S., & Pearce, S. (1995). The Dice Game: A new test of organizational skills in language. *Brain Injury, 9,* 255–271.

Moran, C., & Gillon, G. T. (2004) Language and memory profiles of adolescents with traumatic brain injury. *Brain Injury, 18*(3), 273–288.

Moran, C. A., & Gillon, G. T. (2005). Inference comprehension in adolescents with traumatic brain injury: A working memory hypothesis. *Brain Injury, 19*(10), 743–751.

Moran, C., Nippold, M., Mansfield, T., & Gillon, G. (2005). *Expository language sampling in older children and adolescents.* Poster presented at the annual convention of the American Speech-Language Hearing Association, November 18-20, 2005, San Diego, CA.

Nelson, N. (1993). *Childhood language disorders in context: Infancy through adolescence.* New York: Macmillan.

Nippold, M. A. (2007). *Later language development: School-age children, adolescents, and young adults* (3rd ed.). Austin, TX: PRO-ED.

Nippold, M. A., Hesketh, L. J., Duthie, J. K., & Mansfield, T. C. (2005). Conversational versus expository discourse: A study of syntactic development in children, adolescents, and adults. *Journal of Speech, Language and Hearing Research, 48,* 1048–1064.

Nippold, M. A., Mansfield, T. C., & Billow, J. L. (2007). Peer conflict explanations in children, adolescents, and adults: Examining the development of complex syntax. *American Journal of Speech-Language Pathology, 16,* 179–188.

Nippold, M. A., Moran, C. A., Mansfield, T. C., & Gillon, G. T. (2005, July). *Expository discourse development in American and New Zealand youth: A cross-cultural comparison.* Poster presented at the 10th International Congress for the International Association for the Study of Child Language, Berlin, Germany.

Paul, R. (2007). *Language disorders from infancy through adolescence: Assessment and intervention* (3rd ed.). St. Louis, MO: Mosby.

Portney, L. G., & Watkins, M. P. (2000). *Foundations of clinical research: Applications to practice* (2nd ed.). Norwalk, CT: Prentice Hall.

Richgels, D. J., McGee, L. M., Lomax, R. G., & Sheard, C. (1987). Awareness of four text structures: Effect on recall of expository text. *Reading Research Quarterly, 2,* 177–196.

Schneider, P. (1996). Effects of pictures versus orally presented stories on story-retellings by children with language-impairment. *American Journal of Speech-Language Pathology, 5,* 86–96.

Scott, C. M., & Windsor, J. (2000). General language performance measures in spoken and written narrative and expository discourse of school-age children with language learning disabilities. *Journal of Speech, Language, and Hearing Research, 43,* 324–339.

Semel, E. M., Wiig, E. H., & Secord, W. (1995). *Clinical evaluation of language fundamentals.* San Antonio, TX: The Psychological Corporation.

Snow, P., Douglas, J., & Ponsford, J. (1995). Discourse assessment following traumatic brain injury: A pilot study examining some demographic and methodological issues. *Aphasiology, 9*(4), 365–380.

Snow, P., Douglas, J., & Ponsford, J. (1997). Procedural discourse following traumatic brain injury. *Aphasiology, 11*(10), 947–967.

Stewart, S. (1985). Development of written language proficiency: Methods for teaching text structure. In C. Simon (Ed.), *Communication skills and classroom success* (pp. 341–361). San Diego, CA: College Hill Press.

Strum, J., & Rankin-Erickson, J. (2002). Effects of hand-drawn and computer-generated concept mapping on the expository writing of middle school students with learning disabilities. *Learning Disabilities, Research, and Practice, 17,* 124–139.

Turkstra, L. S. (1999). Language testing in adolescents with brain injury: A consideration of the CELF-3. *Language, Speech and Hearing Services in Schools, 30,* 132–140.

Turkstra, L. S., McDonald, S., & Kaufmann, P. M. (1995). Assessment of pragmatic communication skills in adolescents after traumatic brain injury. *Brain Injury, 10,* 329–345.

Ulatowska, H. K., Allard, L., & Chapman, S. B. (1990). Narrative and procedural discourse in aphasia. In Y. Joanette & H. H. Brownell (Eds.), *Discourse ability and brain damage* (pp. 180–198). New York: Springer-Verlag.

Ward-Lonergan, J. M., Liles, B. Z., & Anderson, A. M. (1999). Verbal retelling abilities in adolescents with and without language-learning disabilities for social studies lectures. *Journal of Learning Disabilities, 32*(3), 213–223.

Westby, C. (1991). Learning to talk-talking to learn: Oral-literate language differences. In C. S. Simon (Ed.), *Communication skills and classroom success* (pp. 181–218). San Diego, CA: College Hill Press.

Westerveld, M., & Gillon, G. T. (2001). Oral language sampling in 6-year-old New Zealand children from different cultural backgrounds. *New Zealand Journal of Speech-Language Therapy, 56,* 5–17.

Wiig, E. H., & Secord, W. (1992). *Test of word knowledge (TOWK).* San Antonio, TX: Harcourt Assessment.

Windsor, J., Scott, C., & Street, C. (2000). Verb and noun morphology in the spoken and written language of children with language learning disabilities. *Journal of Speech, Language, and Hearing Research, 43,* 1322–1336.

Wolfe, M. B. W. (2005). Memory for narrative and expository text: Independent influences of semantic associations and text organization. *Journal of Experimental Psychology Learning Memory and Cognition, 31*(2), 359–364.

Youse, K. M., & Coehlo, C. A. (2005, November). *Treatment of conversational discourse following traumatic brain injury.* Paper presented at the annual convention of the American Speech and Hearing Association, San Diego, CA.

## APPENDIX: TWO EXPOSITORY PASSAGES USED IN THE TREATMENT PROTOCOL

### The Earth

The Earth is a huge mass that weighs thousands of million tons. It is made up of three main layers. The top layer is the crust, which is made of solid rock. In some places, like under the continents, the crust is twenty to thirty miles thick. Under the oceans, the crust is only about three miles thick. The next layer is called the mantle. This is also made of solid rock. It goes down as far as eighteen hundred miles. The mantle is not as solid as the crust. It has so much pressure on it that it will crumble and move very slowly. The very center of the earth is called the core. It measures over two thousand miles across. Scientists believe this core is liquid made up of iron and nickel. They also think the core produces a magnetic field just like a magnet. This field spreads out from the core to the surface of the earth and into space.

### Woodpeckers

Woodpeckers are birds that live in trees in the woods. They build their nests and find their food in the trees. The corners and gaps in the bark of a tree are full of insects and grubs. These are a feast for the woodpecker and he has an inborn instinct to find these goodies. The woodpecker has a beak that is a chisel shaped point. It is both sharp and strong. This is what he uses to drill a hole straight down into the bark of the tree so he can get at those grubs and insects. Inside the sharp beak the woodpecker has a very long and round tongue, which has a hard tip and sharp, tiny points on the side. After the woodpecker has drilled the hole with his beak, he uncoils his tongue and collects the bugs he can get. The woodpecker builds his nest in trees, which are partially hollowed by decay. He pecks away to make two openings, one on each side, like a front door and a back door. The woodpecker is a clever bird.

## STUDY GUIDE QUESTIONS

1. Tasks are more likely to elicit discourse that reflects the effects of TBI on communication if they
   a.  describe simple everyday routines.
   b.  describe complex, multifaceted information.
   c.  are highly familiar.
   d.  are ecologically valid.
2. Individuals with TBI who provide very little relevant information are *most* likely to show deficits in
   a.  number of information units (propositions).
   b.  lexical diversity.
   c.  syntactic complexity.
   d.  number of T-units.
3. The following is *not* an example of an expository generation task:
   a.  Description of a favorite game or sport
   b.  Making up a story while viewing a silent movie
   c.  Peer Conflict Resolution task
   d.  Explaining information that has been presented in a lecture
4. The utilization of expository discourse tasks to evaluate language production following TBI is best suited for
   a.  children.
   b.  adolescents.
   c.  adults.
   d.  individuals across age ranges.
5. Traumatic brain injuries sustained in childhood can affect
   a.  syntax.
   b.  semantics.
   c.  pragmatics.
   d.  all of the above.

# Answers to Study Guide Questions

## CHAPTER 2

1. d
2. b
3. a
4. b
5. c

## CHAPTER 3

1. c
2. a
3. d
4. a
5. b

## CHAPTER 4

1. d
2. a
3. d
4. c
5. b

## CHAPTER 5

1. b
2. a
3. d
4. a
5. c

## CHAPTER 6

1. b
2. a
3. c
4. d
5. c

## CHAPTER 7

1. c
2. c
3. a
4. c
5. d

## CHAPTER 8

1. d
2. a
3. d
4. b
5. b

## CHAPTER 9

1. a
2. c
3. b
4. d
5. a

## CHAPTER 10

1. a
2. c
3. b
4. a
5. d

## CHAPTER 11

1. b
2. a
3. b
4. d
5. d

# Author Index

## A

Abrahamsen, E. P., 225
Adam, J.-M., 64–65
Afflerbach, P. P., 28
Alao, S., 25
Albrecht, J. E., 19, 29
Alexander, A. A., 256
Alexander, P. A., 22–23, 27
Allard, L., 278
Alley, G., 243, 247
Andersen, S., 199
Anderson, A. M., 157–158, 280
Anderson, E., 25
Anderson, L. M., 176, 242, 259
Anderson, R., 26
Anderson, T. H., 165–166, 171, 220, 228, 232
Anderson, V., 164
Anders, P. L., 250
Anglin, J. M., 125
Anthony, H. M., 242, 259
Applebee, A., 162
Armbruster, B. B., 165–166, 171, 218, 220, 228, 232, 260
Au, T. K-F., 142
Avidor, A., 125

## B

Baddeley, A. D., 291
Baker I., 167
Baker, L., 25–26
Baker, S., 219, 249, 259
Bakken, J. P., 217, 226–227, 250, 253, 258–259

Bales, R., 250
Banikoski, A., 182
Barenbaum, E., 174, 176
Barfett, S., 27
Bar-Ilan, L., 101, 111, 125
Barsalou, L. W., 88
Bartlett, F., 64
Barton, M. L., 216
Baruch, E., 103, 107, 143
Bashir, A. S., 225
Bates, E., 67, 87, 104
Battle, J., 250
Beach, R. W., 220
Beck, I. L., 15, 25, 27, 29, 165, 171, 225, 242
Beimiller, A., 15
Benigni, L., 67
Bennett-Armistead, V. S., 164
Bentz, J., 247
Bereiter, C., 176, 178, 217, 260
Bergerud, D., 227
Berko Gleason, J., 43
Berkowitz, S. J., 14
Berman, R. A., 4, 10, 44, 99–105, 107–116, 124–128, 132, 134, 141–146, 192, 203, 206, 209–210
Bernard, R. M., 256
Bernhardt, E., 164
Bernstein Ratner, N., 43
Bertus, E., 18
Best, R. M., 15, 23, 25, 28, 125, 217
Biber, D., 99, 104, 126
Biddle, K. R., 276–277
Billingsley, B., 174
Billow, J. L., 43, 49, 278

Roth, F., 224
Roulet, E., 64
Rowe, M., 217
Rubin, H., 175
Ruiter (de), J. P., 69, 73
Rutland-Brown, W., 276

### S

Saban, R., 125
Sabornie, E. J., 231
Sacks, G., 218
Saenz, L. M., 164, 166
Salvia, J., 245, 249
Samuels, S. J., 14, 170, 217
Samuelstuen, M. S., 24, 27
Saul, E. U., 18
Sawatsky, D., 260
Scarborough, H. S., 173
Scardamalia, M., 176, 178, 217, 260
Schafer, W. D., 259
Schallert, D. L., 256
Scheflen, A. E., 66
Schneider, P., 282
Schraw, G., 225
Schultz, S. K., 23
Schumaker, J. B., 225, 228, 230, 243,
    246–248, 250, 256, 264–265
Schumm, J. S., 242, 250
Schwartz, S. S., 259
Scott, C. M., 1, 6, 9, 43, 110, 125–126,
    156, 160, 162, 164, 172–175,
    191, 199–208, 210, 275, 280,
    282, 286–287
Scott, J., 25, 28
Scruggs, T. E., 217, 231–232, 250, 259
Secord, W., 198, 292
Seely, M. R., 19
Seidenberg, P. L., 218, 222, 226, 230
Semel, F. M., 198, 292
Semenza, C., 124
Seroussi, B., 125, 127
Sfard, A., 126, 130
Shapiro, A. M., 24
Shatz, M., 142
Sheard, C., 170, 284
Sheinker, A., 260
Sheinker, J., 260
Sheldon, J. B., 243, 246, 264–265
Shelton, K. C., 225

Siegler, R. S., 129
Silbert, J., 242
Silver, E. A., 129–132, 143
Silverstein, A. K., 220
Simmonds, E. P. M., 249
Simmons, D. C., 25, 171, 215, 226
Simon, J.-P., 68
Sinatra, G. M., 29, 32, 165, 225
Sinclair, H., 65
Sindelar, P., 174
Singer, M., 19
Skarakis-Doyle, E., 160
Slater, W. H., 220
Slobin, D. I., 109, 134
Smiley, S. S., 32
Smith, C. S., 100
Smith, D. J., 249
Smith, K. J., 2
Snow, C. E., 15
Snow, P., 275, 278, 280, 283, 288
Snyder, B. L., 231
Snyder, L., 3, 10, 13, 19, 30, 32, 43
Songer, N. B., 13, 233
Song, J. X., 290
Sood, S., 218
Spanos, G., 129, 131
Speer, S. A., 100
Spekman, N., 224
Spelke, L., 124
Spence, D., 250, 253–254
Spilich, G. J., 50
Spillich, G. J., 23
Steely, D. G., 165
Steen, G., 127
Stegink, P., 249
Steinberg, L., 114
Stein, N. L., 165
Sternau, M., 111
Steup, M., 41
Stevens, D. D., 259
Stewart, S., 279
Stodolsky, S. S., 217
Stokes, S. E., 199
Street, C. K., 173, 286
Strömqvist, S., 108, 111, 125–126, 210
Strømso, H. I., 27
Strong, C., 282
Sturm, J. M., 172, 179, 294
Stylianou, P., 32
Swales, J., 100

# Subject Index

Note: Page numbers followed by "f" indicate figures. Those followed by "t" indicate tables.